America's Children: Key National Indicators of Well-Being, 2009

Federal Interagency Forum on Child and Family Statistics

The Federal Interagency Forum on Child and Family Statistics was founded in 1994. Executive Order No. 13045 formally established the Forum in April 1997 to foster coordination and collaboration in the collection and reporting of Federal data on children and families. Agencies that are members of the Forum as of Spring 2009 are listed below.

Department of Agriculture
Economic Research Service
http://www.ers.usda.gov

Department of Commerce
U.S. Census Bureau
http://www.census.gov

Department of Defense
Office of the Deputy Under Secretary of Defense, Military Community and Family Policy
http://www.defenselink.mil/prhome/mcfp.html

Department of Education
National Center for Education Statistics
http://nces.ed.gov

Department of Health and Human Services
Administration for Children and Families
http://www.acf.hhs.gov

Agency for Healthcare Research and Quality
http://www.ahrq.gov

Eunice Kennedy Shriver National Institute of Child Health and Human Development
http://www.nichd.nih.gov

Maternal and Child Health Bureau
http://www.mchb.hrsa.gov

National Center for Health Statistics
http://www.cdc.gov/nchs

National Institute of Mental Health
http://www.nimh.nih.gov

Office of the Assistant Secretary for Planning and Evaluation
http://aspe.hhs.gov

Substance Abuse and Mental Health Services Administration
http://www.samhsa.gov

Department of Housing and Urban Development
Office of Policy Development and Research
http://www.huduser.org

Department of Justice
Bureau of Justice Statistics
http://www.ojp.usdoj.gov/bjs

National Institute of Justice
http://www.ojp.usdoj.gov/nij

Office of Juvenile Justice and Delinquency Prevention
http://www.ojjdp.ncjrs.gov

Department of Labor
Bureau of Labor Statistics
http://www.bls.gov

Women's Bureau
http://www.dol.gov/wb

Department of Transportation
National Highway Traffic Safety Administration
http://www.nhtsa.dot.gov

Environmental Protection Agency
Office of Children's Health Protection and Environmental Education
http://yosemite.epa.gov/ochp/ochpweb.nsf

National Science Foundation
Division of Science Resources Statistics
http://www.nsf.gov/statistics

Office of Management and Budget
Statistical and Science Policy Office
http://www.whitehouse.gov/omb/inforeg_statpolicy

Recommended citation: Federal Interagency Forum on Child and Family Statistics. *America's Children: Key National Indicators of Well-Being, 2009.* Washington, DC: U.S. Government Printing Office.

This report was printed by the U.S. Government Printing Office in cooperation with the National Center for Health Statistics, July 2009.

Table of Contents

Foreword

In 1994, the Office of Management and Budget joined with six other Federal agencies to create the Federal Interagency Forum on Child and Family Statistics. Formally established in April 1997 through Executive Order No. 13045, the Forum is charged with developing priorities for collecting enhanced data on children and youth, improving the reporting and dissemination of information on the status of children to the policy community and the general public, and producing more complete data on children at the state and local levels. The Forum, which now has participants from 22 Federal agencies as well as partners in private research organizations, fosters coordination, collaboration, and integration of Federal efforts to collect and report data on conditions and trends for children and families and calls attention to needs for new data about them.

America's Children: Key National Indicators of Well-Being, 2009 is a compendium of indicators illustrating both the promises and the difficulties confronting our Nation's young people. The report presents 40 key indicators on important aspects of children's lives. These indicators are drawn from our most reliable statistics, easily understood by broad audiences, objectively based on substantial research, balanced so that no single area of children's lives dominates the report, measured regularly so that they can be updated to show trends over time, and representative of large segments of the population rather than one particular group.

This year's report continues to present key indicators grouped by the seven sections identified in the restructured 10th anniversary report (2007): family and social environment, economic circumstances, health care, physical environment and safety, behavior, education, and health. The report incorporates several modifications that reflect the Forum's ongoing efforts to improve its quality and comprehensiveness: updates to data sources and substantive expansions or clarifications have been made for several indicators; a regular indicator on adolescent depression has been added, addressing an ongoing data gap on the mental health of children; and a special feature, Children with Special Health Care Needs, has been included.

Each volume of *America's Children* has also highlighted critical data gaps and challenged Federal statistical agencies to do better. Forum agencies are meeting that challenge by working to provide more comprehensive and consistent information on the condition and progress of our Nation's children. Since the last full report (*America's Children: Key National Indicators of Well-Being, 2007*), Forum agencies have continued efforts to strengthen some indicators and to close critical data gaps, particularly in areas such as disability, the mental health of children, and environmental quality. In addition, the Forum has established a new Research and Innovation Committee charged with developing innovative ways of addressing existing gaps in our systems of collecting, reporting, and disseminating information on the status of children and families. This committee made valuable contributions to the identification of "indicators needed" in this year's report. The Forum is confident that, over time, the committee's work will facilitate an even more well-rounded portrait of America's children.

The value of the *America's Children* reports and the extraordinary cooperation they represent reflect the Forum's determination to advance our understanding of where our children are today and what may be needed to bring them a better tomorrow. The Forum agencies should be congratulated once again for joining together to address their common goals: developing a truly comprehensive set of indicators on the well-being of America's children and ensuring that this information is readily accessible in both content and format. Their accomplishments reflect the dedication of the Forum agency staff members who coordinate the assessment of data needs, evaluate strategies to make data presentations more consistent, and work together to produce important publications and provide these products on the Forum's website. Last but not least, none of this work would be possible without the continued cooperation of millions of American citizens who willingly provide the data that are summarized and analyzed by staff in the Federal agencies. We invite you to suggest ways in which we can enhance this annual portrait of the Nation's most valuable resource: its children. I applaud the Forum's collaborative efforts in producing this report and hope that our compendium will continue to be useful in your work.

Katherine K. Wallman
Chief Statistician
Office of Management and Budget

Acknowledgments

This report reflects the commitment of the members of the Federal Interagency Forum on Child and Family Statistics. The report was written by the staff of the Forum, including Dara Blachman, Forum Coordinator; Lynda Laughlin, U.S. Census Bureau; Susan Lukacs, Patricia Pastor, and LaJeana Howie, National Center for Health Statistics; William Sonnenberg, National Center for Education Statistics; Daniel Axelrad, Environmental Protection Agency; Barry Steffen, Department of Housing and Urban Development; Katrina Baum, Bureau of Justice Statistics; Marsha Lopez, National Institute on Drug Abuse; Susan Jekielek, Administration for Children and Families; Mark Nord, Economic Research Service; Teri Morisi, Bureau of Labor Statistics; Shelli Avenevoli, National Institute of Mental Health; James Singleton, Centers for Disease Control and Prevention; Lisa Colpe, Substance Abuse and Mental Health Services Administration; Thomas Fungwe, Center for Nutrition Policy and Promotion; and Reem Ghandour, Maternal and Child Health Bureau.

In addition to the report authors, active members of the Reporting Committee who guided development of the report included Laura Chadwick and Annette Rogers, Office of the Assistant Secretary for Planning and Evaluation, Health and Human Services; Shelly Wilkie Martinez, Office of Management and Budget; Gregory Miller, Environmental Protection Agency; Carrie Mulford, National Institute of Justice; Robert Kominski and Jane Dye, U.S. Census Bureau; Jeffrey Evans, Eunice Kennedy Shriver National Institute of Child Health and Human Development; Ingrid Goldstrom, Substance Abuse and Mental Health Services Administration; Janet Chiancone, Office of Juvenile Justice and Delinquency Prevention; and Syreta Sharp, National Highway Traffic Safety Administration.

Members of the Research and Innovation Committee who provided valuable input for the Indicators Needed sections of the report include Dara Blachman, Forum Coordinator; Patricia Pastor, National Center for Health Statistics; Jeffrey Evans, Eunice Kennedy Shriver National Institute of Child Health and Human Development; Ingrid Goldstrom, Substance Abuse and Mental Health Services Administration; Susan Jekielek, Administration for Children and Families; Michael Planty, National Center for Education Statistics; and Margaret Zahn, National Institute of Justice.

Other staff members of the Forum agencies provided data, developed indicators, or wrote parts of the report. They include Stephen Provasnik, National Center for Education Statistics; David Johnson, Hyon Shin, Rose Kreider, Lea Auman, and Bernadette Proctor, U.S. Census Bureau; Hector Rodriquez and Shalom Williams, Bureau of Labor Statistics; Patricia Guenther and WenYen Juan, Center for Nutrition Policy and Promotion; Margaret Warner, Debra Brody, Li-Hui Chen, Robin Cohen, Cathy Duran, Donna Hoyert, Joyce Martin, T.J. Mathews, Cynthia Ogden, Stephanie Ventura, and Stephen Blumberg, National Center for Health Statistics; Cindy Knighton, Centers for Disease Control and Prevention; Michael Kogan and Bonnie Strickland, Maternal and Child Health Bureau; Beth Han, Substance Abuse and Mental Health Services Administration; Lance McCluney and Jade Lee-Freeman, Environmental Protection Agency; and Kristen Kracke, Office of Juvenile Justice and Delinquency Prevention.

In addition, Mary Ann Fox, Kristen Darling-Churchill, Lauren Drake, Katie Ferguson, Bo Chen, Kevin Bianco, and Tom Nachazel with the American Institutes for Research and Richard Devens with First XV Communications assisted Forum staff in producing the report.

About This Report

The Federal Interagency Forum on Child and Family Statistics' primary mission is to enhance the practice of and improve consistency in data collection and reporting on children and families. *America's Children: Key National Indicators of Well-Being, 2009* continues to follow the restructured format of the 10th anniversary edition (2007), providing the Nation with a summary of national indicators of children's well-being and monitoring changes in these indicators. The purposes of the report are to improve Federal data on children and families and make these data available in an easy-to-use, non-technical format, as well as to stimulate discussions among policymakers and the public and spur exchanges between data providers and policy communities.

Conceptual Framework for *America's Children*

There are many interrelated aspects of children's well-being, and only selected facets can be included in this report. This report draws on various overarching frameworks to identify seven major domains that characterize the well-being of a child and that influence the likelihood that a child will grow to be a well-educated, economically secure, productive, and healthy adult. The seven domains are family and social environment, economic circumstances, health care, physical environment and safety, behavior, education, and health. These domains are interrelated and can have synergistic effects on well-being.

As described below, each section of the report corresponds to one of the seven domains and includes a set of key indicators. These indicators either characterize an aspect of well-being or an influence on well-being. The report does not distinguish between these two types of indicators, nor does it address the relationships between them. Yet all the indicators are important if we are to assess the well-being of children.

- *Family and Social Environment* includes indicators that characterize or are related to children's family and social environment.

- *Economic Circumstances* includes indicators that characterize or are related to children's basic material needs.

- *Health Care* includes indicators that characterize determinants of, or use of, health services among children.

- *Physical Environment and Safety* includes indicators that characterize children's environmental conditions or are related to children's safety.

- *Behavior* includes indicators that characterize personal behaviors and their effects.

- *Education* includes indicators that characterize or are related to how children learn and progress in school.

- *Health* includes indicators that characterize or are related to physical, mental, and social aspects of children's health.

Structure of the Report

America's Children: Key National Indicators of Well-Being, 2009 presents a set of key indicators that measure important aspects of children's lives and are collected regularly, reliably, and rigorously by Federal agencies. The Forum chose these indicators through careful examination of available data. In determining this list of key indicators, the Forum sought input from the Federal policymaking community, foundations, academic researchers, and state and local children's service providers. These indicators were chosen because they meet the following criteria:

- *Easy to understand* by broad audiences;

- *Objectively based* on substantial research connecting them to child well-being and easily estimated using reliable data;

- *Balanced,* so that no single area of children's lives dominates the report;

- *Measured regularly,* so that they can be updated and show trends over time; and

- *Representative* of large segments of the population, rather than one particular group.

America's Children: Key National Indicators of Well-Being, 2009 is designed as a gateway to complement other, more technical or comprehensive reports produced by several Forum agencies. The report not only provides indicators covering seven domains of child well-being, but also includes supplementary information. Appendix A, Detailed Tables, presents tabulated data for each measure and additional details not discussed in the main body of the report. Appendix B, Data Source Descriptions, describes the sources and surveys used to generate the demographic background measures and the indicators.

In addition, this year's report contains a special feature section which offers an opportunity to present additional measures that either are not available with sufficient frequency to be considered as regular key indicators, are new regular measures that the Forum believes merit special attention when first introduced, or provide more detailed information about a particular indicator or topic. The Special Feature for *America's Children: Key National Indicators of Well-Being 2009* is Children with Special Health Care Needs.

Changes to This Year's Report

Wherever possible, we have updated indicators with the latest available data for *America's Children: Key National Indicators of Well-Being, 2009.* In addition, this year's report includes a new, regular indicator on adolescent depression, which fills a long-identified gap in the area of children's mental health. The indicator on diet quality has been updated to reflect changes to the USDA's Healthy Eating Index and was moved to the Health section to better reflect its relation to healthy behavior generally and overweight in particular. The Forum has also worked to enhance the report by revising certain indicators to reflect improvements in the availability of data sources, substantive expansion of the indicator, or clarification of the concept being measured. Specifically, the indoor air quality indicator's data source was updated, the low birthweight indicator now also reports preterm birth, childhood immunization trends are shown for the most recent vaccine series recommendation, finer age breakdowns are provided for child maltreatment, and the measure of lead in the blood of children has been restructured to better reflect available data and trends.

The Forum continues to strive to demonstrate greater consistency and standardization in the presentation of information in this report.

Data on Race and Ethnicity and Poverty Status

Most indicators in *America's Children* include data tabulated by race and ethnicity. In 1997, the Office of Management and Budget (OMB) issued revised standards for data on race and ethnicity (http://www.whitehouse.gov/omb/fedreg/1997standards.html). These revised standards included two changes that had a direct effect on many of the indicators in this report, particularly with respect to trend analyses. First, racial categories expanded from four (White, Black, American Indian or Alaskan Native, or Asian or Pacific Islander) to five (White, Black or African American, American Indian or Alaska Native, Asian, or Native Hawaiian or Other Pacific Islander). Second, respondents were given the opportunity to select multiple races.

The data collection systems used in this report implemented these revised standards at different times, and some indicators have more detailed data on race and ethnicity than others. Yet, where feasible, we utilize the 1997 OMB standards for race and ethnicity in this report. Detailed information on data collection methods for race and ethnicity is provided in footnotes at the end of each table, and additional information can be found in the

Data Source Descriptions section. The Forum strives to consistently report racial and ethnic data across indicators for clarity and continuity.

Many indicators in this report also include data tabulated by family income and poverty status. All poverty calculations in this report are based on the OMB's Statistical Policy Directive 14, which is the official poverty measurement standard for the United States. A family is considered to be living below the poverty level if its before-tax cash income is below a defined level of need, called a poverty threshold. Poverty thresholds are updated annually and vary based on family size and composition. Detailed information about children's poverty status can be found in the Child Poverty and Family Income indicator (ECON1). In addition, where feasible, other indicators present data by poverty status, utilizing the following categories: families with incomes less than 100 percent of the poverty line (poor), families with incomes between 100 and 199 percent of the poverty line (near-poor), and families with incomes 200 percent or more of the poverty line (non-poor). The Forum continues to work on reporting consistent data on family income and poverty status across indicators for clarity and continuity.

Indicators Needed

The Forum recently formed a Research and Innovation Committee to improve the monitoring of important areas of children's lives and to improve the timeliness with which information is made available to policymakers and the public. This committee is tasked with identifying critical gaps in the data available on children and families and developing innovative ways to address those gaps.

With assistance from this committee, the Forum presents a list describing child well-being data in need of development at the end of each section of the report. The lists include many important aspects of children's lives for which regular indicators are lacking or are in development, such as early childhood development, long-term poverty, disability, and social connections and engagement.

In some areas, the Forum is exploring ways to collect new measures and improve existing ones. In others, Forum agencies have successfully fielded surveys incorporating some new measures, but data are not yet available on a regular basis for monitoring purposes.

For Further Information

There are several useful places to obtain additional information on each of the indicators found in this report, including the tables, data source descriptions, and the website.

Tables

For many of the indicators, Appendix A, Detailed Tables, contains additional details not discussed in the main body of the report. When available and feasible to report, tables show data by the following categories: gender, age, race and Hispanic origin, poverty status, parental education, region of the country, and family structure.

Data Source Descriptions

Appendix B, Data Source Descriptions, contains information on and descriptions of the sources and surveys used to generate the indicators, as well as information on how to contact the agency responsible for collecting the data or administering the relevant survey.

It is also important to note that numerous publications of the Federal statistical agencies provide additional details about indicators in this report and on other areas of child well-being. Two such reports include *The Condition of Education,* published annually by the National Center for Education Statistics, and *Health, United States,* published annually by the National Center for Health Statistics.

Website

Finally, the Forum's website, http://childstats.gov, contains data tables, links to previous reports, links for ordering reports, and additional information about the Forum. The website provides downloadable tables (in Microsoft Excel® format) when available, along with additional years of data that cannot all be shown in the printed report. The website also provides links to previous *America's Children* reports (from 1997 to 2008), which are available in PDF format.

Highlights

America's Children: Key National Indicators of Well-Being, 2009 continues a series of annual reports to the Nation on conditions affecting children in the United States. Three demographic background measures and 40 selected indicators describe the population of children and depict child well-being in the areas of family and social environment, economic circumstances, health care, physical environment and safety, behavior, education, and health. This year's report has a special feature on children with special health care needs. Highlights from each section follow.

Demographic Background

- In 2008, there were 73.9 million children ages 0–17 in the United States (or 24 percent of the population) down from a peak of 36 percent at the end of the "baby boom" (1964). Children are projected to remain a fairly stable percentage of the total population through 2021, when they are projected to compose 24 percent of the population.

- Racial and ethnic diversity in the United States continues to increase over time. In 2008, 56 percent of U.S. children were White, non-Hispanic; 22 percent were Hispanic; 15 percent were Black; 4 percent were Asian; and 5 percent were of other races. The percentage of children who are Hispanic has increased faster than that of any other racial or ethnic group, growing from 9 percent of the child population in 1980 to 22 percent in 2008.

Family and Social Environment

- In 2008, 67 percent of children ages 0–17 lived with two married parents, down from 77 percent in 1980.

- The nonmarital birth rate in 2007 was 53 births per 1,000 unmarried women ages 15–44 years. The nonmarital birth rate has increased annually since 2000–2002, when it was relatively stable at 44 births per 1,000. In 2007, 40 percent of all births were to unmarried women, the highest percentage ever reported. This percentage has increased from 34 percent in 2002.

- In 2008, 19 percent of children were native children with at least one foreign-born parent, and 3 percent were foreign-born children with at least one foreign-born parent. Overall, the percentage of all children living in the United States with at least one foreign-born parent rose from 15 percent in 1994 to 22 percent in 2008.

- In 2007, 21 percent of school-age children spoke a language other than English at home and 5 percent of school-age children both spoke a language other than English at home and had difficulty speaking English.

- In 2007, the adolescent birth rate was 22.2 per 1,000 young women ages 15–17, up from the 2006 rate of 22.0 per 1,000. This was the second consecutive year of increase in this rate after dropping by almost half from 1991 to 2005.

Economic Circumstances

- In 2007, 18 percent of all children ages 0–17 lived in poverty, an increase from 17 percent in 2006. Among children living in families, the poverty rate was also 18 percent in 2007.

- The percentage of children who had at least one parent working year round, full time was 77 percent in 2007, down from 78 percent in 2006.

- The percentage of children living in households with very low food security among children increased from 0.6 percent in 2006 to 0.9 percent in 2007. In these households, eating patterns of one or more children were disrupted and food intake was reduced below a level considered adequate by caregivers.

Health Care

- In 2007, 89 percent of children had health insurance coverage at some point during the year, up from 88 percent in 2006. The number of children without health insurance at any time during 2007 was 8.1 million (11 percent of all children).

- In 2007, 77 percent of children ages 19–35 months had received the recommended combined six-vaccine series. Reporting for this combined six-vaccine series began in 2002, and percentages have steadily increased from 66 percent.

- In 2007, 77 percent of children ages 2–17 had a dental visit in the past year. In 2003–2004, 25 percent of children ages 2–17 had untreated dental caries (cavities), an increase from 21 percent in 1999–2002.

Physical Environment and Safety

- In 2007, 66 percent of children lived in counties in which one or more air pollutants were above allowable levels. Ozone is the pollutant that is most often above the allowable levels as defined by the Primary National Ambient Air Quality Standards.

- Children's exposure to secondhand smoke, as indicated by blood cotinine levels, dropped between 1988–1994 and 2005–2006. Overall, 51 percent of children ages 4–11 had cotinine in their blood in 2005–2006, down from 88 percent in 1988–1994. In 2005, 8 percent of children ages 0-6 lived in homes where someone smoked regularly, down from 27 percent in 1994.

- In 2007, 43 percent of households with children had one or more of three housing problems: physical inadequacy, crowding, or a cost burden of more than 30 percent of income. This percentage increased from 30 percent in 1978. The percentage of households with children with severe cost burdens—where more than half of income is spent for housing—rose from 6 percent to 16 percent over the same period.

- In 2005–2006, the leading causes of initial injury-related emergency department (ED) visits among adolescents ages 15–19 were being struck by or against an object or person (26 visits per 1,000); motor vehicle traffic crashes (24 visits per 1,000); and falls (22 visits per 1,000), altogether accounting for about half of all injury-related ED visits for this age group.

Behavior

- Heavy drinking declined from the most recent peaks of 13 percent in 1996 to 8 percent in 2008 for 8th-grade students, from 24 percent in 2000 to 16 percent in 2008 for 10th-grade students, and from 32 percent in 1998 to 25 percent in 2008 for 12th-grade students.

Education

- In 2007, 55 percent of children ages 3–5 who were not yet in kindergarten were read to daily by a family member. This rate is slightly higher than the rate in 1993 (53 percent), but the rate fluctuated in intervening years.

- In 2007, 89 percent of young adults ages 18–24 had completed high school with a diploma or an alternative credential such as a General Education Development (GED) certificate. The high school completion rate has increased slightly since 1980, when it was 84 percent.

- In 2007, 67 percent of high school completers enrolled immediately in a 2-year or 4-year college. Between 1980 and 2007, the rate of immediate college enrollment has trended upward from 49 percent to 67 percent; however, the rate has fluctuated from year to year.

Health

- After several decades of steady increases, the percentage of infants born preterm and the percentage born with low birthweight declined slightly in 2007. The percentage of infants born preterm in 2007 was 12.7, down from 12.8 percent in 2006. The percentage of infants born with low birthweight in 2007 was 8.2, down from 8.3 percent in 2006.

- In 2007, 8 percent of youth ages 12–17 had a Major Depressive Episode (MDE) in the past year, down from 9 percent in 2004. The percentage of youth with MDE receiving treatment for depression in the past year remained stable from 2004 to 2007 (40 percent in 2004 and 39 percent in 2007).

- In 2003–2004, on average, the quality of the diets of younger children was better when compared with that of older children with regard to fruit, milk, and extra calories. The quality of the diets of older children was better with regard to meat, oils, and saturated fat.

- In 2007, about 9 percent of children were reported to currently have asthma, and about 5 percent of children had one or more asthma attacks in the previous year. The prevalence of asthma was particularly high among Black, non-Hispanic children and Puerto Rican children (15 percent in each group).

Children With Special Health Care Needs

- In 2005–2006, an estimated 14 percent of children ages 0–17 had a special health care need, as measured by parents' reports that their child had a health problem expected to last at least 12 months and which required prescription medication, more services than most children, special therapies, or which limited his or her ability to do things most children can do.

America's Children at a Glance

	Previous Value (Year)	Most Recent Value (Year)	Change Between Years
Demographic Background			
Child population*			
Children ages 0–17 in the United States	73.9 million (2007)	73.9 million (2008)	NS
Children as a percentage of the population*			
Children ages 0–17 in the United States	24.5% (2007)	24.3% (2008)	↓
Racial and ethnic composition*			
Children ages 0–17 by race and Hispanic origin			
White	76.0% (2007)	75.9% (2008)	↓
White, Non-Hispanic	56.8% (2007)	56.2% (2008)	↓
Black	15.2% (2007)	15.2% (2008)	NS
Asian	4.1% (2007)	4.2% (2008)	↑
All other races	4.7% (2007)	4.8% (2008)	↑
Hispanic (of any race)	21.2% (2007)	21.8% (2008)	↑
Family and Social Environment			
Family structure and children's living arrangements			
Children ages 0–17 living with two married parents	68% (2007)	67% (2008)	↓
Births to unmarried women			
Births to unmarried women ages 15–44	51 per 1,000 (2006)	53 per 1,000 (2007)	↑
All births that are to unmarried women	38% (2006)	40% (2007)	↑
Child care			
Children ages 0–4, with employed mothers, whose primary child care arrangement is with a relative	Summary statistics excluded due to lack of comparability of data across the previous and most recent years. Please refer to the indicator text for more details.		
Children ages 0–6, not yet in kindergarten, who received some form of nonparental child care on a regular basis	61% (2001)	61% (2005)	NS
Children of at least one foreign-born parent			
Children ages 0–17 living with at least one foreign-born parent	22% (2007)	22% (2008)	NS
Language spoken at home and difficulty speaking English			
Children ages 5–17 who speak a language other than English at home	20.3% (2006)	20.5% (2007)	↑
Children ages 5–17 who speak a language other than English at home and who have difficulty speaking English	5% (2006)	5% (2007)	NS
Adolescent births			
Births to females ages 15–17	22.0 per 1,000 (2006)	22.2 per 1,000 (2007)	↑
Child maltreatment			
Substantiated reports of maltreatment of children ages 0–17	Summary statistics excluded due to lack of comparability of data across the previous and most recent years. Please refer to the indicator text for more details.		

* Population estimates are not sample derived and therefore not subject to statistical testing. Change between years identifies differences in the proportionate size of these estimates as rounded. Percentages may not sum to 100 due to rounding.

Legend: NS = No statistically significant change   ↑ = Statistically significant increase   ↓ = Statistically significant decrease

America's Children at a Glance

	Previous Value (Year)	Most Recent Value (Year)	Change Between Years
Economic Circumstances			
Child poverty and family income			
Related children ages 0–17 in poverty	17% (2006)	18% (2007)	↑
Secure parental employment			
Children ages 0–17 living with at least one parent employed year round, full time	78% (2006)	77% (2007)	↓
Food security			
Children ages 0–17 in households classified by USDA as "food insecure"	17% (2006)	17% (2007)	NS
Health Care			
Health insurance coverage			
Children ages 0–17 covered by health insurance at some time during the year	88% (2006)	89% (2007)	↑
Usual source of health care			
Children ages 0–17 with no usual source of health care	6% (2006)	6% (2007)	NS
Childhood immunization			
Children ages 19–35 months with the 4:3:1:3:3:1 combined series of vaccinations	77% (2006)	77% (2007)	NS
Oral health			
Children ages 2–17 with a dental visit in the past year	76% (2006)	77% (2007)	NS
Physical Environment and Safety			
Outdoor and indoor air quality			
Children ages 0–17 living in counties in which levels of one or more air pollutants were above allowable levels	66% (2006)	66% (2007)	NS
Drinking water quality			
Children served by community water systems that did not meet all applicable health-based drinking water standards	9% (2006)	8% (2007)	NS
Lead in the blood of children			
Children ages 1–5 with blood lead greater than or equal to 10 µg/dL	2% (1999–2002)	* (2003–2006)	NS
Housing problems			
Households with children ages 0–17 reporting shelter cost burden, crowding, and/or physically inadequate housing	40% (2005)	43% (2007)	↑
Youth victims of serious violent crimes			
Serious violent crime victimization of youth ages 12–17	14 per 1,000 (2005)	10 per 1,000 (2007)	NS
Child injury and mortality			
Injury deaths of children ages 1–4	13 per 100,000 (2005)	12 per 100,000 (2006)	NS
Injury deaths of children ages 5–14	8 per 100,000 (2005)	7 per 100,000 (2006)	↓
Adolescent injury and mortality			
Injury deaths of adolescents ages 15–19	50 per 100,000 (2005)	50 per 100,000 (2006)	NS

* Percentage is not shown because sample is too small to provide a statistically reliable estimate.

Legend: NS = No statistically significant change   ↑ = Statistically significant increase   ↓ = Statistically significant decrease

America's Children at a Glance

	Previous Value (Year)	Most Recent Value (Year)	Change Between Years
Behavior			
Regular cigarette smoking			
Students who reported smoking daily in the past 30 days			
8th grade	3% (2007)	3% (2008)	NS
10th grade	7% (2007)	6% (2008)	↓
12th grade	12% (2007)	11% (2008)	NS
Alcohol use			
Students who reported having five or more alcoholic beverages in a row in the past 2 weeks			
8th grade	8% (2007)	8% (2008)	NS
10th grade	20% (2007)	16% (2008)	↓
12th grade	26% (2007)	25% (2008)	NS
Illicit drug use			
Students who reported using illicit drugs in the past 30 days			
8th grade	7% (2007)	8% (2008)	NS
10th grade	17% (2007)	16% (2008)	NS
12th grade	22% (2007)	22% (2008)	NS
Sexual activity			
High school students who reported ever having had sexual intercourse	47% (2005)	48% (2007)	NS
Youth perpetrators of serious violent crimes			
Youth offenders ages 12–17 involved in serious violent crimes	17 per 1,000 (2005)	11 per 1,000 (2007)	↓
Education			
Family reading to young children			
Children ages 3–5 who were read to every day in the last week by a family member	60% (2005)	55% (2007)	↓
Mathematics and reading achievement			
Average mathematics scale score of			
4th-graders (0–500 scale)	238 (2005)	240 (2007)	↑
8th-graders (0–500 scale)	279 (2005)	281 (2007)	↑
12th-graders (0–300 scale)	—	150 (2005)	N/A
Average reading scale score of			
4th-graders (0–500 scale)	219 (2005)	221 (2007)	↑
8th-graders (0–500 scale)	262 (2005)	263 (2007)	↑
12th-graders (0–500 scale)	287 (2002)	286 (2005)	NS

Legend: NS = No statistically significant change   ↑ = Statistically significant increase   ↓ = Statistically significant decrease
           — = Not available   N/A = Not applicable

America's Children at a Glance

	Previous Value (Year)	Most Recent Value (Year)	Change Between Years
Education—continued			
High school academic coursetaking			
High school graduates who completed advanced coursework in			
Mathematics	45% (2000)	49% (2005)	↑
Science	63% (2000)	63% (2005)	NS
English	34% (2000)	31% (2005)	NS
Foreign language	30% (2000)	33% (2005)	↑
High school completion			
Young adults ages 18–24 who have completed high school	88% (2006)	89% (2007)	↑
Youth neither enrolled in school* nor working			
Youth ages 16–19 who are neither enrolled in school nor working	8% (2007)	8% (2008)	NS
College enrollment			
Recent high school completers enrolled in college the October immediately after completing high school	66% (2006)	67% (2007)	NS
Health			
Preterm birth and low birthweight			
Infants less than 37 completed weeks of gestation at birth	12.8% (2006)	12.7% (2007)	↓
Infants weighing less than 5 lb. 8 oz. at birth	8.3% (2006)	8.2% (2007)	↓
Infant mortality			
Deaths before first birthday	6.9 per 1,000 (2005)	6.7 per 1,000 (2006)	↓
Emotional and behavioral difficulties			
Children ages 4–17 reported by a parent to have serious difficulties with emotions, concentration, behavior, or getting along with other people	5% (2006)	5% (2007)	NS
Adolescent depression			
Youth ages 12–17 with past year Major Depressive Episode	8% (2006)	8% (2007)	NS
Activity limitation			
Children ages 5–17 with activity limitation resulting from one or more chronic health conditions	9% (2006)	8% (2007)	NS
Diet quality			
Average diet scores for children ages 2–17	Summary statistics excluded due to lack of comparability of data across the previous and most recent years. Please refer to the indicator text for more details.		
Overweight			
Children ages 6–17 who are overweight	18% (2003–2004)	17% (2005–2006)	NS
Asthma			
Children ages 0–17 who currently have asthma	9% (2006)	9% (2007)	NS

* School refers to high school and college.

Legend:　NS = No statistically significant change　↑ = Statistically significant increase　↓ = Statistically significant decrease

Demographic Background

Understanding the changing demographic characteristics of America's children is critical for shaping social programs and policies. The number of children determines the demand for schools, health care, and other social services that are essential to meet the daily needs of families. While the number of children living in the United States has grown, the ratio of children to adults has decreased. At the same time, the racial and ethnic composition of the Nation's children continues to change. When combined, these measures provide an important context for understanding the key indicators presented in this report and provide a glimpse of what the future may be like for American families.

In 2008, there were 73.9 million children in the United States, 1.6 million more than in 2000. This number is projected to increase to 82 million in 2021. In 2008, there were approximately equal numbers of children in three age groups: 0–5 (25 million), 6–11 (24 million), and 12–17 (25 million) years of age.

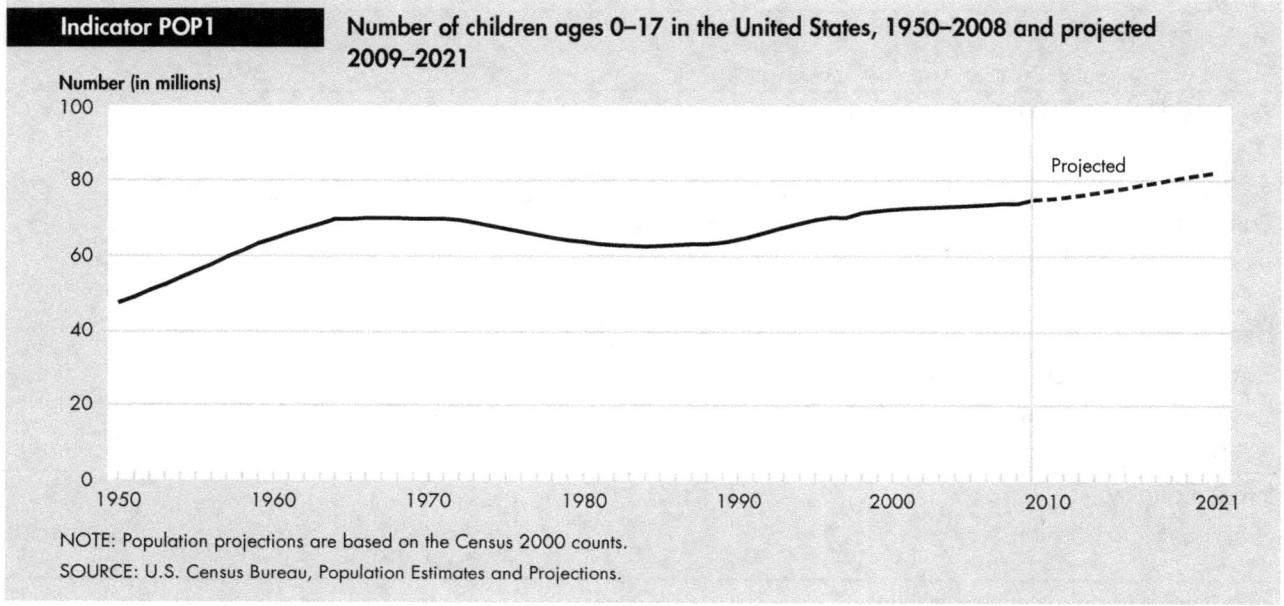

Indicator POP1

Number of children ages 0–17 in the United States, 1950–2008 and projected 2009–2021

NOTE: Population projections are based on the Census 2000 counts.

SOURCE: U.S. Census Bureau, Population Estimates and Projections.

Since the mid-1960s, children have been decreasing as a proportion of the total U.S. population. In 2008, children made up 24 percent of the population, down from a peak of 36 percent at the end of the "baby boom" (1964). Children are projected to remain a fairly stable percentage of the total population through 2021, when they are projected to compose 24 percent of the population.

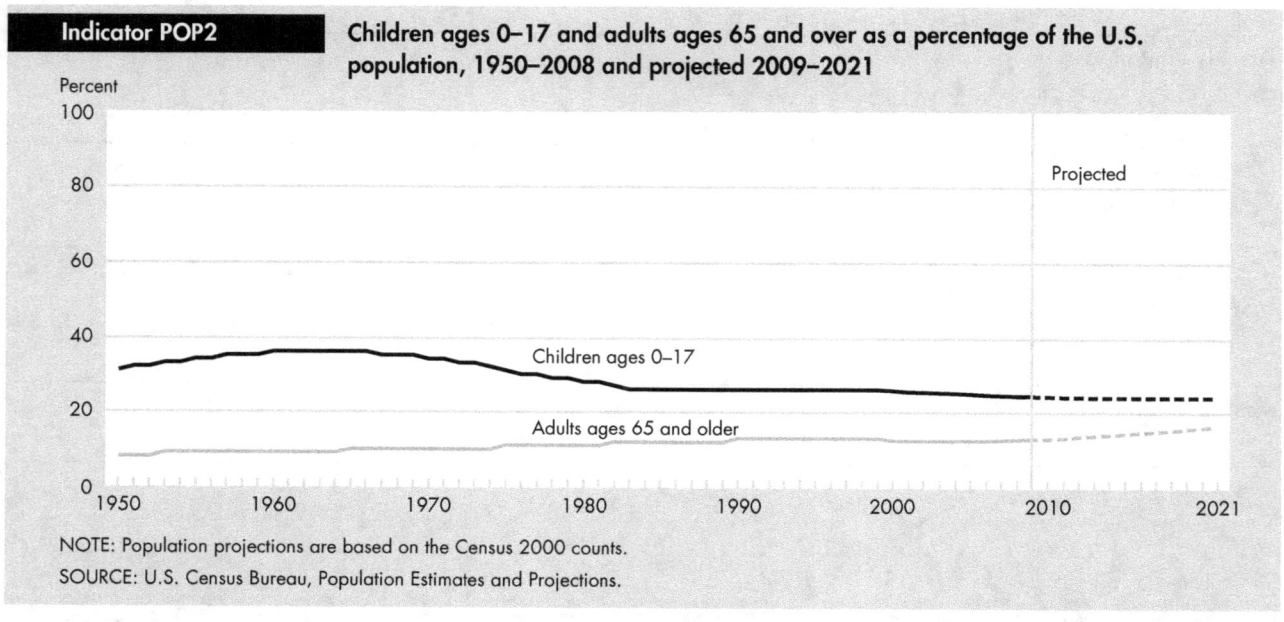

Indicator POP2

Children ages 0–17 and adults ages 65 and over as a percentage of the U.S. population, 1950–2008 and projected 2009–2021

NOTE: Population projections are based on the Census 2000 counts.

SOURCE: U.S. Census Bureau, Population Estimates and Projections.

Racial and ethnic diversity has grown dramatically in the United States in the last three decades. This increased diversity appeared first among children and later in the older population. The population is projected to become even more diverse in the decades to come. In 2008, 56 percent of U.S. children were White, non-Hispanic; 22 percent were Hispanic; 15 percent were Black; 4 percent were Asian; and 5 percent were "All other races." The percentage of children who are Hispanic has increased faster than that of any other racial or ethnic group, growing from 9 percent of the child population in 1980 to 22 percent in 2008. By 2021, it is projected that 1 in 4 children in the United States will be of Hispanic origin.

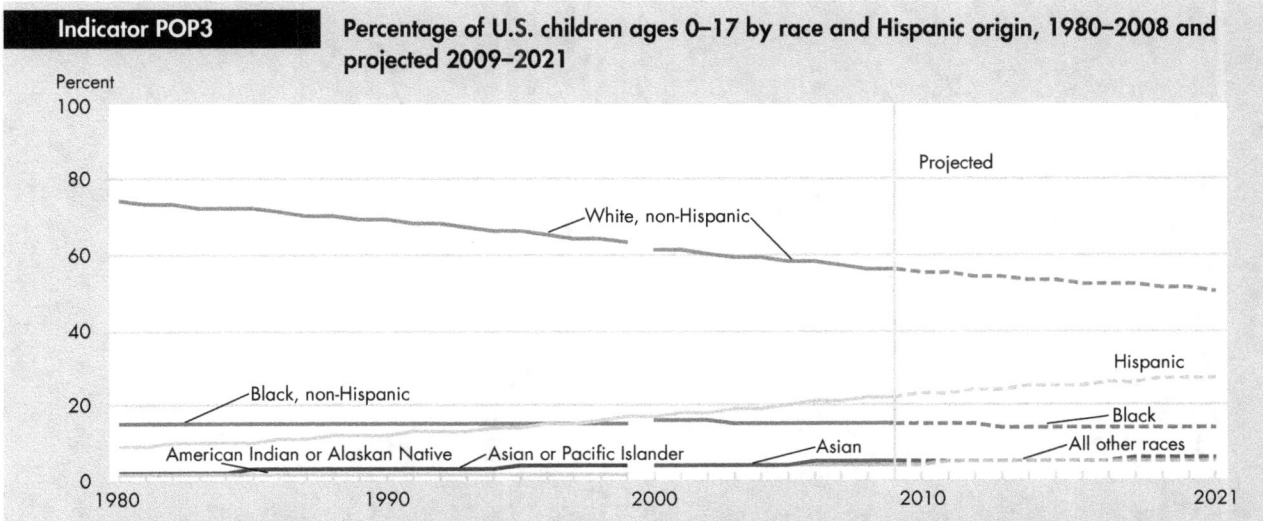

Indicator POP3 — Percentage of U.S. children ages 0–17 by race and Hispanic origin, 1980–2008 and projected 2009–2021

NOTE: Data from 2000 onward are not directly comparable with data from earlier years. Prior to 2000, race data followed a 1977 Office of Management and Budget directive on the collection and presentation of statistics on race and ethnicity. Data for 2000 and subsequent years reflect conversion to OMB's 1997 directive on the collection and presentation of statistics on race and ethnicity. The revised directive refined many race categories and included a provision for identifying multiracial respondents. Identification of Hispanic and other ethnic origins is done independently of race. Thus, Hispanics may be of any race. Except for the "All other races" category, all race groups discussed from 2000 onward refer to people who indicated only one racial identity. Non-Hispanic Whites are used as the comparison group for other race groups and Hispanics. For additional information see http://www.census.gov/population/www/socdemo/race/racefactcb.html and http://www.whitehouse.gov/omb/fedreg/1997standards.html. Unless otherwise specified, statistics by race reported here include persons of Hispanic origin.

SOURCE: U.S. Census Bureau, Population Estimates and Projections.

Data can be found in Tables POP1–POP3 on pages 89–91.

Indicators of Children's Well-Being

Family and Social Environment

The indicators in this section present data on the composition of children's families and the social environment in which they live. The seven indicators include family structure and children's living arrangements, births to unmarried women, child care, presence of a foreign-born parent, language spoken at home and difficulty speaking English, adolescent births, and child maltreatment.

Family Structure and Children's Living Arrangements

The structure of children's families is associated with the economic, parental, and community resources available to children and their well-being.

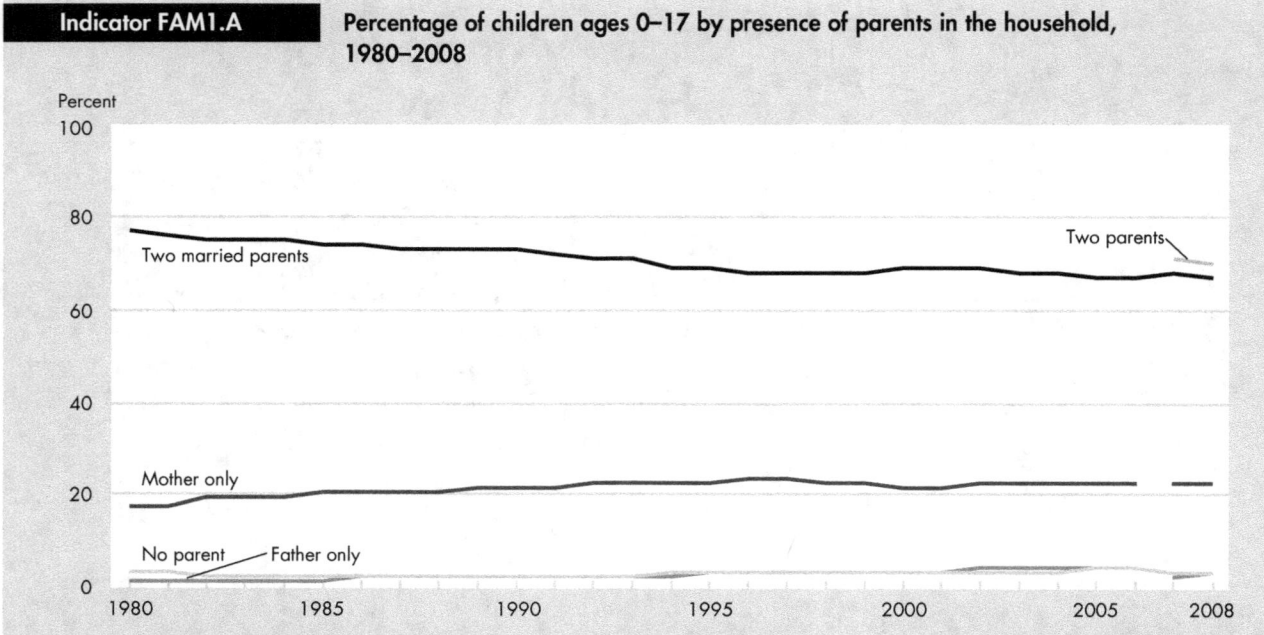

Indicator FAM1.A   **Percentage of children ages 0–17 by presence of parents in the household, 1980–2008**

NOTE: Prior to 2007, Current Population Survey (CPS) data identified only one parent on the child's record. This meant that a second parent could only be identified if they were married to the first parent. In 2007, a second parent identifier was added to CPS. This permits identification of two coresident parents, even if the parents are not married to each other. In this figure "two parents" reflects all children who have both a mother and father identified in the household, including biological, step, and adoptive parents. Before 2007, "mother only" and "father only" included some children who lived with a parent who was living with the other parent of the child, but was not married to them. Beginning in 2007, "mother only" and "father only" refer to children for whom only one parent has been identified, whether biological, step, or adoptive.

SOURCE: U.S. Census Bureau, Current Population Survey, Annual Social and Economic Supplements.

- In 2008, 67 percent of children ages 0–17 lived with two married parents, down from 77 percent in 1980.

- In 2008, 23 percent of children lived with only their mothers, 4 percent lived with only their fathers, and 4 percent lived with neither of their parents.[1]

- In 2008, 75 percent of White, non-Hispanic, 64 percent of Hispanic, and 35 percent of Black children lived with two married parents.[2]

- The proportion of Hispanic children living with two married parents decreased from 75 percent in 1980 to 64 percent in 2008.

- Due to improved measurement, it is now possible to identify children living with two parents who are not married to each other. Three percent of all children lived with two unmarried parents in 2008.

For a detailed measure of living arrangements of children, see FAM1.B on page 3.

While most children spend the majority of their childhood living with two parents, some children have other living arrangements. Information about the presence of parents and other adults in the family, such as the parent's unmarried partner, grandparents, and other relatives, is important for understanding children's social, economic, and developmental well-being.

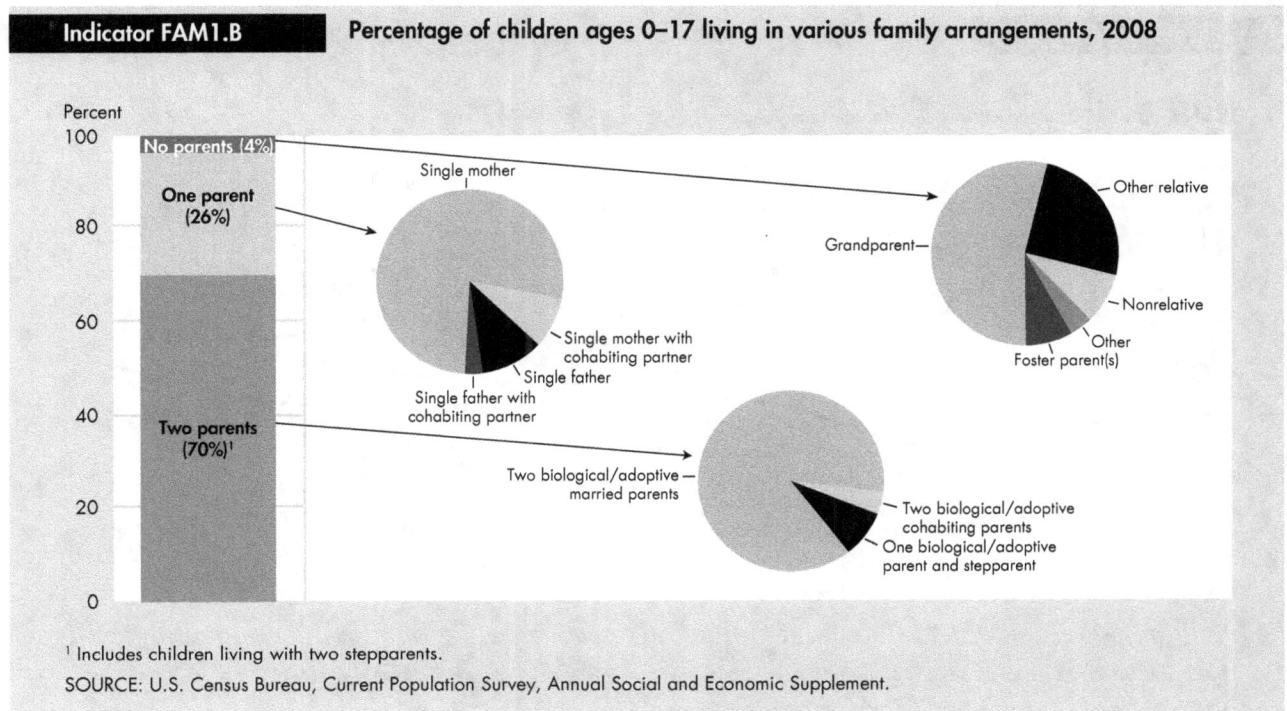

Indicator FAM1.B — Percentage of children ages 0–17 living in various family arrangements, 2008

[1] Includes children living with two stepparents.

SOURCE: U.S. Census Bureau, Current Population Survey, Annual Social and Economic Supplement.

- FAM1.B provides more detailed data about children's living arrangements, using information about the coresident parents for each child, as well as the detailed type of relationship between parent and child—biological, step, or adoptive. In 2008, there were about 74 million children ages 0–17. Seventy percent of them lived with two parents, 26 percent lived with one parent, and about 4 percent lived in households without parents.

- Among children living with two parents, 92 percent lived with both biological or adoptive parents, and 8 percent lived with a biological or adoptive parent and a stepparent. About 74 percent of children living with at least one stepparent lived with their biological mother and stepfather.[3]

- About 4 percent of children who lived with both biological or adoptive parents had parents who were not married.

- The majority of children living with one parent lived with their single mother. Some single parents had cohabiting partners. Nineteen percent of children living with single fathers and 10 percent of children

living with single mothers also lived with their parent's cohabiting partner. Out of all children ages 0–17, 4.6 million (6 percent) lived with a parent or parents who were cohabiting.

- Among the 2.8 million children (4 percent) not living with either parent in 2008, 54 percent (1.5 million) lived with grandparents, 25 percent lived with other relatives, and 21 percent lived with nonrelatives. Of children in nonrelatives' homes, 38 percent (228,000) lived with foster parents.

- Older children were less likely to live with two parents—65 percent of children ages 15–17 lived with two parents, compared with 69 percent of children ages 6–14 and 73 percent of those ages 0–5. Among children living with two parents, older children were more likely than younger children to live with a stepparent and less likely than younger children to live with cohabiting parents.[3]

Bullets contain references to data that can be found in Tables FAM1.A and FAM1.B on pages 92–95. Endnotes begin on page 73.

Births to Unmarried Women

Increases in births to unmarried women are among the many changes in American society that have affected family structure and the economic security of children.[4] Children of unmarried mothers are at higher risk of adverse birth outcomes such as low birthweight and infant mortality than are children of married mothers. They are also more likely to live in poverty than children of married mothers.[5–9]

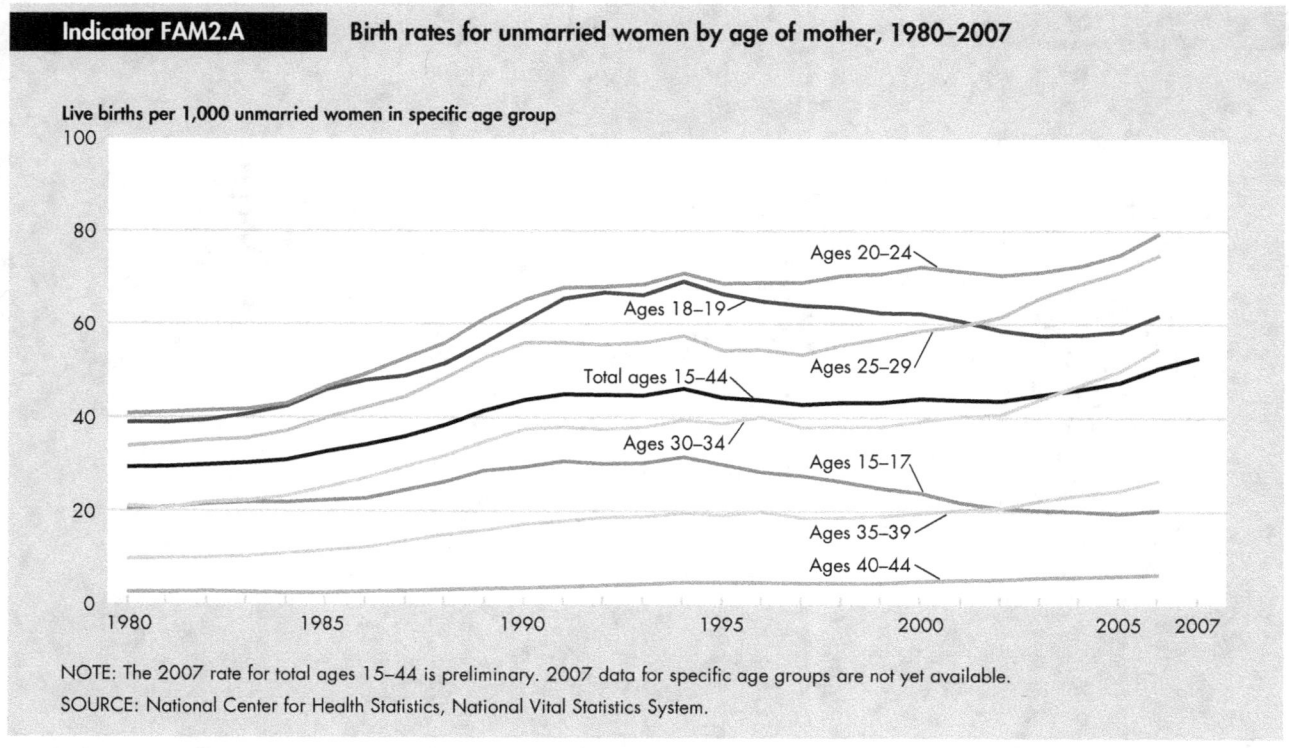

Indicator FAM2.A   **Birth rates for unmarried women by age of mother, 1980–2007**

Live births per 1,000 unmarried women in specific age group

NOTE: The 2007 rate for total ages 15–44 is preliminary. 2007 data for specific age groups are not yet available.
SOURCE: National Center for Health Statistics, National Vital Statistics System.

- There were 53 births for every 1,000 unmarried women ages 15–44 in 2007.[10]

- Between 1980 and 1994, the birth rate for unmarried women ages 15–44 increased from 29 to 46 per 1,000. Between 1995 and 2002, the rate fluctuated little, ranging from 43 to 44 per 1,000; from 2002 to 2007, however, the rate increased from 44 to 53 per 1,000.[8,10,11]

- Rates in 2006 remained highest for women ages 20–24 (79.5 per 1,000), followed closely by the rate for women ages 25–29 (74.9 per 1,000).[6,11]

- The birth rate among unmarried adolescents ages 15–19 declined between 1994 and 2005, and then increased in 2006. Among adolescent subgroups, the rate for adolescents ages 15–17 declined from 31.7 per 1,000 in 1994 to 19.7 in 2005 and increased to 20.4 in 2006. For adolescents ages 18–19 the birth rate declined from 1994 to 2003 and increased annually from 2003 to 2006. Birth rates for unmarried women ages 20–44 changed relatively little during the mid- to late 1990s, but increased in the 2000s. For women ages 20–24 the rate rose from 70.5 per 1,000 in 2002 to 79.5 in 2006. For women ages 25–29 the rate rose from 1997 (53.4

per 1,000) to 2006 (74.9), and for unmarried women ages 30–44 birth rates have steadily increased since the late 1990s.

- The long-term rise between 1960 and 1994 in the nonmarital birth rate is linked to a number of factors.[8] The proportion of women of childbearing age who were unmarried increased from under one-third in 1960 to almost half in 1994. Concurrently, there was an increase in nonmarital cohabitation.[12] The likelihood that an unmarried woman would marry before a child was born declined from the early 1960s to the early 1980s and continued to fall, although more modestly, through the 1990s.[11,13] At the same time, childbearing within marriage fell by almost half between 1960 and 1994.[6–8,11]

- After several years of relative stability beginning in the mid- to late 1990s, the birth rate for unmarried women has increased since 2002. The proportion of women of childbearing age who were unmarried continued to rise to over half in 2007. However, nonmarital cohabitation has remained relatively unchanged: nearly 3 in 10 unmarried women ages 25–29 in 2002 were in cohabiting relationships.[14]

Children are at greater risk for adverse consequences when born to a single mother because the social, emotional, and financial resources available to the family may be more limited.[5] The proportion of births to unmarried women is useful for understanding the extent to which children born in a given year may be affected by any disadvantage—social, financial, or health—associated with being born outside of marriage. The change in the percentage of births to unmarried women reflects changes in the birth rate for unmarried women relative to the birth rate for married women.[15]

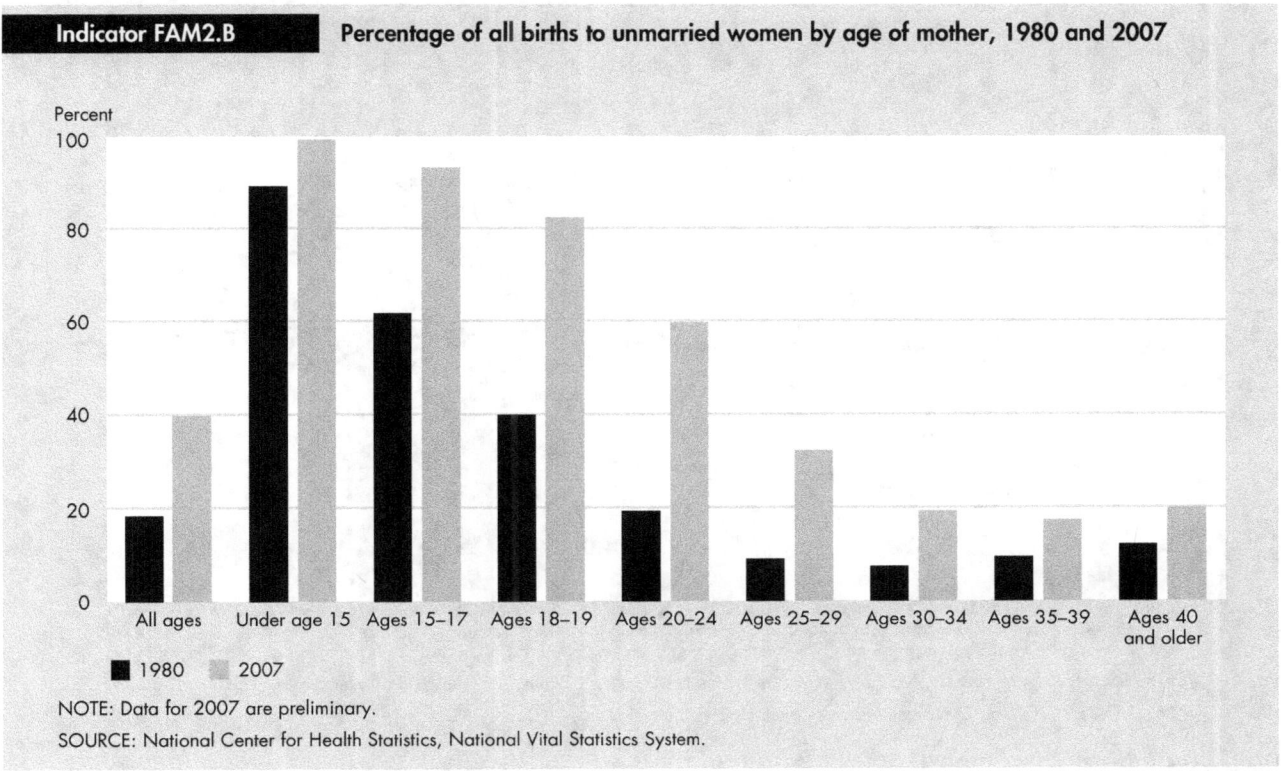

Indicator FAM2.B **Percentage of all births to unmarried women by age of mother, 1980 and 2007**

■ 1980 ■ 2007

NOTE: Data for 2007 are preliminary.

SOURCE: National Center for Health Statistics, National Vital Statistics System.

■ In 2007, 40 percent of all births were to unmarried women.[10]

■ The percentage of all births to unmarried women rose from 18 percent of total births in 1980 to 33 percent in 1994. From 1994 to 2002, the percentage ranged from 32 to 34 percent. The percentage increased more rapidly since 2002, reaching 40 percent in 2007.

■ Between 1980 and 2007, the proportion of births to unmarried women rose for women in all age groups. Among adolescents, the proportion was high throughout the period and rose from 62 to 93 percent for ages 15–17 and from 40 to 82 percent for ages 18–19. The proportion more than tripled for births to women in their twenties, rising from 19 to 60 percent for ages 20–24 and from 9 to 32 percent for ages 25–29. The proportion of births to unmarried women in their thirties more than doubled, from 8 to 19 percent.[8,11]

■ Nearly 4 in 10 total births, including more than 4 in 10 first births, were to unmarried women in 2006. Seven in 10 births to women under age 25 having their first child were nonmarital.[16]

■ The increases in the proportion of births to unmarried women, especially during the 1980s, were linked to increases in the birth rates for unmarried women in all age groups during this period. In addition, the number of unmarried women increased more rapidly than the number of married women increased, as women from the baby boom generation postponed marriage.[8,16,17]

■ During the late 1990s, the rate of increase in the proportion of births to unmarried women slowed. The comparative stability was linked to a renewed rise in birth rates for married women.[6,8] Since 2002, the rate of increase in the proportion of births to unmarried women has grown, reflecting increases, especially among adult women aged 20 and older, in nonmarital birth rates concurrent with relatively little change in birth rates for married women.[8,16]

Bullets contain references to data that can be found in Tables FAM2.A and FAM2.B on pages 96–97. Endnotes begin on page 73.

Child Care

Many children spend time with a child care provider other than their parents. This indicator presents two aspects of early childhood child care usage: a historical trend of the primary child care provider used by employed mothers for their young children and overall use of different providers regardless of parents' work status.[18]

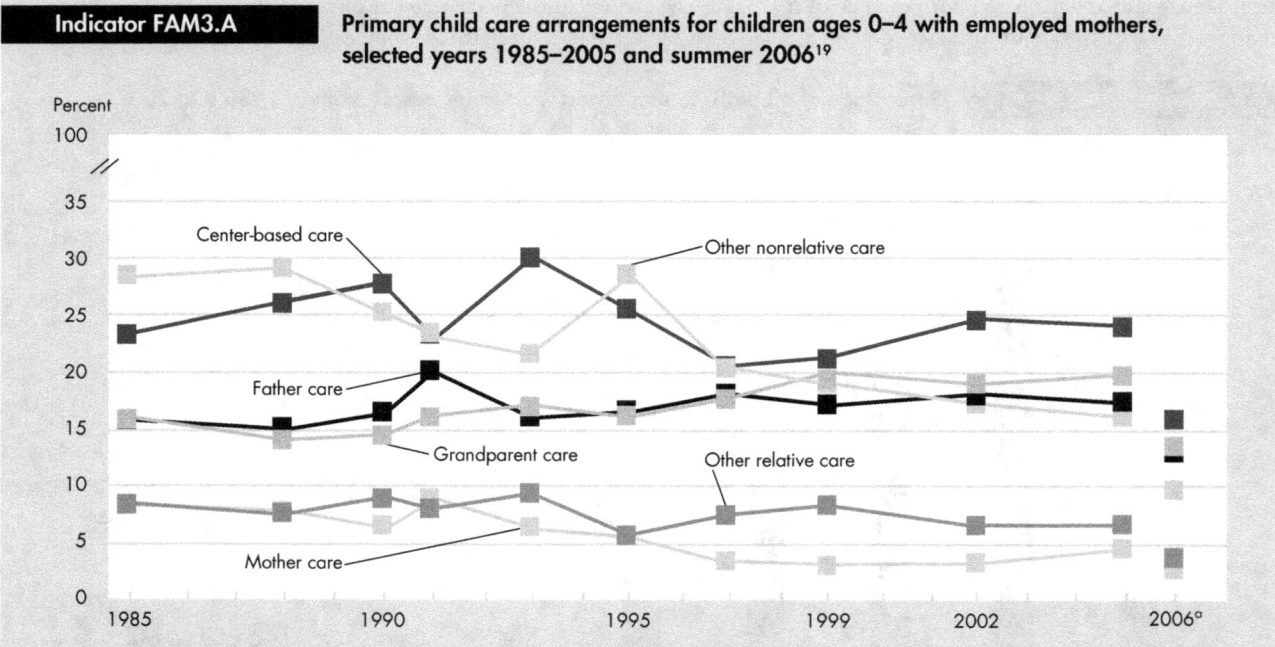

Indicator FAM3.A | **Primary child care arrangements for children ages 0–4 with employed mothers, selected years 1985–2005 and summer 2006[19]**

[a] SIPP child care data collected in 2006 cannot be compared directly with SIPP child care data from previous years due to seasonality differences such as preschool closings, seasonal variations in school activities, and availability of child care arrangements. The 2006 child care data were collected during summer months, whereas previous survey years typically collected data during spring or fall months.

NOTE: The primary arrangement is the arrangement used for the most number of hours per week while the mother worked.

SOURCE: U.S. Census Bureau, Survey of Income and Program Participation.

Indicator FAM3.A

- FAM3.A provides information about primary child care arrangements for preschoolers with employed mothers for selected years and for the summer months of 2006, thus providing a unique opportunity to examine summer child care patterns. Summer child care arrangements for preschoolers follow a similar pattern seen in non-summer months in that relatives play a primary role. Specifically, during the summer months of 2006, 32 percent of children ages 0–4 with employed mothers were primarily cared for by a relative: their father, grandparent, sibling, other relative, or mother while she worked. Sixteen percent spent time in a center-based arrangement (day care, nursery school, preschool, or Head Start). Ten percent were primarily cared for by a nonrelative in a home-based environment such as a family day care provider, nanny, babysitter, or au pair.

- Among children in families in poverty during the summer months of 2006, 12 percent were in center-based care as their primary arrangement, while 5 percent were with other relatives. Comparatively, a larger percentage of children in families at or above the poverty line were in center-based care (16 percent), and a smaller percentage were cared for by other relatives (4 percent).

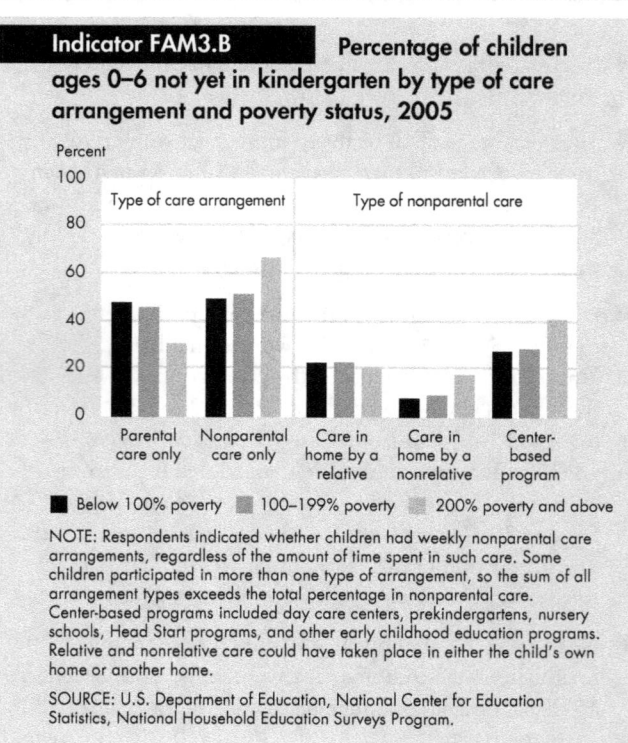

Indicator FAM3.B | **Percentage of children ages 0–6 not yet in kindergarten by type of care arrangement and poverty status, 2005**

■ Below 100% poverty ■ 100–199% poverty ■ 200% poverty and above

NOTE: Respondents indicated whether children had weekly nonparental care arrangements, regardless of the amount of time spent in such care. Some children participated in more than one type of arrangement, so the sum of all arrangement types exceeds the total percentage in nonparental care. Center-based programs included day care centers, prekindergartens, nursery schools, Head Start programs, and other early childhood education programs. Relative and nonrelative care could have taken place in either the child's own home or another home.

SOURCE: U.S. Department of Education, National Center for Education Statistics, National Household Education Surveys Program.

School-age children may spend their weekday, nonschool time in child care arrangements, and also may engage in a variety of enrichment activities such as sports, arts, clubs, academic activities, religious activities, and community service. In addition, some children care for themselves without adult supervision for some time during the week. This measure presents the most recent data available on how grade-school-age children spend their out-of-school time.

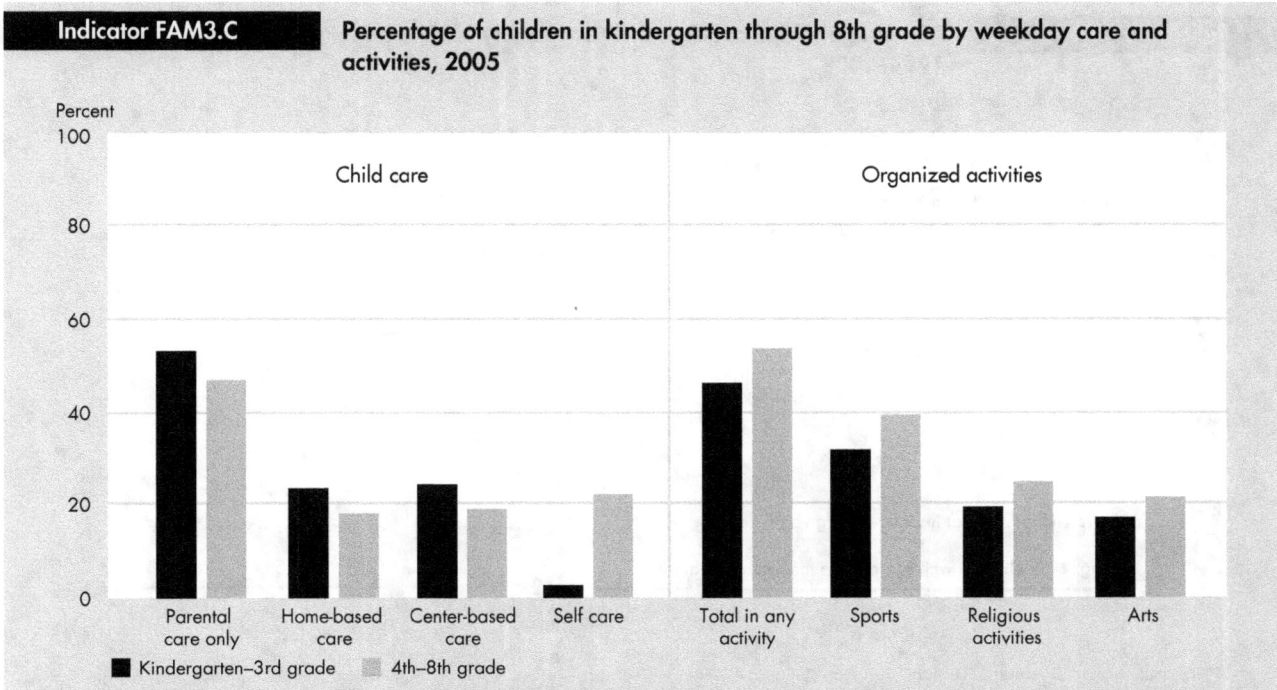

Indicator FAM3.C — Percentage of children in kindergarten through 8th grade by weekday care and activities, 2005

NOTE: Some children participate in more than one type of care arrangement or activity. For self care, parents reported that their child is responsible for himself/herself before or after school on a regular basis. Parents reported on organized before- or after-school activities that are undertaken by their child on a regular basis.

SOURCE: U.S. Department of Education, National Center for Education Statistics, National Household Education Surveys Program.

Indicator FAM3.B

■ In 2005, 61 percent of children ages 0–6 who were not yet in kindergarten (about 12 million children) received some form of child care on a regular basis from persons other than their parents. This is about the same proportion of children in child care as in 1995.

■ Patterns of child care vary by the poverty status of the child's family. In 2005, children ages 0–6 in families with incomes at least twice the poverty level were more likely than children in families with incomes below the poverty level and children in families with incomes 100–199 percent of the poverty level to be in nonparental care (68 percent versus 51 and 53 percent, respectively). In addition, children in families with incomes at least twice the poverty level were more likely than children in families with lower incomes to be in home care by a nonrelative or in center-based programs such as nursery schools and other early childhood education programs.

Indicator FAM3.C

■ In 2005, 47 percent of children in kindergarten through 3rd grade and 53 percent of those in 4th through 8th grade received some nonparental child care.

■ In 2005, parents reported that older children were more likely to care for themselves before or after school than were younger children: 3 percent of children in kindergarten through 3rd grade and 22 percent of children in 4th through 8th grade cared for themselves regularly either before or after school.

■ Children in the higher grades were more likely to engage in some kind of organized before- or after-school activity than were children in the lower grades. Children from families in poverty were less likely than those in families at or above poverty to participate in activities. Children in kindergarten through 8th grade were more likely to participate in sports than in any other activity.

Bullets contain references to data that can be found in Tables FAM3.A–FAM3.C on pages 98–103. Endnotes begin on page 73.

Children of at Least One Foreign-Born Parent

he foreign-born population of the United States has grown since 1970.[20] This increase in the past generation has largely been due to immigration from Latin America and Asia, and has led to an increase in the diversity of language and cultural backgrounds of children growing up in the United States.[21] As a result of language and cultural barriers confronting children and their parents, children with foreign-born parents may need additional resources both at school and at home.[22]

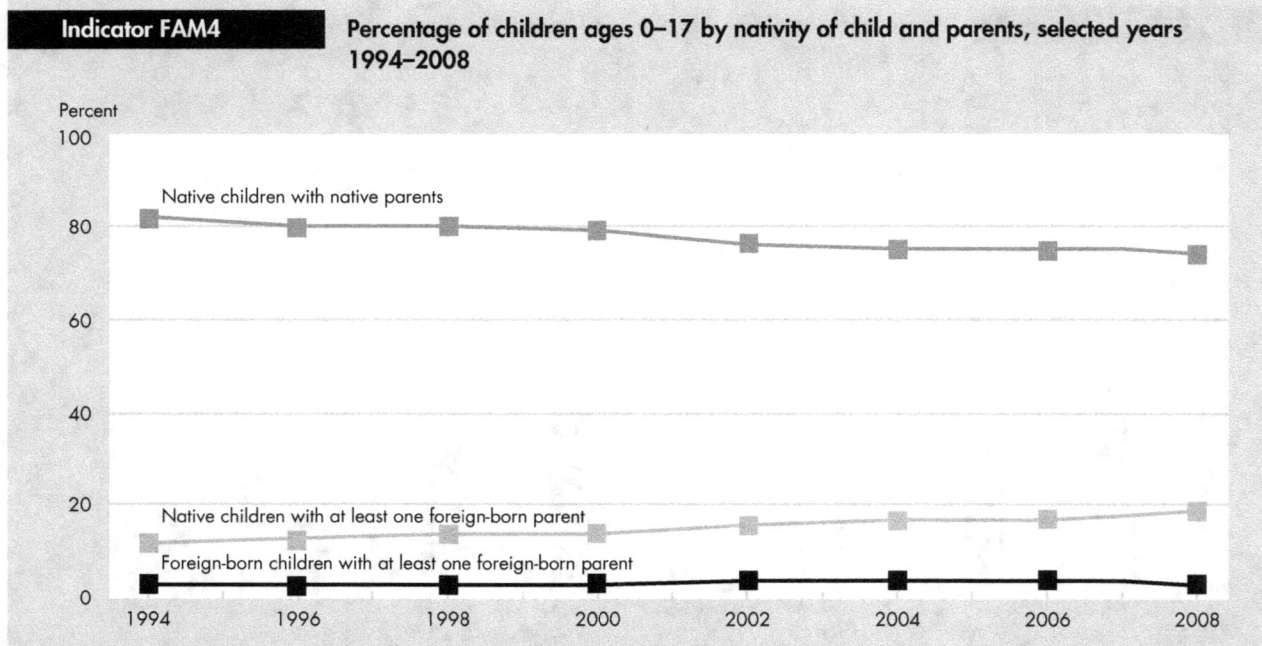

Indicator FAM4

Percentage of children ages 0–17 by nativity of child and parents, selected years 1994–2008

NOTE: Includes children under 18 in households. Children living in households with no parents present are not shown in this figure, but are included in the bases for the percentages. Native parents means that all of the parents that the child lives with are native-born, while foreign-born means that one or both of the child's parents are foreign-born. Anyone with U.S. citizenship at birth is considered native, which includes people born in the United States and in U.S. outlying areas, and people born abroad with at least one American parent. Foreign-born children with native parents are included in the native children with native parents category. Prior to 2007, Current Population Survey (CPS) data identified only one parent on the child's record. This meant that a second parent could only be identified if they were married to the first parent. In 2007, a second parent identifier was added to CPS. This permits identification of two coresident parents, even if the parents are not married to each other.

SOURCE: U.S. Census Bureau, Current Population Survey, Annual Social and Economic Supplements.

- In 2008, 19 percent of children were native children with at least one foreign-born parent, and 3 percent were foreign-born children with at least one foreign-born parent. Overall, the percentage of all children living in the United States with at least one foreign-born parent rose from 15 percent in 1994 to 22 percent in 2008.

- In 2008, 29 percent of foreign-born children with at least one foreign-born parent, 26 percent of native children with at least one foreign-born parent, and 7 percent of native children with native parents had a parent with less than a high school diploma or equivalent credential.[23]

- In 2008, 30 percent of foreign-born children with foreign-born parents lived below the poverty line, compared with 21 percent of native children with foreign-born parents and 16 percent of native children with native parents.

- Regardless of their own nativity status, children with at least one foreign-born parent more often lived in a household with two parents present than did children with no foreign-born parents. In 2008, 84 percent of native children with at least one foreign-born parent lived with two parents, compared with 70 percent of children with two native parents.

Bullets contain references to data that can be found in Table FAM4 on pages 104–106. Endnotes begin on page 73.

Language Spoken at Home and Difficulty Speaking English

Children who speak languages other than English at home and who also have difficulty speaking English[24] may face greater challenges progressing in school and in the labor market. Once it is determined that a student speaks another language, school officials must, by law, evaluate the child's English ability to determine whether the student needs services (such as special instruction to improve his or her English) and provide these services if needed.

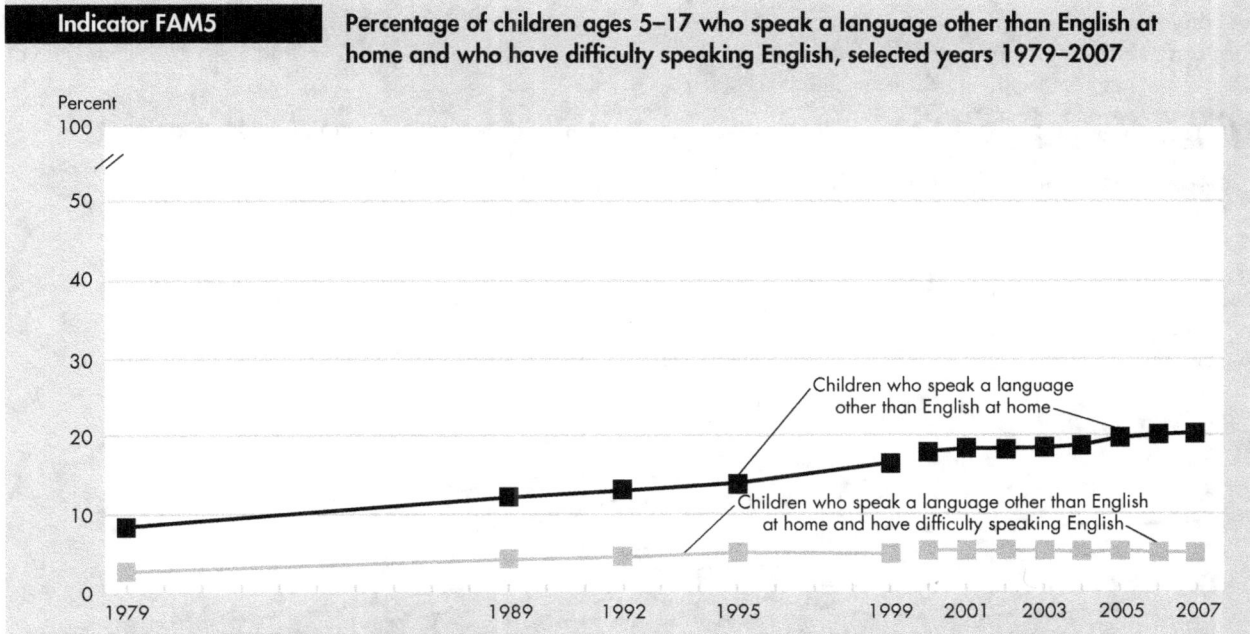

Indicator FAM5

Percentage of children ages 5–17 who speak a language other than English at home and who have difficulty speaking English, selected years 1979–2007

NOTE: Numbers from the 1995 and 1999 Current Population Survey (CPS) may reflect changes in the survey because of newly instituted computer-assisted interviewing techniques and/or because of the change in the population controls to the 1990 Census-based estimates, with adjustments. A break is shown in the lines between 1999 and 2000 because data from 1979 to 1999 come from the CPS, while beginning in 2000 the data come from the American Community Survey (ACS). The questions were the same on the CPS and the ACS questionnaires.

SOURCE: U.S. Census Bureau, October (1992, 1995, and 1999) and November (1979 and 1989) Current Population Surveys, and 2000–2007 American Community Survey.

- In 2007, 21 percent of school-age children spoke a language other than English at home and 5 percent of school-age children both spoke a language other than English at home and had difficulty speaking English.

- In 2007, the percentage of school-age children who spoke a language other than English at home varied by region of the country, from a low of 11 percent in the Midwest to a high of 34 percent in the West.

- In 2007, the percentage of school-age children who had difficulty with English also varied by region, from a low of 3 percent in the Midwest to a high of 9 percent in the West.

- In 2007, 64 percent of school-age Asian children and 68 percent of school-age Hispanic children spoke a language other than English at home, compared with 6 percent of school-age White, non-Hispanic children and 5 percent of school-age Black, non-Hispanic children.[2]

- In 2007, 16 percent of school-age Asian children and 18 percent of school-age Hispanic children both spoke another language at home and had difficulty with English, compared with about 1 percent of both school-age White, non-Hispanic children and school-age Black, non-Hispanic children.[25]

- About 6 percent of school-age children spoke a language other than English at home and lived in a linguistically isolated household in 2007. A linguistically isolated household is one in which all persons age 14 or over speak a language other than English at home and no person age 14 or over speaks English "Very well."

Bullets contain references to data that can be found in Table FAM5 on pages 107–110. Endnotes begin on page 73.

Adolescent Births

Bearing a child during adolescence is often associated with long-term difficulties for the mother and her child. These consequences are often attributable to poverty and other adverse socioeconomic circumstances that frequently accompany early childbearing.[26] Compared with babies born to older mothers, babies born to adolescent mothers, particularly young adolescent mothers, are at higher risk of low birthweight and infant mortality.[6,9,27] They are more likely to grow up in homes that offer lower levels of emotional support and cognitive stimulation and they are less likely to earn high school diplomas. For the mothers, giving birth during adolescence is associated with limited educational attainment, which in turn can reduce employment prospects and earnings potential.[28] The birth rate of adolescents under age 18 is a measure of particular interest because the mothers are still of school age.

| Indicator FAM6 | Birth rates for females ages 15–17 by race and Hispanic origin, 1980–2007 |

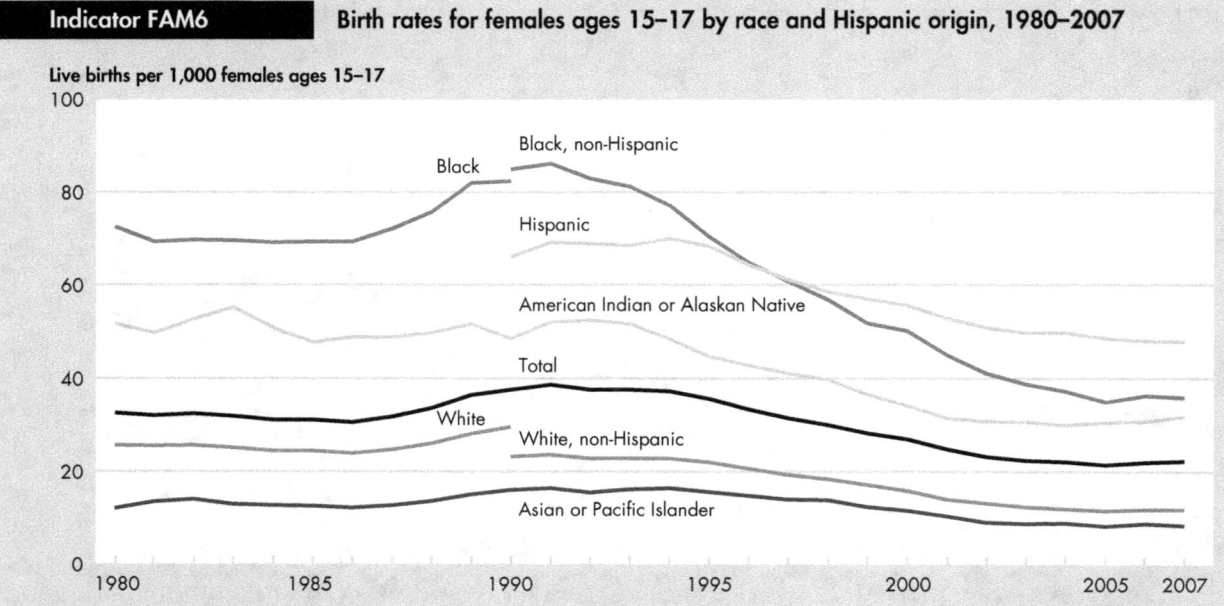

NOTE: Data for 2007 are preliminary. Race refers to mother's race. The 1977 OMB Standards for Data on Race and Ethnicity were used to classify persons into one of the following four racial groups: White, Black, American Indian or Alaskan Native, or Asian or Pacific Islander. Although state reporting of birth certificate data is transitioning to comply with the 1997 OMB standard for race and ethnic statistics, data from states reporting multiple races were bridged to the single-race categories of the 1977 OMB standards for comparability with other states and for trend analysis. Rates for 1980–1989 are not shown for Hispanics; White, non-Hispanics; or Black, non-Hispanics because information on Hispanic origin of the mother was not reported on birth certificates of most states and because population estimates by Hispanic ethnicity for the reporting states were not available. Data on race and Hispanic origin are collected and reported separately. Persons of Hispanic origin may be of any race.

SOURCE: National Center for Health Statistics, National Vital Statistics System.

- In 2007, the adolescent birth rate was 22.2 per 1,000 adolescents ages 15–17. There were 140,640 births to these adolescents in 2007 according to preliminary data. The 2007 rate was higher than the 2006 rate of 22.0 per 1,000. This was the second consecutive year of increase in this measure since the long-term decline beginning 1991–1992.[6,10,11]

- The birth rate among adolescents ages 15–17 declined from 38.6 to 21.4 births per 1,000, between 1991 and 2005. This decline followed an increase between 1986 and 1991.

- There remain substantial racial and ethnic disparities among the birth rates for adolescents ages 15–17. In 2007, the birth rates for this age group were 8.4 for Asians or Pacific Islanders, 11.8 for White, non-Hispanics, 31.7 for American Indians or Alaskan Natives, 35.8 for Black, non-Hispanics, and 47.8 for Hispanics.[10]

- The birth rate for Black, non-Hispanic and White, non-Hispanic females ages 15–17 dropped more than

half between 1991 and 2005, completely reversing the increase between 1986 and 1991. Rates for both groups increased in 2006 and were statistically unchanged in 2007.

- The birth rate for Hispanic adolescents in this age group fell during 1991 to 2007, although at a slower pace than for Black and White non-Hispanic adolescents. Most of the decline for Hispanic adolescents occurred by 2003.[10,11]

- In 2007, 93 percent of births to females ages 15–17 were to unmarried mothers, compared with 62 percent in 1980 (See FAM2.B).

- The rates of first and second births for females ages 15–17 declined by two-fifths and nearly two-thirds, respectively, between 1991 and 2005; both rates rose slightly in 2006.[6]

Bullets contain references to data that can be found in Table FAM6 on pages 111–112. Endnotes begin on page 73.

Child Maltreatment

C hild maltreatment includes physical, sexual, and psychological abuse, as well as neglect (including medical neglect). Maltreatment in general is associated with a number of negative outcomes for children, including lower school achievement, juvenile delinquency, substance abuse, and mental health problems.[29] Certain types of maltreatment can result in long-term physical, social, and emotional problems, and even death. For example, "shaken baby syndrome" can result in mental retardation, cerebral palsy, or paralysis. Child maltreatment includes both fatal and nonfatal maltreatment.

Indicator FAM7	Rate of substantiated maltreatment reports of children ages 0–17 by age, 1998–2007

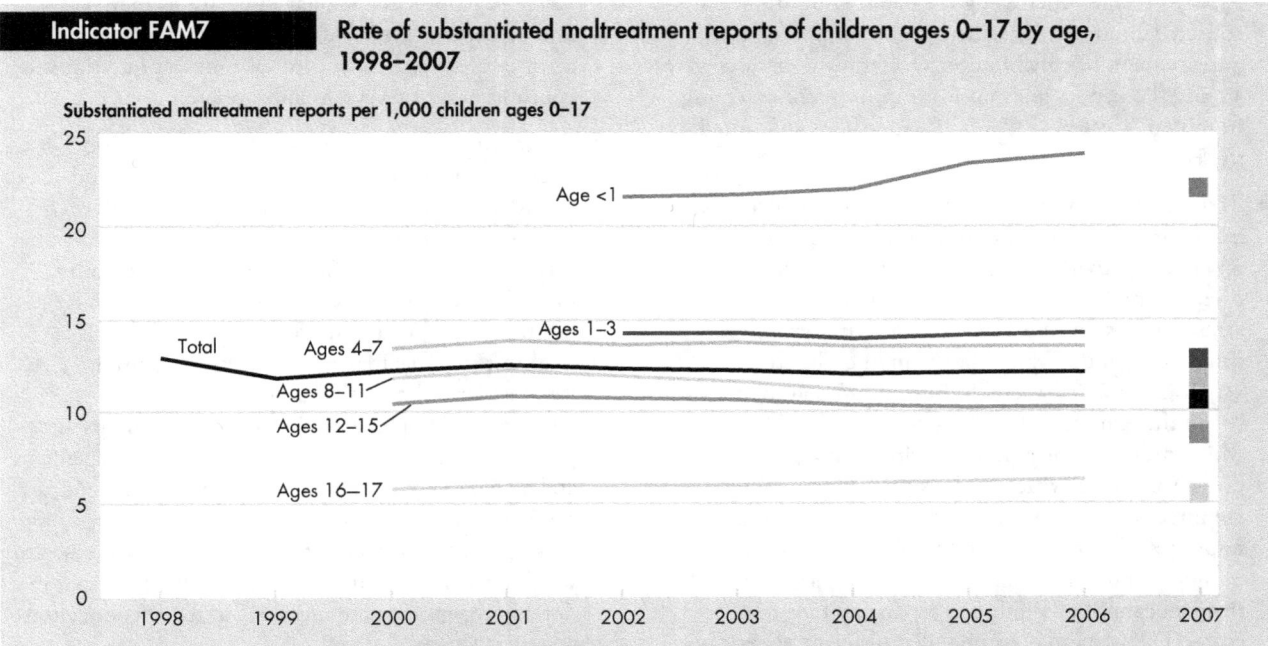

Substantiated maltreatment reports per 1,000 children ages 0–17

NOTE: The count of child victims is based on the number of investigations by Child Protective Services that found the child to be a victim of one or more types of maltreatment. The count of victims is, therefore, a report-based count and is a "duplicated count," since an individual child may have been maltreated more than once. The number of states reporting varies from year to year. States vary in their definition of abuse and neglect. Data from 2007 are not directly comparable with prior years as differences may be partially attributed to changes in one state's procedures for determination of maltreatment. Other reasons include the increase in children who received an "other" disposition, the decrease in the percentage of children who received a substantiated or indicated disposition, and the decrease in the number of children who received an investigation or assessment.

SOURCE: Administration for Children and Families, National Child Abuse and Neglect Data System.

■ In 2007, the rate of substantiated reports of child maltreatment was 11 per 1,000 children ages 0–17.[30]

■ From 1998 through 2002, the rate of substantiated reports of child maltreatment varied between 12 and 13 reports per 1,000 children and remained at approximately 12 reports per 1,000 children between 2002 and 2006.

■ Younger children are more frequently victims of child maltreatment than older children. In 2007, there were 22 substantiated child maltreatment reports per 1,000 children under age 1, compared with 13 for children ages 1–3, 12 for children ages 4–7, 9 for children ages 8–11, 9 for children ages 12–15, and 5 for adolescents ages 16–17.

■ Higher rates of maltreatment were reported for girls than boys (11 reports per 1,000 for females vs. 10 for males).

■ While neglect is the most common type of maltreatment across all age groups, types of

maltreatment vary by age. In 2007, 79 percent of substantiated child maltreatment reports for children ages 0–3 involved neglect, compared to 62 percent for adolescents ages 16–17. Twenty-one percent of substantiated reports for adolescents ages 16–17 involved physical abuse and 17 percent involved sexual abuse. Among substantiated reports for children ages 0–3, 13 percent involved physical abuse and 2 percent involved sexual abuse.

■ In 2007, Black, non-Hispanic children had the highest rates of substantiated child maltreatment reports (17 reports per 1,000 children), followed by American Indian or Alaska Native children (14), children of two or more races (14), Native Hawaiian or Other Pacific Islander children (14), Hispanic children (10), White, non-Hispanic children (9), and Asian children (2).

Bullets contain references to data that can be found in Tables FAM7.A and FAM7.B on pages 113–114. Endnotes begin on page 73.

Indicators Needed

Family and Social Environment

Current data collection systems at the national level do not provide extensive detailed information on children's families, their caregivers, or their social environments. Certain topical databases provide some of this information, but data need to be collected regularly across domains of child well-being. More details are needed on the following topics:

- *Family structure.* Increasing the detail of information collected about family structure and improving the measurement of cohabitation and family dynamics were among the key suggestions for improvement emerging from two "Counting Couples" workshops sponsored by the Forum.

- *Time use.* Currently, some Federal surveys collect information on the amount of time children spend on certain activities such as watching television and on participation rates in specific activities or care arrangements, but no Federal data source examines time spent on the whole spectrum of children's activities. In 2003, the U.S. Bureau of Labor Statistics began the American Time Use Survey (ATUS), which measures the amount of time people spend doing various activities, such as paid work, childcare, volunteering, and socializing. The survey includes responses from persons age 15 and older. Since the numbers of observations for older youth are small, the data cannot be published separately for each year. ATUS data may be included in future *America's*

Children reports as a regular indicator as more years of data become available. Forum agencies continue to be interested in the inclusion of time use questions for youth in other surveys, as appropriate.

- *Social connections and engagement.* The formation of close attachments to family, peers, school, and community have been linked to healthy youth development in numerous research studies. Additional research needs to be conducted to strengthen our understanding of how these relationships promote healthy development and protect youth from risks that, in turn, affect later life success. We currently lack regular indicators on aspects of healthy development, such as relationships with parents and peers, connections to teachers and school engagement, and civic or community involvement. To that end, the Forum co-sponsored the Indicators of Positive Development conference to define and measure healthy youth development and continues to be interested in developing appropriate measures of social connection and engagement.

Economic Circumstances

The well-being of children depends greatly on the economic circumstances and material well-being of their families. This section presents information on the economic resources of children's households and on their food-related well-being. Indicators of economic resources include income and poverty status of children's families and an indicator on secure employment of children's parents. An indicator on food security presents information on families with children that report difficulty obtaining adequate food. These indicators provide a broad perspective on children's economic situations.

Child Poverty and Family Income

Children in low-income families fare less well than children in more affluent families on many of the indicators in this report.[31] Compared with children living in families that are not in poverty, children living in poverty are more likely to have difficulty in school, to become teen parents, and, as adults, to earn less and be unemployed more frequently.[32,33] This indicator is based on the official poverty measure for the United States as defined in Office of Management and Budget Statistical Policy Directive 14.[34]

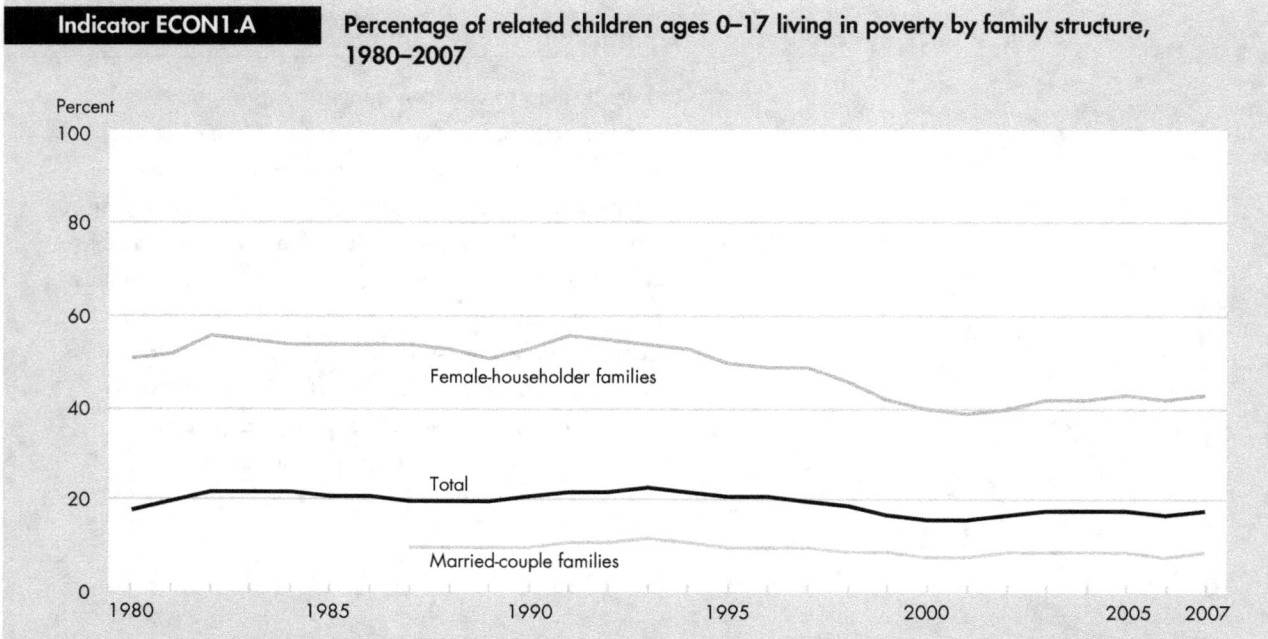

Indicator ECON1.A | **Percentage of related children ages 0–17 living in poverty by family structure, 1980–2007**

NOTE: Estimates for related children ages 0–17 include children related to the householder (or reference person of an unrelated subfamily) who are not themselves a householder or spouse of the householder (or family reference person). In 2007, the average poverty threshold for a family of four was $21,203.

SOURCE: U.S. Census Bureau, Current Population Survey, Annual Social and Economic Supplements.

- In 2007, 18 percent of all children ages 0–17 lived in poverty, an increase from 17 percent in 2006. Compared with White, non-Hispanic children, the poverty rate was higher for Black children and for Hispanic children. In 2007, 10 percent of White, non-Hispanic children, 35 percent of Black children, and 29 percent of Hispanic children lived in poverty.[2,31]

- As was the case for all children, the percentage of related children with family incomes below the poverty threshold was higher in 2007 (18 percent) than in 2006 (17 percent). The poverty rate for related children has fluctuated since the early 1980s, reaching a peak of 22 percent in 1993 and a low of 16 percent in 2000.

- The poverty rate for children living in female-householder families (no spouse present) also fluctuated between 1980 and 1994; it then declined between 1994 and 2000 by more than the decline in the poverty rate for all children in families. In 1994, 53 percent of children living in female-householder families were living in poverty; by 2007, this proportion was 43 percent.

- Children in married-couple families were less likely to live in poverty than children living in female-householder families. In 2007, 9 percent of children in married-couple families were living in poverty, compared with 43 percent in female-householder families.

- Related children ages 0–5 were more likely to be living in families with incomes below the poverty line than those ages 6–17. In 2007, 21 percent of related children ages 0–5 lived in poverty, compared with 16 percent of older related children.

- In 2007, some 5 percent of White, non-Hispanic children in married-couple families lived in poverty, compared with 32 percent of White, non-Hispanic children in female-householder families. Eleven percent of Black children in married-couple families lived in poverty, compared with 50 percent of Black children in female-householder families. Nineteen percent of Hispanic children in married-couple families lived in poverty, compared with 52 percent of Hispanic children in female-householder families.[35]

The distribution of the income of children's families provides a broader picture of children's economic situations.

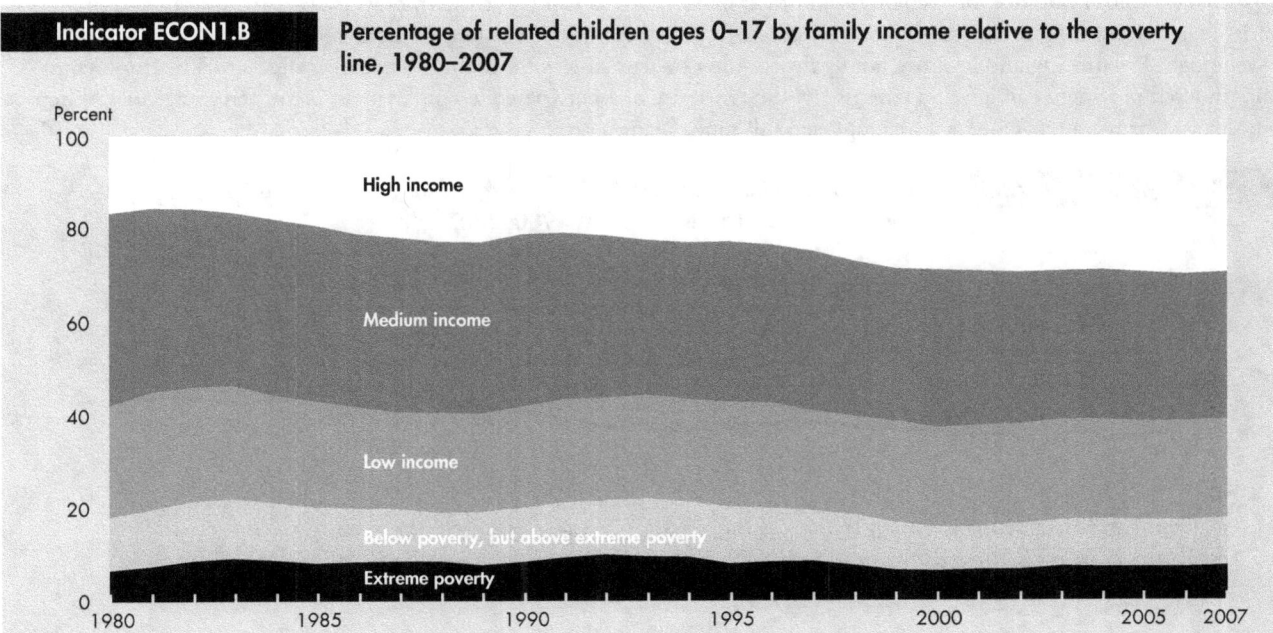

Indicator ECON1.B   **Percentage of related children ages 0–17 by family income relative to the poverty line, 1980–2007**

NOTE: Estimates refer to children ages 0–17 who are related to the householder. The income classes are derived from the ratio of the family's income to the family's poverty threshold. A child living in extreme poverty is defined as a child living in a family with income less than 50 percent of the poverty threshold. Below poverty, but above extreme poverty is defined as 50–99 percent of the poverty threshold. Low income is defined as 100–199 percent of the poverty threshold. Medium income is defined as 200–399 percent of the poverty threshold. High income is defined as being at or above 400 percent of the poverty threshold. For example, in 2007, a family of four with two children would be in extreme poverty if their income was less than $10,514 (50 percent of $21,027). The same family would be classified as low income if their income was at least $21,027 and less than $42,054.

SOURCE: U.S. Census Bureau, Current Population Survey, Annual Social and Economic Supplements.

■ In 2007, more children lived in families with medium income (32 percent) than in families in other income groups. Fewer children lived in families with low income and with high income (21 and 30 percent, respectively) than lived in families with medium income.

■ The percentage of children living in families with medium income was lower in 2007, at 32 percent, than in 1980, at 41 percent. Conversely, the percentage of children living in families with high income was higher in 2007, at 30 percent, than in 1980, at 17 percent.

■ The percentage of children living in families classified as in extreme poverty was 6.6 percent in 1980. This percentage rose to 10 percent in 1992 and decreased to 7.4 percent in 2007. The percentage of children who lived in families with very high incomes (600 percent or more of the poverty threshold) was two times higher in 2007 than in 1980 (13 percent and 4 percent, respectively).

Bullets contain references to data that can be found in Tables ECON1.A and ECON1.B on pages 115–120. Endnotes begin on page 73.

Secure Parental Employment

Secure parental employment reduces the incidence of poverty and its attendant risks to children. Since most parents who obtain health insurance for themselves and their children do so through their employers, a secure job can also be a key variable in determining whether children have access to health care. Secure parental employment may also enhance children's psychological well-being and improve family functioning by reducing stress and other negative effects that unemployment and underemployment can have on parents.[36,37] One measure of secure parental employment is the percentage of children whose resident parent or parents were employed full time during a given year.

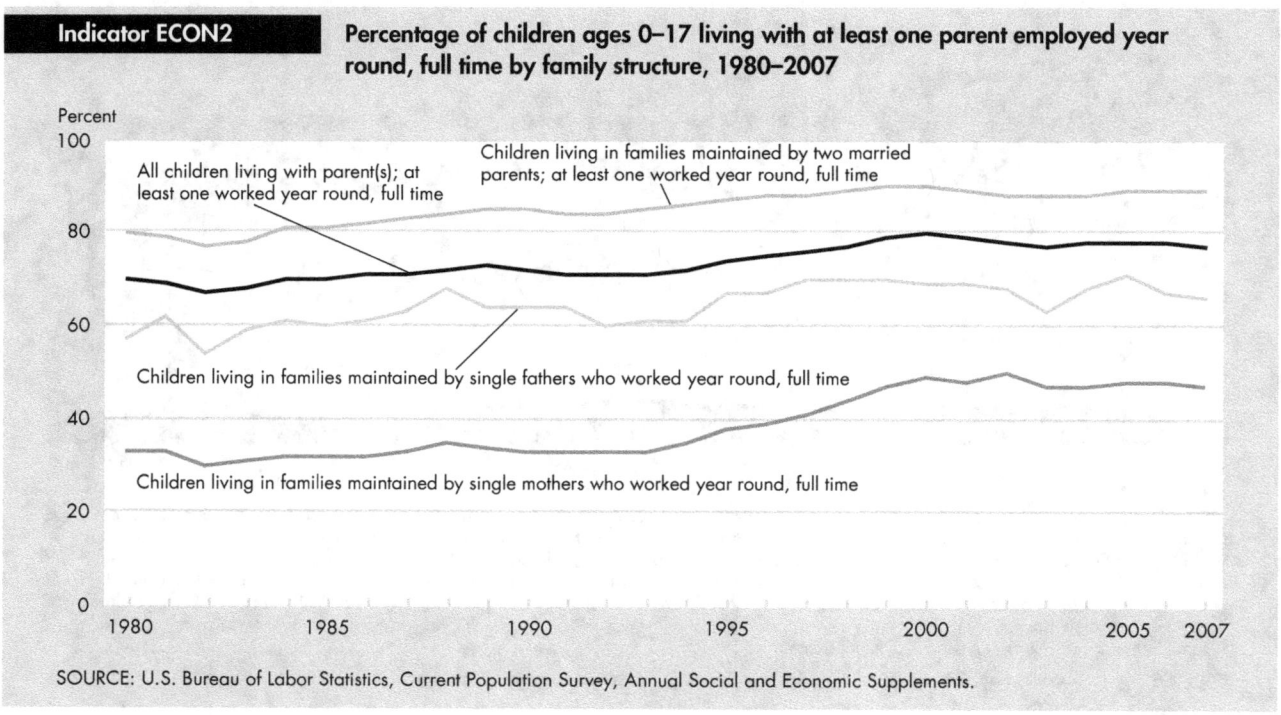

Indicator ECON2 — **Percentage of children ages 0–17 living with at least one parent employed year round, full time by family structure, 1980–2007**

SOURCE: U.S. Bureau of Labor Statistics, Current Population Survey, Annual Social and Economic Supplements.

- The percentage of children who had at least one parent working year round, full time was 77 percent in 2007, down from 78 percent in 2006 and below the peak of 80 percent in 2000. This proportion has remained relatively high, given its historical context; in the early 1990s, the proportion was 72 percent.

- In 2007, 89 percent of children living in families maintained by two married parents had at least one parent who worked year round, full time. In contrast, 66 percent of children living in families maintained by a single father and 47 percent of children living in families maintained by a single mother had a parent who worked year round, full time.

- Children living in poverty were much less likely to have a parent working year round, full time than children living at or above the poverty line (32 percent and 87 percent, respectively, in 2007). In 2007, 54 percent of children living in families maintained by two married parents who were living below the poverty line had at least one parent working year round, full time, compared with 92 percent of children living at or above the poverty line.

- Black, non-Hispanic children and Hispanic children were less likely than White, non-Hispanic children to have a parent working year round, full time. About 72 percent of Hispanic children and 64 percent of Black, non-Hispanic children lived in families with secure parental employment in 2007, compared with 82 percent of White, non-Hispanic children.

- In 2007, 32 percent of children in married two-parent families had both parents working year round, full time. This proportion is up from its most recent low in 2003 (29 percent).

Bullets contain references to data that can be found in Table ECON2 on pages 121–122. Endnotes begin on page 73.

Food Security

A family's ability to provide for its children's nutritional needs is linked to the family's food security—that is, to its access at all times to adequate food for an active, healthy life.[38] The food security status of households is based on self-reports of difficulty in obtaining enough food, reduced food intake, reduced diet quality, and anxiety about an adequate food supply. In some households classified as food insecure, only adults' diets and food intakes were affected, but in a majority of such households, children's eating patterns were also disrupted to some extent and the quality and variety of their diets were adversely affected.[39] In a subset of food-insecure households—those classified as having very low food security among children—a parent or guardian reported that at some time during the year one or more children were hungry, skipped a meal, or did not eat for a whole day because the household could not afford enough food.[40]

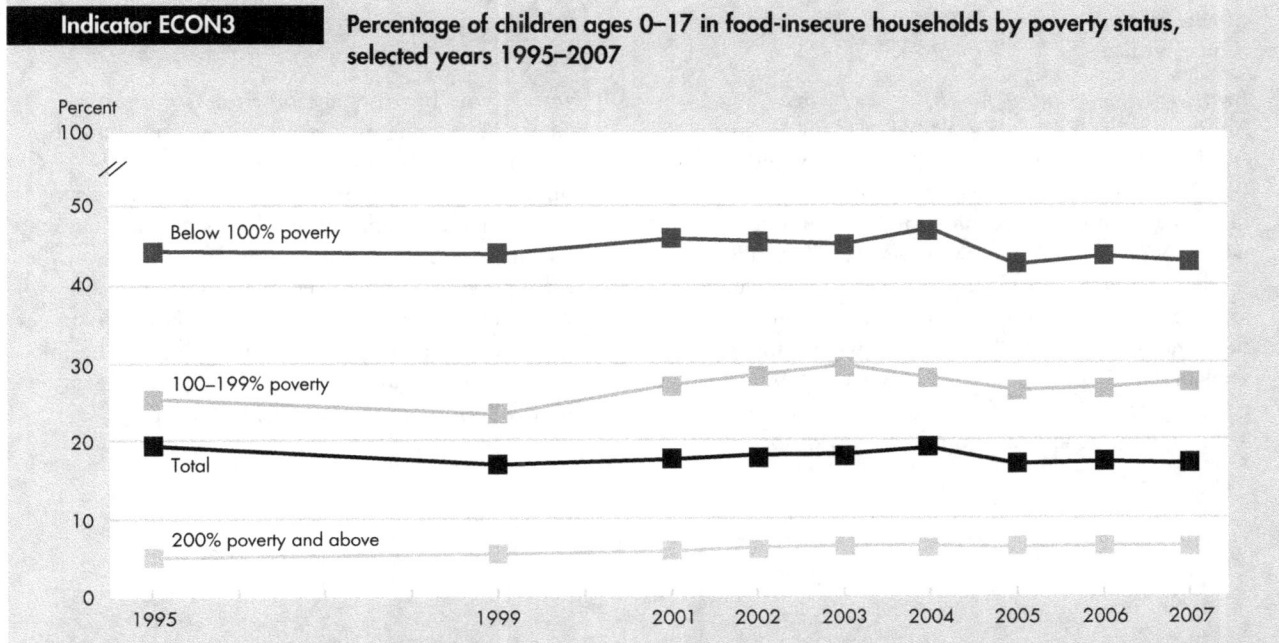

Indicator ECON3 — Percentage of children ages 0–17 in food-insecure households by poverty status, selected years 1995–2007

NOTE: Food-insecure households are those in which either adults or children or both were food insecure. At times they were unable to acquire adequate food for active, healthy living for all household members because they had insufficient money and other resources for food. Statistics for 1996–1998 and 2000 are omitted because they are not directly comparable with those for other years.

SOURCE: U.S. Census Bureau, Current Population Survey Food Security Supplement; tabulated by U.S. Department of Agriculture, Economic Research Service and Food and Nutrition Service.

■ About 12.4 million children (17 percent of all children) lived in households that were classified as food insecure at times in 2007. About 691,000 of these children (0.9 percent of all children) lived in households classified as having very low food security among children.

■ The percentage of children living in food-insecure households in 2007 was essentially unchanged from 2005 and 2006 and was lower than the 19 percent observed in 2004. The percentage of children living in households with very low food security among children increased from 0.6 percent in 2006 to 0.9 percent in 2007.

■ In 2007, the proportions of children living in food-insecure households were substantially above the national average (17 percent) for those living in poverty (43 percent), Black, non-Hispanics (26 percent), Hispanics (27 percent), those whose parents or guardians lacked a high school diploma or GED (38 percent), and those living with a single mother (32 percent).

Bullets contain references to data that can be found in Table ECON3 on pages 123–124. Endnotes begin on page 73.

Indicators Needed

Economic Circumstances

Economic security is multifaceted; therefore, several measures are needed to adequately represent it. While this year's report continues to provide some information on economic and food security, additional indicators are needed on:

- *Economic well-being.* Economic well-being over time needs to be anchored in an average standard of living context. Multiple measures of family income or consumption, some of which might incorporate estimates of various family assets, could produce more reliable estimates of changes in children's economic well-being over time.

- *Long-term poverty among families with children.* Although Federal data are available on child poverty (see Indicators ECON1.A and ECON1.B, Child Poverty and Family Income), the surveys that collect these data do not capture information on long-term poverty. Existing longitudinal survey data are available for identifying children living in poverty continually for a period of time and for producing estimates of the duration of poverty. However, those data are not available on a regular basis. The U.S. Census Bureau currently has longitudinal estimates of poverty for the 2001 to 2003 period based on the Survey of Income and Program Participation (SIPP) 2001 Panel. Estimates from the 2004 Panel of SIPP, covering the period 2004 to 2006, will be available later this year. Data from the 2008 Panel will not be available for several more years. Since long-term poverty can have serious negative consequences for children's well-being, regularly collected and reported estimates are needed.

- *Homelessness.* The Annual Homeless Assessment Report offers Congress a yearly update on the number of homeless people counted at a point in time by communities and of homeless people in shelters over time using local Homeless Management Information System (HMIS) data. The Forum is encouraged by the recent progress that has been made in the availability of data on homelessness. As a result, the U.S. Department of Housing and Urban Development hopes to be able to present information on the number of homeless children in future *America's Children* reports.

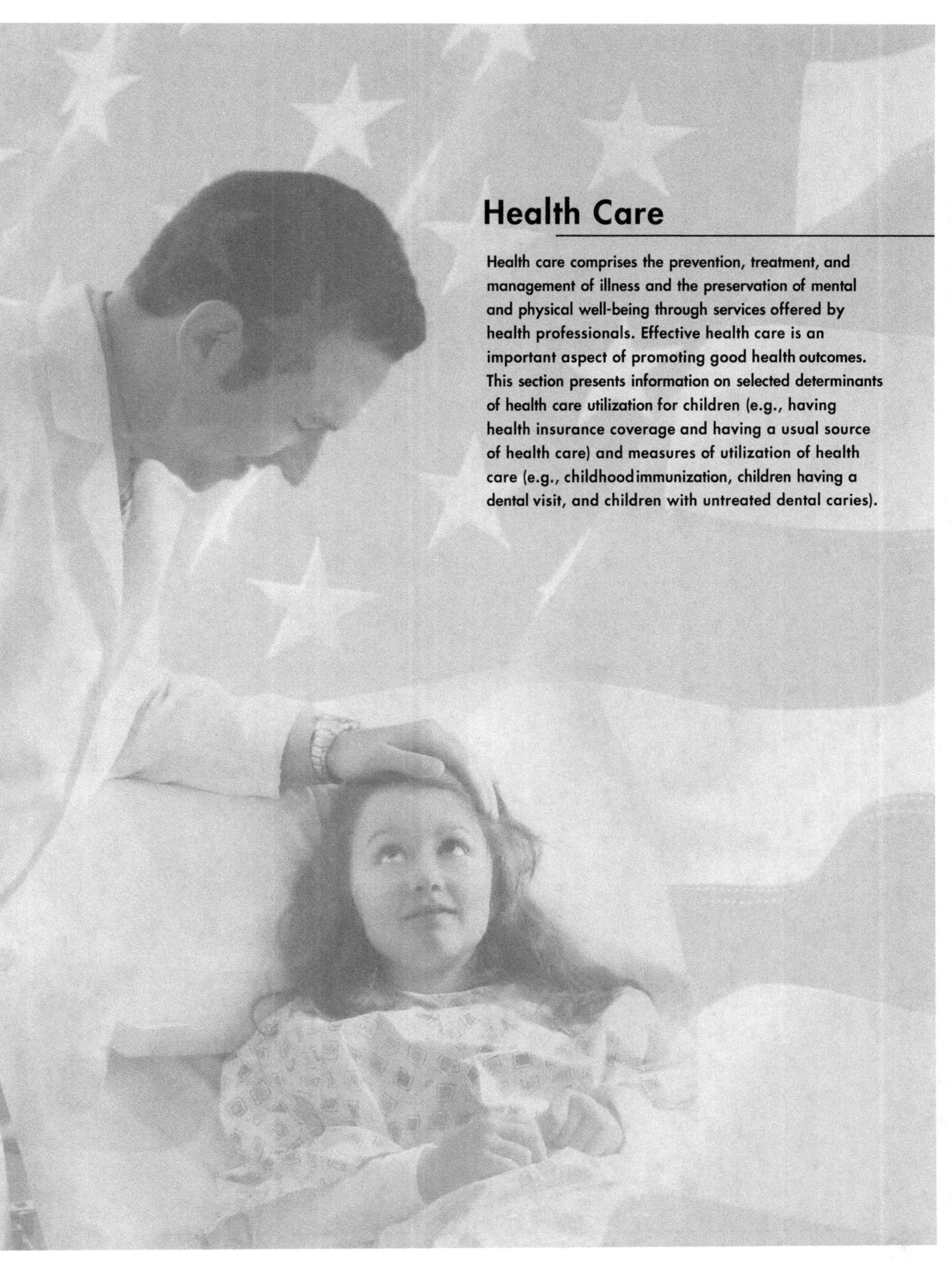

Health Care

Health care comprises the prevention, treatment, and management of illness and the preservation of mental and physical well-being through services offered by health professionals. Effective health care is an important aspect of promoting good health outcomes. This section presents information on selected determinants of health care utilization for children (e.g., having health insurance coverage and having a usual source of health care) and measures of utilization of health care (e.g., childhood immunization, children having a dental visit, and children with untreated dental caries).

Health Insurance Coverage

Children with health insurance, whether public or private, are more likely than children without insurance to have a regular and accessible source of health care. The percentage of children who have health insurance coverage for at least part of the year is one measure of the extent to which families can obtain preventive care or health care for a sick or injured child.

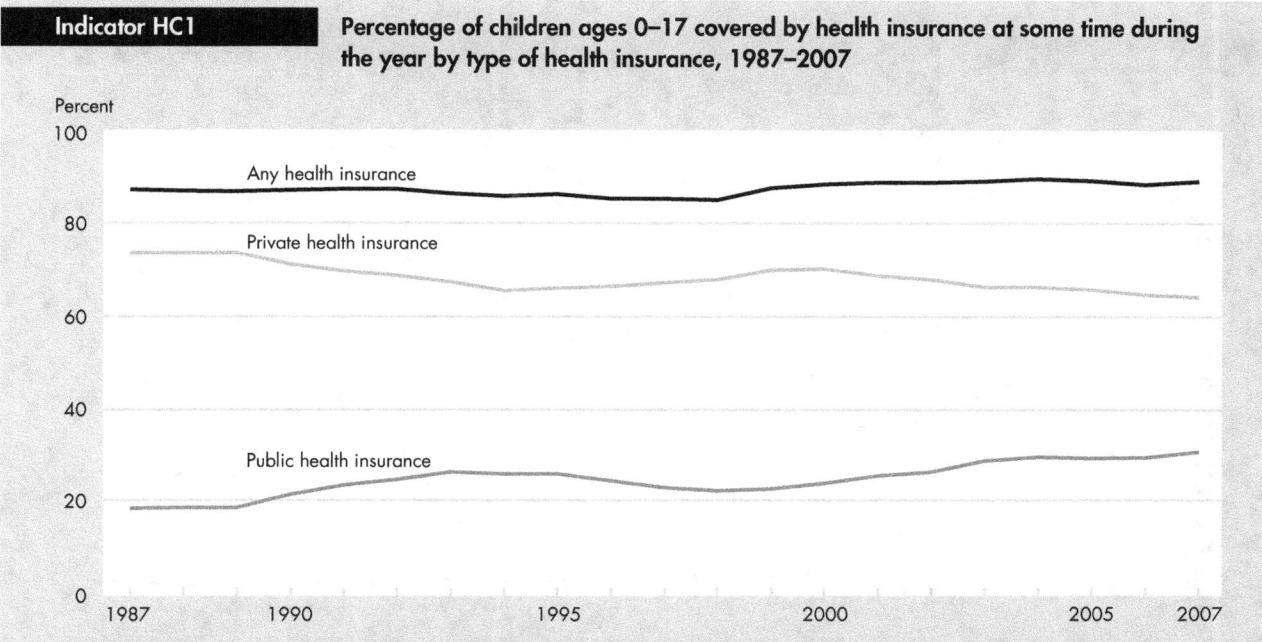

Indicator HC1 — Percentage of children ages 0–17 covered by health insurance at some time during the year by type of health insurance, 1987–2007

NOTE: Public health insurance for children consists primarily of Medicaid, but also includes Medicare, SCHIP (State Children's Health Insurance Programs), and CHAMPUS/Tricare, the health benefit program for members of the armed forces and their dependents. Estimates beginning in 1999 include follow-up questions to verify health insurance status. Children are considered to be covered by health insurance if they had public or private coverage any time during the year. The data from 1996 to 2004 have been revised since initially published. For more information, see http://www.census.gov/hhes/www/hlthins/usernote/schedule.html.

SOURCE: U.S. Census Bureau, unpublished tables from the Current Population Survey, Annual Social and Economic Supplements.

- In 2007, 89 percent of children had health insurance coverage at some point during the year, up from 88 percent in 2006. In each year since 1987, between 85 and 90 percent of children have had health insurance.

- The number of children without health insurance at any time during 2007 was 8.1 million (11 percent of all children).

- In 2007, 64 percent of children were covered by private health insurance at some time during the year and 31 percent were covered by public health insurance at some time during the year. (Both estimates include the children covered by both public and private at some time during the year; hence, the estimates sum to more than the estimated 89 percent of children with coverage.)

- Hispanic children were less likely to have health insurance, compared to White, non-Hispanic or Black children. In 2007, 80 percent of Hispanic children were covered at some time during the year by health insurance, compared with 93 percent of White, non-Hispanic children and 88 percent of Black children.[2]

- The type of insurance varied by the age of the child: younger children were more likely to have public health insurance than older children, while older children were more likely to have private health insurance than younger children.

Bullets contain references to data that can be found in Table HC1 on pages 125–126. Endnotes begin on page 73.

Usual Source of Health Care

T he health of children depends at least partially on their access to health services. Health care for children includes physical examinations, preventive care, health education, observations, screening, immunizations, and sick care.[41] Having a usual source of care—a particular person or place a child goes for sick and preventive care—facilitates the timely and appropriate use of pediatric services.[42,43] Emergency rooms are excluded here as a usual source of care because their focus on emergency care generally excludes the other elements of health care.[44]

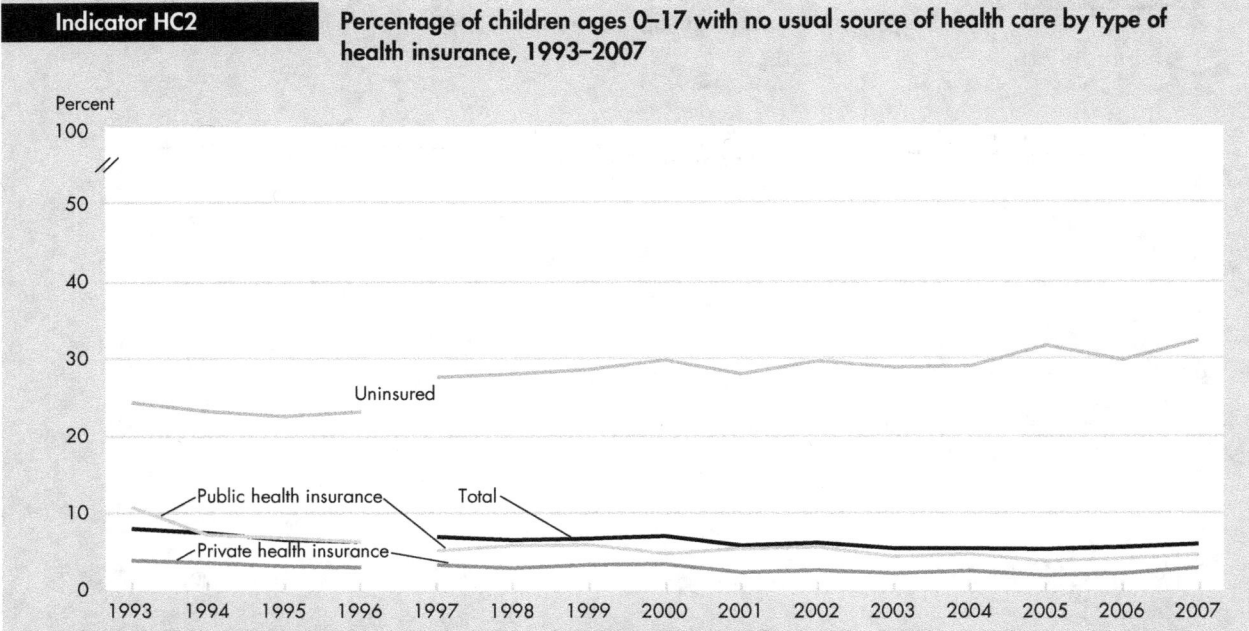

Indicator HC2 — Percentage of children ages 0–17 with no usual source of health care by type of health insurance, 1993–2007

NOTE: Children with both public and private insurance coverage are placed in the private insurance group. Emergency rooms are excluded as a usual source of care. A break is shown in the lines because in 1997 the National Health Interview Survey was redesigned. Data for 1997–2007 are not strictly comparable with earlier data.

SOURCE: National Center for Health Statistics, National Health Interview Survey.

- In 2007, 6 percent of children had no usual source of health care.

- Uninsured children are much more likely to have no usual source of care than are children who have health insurance. For example, 32 percent of children who were not insured had no usual source of health care. This was 11 times the percentage of children with private health insurance who had no usual source of health care (3 percent).

- There are differences in the percentage of children having no usual source of care by type of health insurance coverage. In 2007, children with public insurance, such as Medicaid, were more likely to have no usual source of care than were children with private insurance (5 percent and 3 percent, respectively).

- In 2007, 10 percent of children living below the poverty level and 9 percent of children living in families with incomes 100–199 percent of the poverty level had no usual source of health care, compared to 4 percent of children with family incomes 200 percent or more of the poverty level.

- Older children are slightly more likely than younger children to lack a usual source of health care. In 2007, 7 percent of children ages 6–17 had no usual source of care, compared with 4 percent of children ages 0–5.

Bullets contain references to data that can be found in Table HC2 on page 127. Endnotes begin on page 73.

Childhood Immunization

R ates of childhood immunization are one measure of how extensively children are protected from serious vaccine-preventable illnesses. Combined immunization series (often referred to as the 4:3:1:3:3 or 4:3:1:3:3:1 combined series) rates measure receipt of the number of doses of the five or six vaccinations that have been recommended since 1991 or earlier.

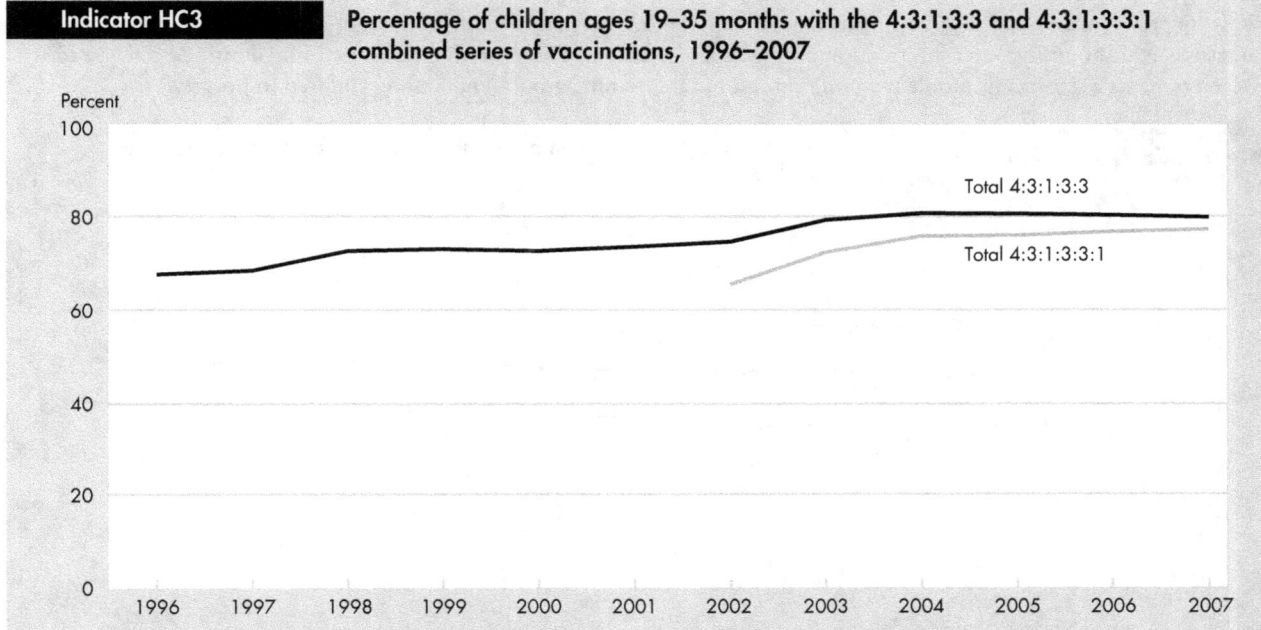

Indicator HC3

Percentage of children ages 19–35 months with the 4:3:1:3:3 and 4:3:1:3:3:1 combined series of vaccinations, 1996–2007

NOTE: The 4:3:1:3:3 series consists of 4 doses (or more) of diphtheria, tetanus toxoids, and pertussis (DTP) vaccines, diphtheria and tetanus toxoids (DT), or diphtheria, tetanus toxoids, and any acellular pertussis (DTaP) vaccines; 3 doses (or more) of poliovirus vaccines; 1 dose (or more) of any measles-containing vaccine; 3 doses (or more) of *Haemophilus influenzae* type b (Hib) vaccines; and 3 doses (or more) of hepatitis B vaccines. The 4:3:1:3:3:1 series consists of the 4:3:1:3:3 series plus 1 dose (or more) of varicella vaccine. The collection of coverage rate estimates for this series began in 2002. The recommended immunization schedule for children is available at http://www.cdc.gov/vaccines/recs/schedules/child-schedule.htm#printable.

SOURCE: Centers for Disease Control and Prevention, National Center for Immunization and Respiratory Diseases and National Center for Health Statistics, National Immunization Survey.

■ In 2007, 80 percent of children ages 19–35 months had received the recommended combined five-vaccine series, and 77 percent of children ages 19–35 months had received the recommended combined six-vaccine series.

■ The combined five-vaccine series percentages have remained relatively stable since 2003. Reporting the combined six-vaccine series began in 2002, and percentages have steadily increased from 66 percent.

■ Children in families below the poverty level had a lower rate of coverage (77 percent) with the combined five-vaccine series than children at or above the poverty level (81 percent), and children in families below the poverty level had a lower rate of coverage (75 percent) with the combined six-vaccine series than children at or above the poverty level (78 percent).

■ Coverage with the combined five-vaccine series was higher among White, non-Hispanic children than among Black, non-Hispanic children. Eighty-one percent of White, non-Hispanic children received these vaccinations, compared with 78 percent of Black, non-Hispanic children. Coverage with the combined six-vaccine series was similar across all racial and ethnic groups.

■ In 2007, the total coverage rate for each individual vaccine in the combination series was greater than or equal to 90 percent, except for children receiving four doses (or more) of the diphtheria, tetanus toxoids, and pertussis (DTP) vaccine. The total coverage rate for DTP was 85 percent and has not changed during the past 5 years (DTP is any diphtheria, tetanus toxoids, and pertussis vaccines, including diphtheria, tetanus toxoids and any acellular pertussis vaccine).

■ In 2007, 75 percent of children ages 19–35 months received four doses (or more) of pneumococcal conjugate vaccine (PCV). This vaccine was recommended in 2000, and the full series includes four doses. Shortages occurred during 2001–2004, so recommendations were made to defer the third dose or third and fourth doses.[45]

Bullets contain references to data that can be found in Table HC3 on pages 128–129. Endnotes begin on page 73.

Oral Health

Oral health is an essential and integral component of health.[46] Good oral health requires both self-care and professional care. Regular dental visits provide an opportunity for prevention, early diagnosis, and treatment of oral and craniofacial diseases and conditions. Routine dental visits are recommended by the American Academy of Pediatric Dentistry beginning at one year of age.[47] Dental caries (cavities) is the single most common disease of childhood.[46] Since the early 1970s, the prevalence of dental caries in permanent teeth has dramatically declined in school-age children due to prevention efforts such as community water fluoridation programs and increased use of toothpastes containing flouride.[46] Dental caries, however, remains a significant problem among certain racial or ethnic groups and among children in poverty.

| Indicator HC4.A | Percentage of children ages 2–17 with a dental visit in the past year by poverty status, 1997–2007 |

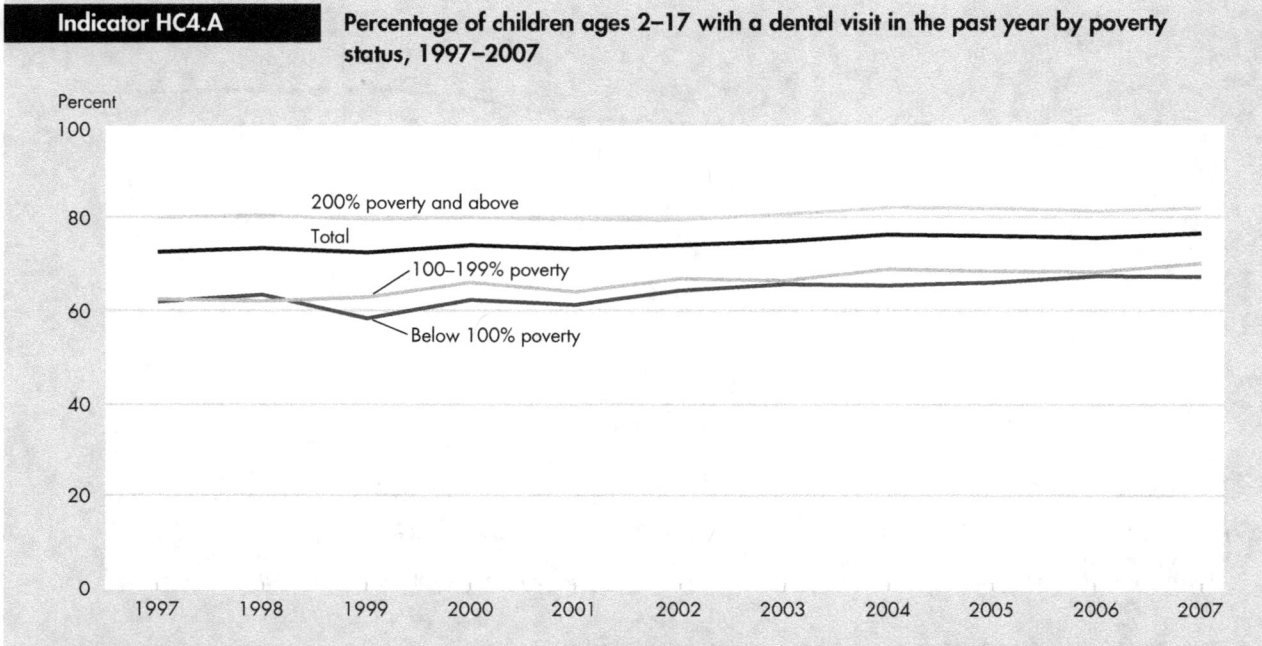

NOTE: From 1997–2000, children were identified as having a dental visit in the past year by asking parents "About how long has it been since your child last saw or talked to a dentist?" In 2001 and later years, the question was "About how long has it been since your child last saw a dentist?" Parents were directed to include all types of dentists, such as orthodontists, oral surgeons, and all other dental specialists, as well as dental hygienists.

SOURCE: National Center for Health Statistics, National Health Interview Survey.

- In 2007, 77 percent of children ages 2–17 had a dental visit in the past year. This percentage has remained relatively constant since 1997, ranging from 73–77 percent.

- In 2007, 67 percent of children living below the poverty level and 70 percent of children living in families with incomes 100–199 percent of the poverty level had a dental visit in the past year, compared to 82 percent of children with family incomes 200 percent or more of the poverty level.

- Fifty-two percent of uninsured children ages 2–17 had a dental visit in the past year, compared with 73 percent of children receiving Medicaid or other public health insurance and 82 percent of children with private health insurance.

- From 1997 to 2007, children ages 2–5 were less likely to have had a dental visit in the past year (56 percent in 2007) than children ages 6–11 (85 percent in 2007) and adolescents ages 12–17 (83 percent in 2007).

- In 2007, among younger children ages 2–5, 58 percent with private health insurance had a dental visit, compared with 40 percent of uninsured children. Among older children ages 6–11, 90 percent with private health insurance had a dental visit in the past year, compared with 60 percent of uninsured children. Among adolescents ages 12–17, 90 percent with private health insurance had a dental visit in the past year, compared with 50 percent of uninsured children.

Percentage of children ages 2–17 with untreated dental caries (cavities) by age and poverty status, 1999–2002 and 2003–2004

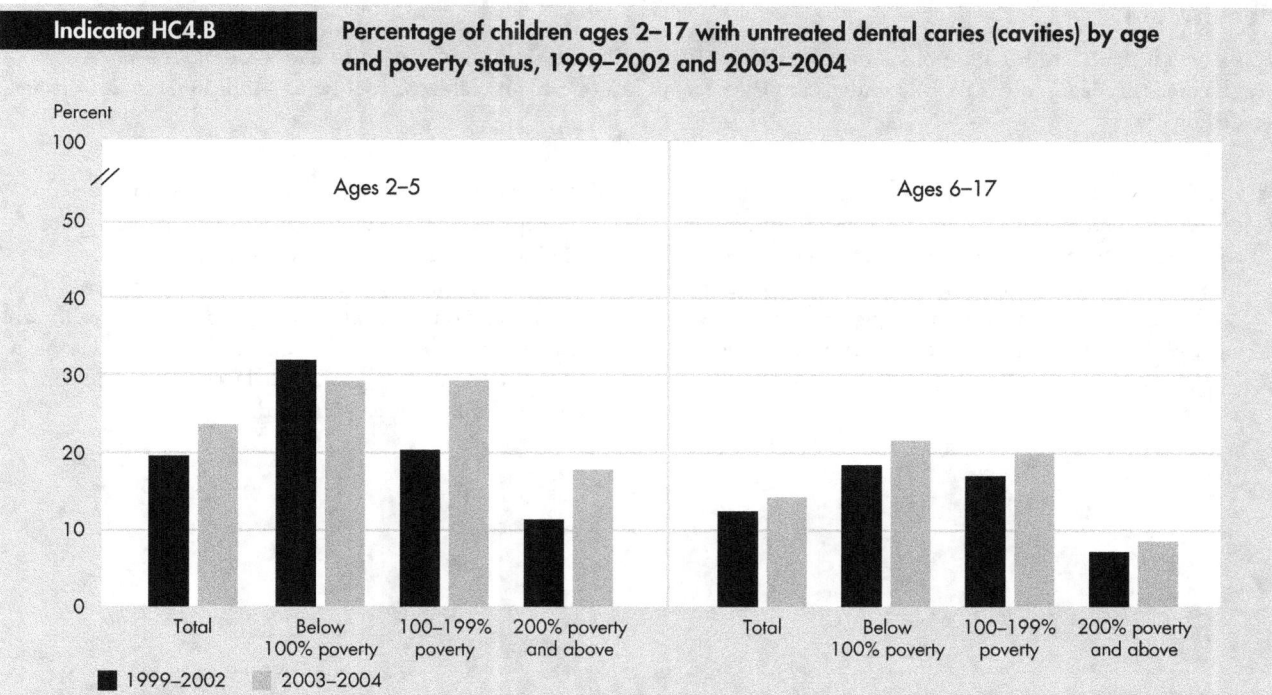

NOTE: Untreated dental caries is defined for children ages 2–5 as having had at least one primary tooth with untreated decay; for children ages 6–17 it is defined as having had at least one permanent tooth with untreated decay; and for children ages 2–17 it is defined as having had at least one primary or permanent tooth with untreated decay. Thus, estimates for children ages 2–17 may be higher than estimates for children ages 2–5 and ages 6–17 combined.

SOURCE: National Center for Health Statistics, National Health and Nutrition Examination Survey.

- In 2003–2004, 25 percent of children ages 2–17 had untreated dental caries (cavities) upon dental examination, an increase from 21 percent in 1999–2002.

- In 2003–2004, 23 percent of children ages 2–5 and 14 percent of children ages 6–17 had untreated dental caries.

- In 2003–2004, among children ages 2–5, 29 percent of children living in poverty or living in families with incomes between 100–199 percent of the poverty level had untreated dental caries, compared with 18 percent of children from families with incomes 200 percent or more of the poverty level.

- From 1999–2002 to 2003–2004, the percentage of children ages 2–5 who had untreated dental caries declined by 3 percentage points among children living in poverty, but increased among children in families with incomes 100–199 percent or 200 percent or more of the poverty line. The percentage of children ages 6–17 with untreated dental caries increased for all levels of family income.

- For both younger and older children, the percentage of children with untreated dental caries was higher among Mexican American children than among White, non-Hispanic and Black, non-Hispanic children.

Bullets contain references to data that can be found in Tables HC4.A and HC4.B on pages 130–132. Endnotes begin on page 73.

Indicators Needed

Health Care

This report provides information on a limited number of key indicators on health care. Information on other aspects of health care is needed in order to fully understand the effect of health care on children's well-being. Additional indicators are needed on:

■ *Adequacy of health care coverage.* This report contains information on whether children had health insurance coverage for at least part of the previous calendar year. Information is also needed on patterns of coverage and on the characteristics of the child's plan to determine whether the plan is adequate to meet health care needs.

■ *Quality and content of health care.* This report contains information on children's usual source of health care and some aspects of health care utilization (e.g., immunizations), but additional regularly collected data are needed on the content and the quality of health care that children receive. High-quality health care has been defined as care that is safe, timely, effective, efficient, equitable, and patient-centered.[48]

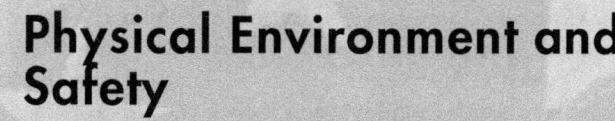

Physical Environment and Safety

The physical environment in which children live plays a role in their health, development, and
safety. This section presents indicators on how environmental conditions such as outdoor and indoor air quality, drinking water quality, and
exposure to lead may affect children. In addition, indicators of housing problems, youth victims of serious violent crimes, and child and adolescent injury and mortality are presented.

Outdoor and Indoor Air Quality

The environment in which children live plays an important role in their health and development. Children may be more vulnerable than adults to the adverse effects of environmental contaminants in air, food, drinking water, and other sources because their bodies are still developing. In addition, children have increased potential for exposure to pollutants because they eat, drink, and breathe more, in proportion to the size of their bodies, than adults. One important measure of children's environmental health is the percentage of children living in areas in which air pollution levels are higher than the allowable levels of the Primary National Ambient Air Quality Standards.[49] These standards, established by the U.S. Environmental Protection Agency under the Clean Air Act, are designed to protect public health, including the health of susceptible populations such as children and individuals with asthma. Ozone, particulate matter, sulfur dioxide, and nitrogen dioxide are air pollutants associated with increased asthma episodes and other respiratory illnesses.[50–53] Lead can affect the development of the central nervous system in young children,[54] and exposure to carbon monoxide can reduce the capacity of blood to carry oxygen.[55]

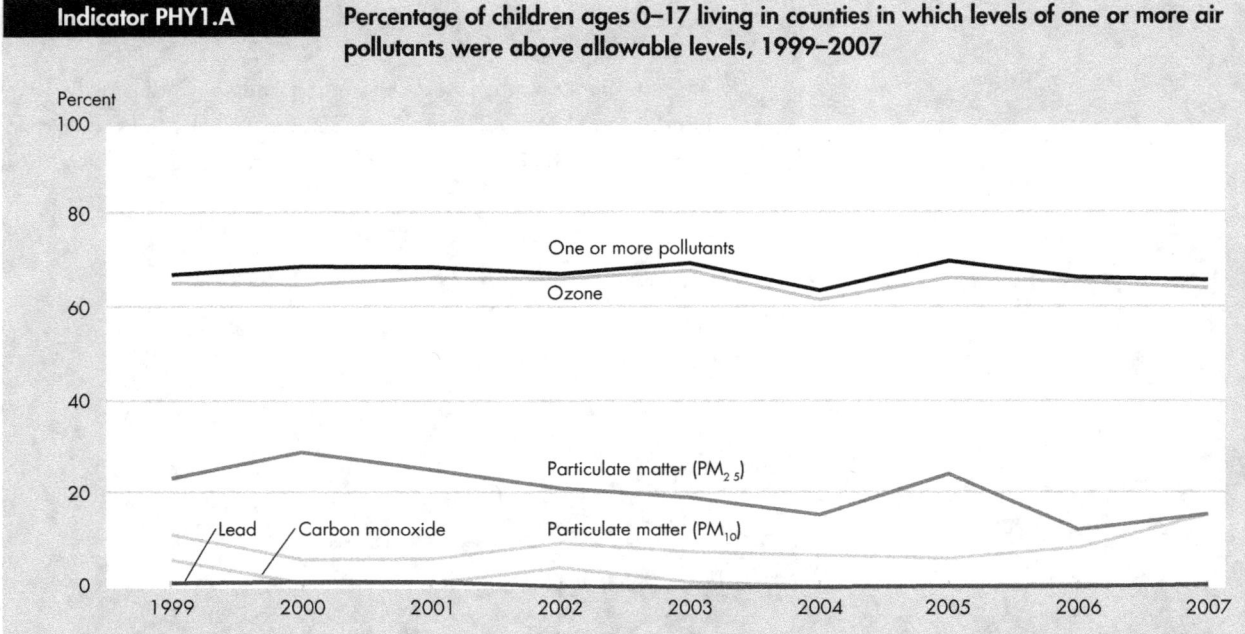

Indicator PHY1.A

Percentage of children ages 0–17 living in counties in which levels of one or more air pollutants were above allowable levels, 1999–2007

NOTE: The U.S. Environmental Protection Agency has set national air quality standards for six principal pollutants: carbon monoxide (CO), lead (Pb), nitrogen dioxide (NO_2), ozone (O_3), particulate matter (PM_{10} and $PM_{2.5}$), and sulfur dioxide (SO_2). Nitrogen dioxide and sulfur dioxide are not included in the graph because all areas meet the Primary National Ambient Air Quality Standards for these pollutants. This analysis incorporates a new Primary National Ambient Air Quality Standard for ozone that was promulgated in 2008.

SOURCE: U.S. Environmental Protection Agency, Office of Air and Radiation, Air Quality System.

- In 2007, 66 percent of children lived in counties in which one or more air pollutants were above allowable levels.

- Ozone is the pollutant that is most often above the allowable levels as defined by the Primary National Ambient Air Quality Standards. Ozone, as well as particulate matter, can cause respiratory problems and aggravate respiratory diseases, such as asthma, in children.[50,52,53] These problems can lead to increased emergency room visits and hospitalizations.[56–59] In 2007, 64 percent of children lived in counties in which ozone concentrations were above allowable levels.

- In 2007, approximately 16 percent of children lived in counties where levels of fine particulate matter ($PM_{2.5}$) were above the annual allowable standard, compared with 24 percent in 1999. The term "particulate matter" (PM) includes both solid particles and liquid droplets found in air.[53] Airborne particles measuring less than 10 micrometers in diameter (PM_{10}) pose a health concern because they can be inhaled into and accumulate in the respiratory system. Particles less than 2.5 micrometers in diameter ($PM_{2.5}$) are referred to as "fine" particles and are believed to pose the largest health risks because they can lodge deeply in the lungs.

Children who are exposed to environmental tobacco smoke, also known as secondhand smoke, have an increased probability of experiencing such adverse health effects as infections of the lower respiratory tract, bronchitis, pneumonia, middle ear disease, sudden infant death syndrome (SIDS), and respiratory symptoms.[60] Secondhand smoke can also play a role in the development and exacerbation of asthma.[60] The U.S. Surgeon General has determined that there is no risk-free level of exposure to secondhand smoke.[60] Cotinine, a breakdown product of nicotine, is a marker for recent (previous 1–2 days) exposure to secondhand smoke.

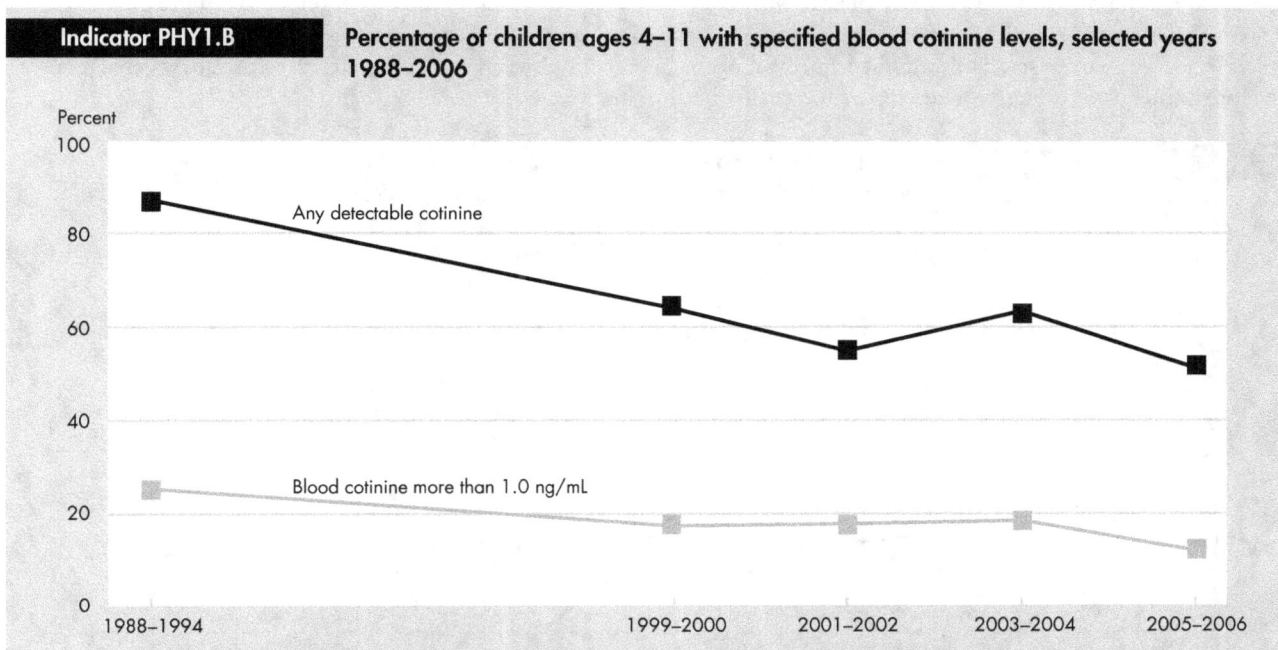

Indicator PHY1.B — **Percentage of children ages 4–11 with specified blood cotinine levels, selected years 1988–2006**

NOTE: "Any detectable cotinine" indicates blood cotinine levels at or above 0.05 nanograms per milliliter (ng/mL), the detectable level of cotinine in the blood in 1988–1994. Cotinine levels are reported for nonsmoking children only. The average (geometric mean) blood cotinine level in children living in homes where someone smoked was 1.0 ng/mL in 1988–1994.

SOURCE: National Center for Health Statistics, National Health and Nutrition Examination Survey.

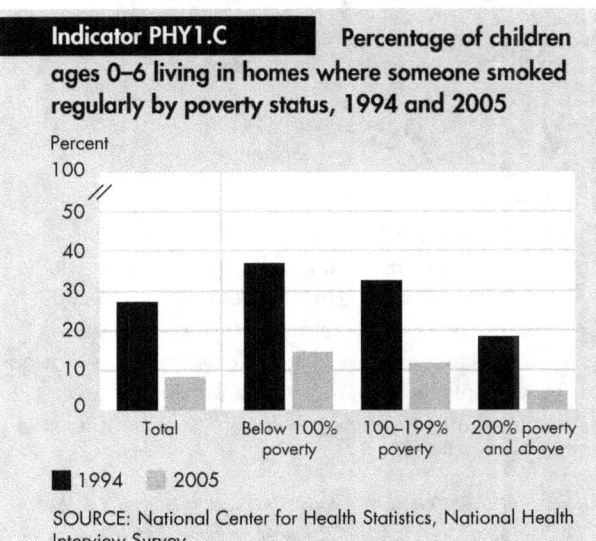

Indicator PHY1.C — **Percentage of children ages 0–6 living in homes where someone smoked regularly by poverty status, 1994 and 2005**

SOURCE: National Center for Health Statistics, National Health Interview Survey.

- The percentage of children ages 4–11 with detectable blood cotinine levels decreased from 88 percent in 1988–1994 to 51 percent in 2005–2006. In 2005–2006, 12 percent had blood cotinine levels more than 1.0 nanograms per milliliter (ng/mL), down from 26 percent in 1988–1994.

- In 2005, the percentage of children ages 0–6 living in homes where someone smoked regularly was 8 percent, compared with 27 percent in 1994.[61] Children living below the poverty level and Black, non-Hispanic children were more likely than their peers to be living in homes where someone smoked regularly.

Bullets contain references to data that can be found in Tables PHY1.A–PHY1.C on pages 133–134. Endnotes begin on page 73.

Drinking Water Quality

Contaminants in surface and ground waters that serve as sources of drinking water may be quite varied and may cause a range of diseases in children, including acute diseases such as gastrointestinal illness, developmental effects such as learning disorders, and serious long-term illnesses such as cancer.[62] The U.S. Environmental Protection Agency (EPA) sets drinking water standards designed to protect people against adverse health effects. These standards currently include Maximum Contaminant Levels (MCLs) and treatment technique requirements for over 90 chemical, radiological, and microbiological contaminants.[63] One way to gain insight into children's potential exposure to drinking water contaminants is to look at community water system compliance with these standards. EPA's drinking water regulations require public water systems, including community water systems, to monitor for compliance with Federal health-based standards and treat their water if needed to meet standards. About 15 percent of the population receives drinking water from private water systems that are not required to monitor and report the quality of drinking water.[64]

Indicator PHY2 — **Percentage of children served by community water systems that did not meet all applicable health-based drinking water standards, 1993–2007**

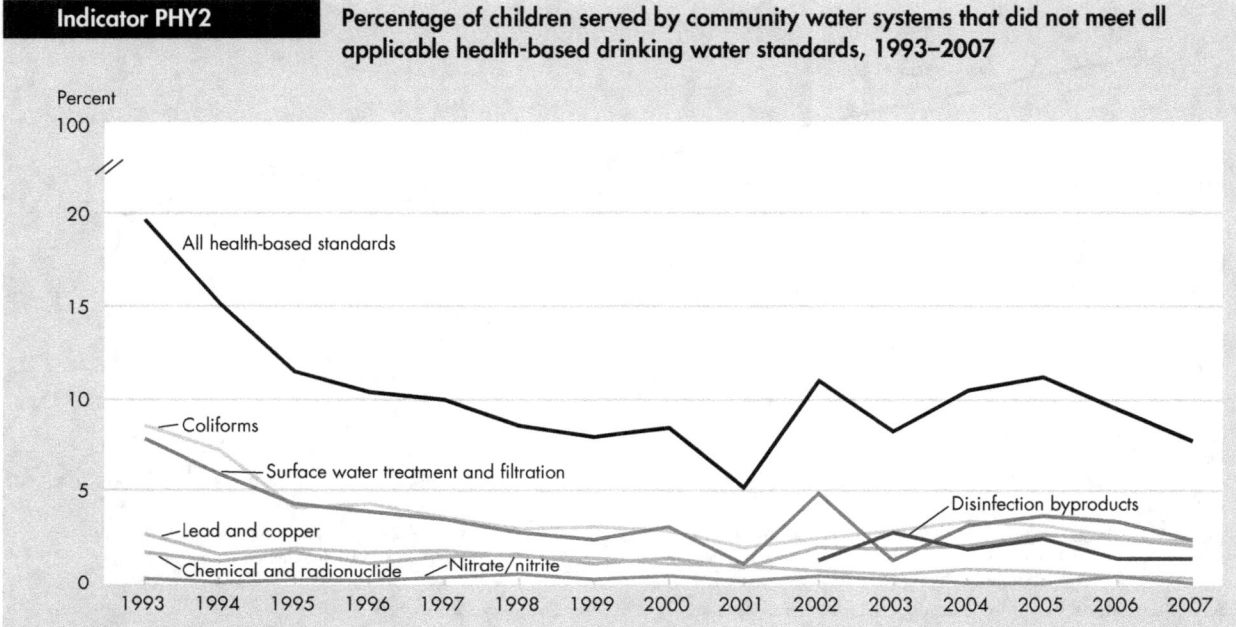

NOTE: A new standard for disinfection byproducts was implemented beginning in 2002 for larger drinking water systems and in 2004 for smaller systems. Revisions to the standard for surface water treatment took effect in 2002. A revised standard for radionuclides went into effect in 2003. A revised standard for arsenic (included in the chemical and radionuclide category) went into effect in 2006. No other revisions to the standards have taken effect during the period of trend data (beginning with 1993). Data have been revised since previous publication in *America's Children*. Values for years prior to 2007 have been recalculated based on updated data in the Safe Drinking Water Information System.

SOURCE: U.S. Environmental Protection Agency, Office of Water, Safe Drinking Water Information System.

- The percentage of children served by community drinking water systems that did not meet all applicable health-based standards declined from 20 percent in 1993 to about 8 percent in 1999. Since 1999, this percentage has fluctuated between 5 and 12 percent and was 8 percent in 2007.

- Coliforms indicate the potential presence of harmful bacteria associated with infectious illnesses. The percentage of children served by community drinking water systems that did not meet the health-based standard for coliforms was about 9 percent in 1993 and about 2 percent in 2007.

- EPA adopted a new standard for disinfection byproducts in 2001. Disinfection byproducts are formed when drinking water disinfectants react with naturally-occurring organic matter in water. In 2007, about 1 percent of all children served by community water systems were served by systems that had violations of the disinfection byproducts standard. Exposure to disinfection byproducts may lead to cancer and have developmental effects.[65]

Bullets contain references to data that can be found in Table PHY2 on page 135. Endnotes begin on page 73.

Lead in the Blood of Children

Lead is a major environmental health hazard for young children. Childhood exposure to lead contributes to learning problems and behavioral problems.[66–69] A blood lead level of 10 micrograms per deciliter (µg/dL) or greater is considered elevated, but adverse health effects can occur at much lower concentrations.[70,71] A child with a 10 µg/dL blood lead level will experience, on average, a decrease in IQ of 6 points.[72] Lead exposures have declined since the 1970s, due largely to the removal of lead from gasoline and fewer homes with lead-based paint. However, 25 percent of U.S. homes have significant lead-based paint hazards, such as high lead levels in dust and soil, which may contribute to childhood exposure.[73] Children ages 1–5 years are particularly vulnerable because they frequently engage in hand-to-mouth behavior.

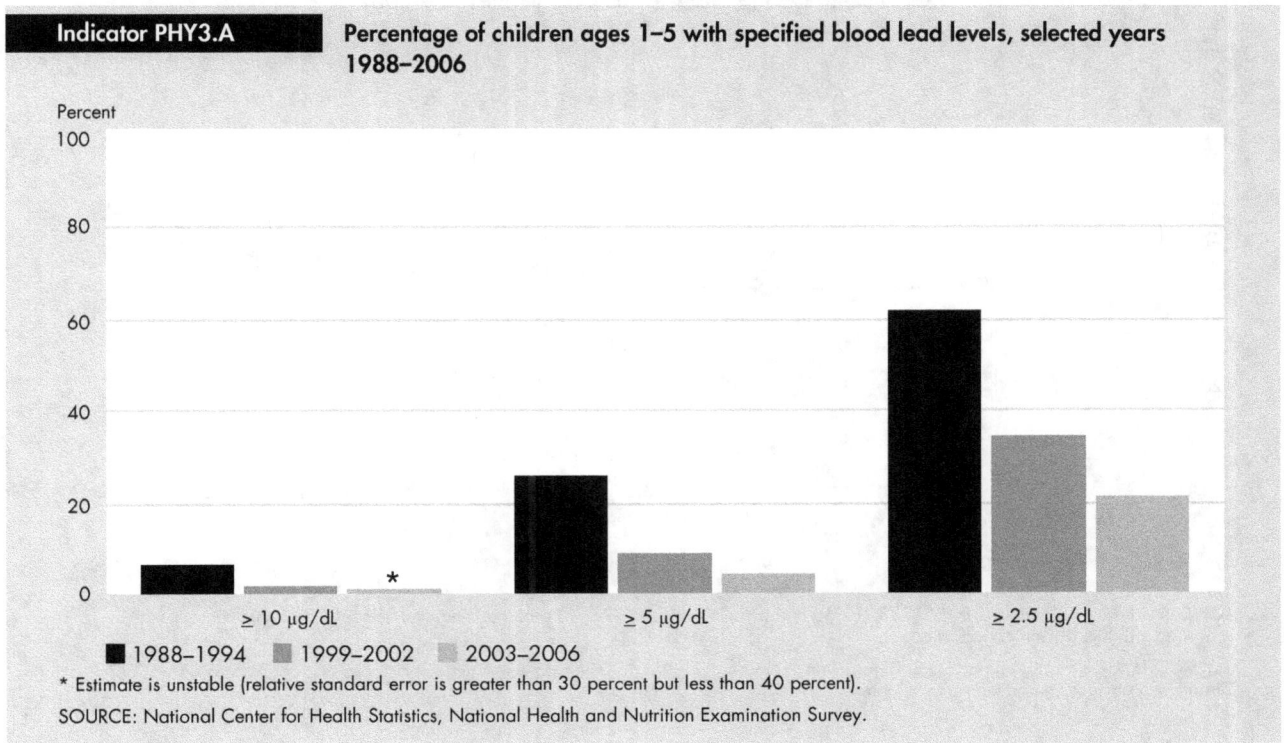

Indicator PHY3.A — Percentage of children ages 1–5 with specified blood lead levels, selected years 1988–2006

■ 1988–1994   ■ 1999–2002   ■ 2003–2006

* Estimate is unstable (relative standard error is greater than 30 percent but less than 40 percent).

SOURCE: National Center for Health Statistics, National Health and Nutrition Examination Survey.

- Children's blood lead levels in 2003–2006 were lower than in 1988–1994.

- In 2003–2006 about 21 percent of children ages 1–5 had blood lead levels greater than 2.5 µg/dL, and 4 percent had levels greater than 5 µg/dL. The estimate of children with levels greater than 10 µg/dL is a low percentage, and the available sample is too small to provide a statistically reliable estimate.

- About 12 percent of Black, non-Hispanic children and 2 percent of White, non-Hispanic children had blood lead levels at or above 5 µg/dL in 2003–2006.

- Children living in poverty generally had greater blood lead levels than children in families with incomes at or above the poverty line.

- The median blood lead concentration for children ages 1–5 dropped from about 14 µg/dL in 1976–1980 to about 2 µg/dL in 2003–2006.[74]

Bullets contain references to data that can be found in Tables PHY3.A and PHY3.B on page 136. Endnotes begin on page 73.

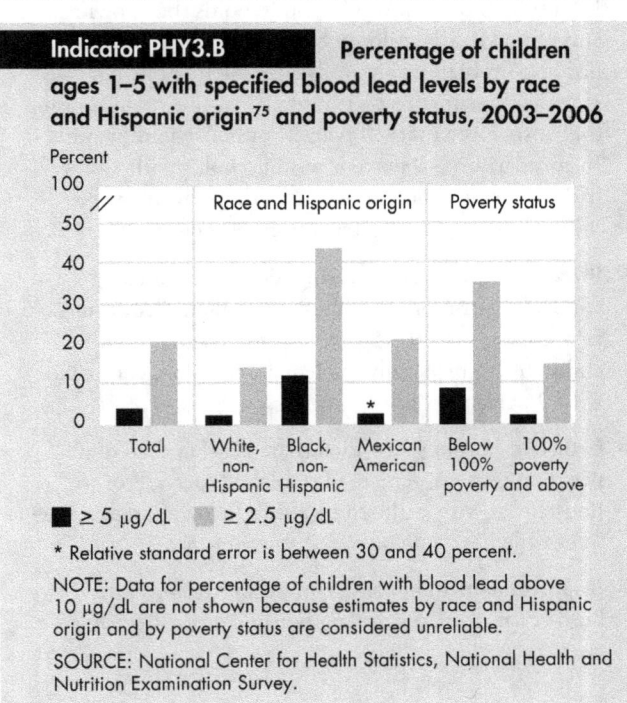

Indicator PHY3.B — Percentage of children ages 1–5 with specified blood lead levels by race and Hispanic origin[75] and poverty status, 2003–2006

■ ≥ 5 µg/dL   ■ ≥ 2.5 µg/dL

* Relative standard error is between 30 and 40 percent.

NOTE: Data for percentage of children with blood lead above 10 µg/dL are not shown because estimates by race and Hispanic origin and by poverty status are considered unreliable.

SOURCE: National Center for Health Statistics, National Health and Nutrition Examination Survey.

Housing Problems

Inadequate, crowded, or costly housing can pose serious problems to children's physical, psychological, and material well-being.[76] Housing cost burdens, especially at high levels, are a risk factor for negative child outcomes, including homelessness, overcrowding, poor nutrition, frequent moving, and lack of supervision while parents are at work.[77] The percentage of households with children that report that they are living in physically inadequate,[78] crowded, or costly housing provides an estimate of the percentage of children whose well-being may be affected by their family's housing.

Indicator PHY4

Percentage of households with children ages 0–17 that reported housing problems by type of problem, selected years 1978–2007

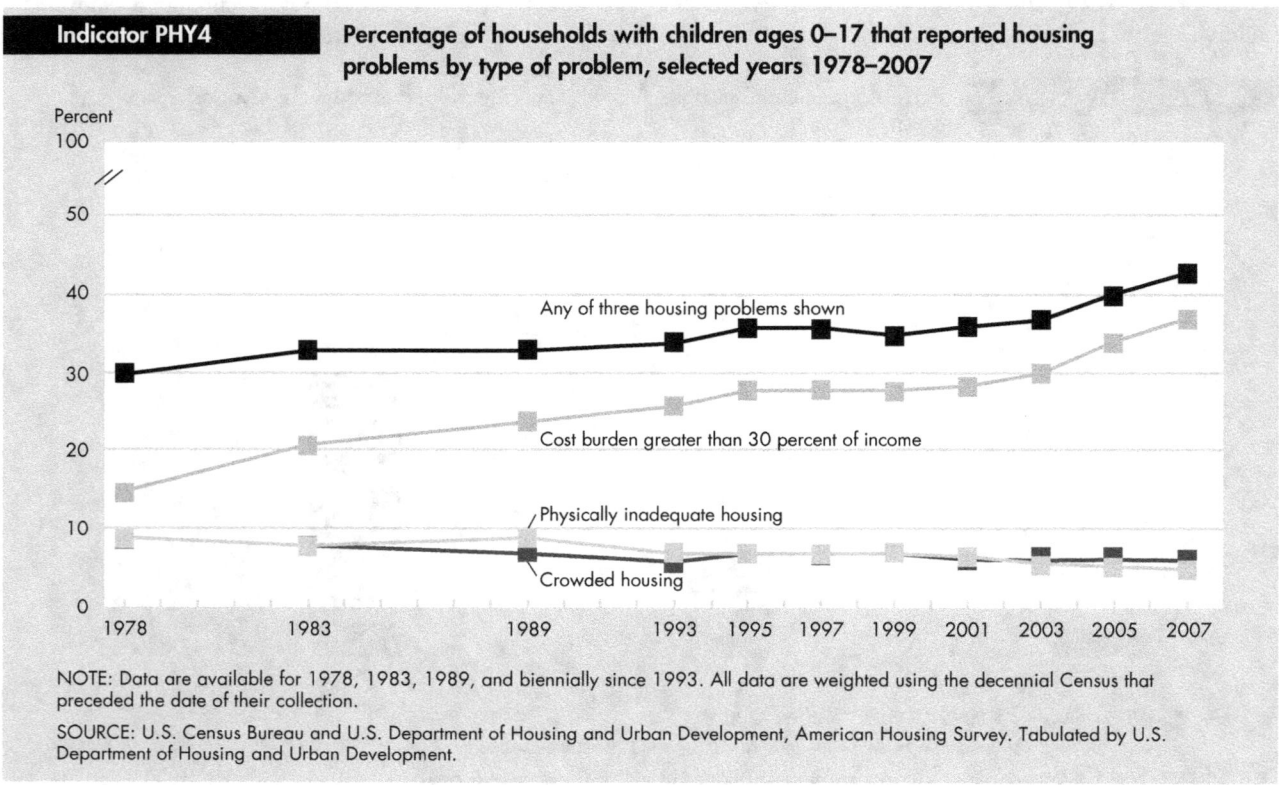

NOTE: Data are available for 1978, 1983, 1989, and biennially since 1993. All data are weighted using the decennial Census that preceded the date of their collection.

SOURCE: U.S. Census Bureau and U.S. Department of Housing and Urban Development, American Housing Survey. Tabulated by U.S. Department of Housing and Urban Development.

- In 2007, 43 percent of U.S. households (both owners and renters) with children had one or more of three housing problems: physically inadequate housing, crowded housing, or cost burden resulting from housing that costs more than 30 percent of household income.[79] In comparison, 40 percent of households with children had a housing problem in 2005. This percentage has increased over the long term from 30 percent in 1978.

- Physically inadequate housing, defined as housing with severe or moderate physical problems, continues to decrease. In 2007, 5 percent of households with children had physically inadequate housing, compared with 9 percent in 1978.

- Crowded housing, in which there is more than one person per room, remained stable at 6 percent of households with children in 2007, following reductions in crowded housing observed through 1993.

- Improvements in housing conditions, however, have been accompanied by rising housing costs. Between

1978 and 2007, the incidence of cost burdens among households with children more than doubled, from 15 percent to 37 percent. The proportion with severe cost burdens, paying more than half of their income for housing, rose from 6 percent to 16 percent over the same period.

- Households that receive no rental assistance and have severe cost burdens or physical problems are defined as having severe housing problems.[80] The percentage of households with children facing severe housing problems increased from 14 percent in 2005 to 15 percent in 2007.

- Severe housing problems are especially prevalent among very-low-income renters.[81] The incidence of severe problems among very-low-income renters with children changed from 36 percent to 35 percent between 2005 and 2007.

Bullets contain references to data that can be found in Table PHY4 on page 137. Endnotes begin on page 73.

Youth Victims of Serious Violent Crimes

Violence impacts the lives of young people who experience, witness, or feel threatened by it. In addition to the direct physical harm suffered by victims of serious violence, such violence can adversely affect young victims' mental health and development and increase the likelihood that they themselves will commit acts of serious violence.[82,83] Youth ages 12–17 were more than twice as likely as adults to be victims of serious violent crimes.[84]

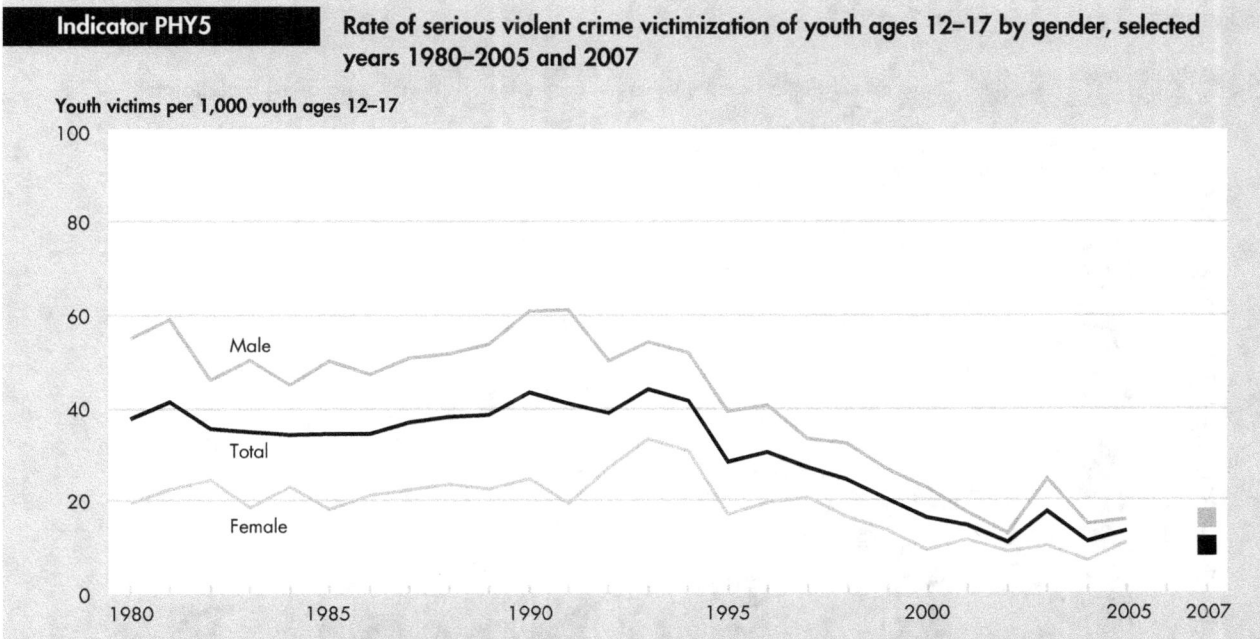

Indicator PHY5 **Rate of serious violent crime victimization of youth ages 12–17 by gender, selected years 1980–2005 and 2007**

Youth victims per 1,000 youth ages 12–17

NOTE: Serious violent crimes include aggravated assault, rape, robbery (stealing by force or threat of violence), and homicide. Because of changes, data prior to 1992 are adjusted to make them comparable with data collected under the redesigned methodology. Data from 2006 are not included because, due to changes in methodology, 2006 crime victimization rates are not comparable to other years and cannot be used for yearly trend comparisons. See *Criminal Victimization, 2006,* http://www.ojp.usdoj.gov/bjs/abstract/cv06.htm. Reporting standards were not met for the 2007 estimate for females.

SOURCE: Bureau of Justice Statistics, National Crime Victimization Survey and Federal Bureau of Investigation, Uniform Crime Reporting Program, Supplementary Homicide Reports.

■ In 2007, the rate at which youth were victims of serious violent crimes was 10 crimes per 1,000 youth ages 12–17. A total of 248,900 such crimes occurred in 2007.

■ Serious violent crime involving youth victims stayed about the same in 2005 and 2007. However, rates are still significantly lower than their peak in 1993. In 1993, the serious violent crime victimization rate was 44 per 1,000 youth, compared to the 2007 rate of 10 per 1,000 youth.

■ In 2007, White, non-Hispanic youth were as likely as Hispanic youth to be victims of a serious violent crime.

■ Older youth (ages 15–17) were as likely to be victims of a serious violent crime as younger youth (ages 12–14) were in 2007.

Bullets contain references to data that can be found in Table PHY5 on page 138. Endnotes begin on page 73.

Child Injury and Mortality

Although injury death rates have declined over the past two decades, unintentional injuries remain the leading cause of death for children ages 1–4 and ages 5–14. In addition, nonfatal injuries continue to be important causes of child morbidity, disability, and reduced quality of life.[85] In 2000, the total lifetime costs (medical expenses and productivity losses) of injuries among children ages 0–14 were estimated to be over $50 billion.[86] For every fatal injury among children ages 1–14, there are 33 hospitalizations and 1,350 emergency department visits for injuries.[87] The leading causes of injury differ for children and adolescents (see PHY7.A).

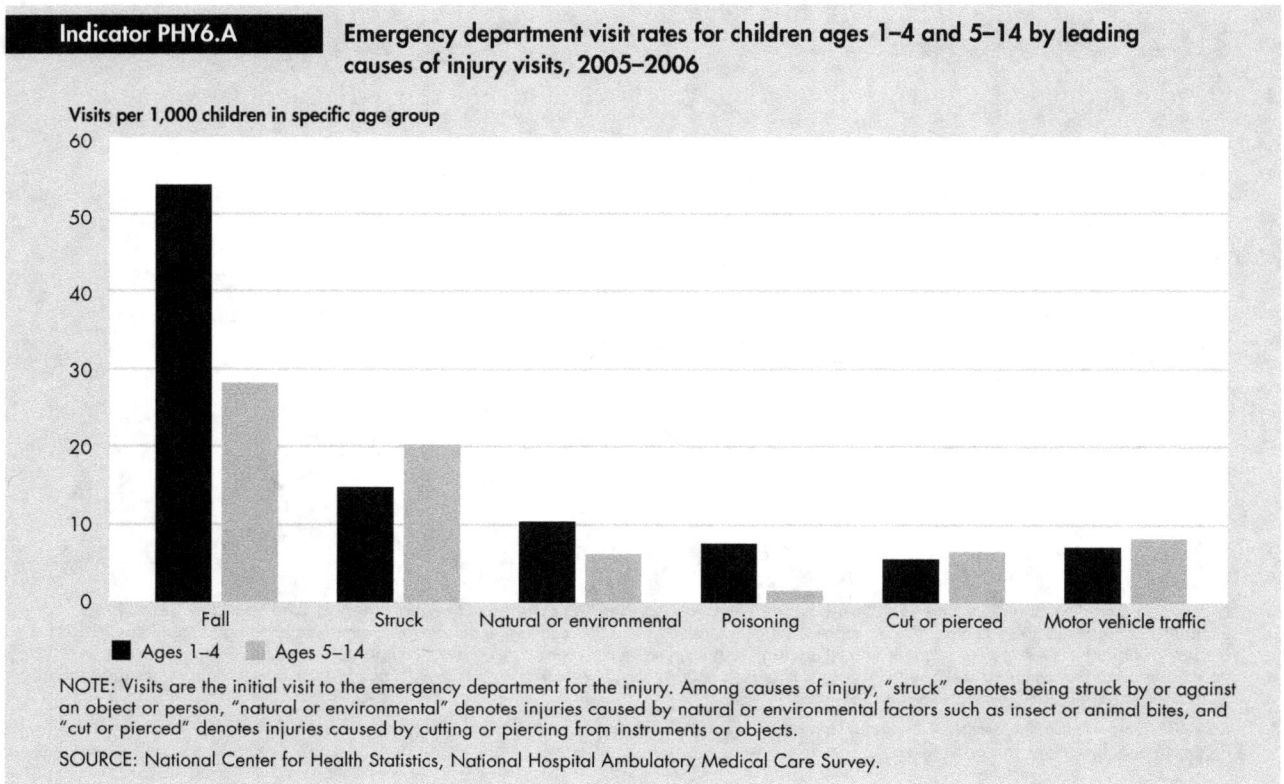

Indicator PHY6.A   Emergency department visit rates for children ages 1–4 and 5–14 by leading causes of injury visits, 2005–2006

Visits per 1,000 children in specific age group

■ Ages 1–4 ■ Ages 5–14

NOTE: Visits are the initial visit to the emergency department for the injury. Among causes of injury, "struck" denotes being struck by or against an object or person, "natural or environmental" denotes injuries caused by natural or environmental factors such as insect or animal bites, and "cut or pierced" denotes injuries caused by cutting or piercing from instruments or objects.

SOURCE: National Center for Health Statistics, National Hospital Ambulatory Medical Care Survey.

■ Among children ages 1–14, falls and being struck by or against an object or person are the two leading causes of initial injury-related emergency department visits. In 2005–2006, there were 54 annual emergency department visits for falls per 1,000 children ages 1–4, whereas the rate was 28 visits per 1,000 children ages 5–14. Falls accounted for 38 percent of initial injury visits for children ages 1–4 and 27 percent of initial injury visits for children ages 5–14.[88]

■ Younger children frequently strike furniture after running, tripping, or falling, whereas older children are often struck as a result of play or sports. Emergency department visit rates for being struck by or against an object or person were 15 emergency department visits per 1,000 for children ages 1–4 and 20 emergency department visits per 1,000 for children ages 5–14. Among children ages 1–4, 24 percent of the emergency department visits resulting from being struck by or against an object or person were related to striking furniture. Among children ages 5–14, 28 percent of the emergency department visits resulting from being struck by or against an object or person were sports related.[88]

■ Emergency department visit rates for injuries caused by natural and environmental factors, poisonings, cutting or piercing from instruments or objects, and motor vehicle traffic crashes ranged between 6–10 visits per 1,000 children for children ages 1–4 and ranged between 2–8 visits per 1,000 children for children ages 5–14.

■ Emergency department visit rates for poisoning were higher among children ages 1–4 (8 per 1,000) than among children ages 5–14 (2 per 1,000).

■ For children ages 1–4 and 5–14, 2 percent of injury-related emergency department visits resulted in hospitalizations, although the percentage varied by cause.[88]

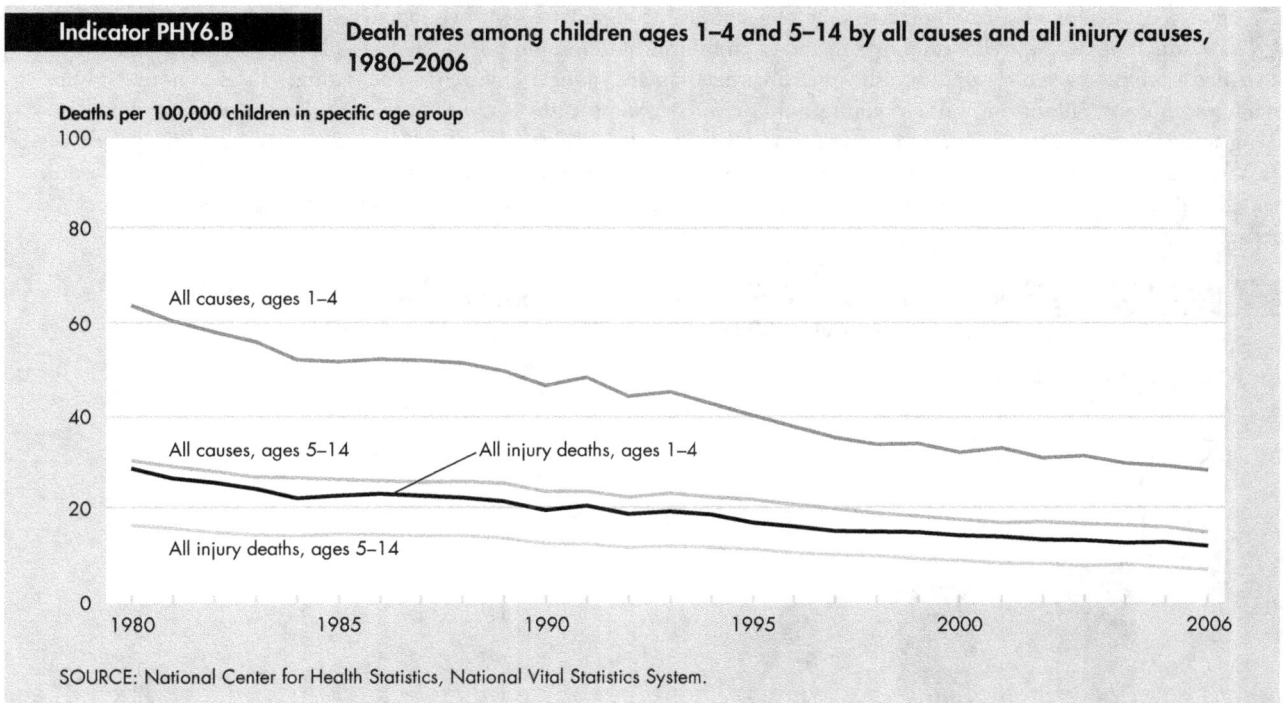

Indicator PHY6.B Death rates among children ages 1–4 and 5–14 by all causes and all injury causes, 1980–2006

Deaths per 100,000 children in specific age group

All causes, ages 1–4

All causes, ages 5–14 / All injury deaths, ages 1–4

All injury deaths, ages 5–14

SOURCE: National Center for Health Statistics, National Vital Statistics System.

- In 2006, the death rate for children ages 1–4 was 28 per 100,000 children and for children ages 5–14 was 15 per 100,000 children. Between 1980 and 2006, the death rate declined by half or more for both age groups.

- Among both younger and older children, Black children had the highest death rates in 2006, at 43 per 100,000 children ages 1–4 and 21 per 100,000 children ages 5–14. Asian or Pacific Islander children had the lowest death rates.

- Among children ages 1–4 and 5–14, unintentional injuries (accidents) were the leading cause of death: 10 deaths per 100,000 children ages 1–4 and 6 deaths per 100,000 children ages 5–14. For children ages 1–4, the next most frequent causes of death were birth defects (3 per 100,000 children) and cancer and homicide (2 per 100,000 each). Among children ages 5–14, the next most frequent causes of death were cancer (2 per 100,000) and homicide and birth defects (1 per 100,000 children each).

- In 2006, the injury death rate was 12 per 100,000 for children ages 1–4 and 7 per 100,000 for children ages 5–14.

- Between 1980 and 2006, motor vehicle traffic and drowning death rates declined by one-half or more among children ages 1–4.

- Among children ages 10–14, homicide and suicide were the third and fourth leading causes of death (1.2 and 1.0 deaths per 100,000, respectively), after unintentional injuries and cancer.[89]

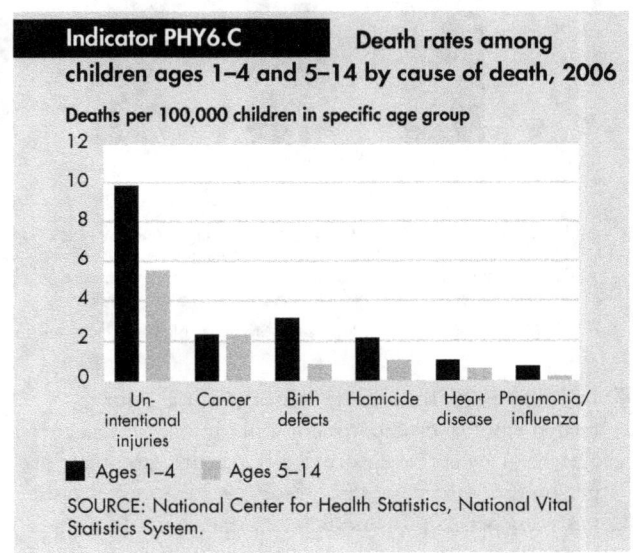

Indicator PHY6.C Death rates among children ages 1–4 and 5–14 by cause of death, 2006

Deaths per 100,000 children in specific age group

Un-intentional injuries | Cancer | Birth defects | Homicide | Heart disease | Pneumonia/ influenza

■ Ages 1–4   ■ Ages 5–14

SOURCE: National Center for Health Statistics, National Vital Statistics System.

Bullets contain references to data that can be found in Tables PHY6.A–PHY6.B on pages 139–141. Endnotes begin on page 73.

Adolescent Injury and Mortality

Injury accounts for close to 80 percent of adolescent deaths. Compared with younger children, adolescents ages 15–19 have much higher mortality rates overall and from injuries. Adolescents are much more likely to die from injuries sustained from motor vehicle traffic crashes and firearms than are younger children.[90] The leading causes of nonfatal injuries in adolescents also differ from those in younger children. For example, the leading cause of adolescent nonfatal injury is being struck by or against an object or person, whereas for younger children, the leading cause of nonfatal injury is falls (see PHY6.A). In addition, nonfatal injuries for adolescents more often result from violence, sports-related activities, or motor vehicle traffic crashes. For each fatal injury among adolescents, there are 11 hospitalizations and nearly 300 emergency department visits for injuries.[87]

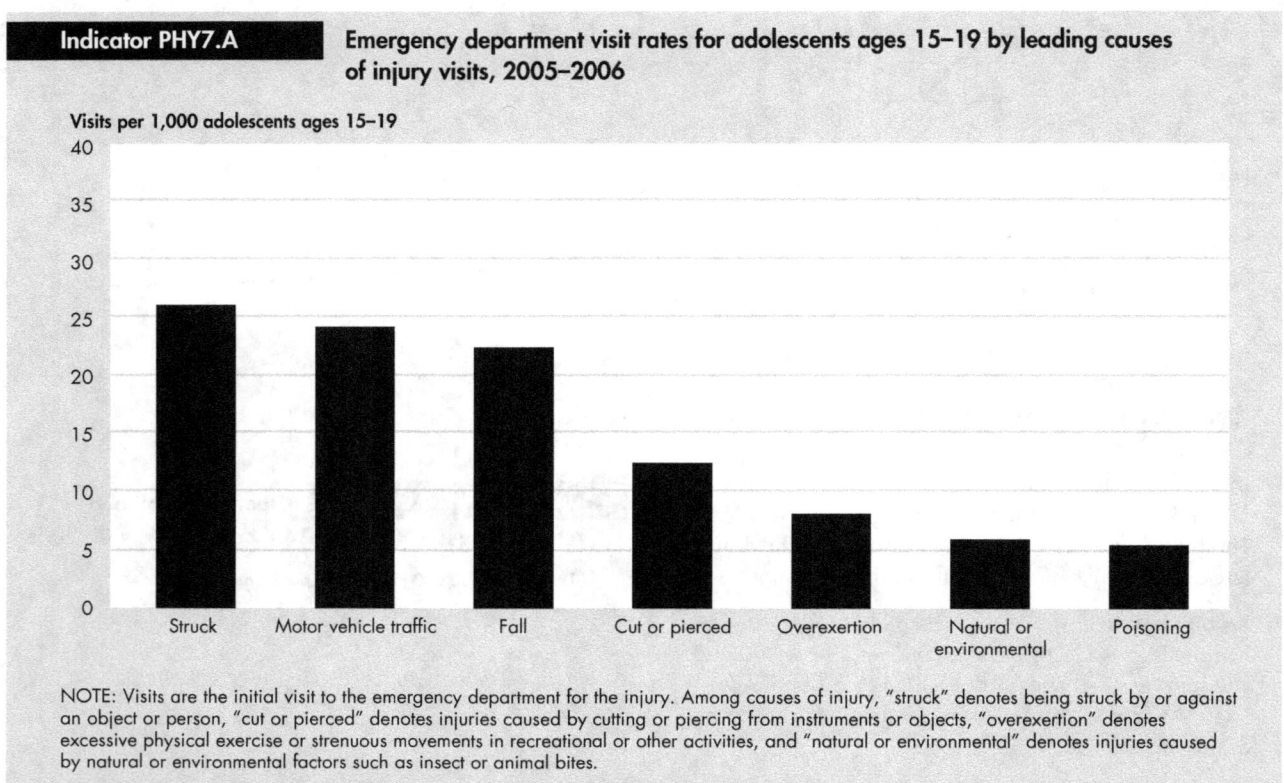

Indicator PHY7.A **Emergency department visit rates for adolescents ages 15–19 by leading causes of injury visits, 2005–2006**

Visits per 1,000 adolescents ages 15–19

NOTE: Visits are the initial visit to the emergency department for the injury. Among causes of injury, "struck" denotes being struck by or against an object or person, "cut or pierced" denotes injuries caused by cutting or piercing from instruments or objects, "overexertion" denotes excessive physical exercise or strenuous movements in recreational or other activities, and "natural or environmental" denotes injuries caused by natural or environmental factors such as insect or animal bites.

SOURCE: National Center for Health Statistics, National Hospital Ambulatory Medical Care Survey.

- In 2005–2006, the leading causes of initial injury-related emergency department visits among adolescents ages 15–19 were being struck by or against an object or person (26 visits per 1,000), motor vehicle traffic crashes (24 visits per 1,000), and falls (22 visits per 1,000), altogether accounting for about half of all injury-related emergency department visits for this age group.

- Injury emergency department visits for adolescents being struck by or against an object or person were most often the result of a sports-related activity (33 percent) or an assault (26 percent).[88]

- Injuries caused by cutting or piercing from instruments or objects, overexertion from excessive physical exercise or strenuous movements in recreational or other activities, natural or environmental factors, and poisonings were also among the leading causes of injury-related emergency department visits among adolescents ages 15–19, ranging from 5–12 visits per 1,000 adolescents.

- For adolescents ages 15–19, 3 percent of injury-related emergency department visits resulted in hospitalizations.[88]

Death rates among adolescents ages 15–19 by all causes and all injury causes and selected mechanisms of injury, 1980–2006

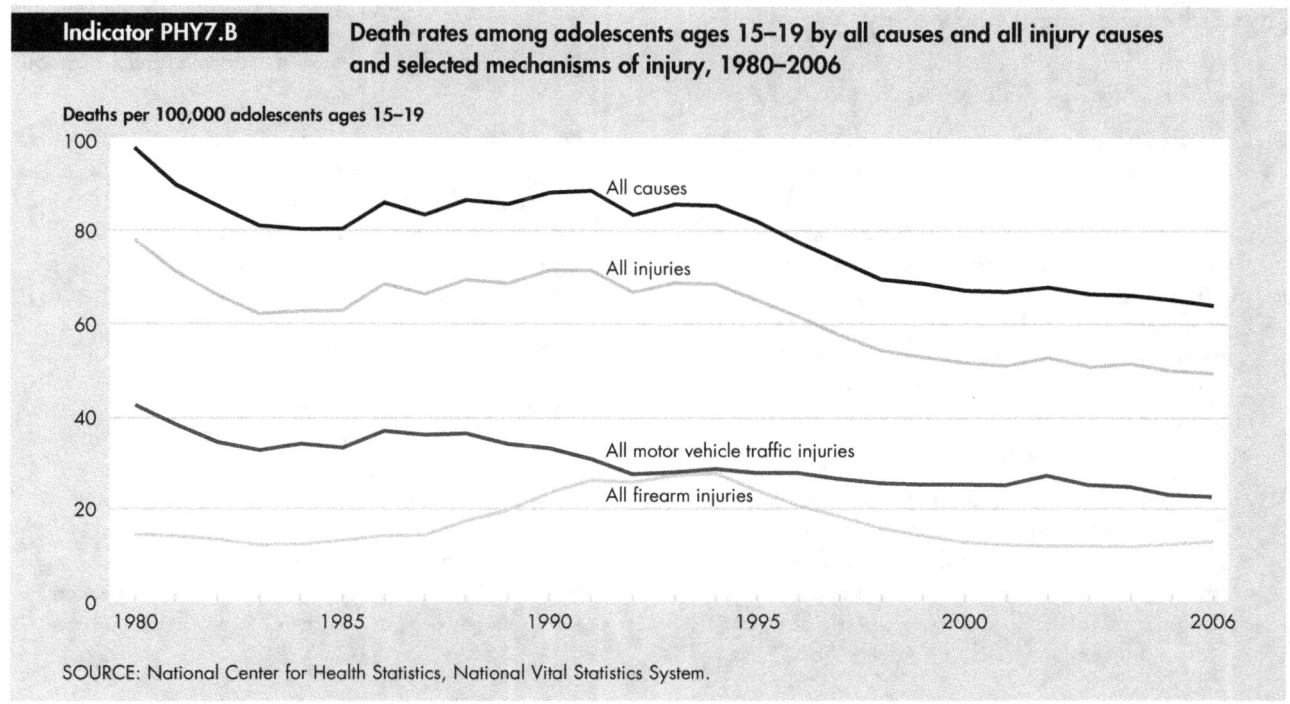

Deaths per 100,000 adolescents ages 15–19

SOURCE: National Center for Health Statistics, National Vital Statistics System.

■ In 2006, the death rate for adolescents ages 15–19 was 64 per 100,000. Nearly 80 percent of adolescent deaths occurred from injuries (50 per 100,000). Both the total and injury death rates have declined substantially since 1980, despite a period of increase from 1986 to 1991.

■ Motor vehicle traffic and firearm injuries accounted for 71 percent of adolescent injury deaths in 2006. The motor vehicle traffic death rate declined since 1980. The firearm death rate was steady from 1980 to 1987, increased from 1987 to 1994, and declined by more than half since 1994. In 2006, the firearm death rate was 13 per 100,000 adolescents, an increase from 2005.

■ Injury deaths can also be reported by intent. Unintentional injury accounts for more than 60 percent of all injury deaths among adolescents. In 2006, this rate was 31 deaths per 100,000 adolescents ages 15–19, unchanged from 2005.

■ For intentional injuries, there were 11 homicides per 100,000 adolescents ages 15–19 in 2006, an increase from 2005. In 2006, there were 9 firearm homicides per 100,000, an increase from 2005. There were 7 suicide deaths per 100,000 adolescents ages 15–19 in 2006, unchanged from 2005.

Bullets contain references to data that can be found in Tables PHY7.A and PHY7.B on pages 142–145. Endnotes begin on page 73.

Indicators Needed

Physical Environment and Safety

A broader set of indicators than those presented in this section is needed to fully understand and monitor children's physical environment and safety. Additional indicators are needed on:

- *Body burden measurements.* Children are exposed to many different contaminants in the environment. Measures of contaminants in air, water, land and food provide indirect indications of children's potential exposure to these contaminants. Both environmental and body burden measurements (i.e., levels of contaminants in blood and urine) are needed to characterize children's exposures. Increasing efforts are under way to assess exposures through body burden measurements and to develop children's indicators based on these measurements.

- *Environmental quality.* Although this report provides indicators for contaminants in both outdoor and indoor air, regular sources of national data are needed to assess indoor air contaminants other than environmental tobacco smoke (e.g., pesticides) that are commonly encountered in homes, schools, and day care settings. Data are needed to more thoroughly characterize children's potential exposure to drinking water contaminants. Indicators are also needed for food and soil contaminants and for cumulative exposures to multiple environmental contaminants that children encounter daily.

- *Exposure to violence.* Although this report provides indicators for direct crime victimization, child maltreatment, and child and adolescent injury and mortality, regular sources of national data are needed to assess children's exposure to violence, including witnessing violence in the home, school, and community. Research suggests that witnessing violence can have detrimental effects similar to being a direct victim of violence. Additional work is needed to develop a national indicator for exposure to violence.

Behavior

The well-being of young people can be affected by aspects of their behavior and social environments. The indicators in this section focus on illegal and high-risk behaviors. Substance use behaviors are shown for regular cigarette smoking, alcohol use, and illicit drug use. Other indicators in this section present data on behaviors such as sexual activity and perpetration of serious violent crime.

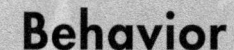

Regular Cigarette Smoking

Smoking has serious long-term consequences, including the risk of smoking-related diseases and premature death, as well as the increased health care costs associated with treating the illnesses.[91] Many adults who are currently addicted to tobacco began smoking as adolescents, and it is estimated that more than 6 million of today's underage smokers will die of tobacco-related illnesses.[92] These consequences underscore the importance of studying patterns of smoking among adolescents.

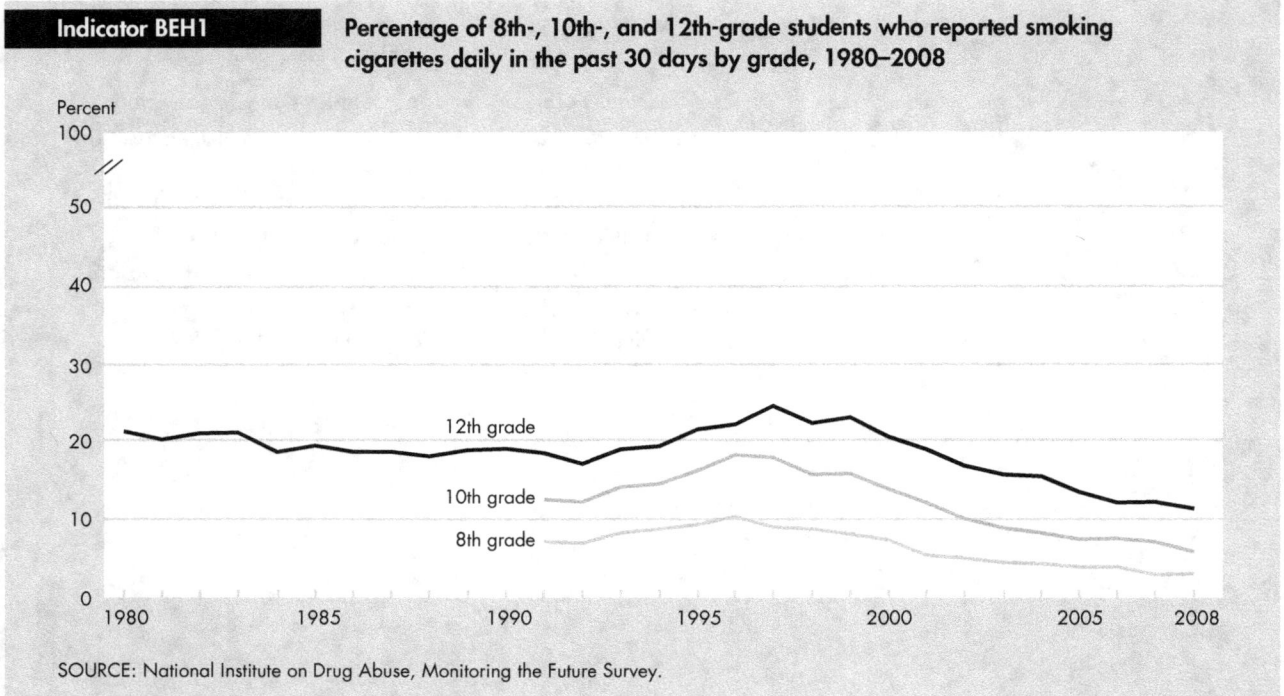

Indicator BEH1 — Percentage of 8th-, 10th-, and 12th-grade students who reported smoking cigarettes daily in the past 30 days by grade, 1980–2008

SOURCE: National Institute on Drug Abuse, Monitoring the Future Survey.

- Among 8th-, 10th-, and 12th-grade students in 2008, the percentage who reported smoking cigarettes daily in the past 30 days was about a third to a half of the percentage for the same groups in the peak years of 1996 and 1997. The most dramatic declines were seen among the youngest students. In 2008, 3 percent of 8th-grade students, 6 percent of 10th-grade students, and 11 percent of 12th-grade students reported smoking cigarettes daily in the past 30 days, compared with the respective peaks of 10, 18, and 25 percent.

- Three percent of both male and female 8th-grade students, 6 percent of both male and female 10th-grade students, and 12 percent of male and 11 percent of female 12th-grade students reported daily smoking.

- In 2008, 14 percent of White 12th-grade students reported smoking cigarettes daily in the past 30 days, compared with 6 percent of Black and 7 percent of Hispanic 12th-grade students.

Bullets contain references to data that can be found in Table BEH1 on page 146. Endnotes begin on page 73.

Alcohol Use

Alcohol is the most common psychoactive substance used during adolescence. Its use is associated with motor vehicle accidents, injuries, and deaths; problems in school and in the workplace; and fighting, crime, and other serious consequences.[93] Early onset of heavy drinking, defined here as five or more alcoholic beverages in a row or during a single occasion in the previous 2 weeks, may be especially problematic, potentially increasing the likelihood of these negative outcomes.

Indicator BEH2 — Percentage of 8th-, 10th-, and 12th-grade students who reported having five or more alcoholic beverages in a row in the past 2 weeks by grade, 1980–2008

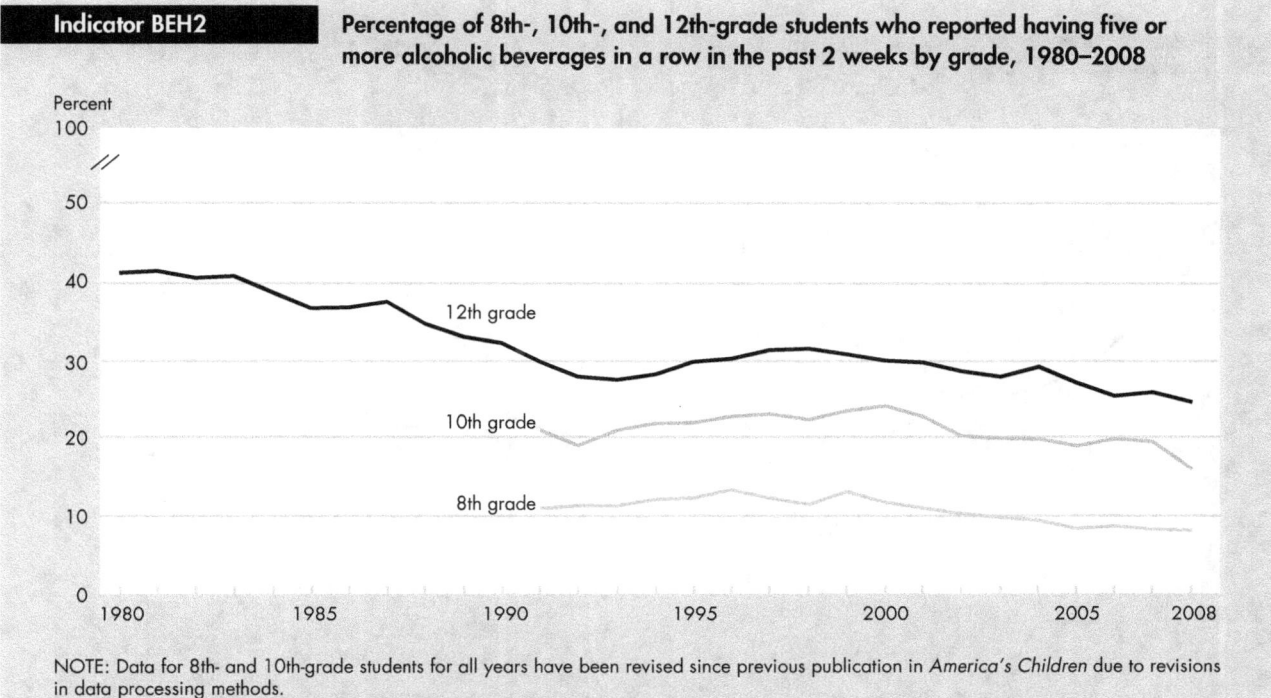

NOTE: Data for 8th- and 10th-grade students for all years have been revised since previous publication in *America's Children* due to revisions in data processing methods.

SOURCE: National Institute on Drug Abuse, Monitoring the Future Survey.

- Heavy drinking declined from the most recent peaks of 13 percent in 1996 to 8 percent in 2008 for 8th-grade students, from 24 percent in 2000 to 16 percent in 2008 for 10th-grade students, and from 32 percent in 1998 to 25 percent in 2008 for 12th-grade students.

- In 2008, 8 percent of both male and female 8th-grade students reported heavy drinking; among 10th-grade students, the proportion was 17 percent for males and 15 percent for females. Twenty-eight percent of 12th-grade males reported heavy drinking, compared with 21 percent of 12th-grade females.

- For 10th- and 12th-grade students in 2008, the percentage of White and Hispanic students who were heavy drinkers was approximately double the percentage of Black students. The percentages of 10th-grade White, Hispanic, and Black students who were heavy drinkers were 20, 20, and 10 percent, respectively. The percentages of White, Hispanic, and Black 12th-graders who were heavy drinkers were 30, 22, and 11 percent, respectively. Among 8th-grade students, the rate of heavy drinking was 8 percent for White, 12 percent for Hispanic, and 6 percent for Black students.

Bullets contain references to data that can be found in Table BEH2 on page 147. Endnotes begin on page 73.

Illicit Drug Use

Drug use by adolescents can have immediate as well as long-term health and social consequences. Cocaine use is linked with health problems that range from eating disorders to disability to death from heart attacks and strokes.[94] Marijuana use poses both health and cognitive risks, particularly for damage to pulmonary functions as a result of chronic use.[95,96] Hallucinogens can affect brain chemistry and result in problems with memory and learning new information.[97] As is the case with alcohol use and smoking, illicit drug use is a risk-taking behavior that has potentially serious negative consequences.

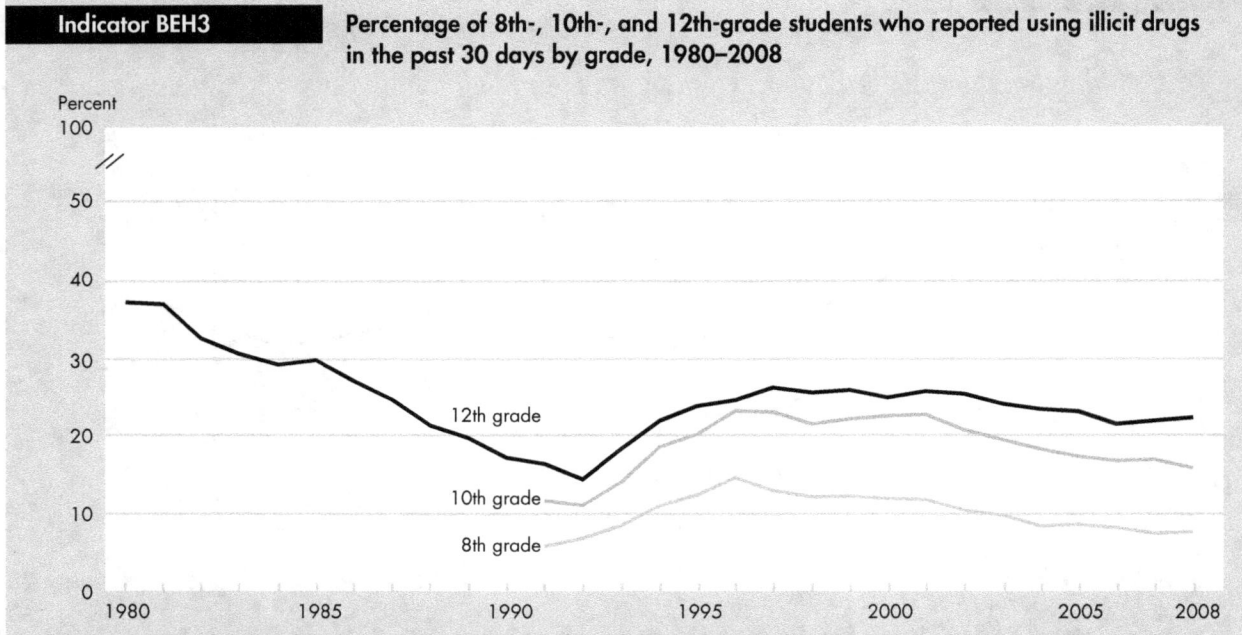

| Indicator BEH3 | Percentage of 8th-, 10th-, and 12th-grade students who reported using illicit drugs in the past 30 days by grade, 1980–2008 |

NOTE: Use of "any illicit drug" includes any use of marijuana, LSD, other hallucinogens, crack, other cocaine, or heroin, or any use of other narcotics, amphetamines, barbiturates, or tranquilizers not under a doctor's orders. For 8th- and 10th-graders, the use of other narcotics and barbiturates has been excluded because these younger respondents appear to overreport use (perhaps because they include the use of nonprescription drugs in their responses).

SOURCE: National Institute on Drug Abuse, Monitoring the Future Survey.

- Illicit drug use in the past 30 days was unchanged from 2007 to 2008. Eight percent of 8th-grade students, 16 percent of 10th-grade students, and 22 percent of 12th-grade students reported use in the past 30 days in 2008.

- Eight percent of male and 7 percent of female 8th-grade students reported using illicit drugs in the past 30 days. Among 10th-grade students, the percentages were 17 percent for males and 14 percent for females. Among 12th-grade students, the percentages were 25 percent for males and 19 percent for females.

- Reports of illicit drug use in the past 30 days have declined from the most recent peaks of 15 percent for 8th-grade students and 23 percent for 10th-grade students in 1996, and 26 percent for 12th-grade students in 1997.

Bullets contain references to data that can be found in Table BEH3 on page 148. Endnotes begin on page 73.

Sexual Activity

Early sexual activity is associated with emotional[98] and physical health risks. Youth who engage in sexual activity are at risk of contracting sexually transmitted infections (STIs) and becoming pregnant. STIs, including HIV, can infect a person for a lifetime and have consequences including disability and early death. Meanwhile, delaying sexual initiation is associated with a decrease in the number of lifetime sexual partners,[99] and decreasing the number of lifetime partners is associated with a decrease in the rate of STIs.[100,101] Additionally, teen pregnancy is associated with a number of negative risk factors, not only for the mother but also for her child (see FAM6).

Indicator BEH4 — Percentage of high school students who reported ever having had sexual intercourse by gender and selected grades, selected years 1991–2007

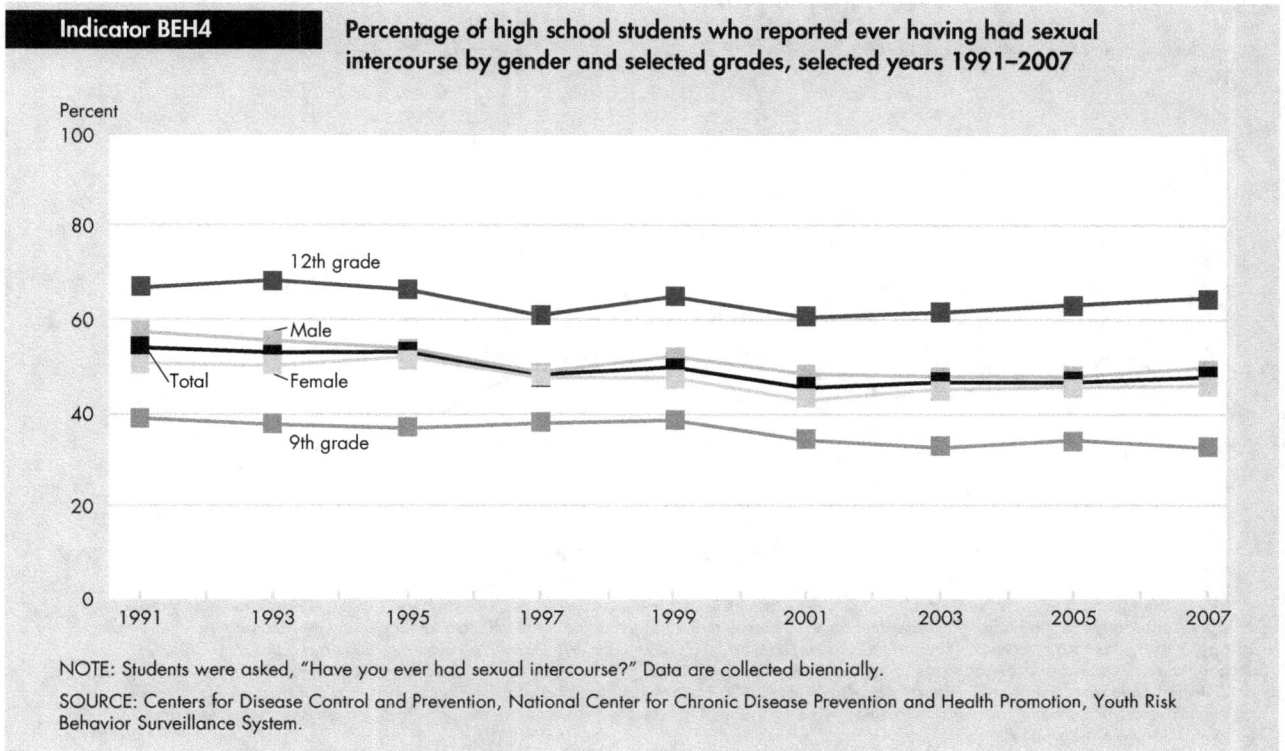

NOTE: Students were asked, "Have you ever had sexual intercourse?" Data are collected biennially.

SOURCE: Centers for Disease Control and Prevention, National Center for Chronic Disease Prevention and Health Promotion, Youth Risk Behavior Surveillance System.

- In 2007, 48 percent of high school students reported ever having had sexual intercourse.

- The proportion of students who reported ever having had sexual intercourse declined significantly from 1991 (54 percent) to 2001 (46 percent) and has remained relatively stable from 2001 to 2007.

- The percentage of students who reported ever having had sexual intercourse differs by grade. In 2007, 33 percent of 9th-grade students reported ever having had sexual intercourse, compared with 65 percent of 12th-grade students.

- Trends differed by race and ethnicity. The percentage of White, non-Hispanic students who reported ever having had sexual intercourse declined from 50 percent in 1991 to 43 percent in 2001, and remained between 42 percent and 44 percent from 2003 to 2007. This rate also declined among Black, non-Hispanic students, from 82 percent in 1991 to 67 percent in 2003, and remained between 67 percent and 68 percent from 2003 to 2007. There was no statistically significant change among Hispanic students between 1991 and 2007 (when the proportion was 52 percent).

- Overall, rates of sexual intercourse did not differ by gender, though they did differ by gender within some racial and ethnic groups. In 2007, 73 percent of Black, non-Hispanic male students reported ever having had sexual intercourse, compared with 61 percent of Black, non-Hispanic female students, and 58 percent of Hispanic male students reported ever having had sexual intercourse, compared with 46 percent of Hispanic female students.[102]

- In 2007, 16 percent of students who had sexual intercourse in the past 3 months reported that they or their partner had used birth control pills before their last sexual intercourse, and 62 percent reported condom use. Of note, condom use increased since 1991 (from 46 percent) among high school students, while there was a statistically significant decrease in the use of birth control pills (from 21 percent).

Bullets contain references to data that can be found in Tables BEH4.A and BEH4.B on page 149. Endnotes begin on page 73.

Youth Perpetrators of Serious Violent Crimes

The level of youth violence in society can be viewed as an indicator of youths' ability to control their behavior and the adequacy of socializing agents such as families, peers, schools, and religious institutions to supervise or channel youth behavior to acceptable norms. One measure of the serious violent crime committed by juveniles is the extent to which at least one juvenile offender is reported by the victim to have been involved in a crime.

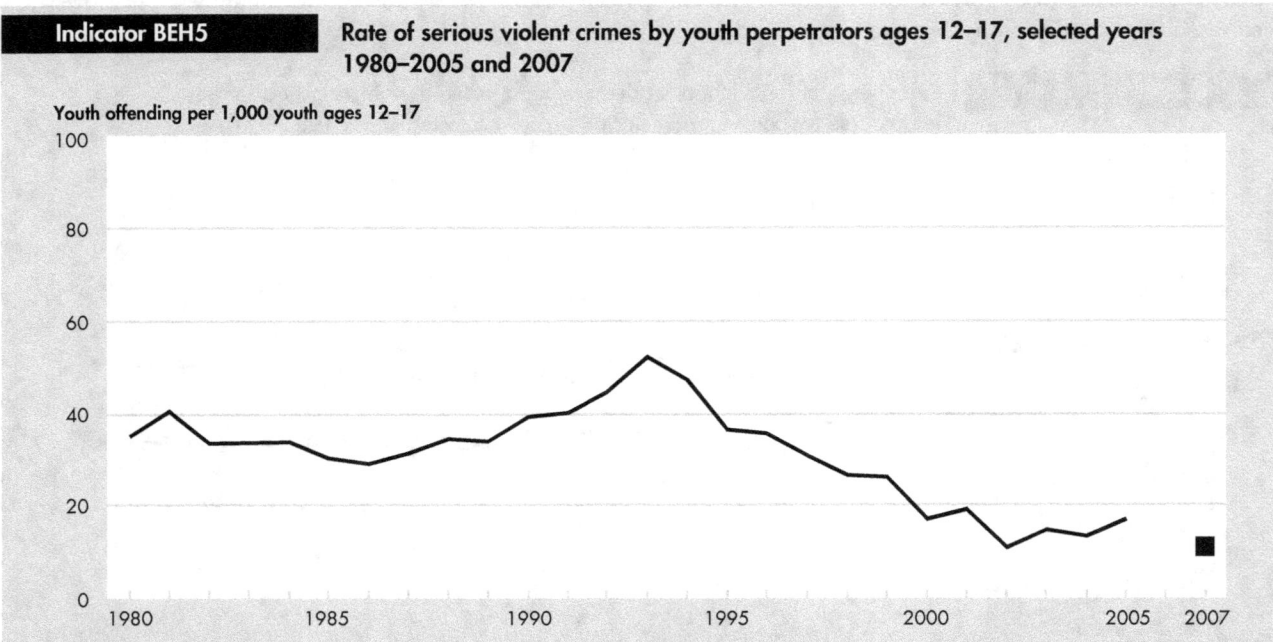

Indicator BEH5

Rate of serious violent crimes by youth perpetrators ages 12–17, selected years 1980–2005 and 2007

Youth offending per 1,000 youth ages 12–17

NOTE: The offending rate is the ratio of the number of crimes (aggravated assault, rape, and robbery, i.e., stealing by force or threat of violence) reported to the National Crime Victimization Survey that involved at least one offender perceived by the victim to be 12–17 years of age, plus the number of homicides reported to the police that involved at least one juvenile offender, to the number of juveniles in the population. Because of changes made in the victimization survey, data prior to 1992 are adjusted to make them comparable with data collected under the redesigned methodology. Data from 2006 are not included because, due to changes in methodology, 2006 crime perpetration rates are not comparable to other years and cannot be used for yearly trend comparisons. See *Criminal Victimization, 2006,* http://www.ojp.usdoj.gov/bjs/abstract/cv06.htm.

SOURCE: Bureau of Justice Statistics, National Crime Victimization Survey and Federal Bureau of Investigation, Uniform Crime Reporting Program, Supplementary Homicide Reports.

- In 2007, the serious violent crime offending rate was 11 crimes per 1,000 juveniles ages 12–17, with a total of 277,000 such crimes involving juveniles. This is lower than the rate in 2005, and it is substantially lower than the 1993 peak rate of 52 crimes per 1,000 juveniles ages 12–17.

- Since 1980, serious violent crime involving youth offenders has ranged from 19 percent of all serious violent crimes in 1982 to 26 percent in 1993, the peak year for youth violence. In 2007, 17 percent of all such victimizations reportedly involved a juvenile offender.

- In over half of all serious violent juvenile crimes reported by victims in 2007, more than one offender was involved in the incident. Because insufficient information exists to determine the ages of each individual offender when a crime is committed by more than one perpetrator, the number of additional juvenile offenders cannot be determined. Therefore, this rate of serious violent crime offending does not represent the number of juvenile offenders in the population, but rather the rate of crimes involving a juvenile.

Bullets contain references to data that can be found in Table BEH5 on page 150.

Indicators Needed

Behavior

A broader set of indicators than those presented in this section is needed to adequately monitor the behaviors of youth. Additional behavioral measures are needed on:

- *Activities promoting health and development.* The participation of youth in a broad range of activities (e.g., volunteering, part-time employment, after-school activities) has been linked to positive developmental outcomes. However, additional research is needed to ascertain how and under what circumstances such activities relate to success in later life. The Forum has presented "Youth Employment While in School" and "Participation in Volunteer Activities" as special features in past *America's Children* reports. However, we currently lack regular indicators on youth involvement in various organized activities as well as data to monitor specific health-promoting behaviors such as exercise.

- *Youth in the justice system.* The youth perpetrators of serious violent crime indicator does not provide critical information on the involvement of youth in the juvenile and criminal justice systems, including the characteristics of youthful offenders and the number and characteristics of youth arrestees and detainees, those prosecuted in juvenile and adult courts, and those incarcerated in the Nation's jails, prisons, and juvenile facilities. Additional work is needed to produce a more comprehensive and useful picture of the number, experiences, and characteristics of youth within the criminal justice system.

Education

The education of children shapes their own personal development and life chances, as well as the economic and social progress of our Nation. This section presents key indicators of how well children are learning and progressing from early childhood through postsecondary school. An indicator on family reading to young children suggests the extent of home support for early learning. Scores on national assessments of mathematics and reading for elementary, middle, and high school students are presented, followed by an indicator on advanced coursetaking. High school completion and college enrollment rates indicate the extent to which students have attained a basic education and are prepared for higher levels of education or the workforce. By contrast, the indicator on youth neither enrolled in school nor working tracks the extent to which youth are at risk of limiting their future prospects at a critical stage of their lives.

Family Reading to Young Children

Reading to young children promotes language acquisition and is linked with literacy development and, later on, with achievement in reading comprehension and overall success in school.[103] The percentage of young children read to daily by a family member is one indicator of how well young children are being prepared for school.

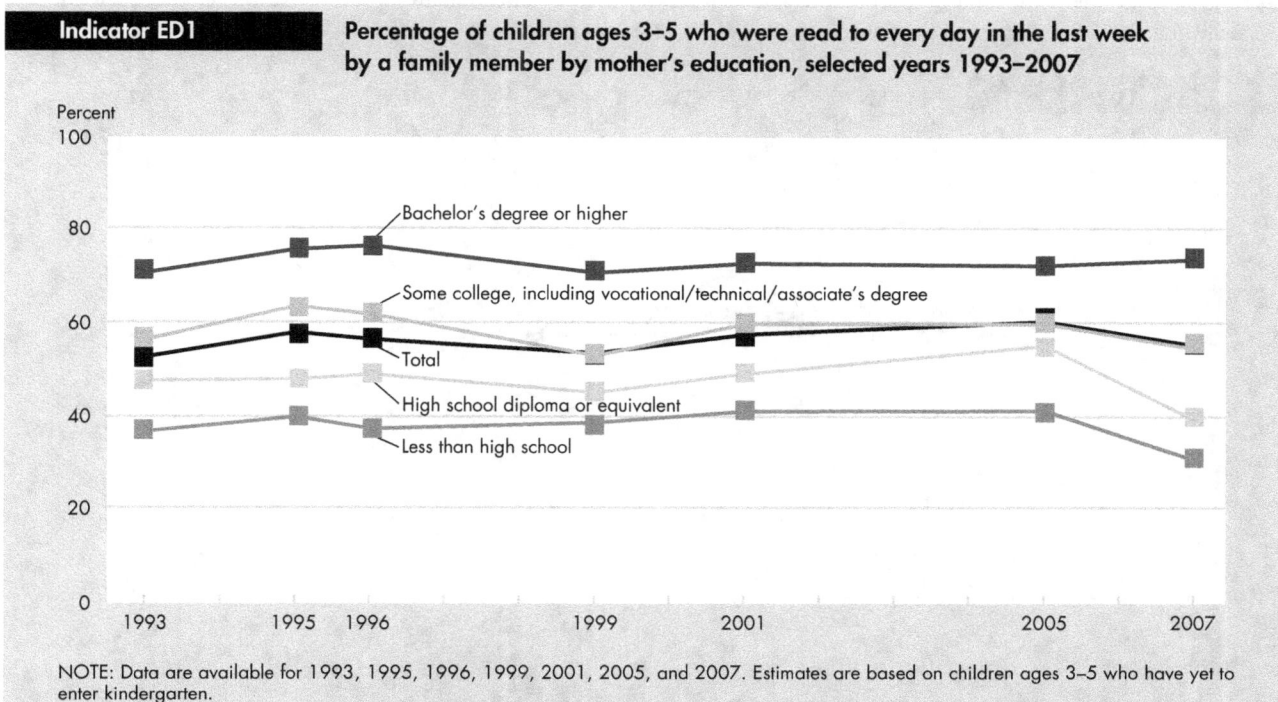

Indicator ED1 — Percentage of children ages 3–5 who were read to every day in the last week by a family member by mother's education, selected years 1993–2007

NOTE: Data are available for 1993, 1995, 1996, 1999, 2001, 2005, and 2007. Estimates are based on children ages 3–5 who have yet to enter kindergarten.

SOURCE: U.S. Department of Education, National Center for Education Statistics, National Household Education Surveys Program.

- In 2007, 55 percent of children ages 3–5 who were not yet in kindergarten were read to daily by a family member. This rate is slightly higher than the rate in 1993 (53 percent), but the rate fluctuated in intervening years.

- In 2007, 74 percent of children whose mothers had at least a bachelor's degree were read to every day. In comparison, daily reading occurred for 55 percent of children whose mothers had some college education, 39 percent of children whose mothers had a high school diploma or equivalent but no further education, and 31 percent of children whose mothers had less than a high school diploma.

- Higher percentages of White, non-Hispanic and Asian, non-Hispanic children than either Black, non-Hispanic or Hispanic children were read to every day in 2007. Sixty-seven percent of White, non-Hispanic children, 60 percent of Asian, non-Hispanic children, 35 percent of Black, non-Hispanic children, and 37 percent of Hispanic children were read to every day by a family member.

- The percentage of children in families with incomes 200 percent or more of the poverty level read to daily by a family member (64 percent) was higher than the percentages of children in families with incomes below the poverty level (40 percent) or those in families with incomes 100–199 percent of the poverty level (50 percent) in 2007.

- The percentage of children living with two parents who were read to every day was higher than the percentage of children living with one parent who were read to every day. Fifty-nine percent of children in two-parent households and 43 percent of children living with one parent were read to every day in 2007.

- The percentages of children in the Northeast (59 percent) and Midwest (59 percent) were not statistically different than the percentages of children in the West (54 percent) and South (52 percent) who were read to daily by a family member in 2007.

Bullets contain references to data that can be found in Table ED1 on page 151. Endnotes begin on page 73.

Mathematics and Reading Achievement

The extent and content of students' knowledge, as well as their ability to think, learn, and communicate, affect their likelihood of becoming productive adults and active citizens. Mathematics and reading achievement test scores are important measures of students' skills in these subject areas, as well as good indicators of overall achievement in school. To assess progress in mathematics and reading, the National Assessment of Educational Progress (NAEP) measures national trends in the academic performance of students in grades 4, 8, and 12.

Indicator ED2.A — Average mathematics scale scores for students in grades 4, 8, and 12, selected years 1990–2007

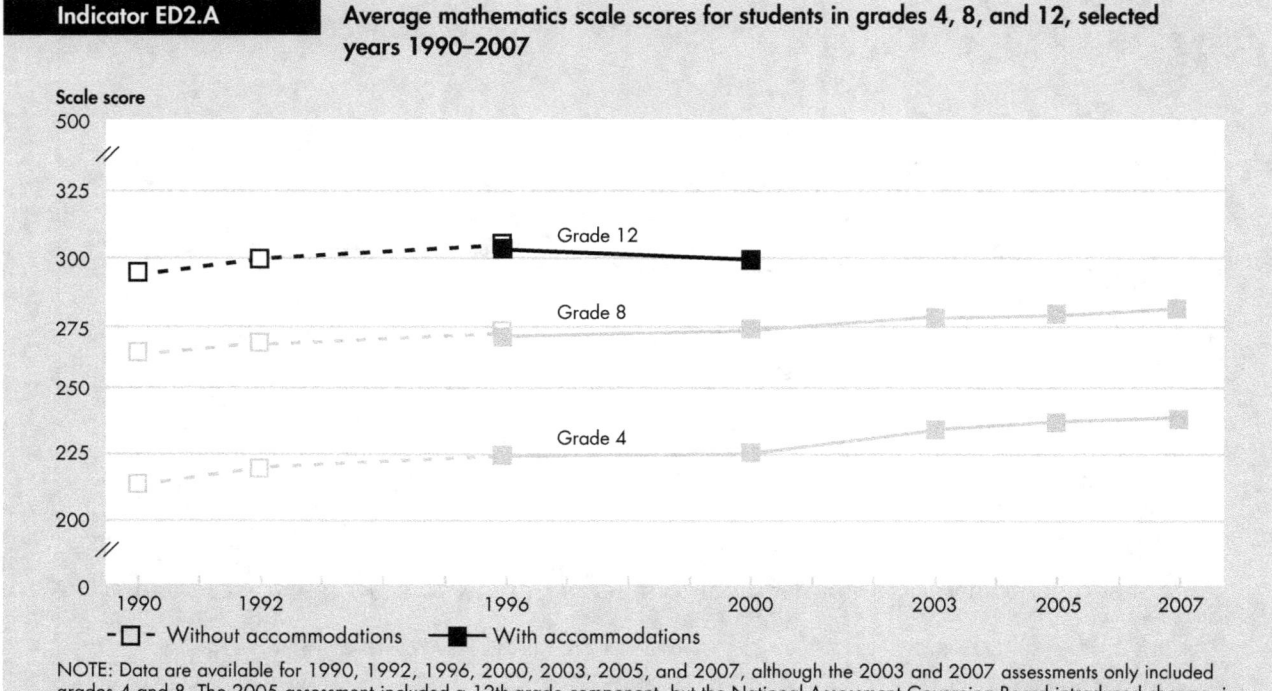

NOTE: Data are available for 1990, 1992, 1996, 2000, 2003, 2005, and 2007, although the 2003 and 2007 assessments only included grades 4 and 8. The 2005 assessment included a 12th-grade component, but the National Assessment Governing Board introduced changes in the 2005 NAEP mathematics framework for grade 12 in both the assessment content and administration procedures. As a result, the 12th-grade assessment results cannot be compared with those of previous assessments. In early years of the assessment, testing accommodations (e.g., extended time, small group testing) for children with disabilities and limited-English-proficient students were not permitted. In 1996, scores are shown for both the assessments with and without accommodations to show comparability across the assessments.

SOURCE: U.S. Department of Education, National Center for Education Statistics, National Assessment of Educational Progress.

- At grades 4 and 8, average mathematics scores were higher in 2007 than in all previous assessments.

- There was no 12th-grade NAEP mathematics assessment in 2007. Moreover, the 12th-grade NAEP mathematics assessment in 2005 was based on a mathematics framework that was revised to reflect changes in high school mathematics standards and coursework. As a result, the 2005 results cannot be compared with those from previous years.[104]

- In 2007, 39 percent of 4th-graders and 32 percent of 8th-graders were at or above the *Proficient* level in mathematics, indicating solid academic achievement. The percentages of 4th- and 8th-graders at or above *Basic* (indicating partial mastery of prerequisite knowledge and skills), at or above *Proficient,* and at *Advanced* (indicating superior performance) in mathematics in 2007 were higher than in all previous assessments.[105]

- At grades 4 and 8 in 2007, Asian or Pacific Islander and White, non-Hispanic students scored higher on average in mathematics than their Black, non-Hispanic, American Indian or Alaska Native, and Hispanic peers; also, Hispanic and American Indian or Alaska Native students had higher average scores than Black, non-Hispanic students.

- In mathematics, males outperformed females at grades 4 and 8 in 2007 and at grade 12 in 2005.

Average reading scale scores for students in grades 4, 8, and 12, selected years 1992–2007

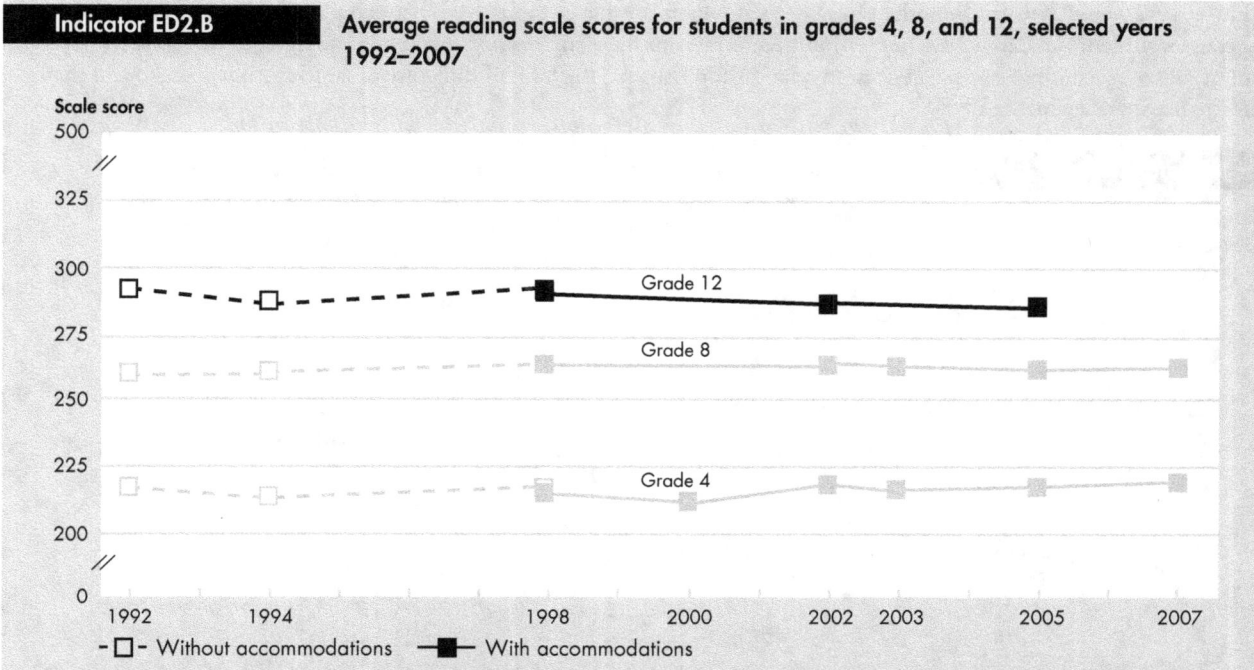

Scale score

- □ - Without accommodations   ■ With accommodations

NOTE: Data are available for 1992, 1994, 1998, 2000, 2002, 2003, 2005, and 2007, although the 2000 assessment only included grade 4, and the 2003 and 2007 assessments only included grades 4 and 8. In early years of the assessment, testing accommodations (e.g., extended time, small group testing) for children with disabilities and limited-English-proficient students were not permitted. In 1998, scores are shown for both the assessments with and without accommodations to show comparability across the assessments.

SOURCE: U.S. Department of Education, National Center for Education Statistics, National Assessment of Educational Progress.

■ At grade 4, there was a 4-point increase in the average reading score between 1992 and 2007. At grade 8, reading scores in 2007 had increased 1 point from 2005 and 3 points from 1992.

■ There was no 12th-grade NAEP reading assessment in 2007. However, in 2005 the average score at grade 12 was 6 points lower than in 1992.

■ In 2007, 33 percent of 4th-graders were at or above the *Proficient* achievement level in reading, indicating solid academic achievement, a higher percentage than in all previous assessments. Thirty-one percent of students in grade 8 were at or above *Proficient,* a percentage not statistically different from the percentage in 1992. Thirty-five percent of students in grade 12 were at or above *Proficient* in 2005, a lower percentage than the percentage in 1992 and 1998 but not statistically different than the percentage in 2002.[105]

■ In reading, Asian or Pacific Islander and White, non-Hispanic students scored higher on average in 2007 than their Black, non-Hispanic, American Indian or Alaska Native, and Hispanic peers at grades 4 and 8. The gap between White, non-Hispanic students and their Black, non-Hispanic peers decreased 5 points between 1992 and 2007 at grade 4; however, there was no change in the gap between White, non-Hispanic students and their Hispanic peers between 1992 and 2007 at grade 4. There were no changes in the gaps between White, non-Hispanic students and their Black, non-Hispanic or Hispanic peers from 1992 to 2007 at grade 8 or between 1992 and 2005 at grade 12.

■ Females had higher reading scores than males at grades 4 and 8 in 2007 and at grade 12 in 2005.

■ In both mathematics and reading, higher parental education levels were associated with higher achievement scores.[106]

Bullets contain references to data that can be found in Tables ED2.A and ED2.B on pages 152–155. Endnotes begin on page 73.

High School Academic Coursetaking

Since *A Nation at Risk* was published in 1983, school reforms have emphasized increasing the number of academic courses students take in high school. More recent reforms have emphasized increasing the rigor, as well as the amount, of coursetaking. Research suggests a relationship between the level of difficulty of courses students take and their performance on assessments.[107, 108]

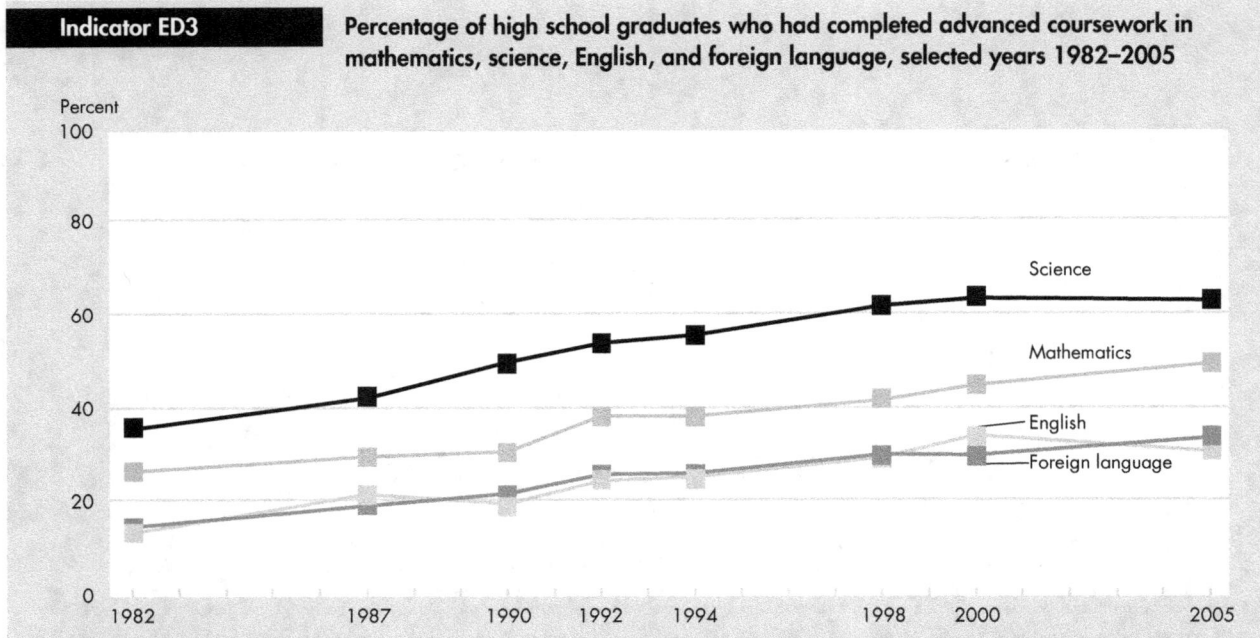

Indicator ED3

Percentage of high school graduates who had completed advanced coursework in mathematics, science, English, and foreign language, selected years 1982–2005

NOTE: Data for 1982 and 1992 are from a series of longitudinal studies, whereas data for 1987, 1990, 1994, 1998, 2000, and 2005 are from the National Assessment of Educational Progress High School Transcript Studies. Due to differences in survey methodology among the data collections, users should use caution when comparing data across the years. Advanced coursework includes the following: mathematics: courses above Algebra II; science: chemistry, physics, or advanced biology; English: some courses at the honors level; and foreign language: a year 3, year 4, or advanced placement course.

SOURCE: U.S. Department of Education, National Center for Education Statistics, High School Transcript Studies: High School and Beyond Study, National Education Longitudinal Study of 1988, and National Assessment of Educational Progress Transcript Study.

- Forty-nine percent of students who graduated from high school in 2005 had taken at least one advanced mathematics course (defined as a course above Algebra II), which was higher than the percentage in 1982 (26 percent). The percentage of graduates in 2005 who had taken a nonacademic or low-level academic course as their most advanced mathematics course was 4 percent, compared with 24 percent of graduates in 1982.

- In science, 63 percent of all high school graduates in 2005 had taken a chemistry, physics, or advanced biology course, compared to 35 percent of the graduates in 1982 who had taken this level of science course. The percentage of graduates whose most advanced science course was classified as a low-level academic course dropped from 27 percent in 1982 to 7 percent in 2005.

- In English, 31 percent of all high school graduates in 2005 had taken honors-level courses, an increase from 13 percent of graduates in 1982. There was no measurable difference between the percentages of graduates in 1982 and 2005 who had taken low-level academic courses in English (10 and 12 percent, respectively).

- In foreign languages, 33 percent of high school graduates had taken a year 3, year 4, or advanced placement course in 2005; this was double the percentage in 1982 (15 percent). Sixteen percent of high school graduates in 2005 had not taken any foreign language course, compared with 46 percent of graduates in 1982.

- While the level of high school academic coursetaking rose between 1982 and 2005, the reading, mathematics, or science scores of 12th-graders did not improve on the National Assessment of Educational Progress.[109]

Bullets contain references to data that can be found in Tables ED3.A–ED3.D on pages 156–159. Endnotes begin on page 73.

High School Completion

A high school diploma or its equivalent is an indicator that a person has acquired the basic reading, writing, and mathematics skills a person needs to function in modern society. The percentage of young adults ages 18–24 with a high school diploma or an equivalent credential is a measure of the extent to which young adults have completed a basic prerequisite for many entry-level jobs and for higher education.

Indicator ED4 — **Percentage of young adults ages 18–24 who have completed high school by race and Hispanic origin, 1980–2007**

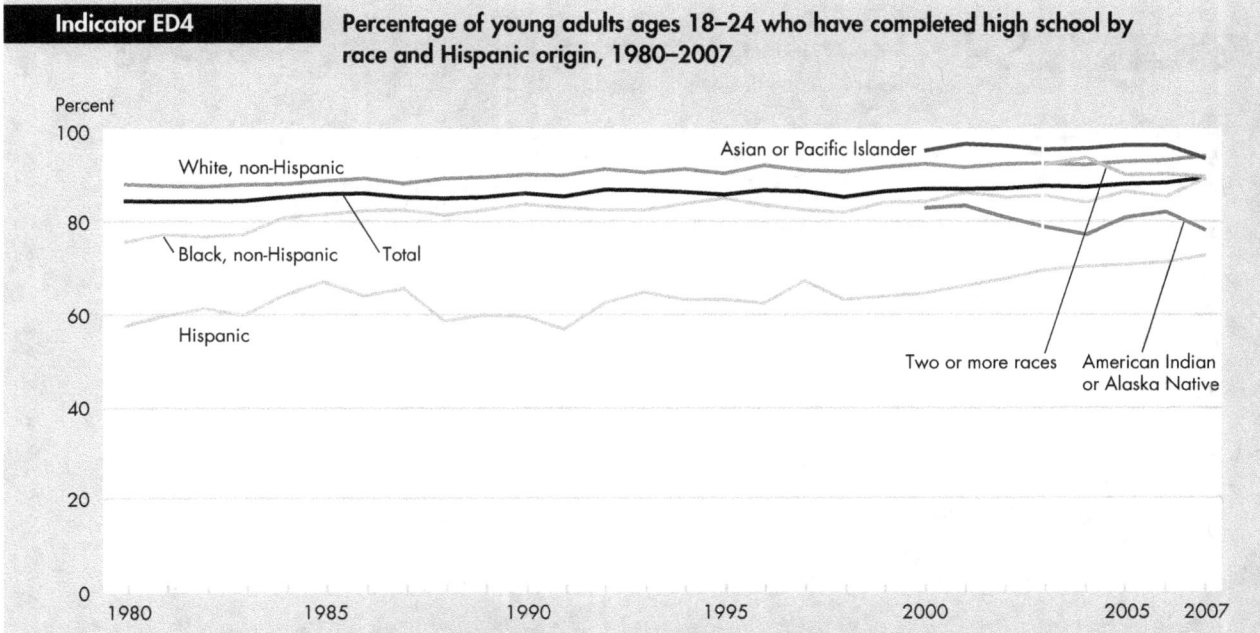

NOTE: Percentages are based only on those not currently enrolled in high school or below. Prior to 1992, this indicator was measured as completing 4 or more years of high school rather than the actual attainment of a high school diploma or equivalent. For data before 2003, the 1977 OMB Standards for Data on Race and Ethnicity were used to classify persons into one of the following four racial groups: White, Black, American Indian or Alaskan Native, or Asian or Pacific Islander. The revised 1997 OMB standards were used for data for 2003 and later years. Persons could select one or more of five racial groups: White, Black or African American, American Indian or Alaska Native, Asian, or Native Hawaiian or Other Pacific Islander. Those reporting more than one race were classified as "Two or more races." For continuity purposes, respondents who reported being Asian or Native Hawaiian or Other Pacific Islander were combined. Beginning in 2003, those in each racial category represent those reporting only one race. Data from 2003 onward are not directly comparable with data from earlier years. Data on race and Hispanic origin are collected separately. Persons of Hispanic origin may be of any race.

SOURCE: U.S. Census Bureau, Current Population Survey, School Enrollment Supplement.

- In 2007, 89 percent of young adults ages 18–24 had completed high school with a diploma or an alternative credential such as a General Education Development (GED) certificate. The high school completion rate has increased slightly since 1980, when it was 84 percent.

- The rate at which Black, non-Hispanic young adults completed high school increased from 75 percent to 89 percent between 1980 and 2007. Among White, non-Hispanics, the high school completion rate increased from 88 percent in 1980 to 93 percent in 2007.

- Hispanic young adults have had a consistently lower high school completion rate than White, non-Hispanic

and Black, non-Hispanic young adults. Nonetheless, the high school completion rate for Hispanic young adults has increased from 57 percent in 1980 to 72 percent in 2007.

- In 2007, higher percentages of White, non-Hispanic and Asian or Pacific Islander young adults (93 percent each) had completed high school, compared with Black, non-Hispanic young adults and young adults of two or more races (89 percent each), American Indian or Alaska Native young adults (78 percent), and Hispanic young adults (72 percent).

Bullets contain references to data that can be found in Table ED4 on page 160.

Youth Neither Enrolled in School nor Working

Youth ages 16–19 who are neither in school nor working are detached from both of these core activities that usually occupy teenagers during their transition from adolescence to adulthood. Such detachment, particularly if it lasts for several years, puts youth at increased risk of having lower earnings and a less stable employment history than their peers who stayed in school, secured jobs, or both.[110] The percentage of youth who are not enrolled in school and not working is one measure of the proportion of young people who are at risk of limiting their future prospects.

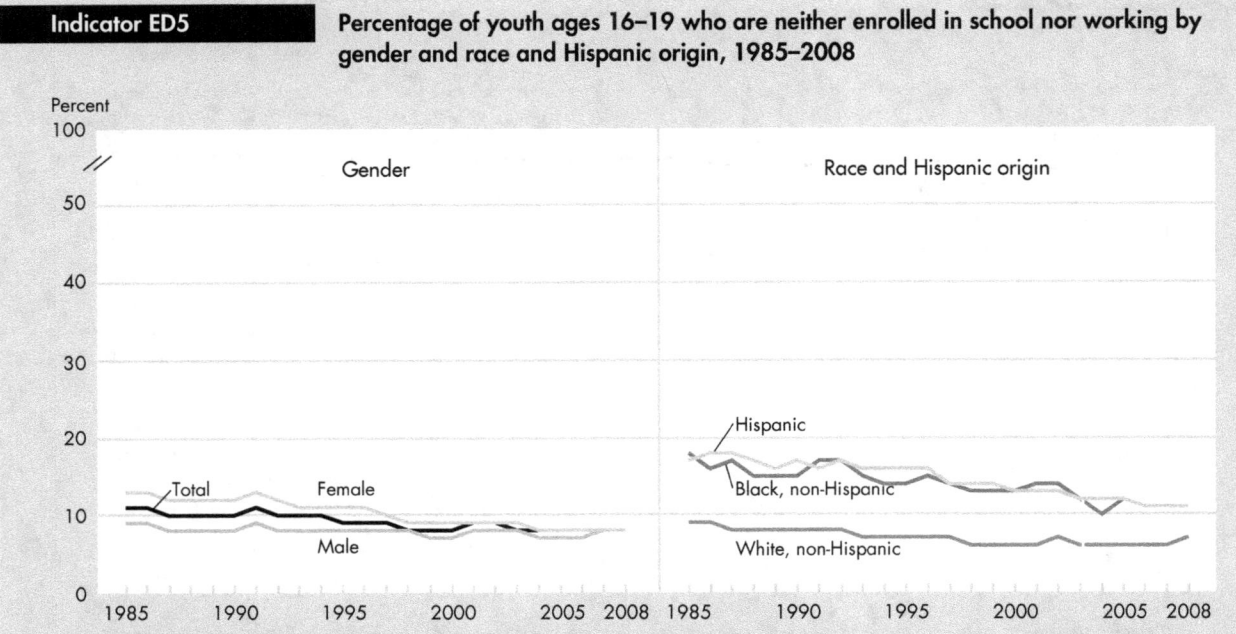

Indicator ED5

Percentage of youth ages 16–19 who are neither enrolled in school nor working by gender and race and Hispanic origin, 1985–2008

NOTE: The information relates to the labor force and enrollment status of persons 16–19 years old in the civilian noninstitutionalized population during an "average" week of the school year. School refers to both high school and college. For data before 2003, the 1977 OMB Standards for Data on Race and Ethnicity were used to classify persons into one of the following four racial groups: White, Black, American Indian or Alaskan Native, or Asian or Pacific Islander. The revised 1997 OMB standards were used for data for 2003 and later years. Persons could select one or more of five racial groups: White, Black or African American, American Indian or Alaska Native, Asian, or Native Hawaiian or Other Pacific Islander. Included in the total but not shown separately are American Indian or Alaska Native, Asian, Native Hawaiian or Other Pacific Islander, and "Two or more races." Beginning in 2003, those in each racial category represent those reporting only one race. Data from 2003 onward are not directly comparable with data from earlier years. Data on race and Hispanic origin are collected separately. Persons of Hispanic origin may be of any race.

SOURCE: U.S. Bureau of Labor Statistics, Current Population Survey.

■ In an average week during the 2008 school year, 8 percent of youth ages 16–19 were neither enrolled in school nor working. The proportion of youth neither enrolled in school nor working has been on a downward trend, and most of the decline has occurred among females. In 1991, 13 percent of young females were neither in school nor working; by 2008, this proportion was 8 percent.

■ Black, non-Hispanic youth and Hispanic youth are more likely to be neither enrolled nor working than White, non-Hispanic youth. In 2008, 11 percent of Hispanic youth and 11 percent of Black, non-Hispanic youth were neither in school nor working, compared with 7 percent of White, non-Hispanic youth.

■ Older youth, ages 18–19, are more than three times as likely to be detached from school and work activities as youth ages 16–17. In 2008, 14 percent of youth ages 18–19 were neither enrolled in school nor working, compared with 4 percent of youth ages 16–17.

■ The percentage of youth who were enrolled in school and not employed was 61 percent in 2008. This proportion has been trending up since 2000, when it was 48 percent.[111]

■ The percentage of youth who were both enrolled in school and employed was 22 percent in 2008, down from 31 percent in 1998.

Bullets contain references to data that can be found in Tables ED5.A and ED5.B on pages 161–162. Endnotes begin on page 73.

College Enrollment

A college education generally enhances a person's employment prospects and increases his or her earning potential.[112] The percentage of high school completers who enroll in college in the fall immediately after high school is one measure of the accessibility and perceived value of a college education by high school completers.[113]

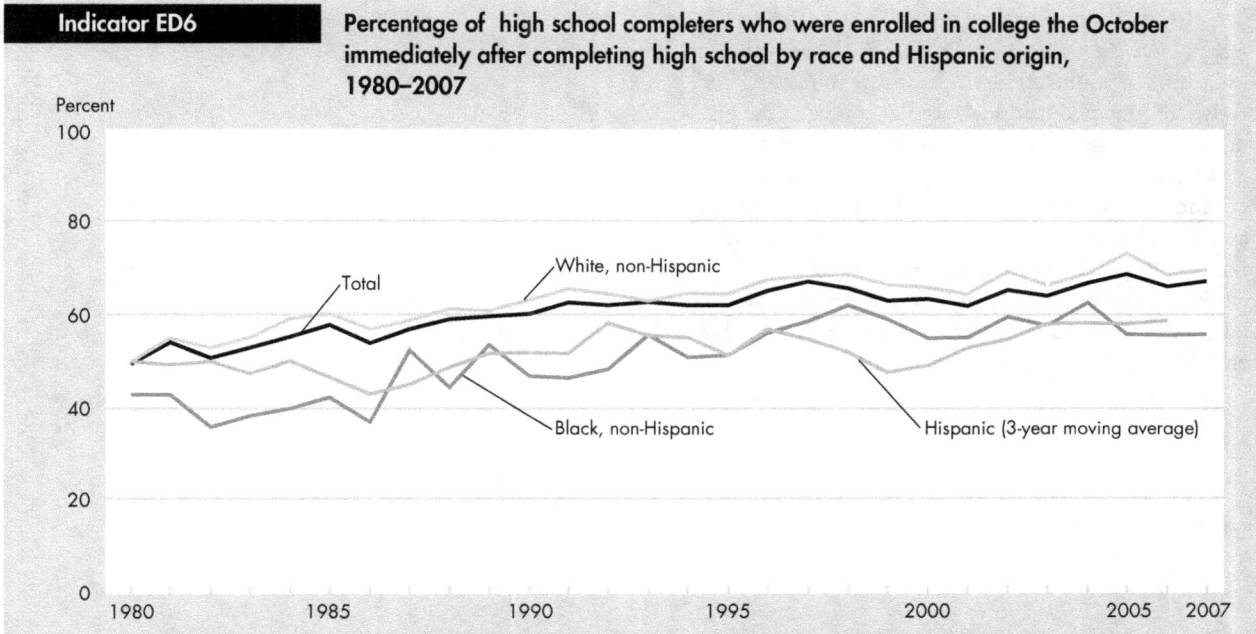

Indicator ED6

Percentage of high school completers who were enrolled in college the October immediately after completing high school by race and Hispanic origin, 1980–2007

NOTE: Enrollment in college as of October of each year for individuals ages 16 to 24 who completed high school during the preceding 12 months. High school completion includes GED recipients. A 3-year moving average is the average of the estimates for the year prior to the reported year, the reported year, and the following year. Thus a moving average cannot be calculated for the most recent year. For data before 2003, the 1977 OMB Standards for Data on Race and Ethnicity were used to classify persons into one of the following four racial groups: White, Black, American Indian or Alaskan Native, or Asian or Pacific Islander. The revised 1997 OMB standards were used for data for 2003 and later years. Persons could select one or more of five racial groups: White, Black or African American, American Indian or Alaska Native, Asian, or Native Hawaiian or Other Pacific Islander. Included in the total but not shown separately are American Indian or Alaska Native, Asian, Native Hawaiian or Other Pacific Islander, and "Two or more races." Beginning in 2003, those in each racial category represent those reporting only one race. Data from 2003 onward are not directly comparable with data from earlier years. Data on race and Hispanic origin are collected separately. Persons of Hispanic origin may be of any race.

SOURCE: U.S. Census Bureau, Current Population Survey, School Enrollment Supplement.

- In 2007, 67 percent of high school completers enrolled immediately in a 2-year or 4-year college.

- Between 1980 and 2007, the rate of immediate college enrollment has trended upward from 49 percent to 67 percent; however, the rate has fluctuated from year to year.

- In 1980, 50 percent of White, non-Hispanic high school completers immediately enrolled in college; this rate increased to 69 percent by 1998 and decreased to 64 percent by 2001. Although this rate fluctuated between 2001 and 2007, the immediate college enrollment rate was higher in 2007 (70 percent) than in 2001.

- In 1980, the immediate enrollment rate for Black, non-Hispanics was 43 percent; this rate increased to 56 percent in 2007.

- For Hispanics, the immediate college enrollment rate has fluctuated greatly since 1980, very likely due to

small sample sizes. For this reason, a 3-year moving average is used to measure the trend. Even so, due to large standard errors, there is no measurable difference between the moving average in 1980 (50 percent) and 2006 (59 percent).

- From 1980 to 2007, the immediate enrollment rate for male high school completers increased from 47 percent to 66 percent, while for female high school completers it increased from 52 percent to 68 percent.

- Between 1980 and 1995, there were no statistically significant differences between the immediate enrollment rates for males and females. Between 1996 and 2004, however, the female rate was significantly greater than the male rate every year except 1999 and 2001. Since 2005, there again were no statistically significant differences between the rates for males and females.

Bullets contain references to data that can be found in Table ED6 on page 163. Endnotes begin on page 73.

Indicator Needed

Education

Regular, periodic data collections are needed to provide information on young children's cognitive, social, and emotional development.

- *Early childhood development.* Although this report offers indicators of young children's exposure to reading and early childhood education, a regular source of data is needed to measure specific cognitive, emotional, and social skills of preschoolers over time. One assessment of kindergartners' skills and knowledge was presented as a special feature in *America's Children, 2000.* The Forum's Research and Innovation committee is working to strengthen our understanding of how to best conceptualize, define, and measure aspects of early childhood socio-emotional development.

Health

The World Health Organization defines health as a "state of complete physical, mental, and social well-being, and not merely the absence of disease or infirmity." This section presents indicators of several important aspects or determinants of child health. Some of the indicators in this section relate to birth outcomes such as low birthweight, preterm birth, and infant mortality. Other indicators describe key health conditions, including emotional or behavioral difficulties,adolescent depression, overweight, and asthma. An indicator on the quality of children'sdiets compares children's dietary intake to recommended national dietary guidelines. The indicator on activity limitation presents a global measure that gauges the effect of chronic health conditions on children's functioning.

Preterm Birth and Low Birthweight

Infants born preterm (less than 37 completed weeks of gestation) or with low birthweight (less than 2,500 grams or 5 lbs. 8 oz.) are at higher risk of early death and long-term health and developmental issues than infants born later in pregnancy or at higher birthweights.[9,114–115] Many, but not all, preterm infants are also low birthweight, and vice versa. In 2006, infants born preterm accounted for two-thirds of all low birthweight infants, and over 40 percent of preterm births were low birthweight.[6] Preterm infants born at less than 34 weeks (very and moderately preterm) are at high risk for poor outcomes, including chronic health conditions, long-term disability, and death. The majority of preterm births are infants born at 34–36 weeks (late preterm). Late preterm infants are at lower risk of poor outcomes than infants born earlier but are at higher risk than infants delivered at term or later.[9] Disorders related to preterm birth and low birthweight are the second leading cause of infant death in the United States.[9]

Indicator HEALTH1.A	Percentage of infants born preterm and percentage of infants born with low birthweight, 1990–2007

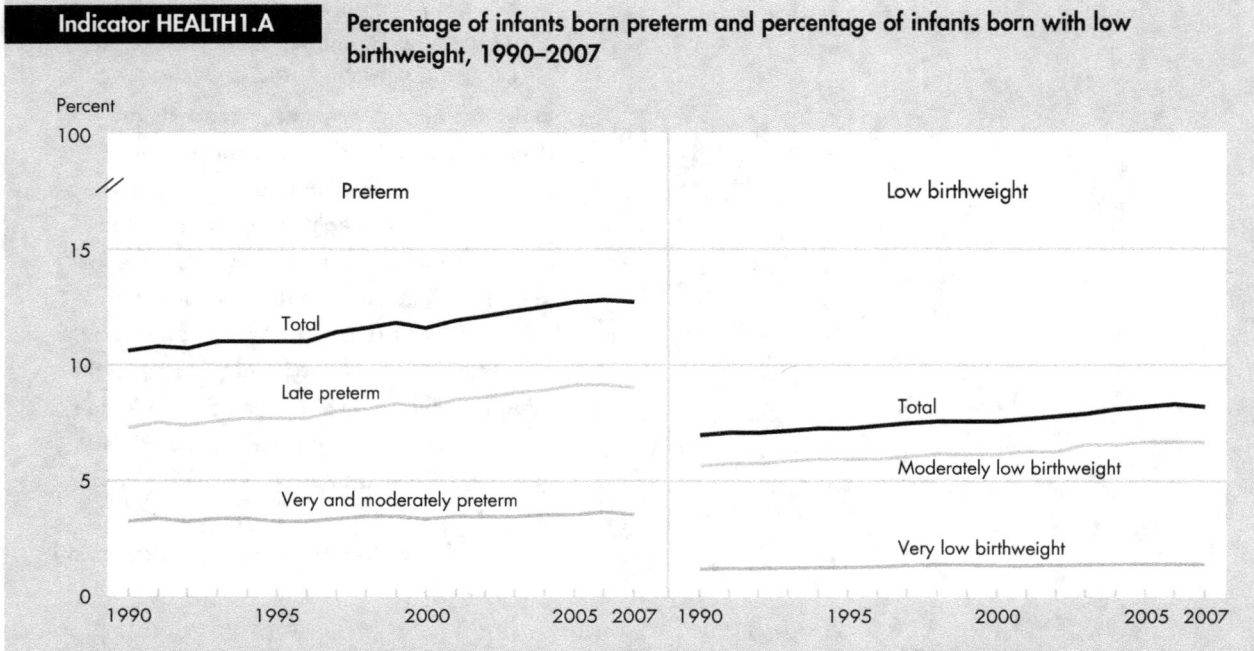

NOTE: Late preterm infants are born at 34–36 weeks of gestation; very and moderately preterm infants are born at less than 34 weeks gestation. Moderately low birthweight infants weigh 1,500–2,499 grams at birth; very low birthweight infants weigh less than 1,500 grams at birth.

SOURCE: National Center for Health Statistics, National Vital Statistics System.

■ After several decades of steady increases, the percentage of infants born preterm and the percentage born with low birthweight declined slightly in 2007. The percentage of infants born preterm was 12.7 percent in 2007, down from 12.8 percent in 2006; most of the decline was among late preterm infants (from 9.1 percent in 2006 to 9.0 percent in 2007). The percentage of infants born with low birthweight declined to 8.2 percent in 2007 from 8.3 percent in 2006; all of the decline was among moderately low birthweight infants.

■ From 1990 to 2006, the percentage of preterm births rose from 10.6 percent to 12.8 percent. The increase in late preterm births (from 7.3 to 9.1 percent) accounted for most of this increase. The percentage of births that were very and moderately preterm changed little in recent years (3.6 percent in 2007).

■ The percentage of low birthweight infants rose from 7.0 percent of all births in 1990 to 8.3 percent in 2006. In 2006 and 2007, 1.5 percent of infants were very low birthweight, up from 1.3 percent in 1990. The percentage of moderately low birthweight infants rose from 5.7 percent in 1990 to 6.8 percent in 2006, but declined slightly to 6.7 percent in 2007.

■ The increasing multiple birth rate was a contributing factor to the rise in preterm birth and low birthweight between 1990 and 2006. However, both the percentage of preterm births and low birthweight infants rose substantially among singleton births as well.[6]

Percentage of infants born with low birthweight by race and Hispanic origin of mother, 1990, 2006, and 2007

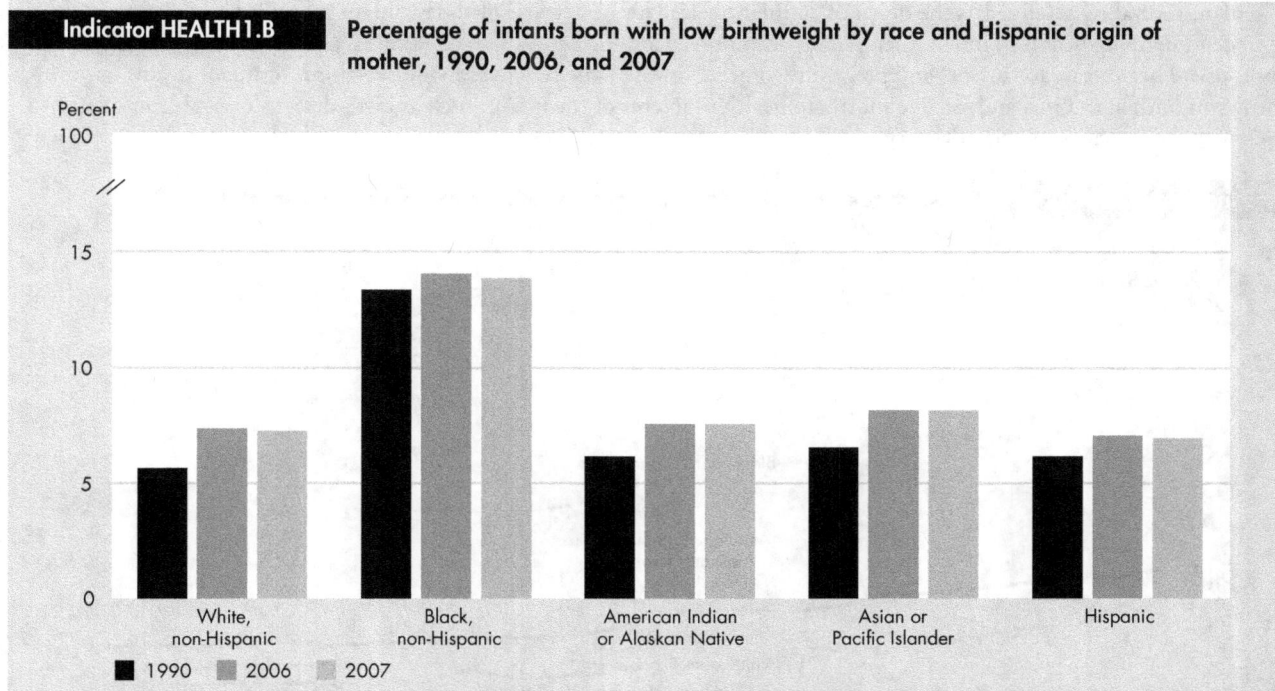

NOTE: Data for 2007 are preliminary. Race refers to mother's race. The 1977 OMB Standards for Data on Race and Ethnicity were used to classify persons into one of the following four racial groups: White, Black, American Indian or Alaskan Native, or Asian or Pacific Islander. Although state reporting of birth certificate data is transitioning to comply with the 1997 OMB standard for race and ethnic statistics, 2006 and 2007 data from states reporting multiple races were bridged to the single-race categories of the 1977 OMB standards for comparability with other states. Data on race and Hispanic origin are collected and reported separately. Persons of Hispanic origin may be of any race.

SOURCE: National Center for Health Statistics, National Vital Statistics System.

■ The percentage of Black, non-Hispanic infants born with low birthweight was higher than that of other racial or ethnic groups. The Black, non-Hispanic percentage declined to a low of 13.1 percent in 1996 and 1997, rose to 14.0 percent in 2006, and declined to 13.8 percent in 2007. The percentage of low birthweight infants rose among White, non-Hispanic infants, from 5.6 percent in 1990 to 7.3 percent in 2006, but declined slightly to 7.2 percent in 2007. Between 1990 and 2006, low birthweight percentages increased for American Indian or Alaskan Native infants (6.1 to 7.5 percent) and Asian or Pacific Islander infants (6.5 to 8.1 percent); the percentages for both groups, however, were unchanged between 2006 and 2007. Among Hispanic infants, the percentage of low birthweight infants rose between 1990 and 2006 (6.1 to 7.0 percent) and declined slightly for 2007 (6.9 percent).

■ In 2007, Black, non-Hispanic infants were also more likely to be born preterm (18 percent) than White, non-Hispanic (11 percent) and Hispanic (12 percent) infants.

■ The percentage of Black, non-Hispanic infants born preterm declined from 19.0 percent in 1991 to 17.4 percent in 2000, rose to 18.5 percent in 2006, and declined slightly in 2007 (18.3 percent). From 1990 to 2006, the percentage of preterm births increased steadily for White, non-Hispanic infants (8.5 to 11.7 percent), then declined slightly in 2007 (11.5 percent). The percentage of preterm Hispanic infants increased from 11.0 to 12.3 percent between 1990 and 2007.

Bullets contain references to data that can be found in Tables HEALTH1.A and HEALTH1.B on pages 164–165. Endnotes begin on page 73.

Infant Mortality

Infant mortality is defined as the death of an infant before his or her first birthday. Infant mortality is related to the underlying health of the mother, public health practices, socioeconomic conditions, and availability and use of appropriate health care for infants and pregnant women.[10] In the United States, about two-thirds of infant deaths occur in the first month after birth and are due mostly to health problems of the infant, such as birth defects, or problems related to the pregnancy, such as preterm delivery.

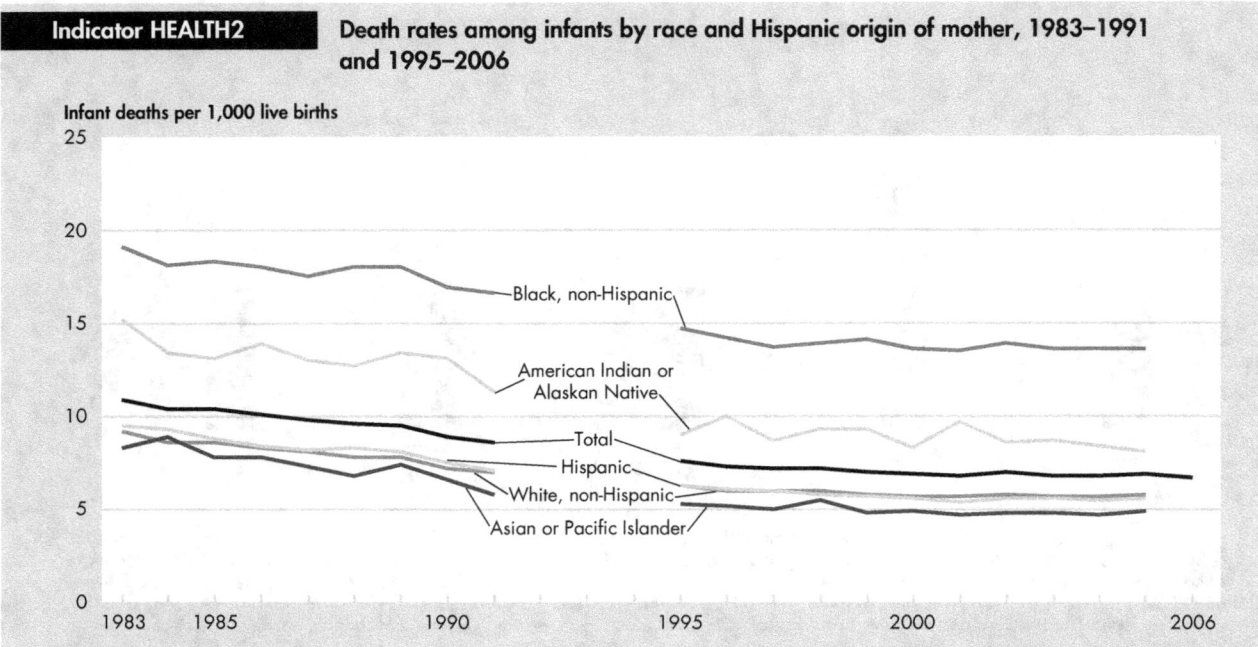

Indicator HEALTH2 **Death rates among infants by race and Hispanic origin of mother, 1983–1991 and 1995–2006**

Infant deaths per 1,000 live births

NOTE: Infant deaths are deaths before an infant's first birthday. Data from the file linking live births to infant deaths are available for 1983–1991 and 1995–2005 only. The infant mortality rate for 2006 was obtained from unlinked death records from the National Vital Statistics System because data for 2006 are not currently available from the National Linked Files of Live Births and Infant Deaths. 2006 data for specific race and ethnicity groups in this figure are not available. Race refers to mother's race. The 1977 OMB Standards for Data on Race and Ethnicity were used to classify persons into one of the following four racial groups: White, Black, American Indian or Alaskan Native, or Asian or Pacific Islander. Although state reporting of birth certificate data is transitioning to comply with the 1997 OMB standard for race and ethnic statistics, data from states reporting multiple races were bridged to the single-race categories of the 1977 OMB standards for comparability with other states. Data on race and Hispanic origin are collected and reported separately. Persons of Hispanic origin may be of any race. Trends for the Hispanic population are affected by an expansion in the number of registration areas that included an item on Hispanic origin on the birth certificate.

SOURCE: National Center for Health Statistics, National Vital Statistics System.

- The infant mortality rate was 6.7 deaths per 1,000 live births in 2006, a decline from 6.9 in 2005.

- Substantial racial and ethnic disparities in infant mortality continue. Black, non-Hispanic and American Indian or Alaskan Native infants have consistently had higher infant mortality rates than those of other racial or ethnic groups. For example, in 2005, the Black, non-Hispanic infant mortality rate was 13.6 infant deaths per 1,000 live births and the American Indian or Alaskan Native rate was 8.1; both rates were higher than the rates among White, non-Hispanic (5.8), Hispanic (5.6), and Asian or Pacific Islander (4.9) infants in 2005.

- Infant mortality rates also vary within racial and ethnic populations. For example, among Hispanics in the United States, the infant mortality rate for 2005 ranged from 4.4 deaths per 1,000 live births for infants of Cuban origin to a high of 8.3 for Puerto Rican infants.

Bullets contain references to data that can be found in Table HEALTH2 on page 166. Endnotes begin on page 73.

Emotional and Behavioral Difficulties

Good emotional and behavioral health enhances a child's sense of well-being, supports satisfying social relationships at home and with peers, and leads to achievement of full academic potential.[116] Children with emotional or behavioral difficulties may have problems managing their emotions, focusing on tasks, and/or controlling their behavior. These difficulties, which may persist throughout a child's development and can lead to lifelong problems, are usually noticed first by parents.[117] Parents play a crucial role in informing health professionals about a child's emotional and behavioral difficulties and obtaining mental health services.[118]

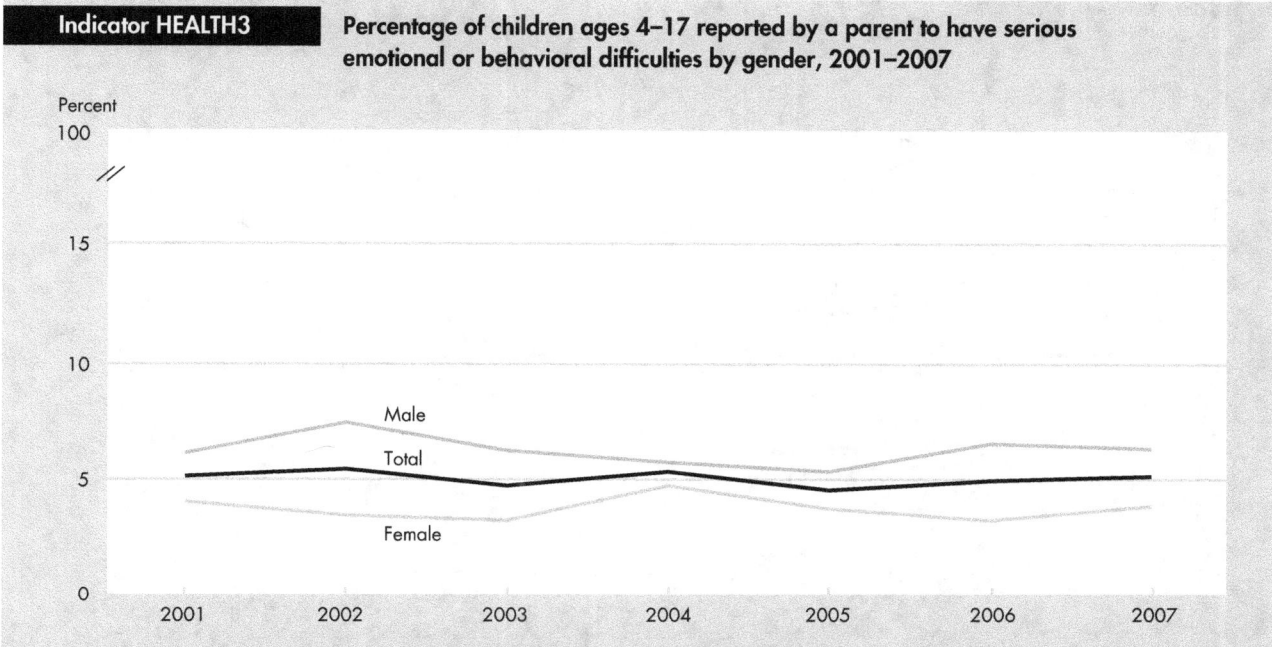

Indicator HEALTH3   Percentage of children ages 4–17 reported by a parent to have serious emotional or behavioral difficulties by gender, 2001–2007

NOTE: Children with serious emotional or behavioral difficulties are defined as those whose parent responded "yes, definite" or "yes, severe" to the following question on the Strengths and Difficulties Questionnaire (SDQ):[119] "Overall, do you think that (child) has difficulties in any of the following areas: emotions, concentration, behavior, or being able to get along with other people?" Response choices were: (1) no; (2) yes, minor difficulties; (3) yes, definite difficulties; (4) yes, severe difficulties. These difficulties may be similar to but do not equate with the Federal definition of serious emotional disturbances (SED), used by the Federal government for planning purposes.

SOURCE: National Center for Health Statistics, National Health Interview Survey.

- In 2007, slightly more than 5 percent of children ages 4–17 were reported by a parent to have serious difficulties with emotions, concentration, behavior, or being able to get along with other people.

- Between 2001 and 2007, the percentage of children with serious emotional or behavioral difficulties remained stable at about 5 percent.

- In 2007, the percentage of children with serious emotional or behavioral difficulties differed by gender. More males than females ages 4–17 years were reported by a parent to have such difficulties.

- In 2007, 7 percent of children living below the poverty level or in families with incomes 100–199 percent of the poverty level had serious emotional or behavioral difficulties, compared with 4 percent of children with family incomes 200 percent or more of the poverty level.

- Among the parents of children with serious difficulties, 86 percent reported contacting a health care provider or school staff about their child's difficulties, 46 percent reported their child was prescribed medication for their emotional or behavioral difficulties, and 51 percent reported their child had received treatment or help other than medication.[120]

Bullets contain references to data that can be found in Tables HEALTH3.A and HEALTH3.B on pages 167–168. Endnotes begin on page 73.

Adolescent Depression

Depression has a significant impact on adolescent development and well being. Adolescent depression can adversely affect school and work performance, impair peer and family relationships, and exacerbate the severity of other health conditions such as asthma and obesity.[121–125] Depressive episodes often persist, recur, or continue into adulthood.[126] Youth who have had a Major Depressive Episode (MDE) in the past year are at greater risk for suicide and are more likely than other youth to initiate alcohol and other drug use, experience concurrent substance use disorders, and smoke daily.[127–129]

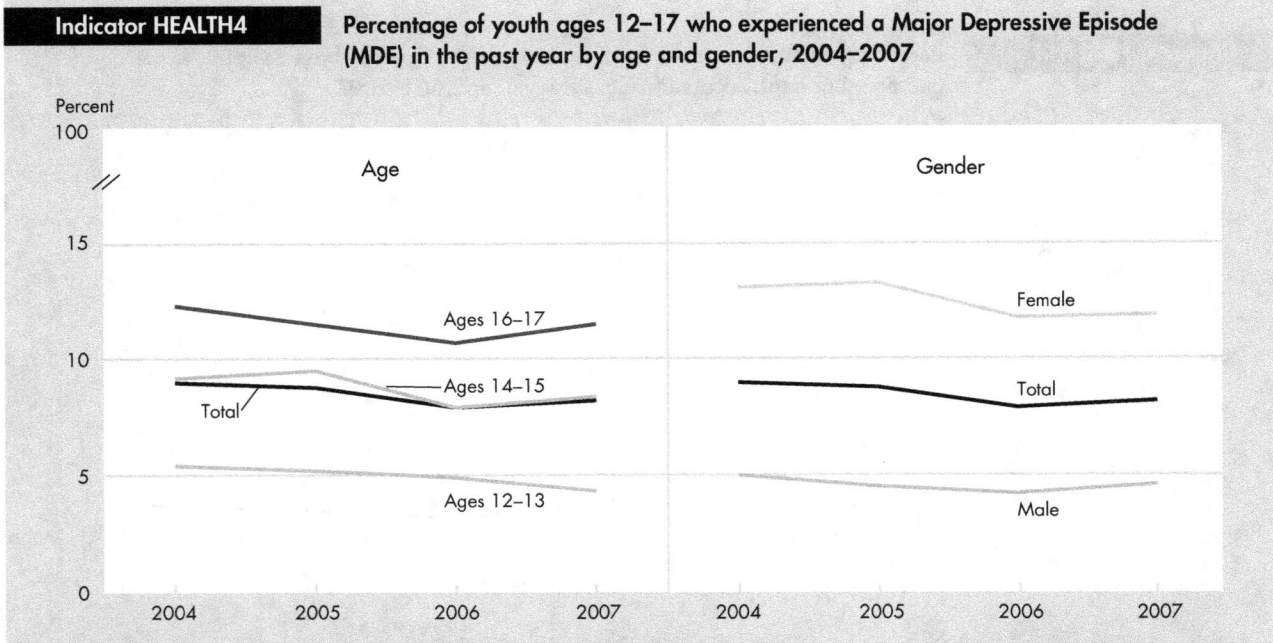

Indicator HEALTH4 — **Percentage of youth ages 12–17 who experienced a Major Depressive Episode (MDE) in the past year by age and gender, 2004–2007**

NOTE: Major Depressive Episode (MDE) is defined as a period of at least 2 weeks when a person experienced a depressed mood or loss of interest or pleasure in daily activities plus at least 4 additional symptoms of depression (such as problems with sleep, eating, energy, concentration and feelings of self-worth) as described in the 4th edition of the *Diagnostic and Statistical Manual of Mental Disorders (DSM-IV)*.[130]

SOURCE: Substance Abuse and Mental Health Services Administration, National Survey on Drug Use and Health.

- In 2007, 8 percent of the population ages 12–17 had a Major Depressive Episode (MDE) during the past year, a lower rate than that reported in 2004 (9 percent).

- From 2004 to 2007, the prevalence of MDE among youth was more than twice as high among females (12 percent to 13 percent) as among males (4 percent to 5 percent).

- The past-year prevalence of MDE in 2007 was lowest in youth ages 12–13 (4 percent), compared to youth ages 14–15 (8 percent) and youth ages 16–17 (12 percent).

- In 2007, 67 percent of youth with MDE (5.5 percent of the population ages 12–17) reported that the MDE caused severe problems in at least one major role domain (home, school/work, family relationships, social life).

- The percentage of youth with MDE receiving treatment for depression, defined as seeing or talking to a medical doctor or other professional about the depressive episode and/or using prescription medication for depression in the past year, remained stable from 2004 to 2007 (40 percent in 2004 and 39 percent in 2007).

Bullets contain references to data that can be found in Tables HEALTH4.A–HEALTH4.C on pages 169–171. Endnotes begin on page 73.

Activity Limitation

Activity limitation refers to a person's inability, due to a chronic physical, mental, emotional, or behavioral condition, to participate fully in age-appropriate activities. Age-appropriate activities for children ages 5–17 consist of a child's ability to complete regular school work and perform other activities, including self-care and walking. Activity limitation is a broad measure of health and functioning affected by a variety of chronic health conditions. The causes of activity limitation most often reported by parents of children ages 5–17 include learning disabilities, speech problems, and other mental, emotional, and behavioral problems.[131]

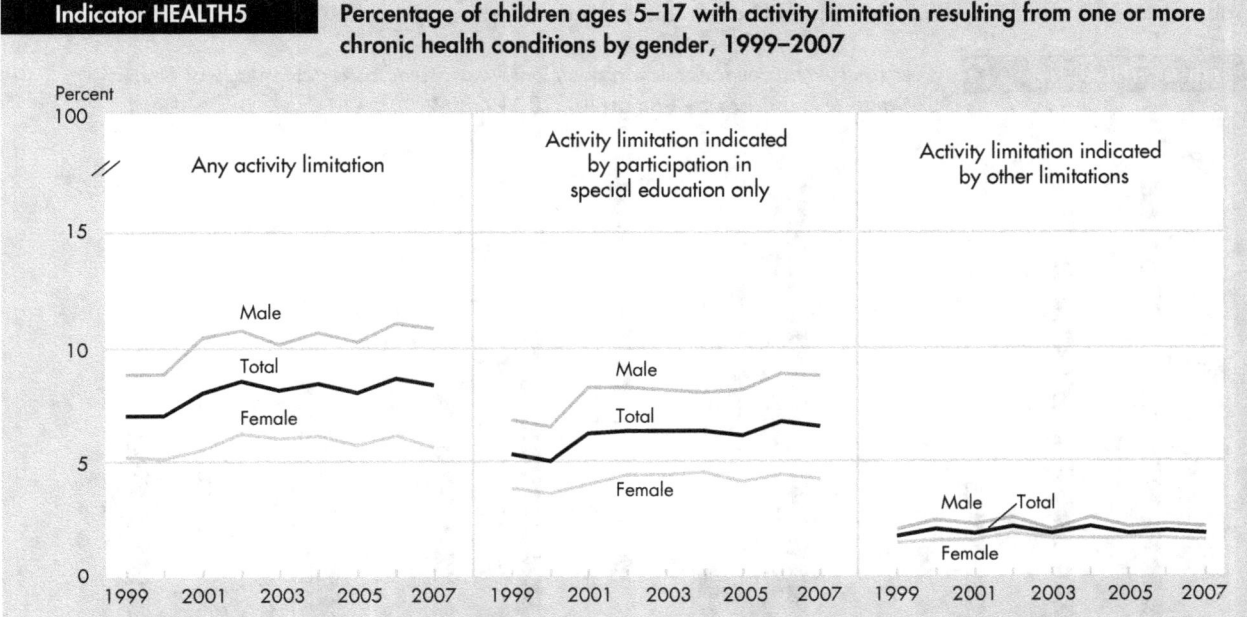

Indicator HEALTH5 — Percentage of children ages 5–17 with activity limitation resulting from one or more chronic health conditions by gender, 1999–2007

NOTE: Children are identified as having activity limitation by asking parents (1) whether children receive special education services and (2) whether they are limited in their ability to walk, care for themselves, or participate in other activities. "Activity limitation indicated by participation in special education" only includes children identified solely by their use of special education services. "Activity limitation indicated by all other limitations" includes limitations in self-care, walking, or other activities; children in this category may also receive special education services. Chronic health conditions are conditions that once acquired are not cured or have a duration of 3 months or more.

SOURCE: National Center for Health Statistics, National Health Interview Survey.

- In 2007, approximately 8 percent of children ages 5–17 were reported by parents to have activity limitation due to chronic conditions. Seven percent of children ages 5–17 were identified as having activity limitation solely by their participation in special education, and 2 percent had limitations in their ability to walk, care for themselves, or participate in other activities.

- Activity limitation, particularly when identified only by participation in special education, was reported more often for male children than for female children.

- In 2007, approximately 12 percent of children living below the poverty level and 10 percent of children living in families with incomes 100–199 percent of the poverty level had activity limitation, compared with 7 percent of children with family incomes 200 percent or more of the poverty level.

- Among children of different racial and ethnic origins, Hispanic children were less likely than White, non-Hispanic and Black, non-Hispanic children to have a parental report of activity limitation.[2]

Bullets contain references to data that can be found in Table HEALTH5 on page 172. Endnotes begin on page 73.

Diet Quality

The diet quality of children and adolescents is of concern. Poor eating patterns established in childhood may transfer to adulthood; such patterns are major factors in the increasing rate of childhood obesity over the past decades and are contributing factors to related health outcomes (see HEALTH7). The Healthy Eating Index-2005 (HEI-2005) is a dietary assessment tool comprising the 12 components shown below. HEI measures quality in terms of how well diets meet the recommendations of the 2005 Dietary Guidelines for Americans and MyPyramid, USDA's food guidance system (www.MyPyramid.gov).[132–134] The HEI-2005 component scores are averages across all children which reflect usual dietary intakes.[135] Nine components of the HEI-2005 address nutrient adequacy. The remaining three components assess saturated fat, sodium, and extra calories, all of which should be consumed in moderation.

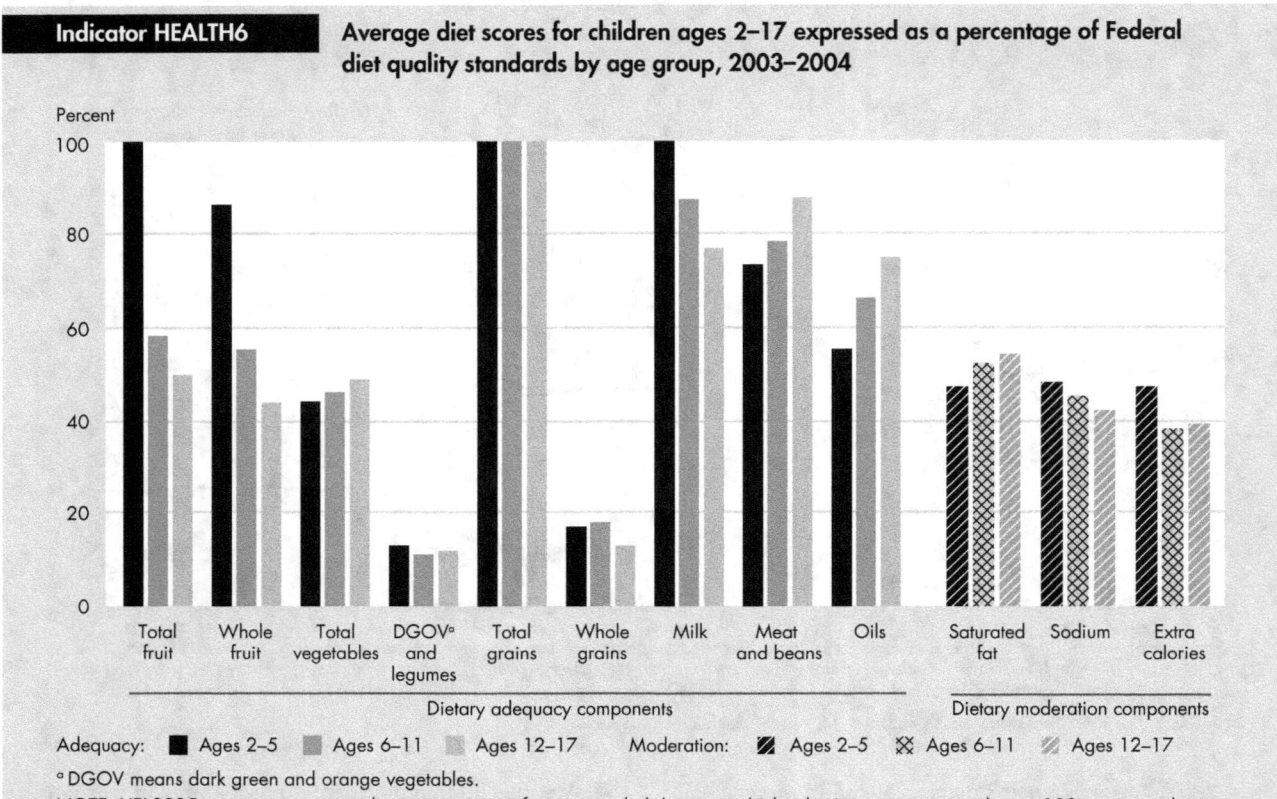

Indicator HEALTH6 — Average diet scores for children ages 2–17 expressed as a percentage of Federal diet quality standards by age group, 2003–2004

Adequacy: ■ Ages 2–5 ■ Ages 6–11 ■ Ages 12–17   Moderation: ▨ Ages 2–5 ▨ Ages 6–11 ▨ Ages 12–17

ªDGOV means dark green and orange vegetables.

NOTE: HEI-2005 scores are expressed as percentages of recommended dietary intake levels. A score corresponding to 100 percent indicates that the recommendation was met or exceeded on average. A score below 100 percent indicates that average intake does not meet the recommendations for that component. For the adequacy components, higher scores reflect higher intakes. For the moderation components, higher scores reflect lower intakes because lower intakes are more desirable. For all components, a higher percentage indicates a higher quality diet. "Extra calories" refers to calories from other sources, such as solid fats and added sugars.

SOURCE: National Center for Health Statistics, National Health and Nutrition Examination Survey, 2003–2004 and U.S. Department of Agriculture, Center for Nutrition Policy and Promotion, Healthy Eating Index-2005.

- In 2003–2004, on average, the quality of the diets of younger children was better when compared with that of older children with regard to fruit, milk, and extra calories. The quality of the diets of older children was better with regard to meat, oils, and saturated fat.

- The average diet score for all age groups (2–5, 6–11, and 12–17) met the quality standards for total grains, but only children ages 2–5 met the standards for total fruit and milk.

- The average diet score across all age groups, especially those of children ages 6–11 and 12–17, did not meet quality standards for a number of food groups, indicating a need to increase intakes of all types of fruit and vegetables, but especially dark green and orange vegetables (DGOV) and cooked dry beans and peas (legumes); whole grains; and oils.[136]

- Average intakes of sodium, saturated fat, and calories from solid fats and added sugars in foods and beverages did not meet the quality standards in any age group. This indicates a need to limit intake of foods high in salt, added sugar (i.e., not naturally occurring), and solid fat. For example, non-fat or low-fat milk and lean meat products should replace foods that have a higher fat content.[132]

Bullets contain references to data that can be found in Table HEALTH6 on page 173. Endnotes begin on page 73.

Overweight

Overweight adolescents often become overweight adults, with increased risks for a wide variety of poor health outcomes, including diabetes, stroke, heart disease, arthritis, and certain cancers.[137,138] The immediate consequences of overweight in childhood are often psychosocial, but also include cardiovascular risk factors such as high blood pressure, high cholesterol, and the precursors to diabetes.[139] The prevalence of overweight among U.S. children changed relatively little from the early 1960s through 1980; however, after 1980 it increased sharply.[140] Between 1999 and 2006, the prevalence of overweight was stable in both boys and girls.[141] Recent national estimates indicate that only 35 percent of adolescents meet current physical activity recommendations and only about 21 percent eat the recommended five or more servings of fruits and vegetables per day.[142] In addition to individual factors such as these, social, economic, and environmental forces (e.g., advances in technology and trends in eating out) may contribute to the increasing prevalence of being overweight.

Indicator HEALTH7 — **Percentage of children ages 6–17 who are overweight by gender, selected years 1976–2006**

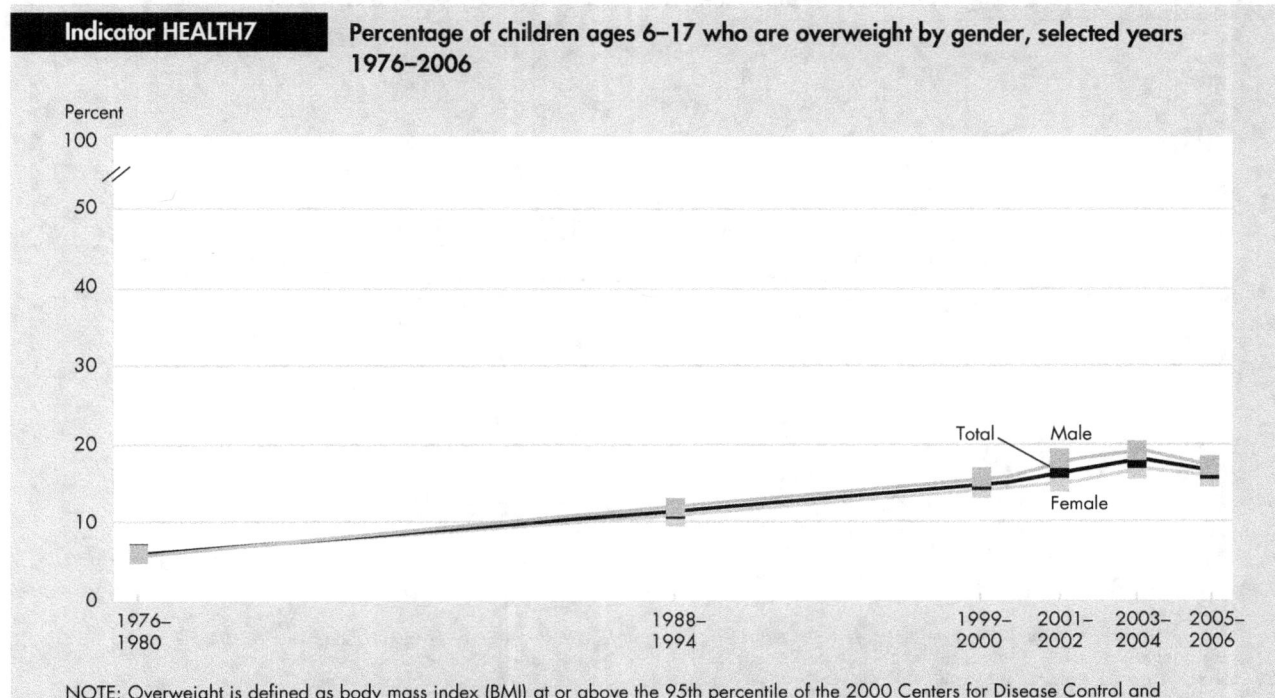

NOTE: Overweight is defined as body mass index (BMI) at or above the 95th percentile of the 2000 Centers for Disease Control and Prevention sex-specific BMI-for-age growth charts. BMI is calculated as weight in kilograms divided by the square of height in meters.

SOURCE: National Center for Health Statistics, National Health and Nutrition Examination Survey.

- Since the 1980s, there has been an increase in the percentage of children who are overweight. During the period 1976–1980, only 6 percent of children ages 6–17 were overweight. By 1988–1994, this percentage had risen to 11 percent of children ages 6–17, and in 1999–2000 it was 15 percent. In 2005–2006, 17 percent of children were overweight. There was no significant change in the percentage of overweight children between 2003–2004 and 2005–2006.

- In 2005–2006, there was no difference between boys and girls in the percentage of children who were overweight.

- In 2005–2006, 15 percent of children ages 6–11 were overweight and 18 percent of adolescents ages 12–17 were overweight. There was no statistical difference between the percentages of the younger and older age groups.

Bullets contain references to data that can be found in Table HEALTH7 on page 174. Endnotes begin on page 73.

Asthma

Asthma is a disease of the lungs that can cause wheezing, difficulty in breathing, and chest pain. It is one of the most common chronic diseases among children and is costly in both health and monetary terms. Asthma varies greatly in severity. Some children who have been diagnosed with asthma may not experience any serious respiratory effects. Other children may have mild symptoms or may respond well to management of their asthma, typically through the use of medication. Some children with asthma may, however, suffer serious attacks that greatly limit their activities, result in visits to emergency rooms or hospitals, or, in rare cases, cause death. Environmental factors such as air pollution and secondhand tobacco smoke, along with infections, exercise, and allergens, can trigger asthma attacks in children who have the disease.[143–145]

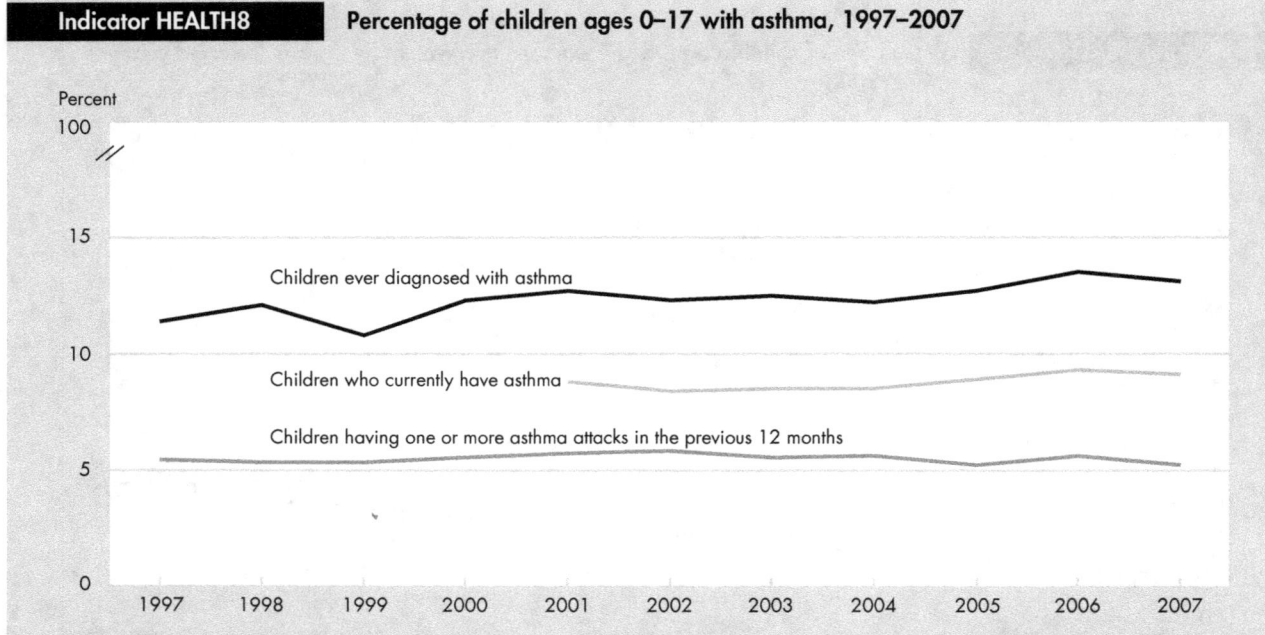

Indicator HEALTH8   **Percentage of children ages 0–17 with asthma, 1997–2007**

NOTE: Children are identified as ever diagnosed with asthma by asking parents, "Has a doctor or other health professional EVER told you that your child has asthma?" If the parent answers YES to this question, they are then asked (1) "Does your child still have asthma?" and (2) "During the past 12 months, has your child had an episode of asthma or an asthma attack?" The question "Does your child still have asthma?" was introduced in 2001 and identifies children who currently have asthma.

SOURCE: National Center for Health Statistics, National Health Interview Survey.

- In 2007, about 13 percent of children had been diagnosed with asthma at some time in their lives.

- About 9 percent of children were reported to currently have asthma in 2007. These include children with active asthma symptoms and those whose asthma is well controlled.

- Approximately 5 percent of all children had one or more asthma attacks in the previous 12 months. These children have ongoing asthma symptoms that could put them at risk for poorer health outcomes, including hospitalizations and death. About 3 children out of 5 who currently have asthma have ongoing asthma symptoms.

- In 2007, about 15 percent of Black, non-Hispanic children were reported to currently have asthma, compared with 7 percent of White, non-Hispanic

and 9 percent of Hispanic children. Disparities exist within the Hispanic population such that 15 percent of Puerto Rican children were reported to currently have asthma, compared with 9 percent of children of Mexican origin.

- From 1997 to 2007, the trends for these three asthma indicators remained fairly stable. Between 1980 and 1995, childhood asthma more than doubled (from about 4 percent in 1980 to approximately 8 percent in 1995). Methods for measurement of childhood asthma changed in 1997, so earlier data cannot be compared to data from 1997–2007.

Bullets contain references to data that can be found in Tables HEALTH8.A and HEALTH8.B on page 175. Endnotes begin on page 73.

Indicator Needed

Health

National indicators on several key dimensions of health are not yet available because of the difficulties in reaching consensus on relevant definitions and measurements. The following health-related area has been identified as a priority for indicator development:

- *Disability.* The Forum has had a longstanding interest in developing an improved measure of child disability based on the functional difficulties experienced by children. The recently adopted *International Classification of Functioning, Disability, and Health for Children and Youth* (ICF-CY)[146] provides a broad conceptual framework and terminology that may be a useful guide for the development of a new measure of child disability. Currently, there is little agreement about which domains of functioning should be included in a child disability measure and how functioning difficulties within these domains should be measured for children of different ages. However, recent progress in the development of an adult disability measure derived from regularly collected survey data is encouraging and underscores the need to devise a similar concise measure of child disability.

Special Feature

Children with Special Health Care Needs

Special features provide an opportunity to present important information in addition to the key national indicators highlighted in this report. This year's special feature reports on children with special health care needs.

Children with Special Health Care Needs

Children with special health care needs (CSHCN) are defined as those children who have a chronic physical, developmental, behavioral, or emotional condition who also require health and related services of a type or amount beyond that required by children generally.[147,148] Based on this definition, CSHCN are identified by parents' reports that their child has a health problem expected to last at least 12 months and which requires prescription medication, more services than most children, special therapies, or which limits his or her ability to do things most children can do. The use of or need for specialized medical, educational, and social services associated with having a special health care need can have a significant impact on both families and service systems charged with meeting these needs.[149] Understanding the extent and nature of special health care needs among children is critical not only for providing services today, but for planning to meet future demands.[150]

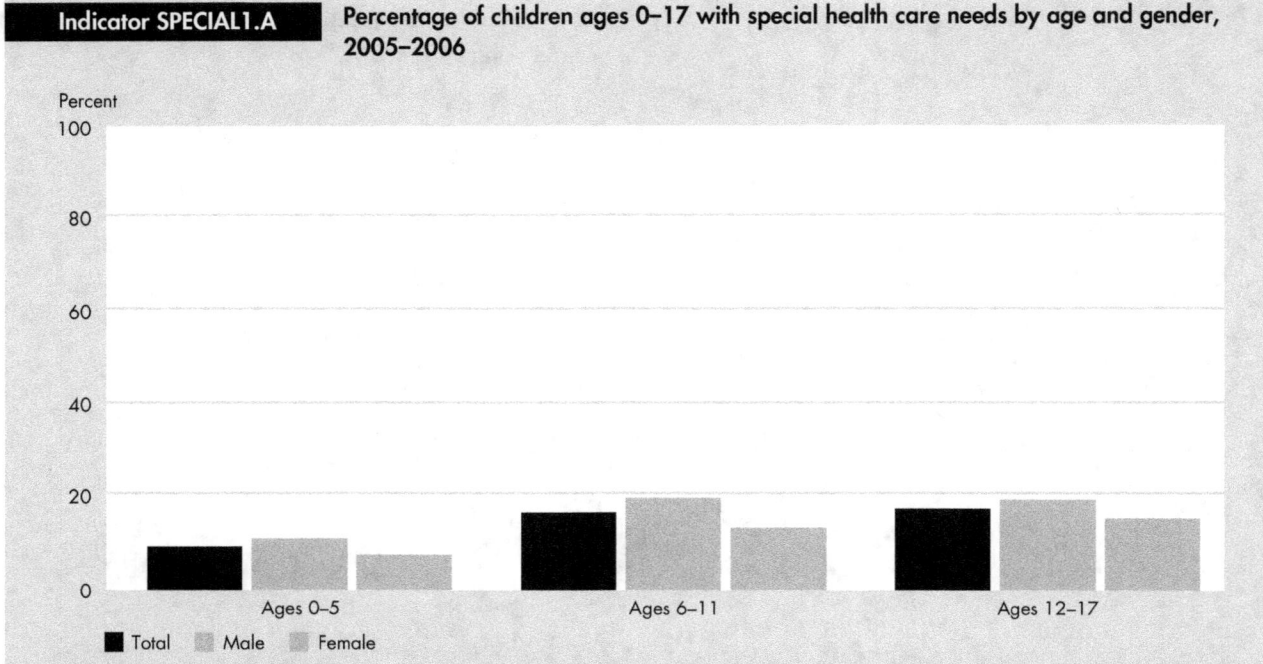

Indicator SPECIAL1.A   **Percentage of children ages 0–17 with special health care needs by age and gender, 2005–2006**

NOTE: Children are considered to have a special health care need if they have a parent-reported medical, behavioral, or other health condition that has lasted or is expected to last 12 months or longer and that has resulted in functional limitations and/or elevated use of or need for medical care, mental health or educational services, specialized therapy, or prescription medications beyond what is usual for other children of the same age.

SOURCE: Maternal and Child Health Bureau and National Center for Health Statistics, State and Local Area Integrated Telephone Survey, National Survey of Children with Special Health Care Needs, 2005–2006.

- In 2005–2006, an estimated 14 percent of children ages 0–17 had a special health care need.[151,152] Overall, 22 percent of all U.S. households with children had at least one child with special health care needs.[153] The proportion of children with special health care needs increased from 13 percent in 2001 to 14 percent in 2005–2006.[154]

- The prevalence of special health care needs was higher among older children. Approximately 17 percent of children ages 12–17 had special health care needs while, 16 percent of children ages 6–11 and about 9 percent of children ages 0–5 were identified as having special health care needs.

- The prevalence of special health care needs was greater among males than females in 2005–2006. About 16 percent of males had a special health care need, compared to 12 percent of females.

- In 2005–2006, the proportion of CSHCN varied by race and ethnicity. The prevalence of special health care needs was highest among children of two or more races (18 percent), followed by White, non-Hispanic (15 percent), Black, non-Hispanic (15 percent), American Indian or Alaska Native (15 percent), and Native Hawaiian or Other Pacific Islander (12 percent) children. The prevalence of special health care needs was lowest among Hispanic and Asian children (8 percent and 6 percent respectively).

- The majority of CSHCN were covered by private health insurance (59 percent), while 28 percent had public health insurance only and approximately 7 percent were covered by some combination of public and private health insurance. About 3 percent were uninsured at the time of the survey. Among CSHCN with health insurance, one-third of parents reported that the coverage was not adequate.[153]

- The most commonly reported health conditions among CSHCN include allergies (53 percent); asthma (39 percent); attention-deficit and attention-deficit/hyperactivity disorder (30 percent); depression, anxiety, or other emotional problems (21 percent); and migraine or frequent headaches (15 percent).[153]

- About one-quarter of CSHCN have health conditions that usually or always affect their daily activities, while 38 percent have health conditions that moderately or sometimes affect their daily activities and 38 percent have health conditions that never affect their daily activities.

- A child's special health care need status is determined by parents' reports about the effects of their child's health problems. About 78 percent of CSHCN used or needed prescription medications, while only 18 percent used or needed special therapies. CSHCN could have met more than one criterion.

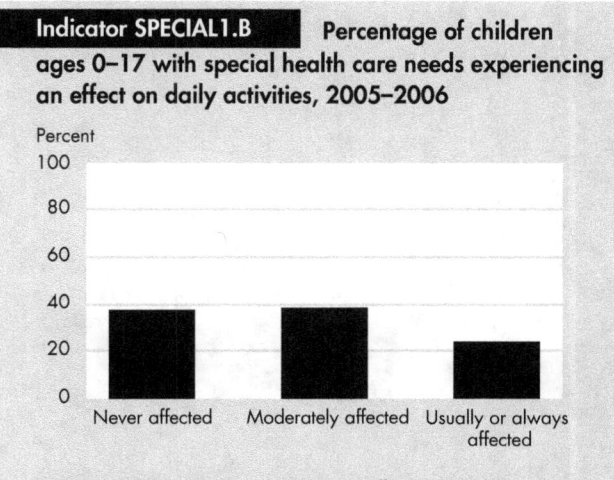

Indicator SPECIAL1.B Percentage of children ages 0–17 with special health care needs experiencing an effect on daily activities, 2005–2006

NOTE: Children whose conditions never affected their daily activities reflect either the effects of treatment used to manage the condition or the nature of the condition.

SOURCE: Maternal and Child Health Bureau and National Center for Health Statistics, State and Local Area Integrated Telephone Survey, National Survey of Children with Special Health Care Needs, 2005–2006.

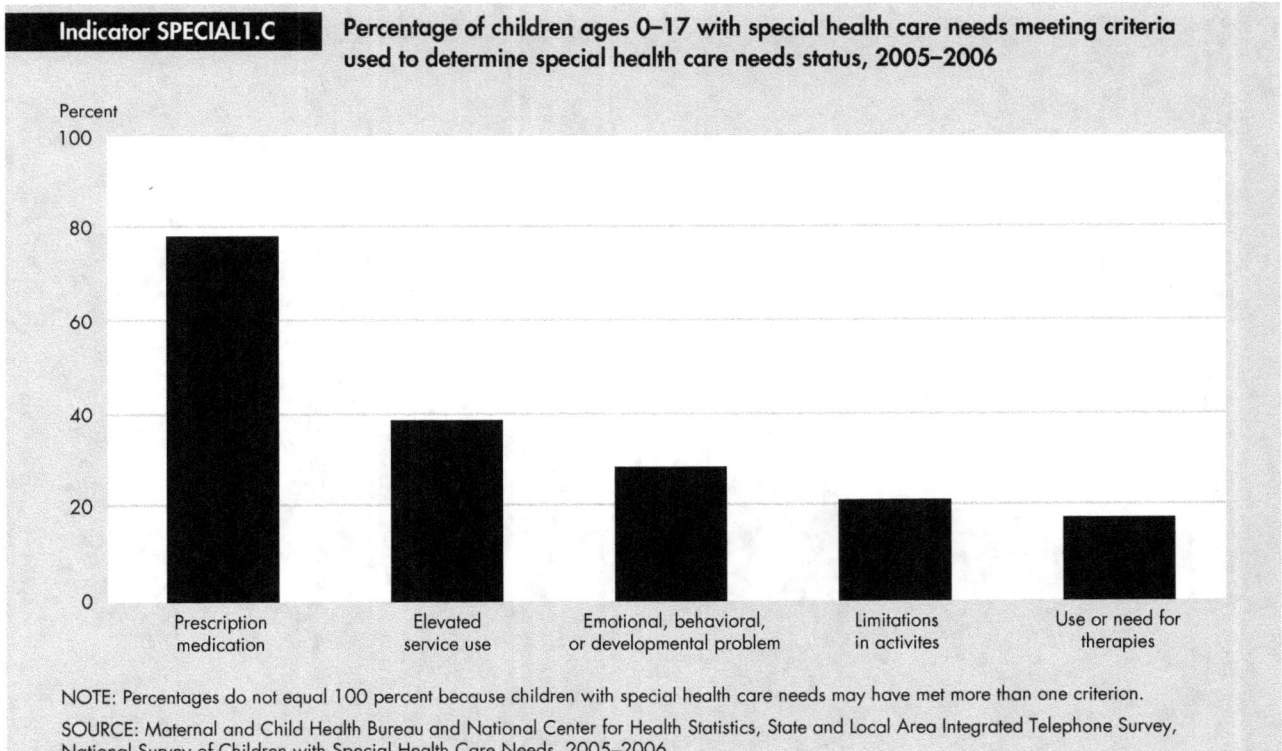

Indicator SPECIAL1.C Percentage of children ages 0–17 with special health care needs meeting criteria used to determine special health care needs status, 2005–2006

NOTE: Percentages do not equal 100 percent because children with special health care needs may have met more than one criterion.

SOURCE: Maternal and Child Health Bureau and National Center for Health Statistics, State and Local Area Integrated Telephone Survey, National Survey of Children with Special Health Care Needs, 2005–2006.

Bullets contain references to data that can be found in Tables SPECIAL1.A and SPECIAL1.B on pages 176–177. Endnotes begin on page 73.

Notes to Indicators

Notes to Indicators

[1] The majority of children who live with neither of their parents are living with grandparents or other relatives. Others who live with neither parent live with foster parents or other nonrelatives.

[2] Federal surveys now give respondents the option of reporting more than one race. Therefore, two basic ways of defining a race group are possible. A group such as Black may be defined as those who reported Black and no other race (the race-alone or single-race concept) or as those who reported Black regardless of whether they also reported another race (the race-alone-or-in-combination concept). This indicator shows data using the first approach (race alone). Use of the single-race population does not imply that it is the preferred method of presenting or analyzing data. The U.S. Census Bureau uses a variety of approaches. Data on race and Hispanic origin are collected separately. Persons of Hispanic origin may be of any race.

[3] For more information, refer to America's Families and Living Arrangements 2008 detailed tables, available at http://www.census.gov/population/www/socdemo/hh-fam/cps2008.html.

[4] National Center for Health Statistics. (1995). *Report to Congress on out-of-wedlock childbearing*. Hyattsville, MD: Author.

[5] McLanahan, S. (1995). The consequences of nonmarital childbearing for women, children, and society. In National Center for Health Statistics, *Report to Congress on out-of-wedlock childbearing*. Hyattsville, MD: National Center for Health Statistics.

[6] Martin, J.A., Hamilton, B.E., Sutton, P.D., Ventura, S.J., Menacker, F.J. Kirmeyer, S., and Mathews, T.J. (2009). Births: Final data for 2006. *National Vital Statistics Reports 57*(7). Hyattsville, MD: National Center for Health Statistics.

[7] Ventura, S.J. (1995). Births to unmarried mothers: United States, 1980–1992. *Vital and Health Statistics, 53*(21). Hyattsville, MD: National Center for Health Statistics.

[8] Ventura, S.J., and Bachrach, L.A. (2000). Nonmarital childbearing in the United States, 1940–1999. *National Vital Statistics Reports, 48*(16). Hyattsville, MD: National Center for Health Statistics.

[9] Mathews, T.J., and MacDorman, M.F. (2008). Infant mortality statistics from the 2005 period linked birth/infant death data set. *National Vital Statistics Reports, 57*(2). Hyattsville, MD: National Center for Health Statistics.

[10] Hamilton, B.E., Martin, J.A., and Ventura, S.J. (2009). Births: Preliminary data for 2007. *National Vital Statistics Reports, 57*(12). Hyattsville, MD: National Center for Health Statistics.

[11] Hamilton, B.E., Sutton, P.D., and Ventura, S.J. (2003). Revised birth and fertility rates for the 1990s: United States, and new rates for Hispanic populations, 2000 and 2001. *National Vital Statistics Reports, 51*(12). Hyattsville, MD: National Center for Health Statistics.

[12] Bumpass, L.L., and Lu, H.H. (2000). Trends in cohabitation and implications for children's family contexts in the United States. *Population Studies, 54,* 29–41.

[13] Bachu, A. (1999). Trends in premarital childbearing: 1930 to 1994. *Current Population Reports* (P23–197). Washington, DC: U.S. Census Bureau.

[14] Chandra, A., Martinez, G.M., Mosher, W.D., Abma, J.C., and Jones, J. (2005). Fertility, family planning, and reproductive health of U.S. women: Data from the 2002 National Survey of Family Growth. *Vital and Health Statistics, 23*(25). Hyattsville, MD: National Center for Health Statistics.

[15] The birth rate for unmarried women is the number of births per 1,000 unmarried women in a given age group, for example, 20–24 years. The percentage of all births that are to unmarried women is the number of births occurring to unmarried women divided by the total number of births. The percentage of all births that are to unmarried women is affected by the birth rate for married women, the birth rate for unmarried women (who account for about 40 percent of all births), and the proportion of women of childbearing age who are unmarried. The percentage of births to unmarried women increased in recent years, because there were rapid increases in the birth rate for unmarried women while births for married women changed little.

[16] National Center for Health Statistics. National Vital Statistics System. (2009). Unpublished tabulations.

[17] U.S. Census Bureau. (various years). Marital status and living arrangements (annual reports) and, beginning in 1999, America's families and living arrangements. *Current Population Reports,* Series P–20. Beginning in 1995, reports are available on the U.S. Census Bureau website at http://www.census.gov/population/www/socdemo/ms-la.html and, since 1999, at http://www.census.gov/population/www/socdemo/hh-fam.html.

[18] To provide a comprehensive picture of the child care arrangements parents use to care for their preschoolers, this indicator draws on the strengths of two different Federal data sets—the National Household Education Surveys Program (NHES) and the Survey of Income and Program Participation (SIPP). Using NHES (FAM3.B) data, the percentage of children in each type of arrangement is shown, to provide total usage rates. Because some children are cared for by more than one type of provider, the numerator is the number of children in the particular arrangement and the denominator is all children. Using SIPP (FAM3.A) data, the historical trend of the primary child care provider is shown because there is an interest in the care arrangement that is used by employed mothers for the greatest number of hours each week. In this case, the numerator is the number of children of employed mothers who spend the greatest number of hours in the particular arrangement each week and the denominator is all children of employed mothers.

[19] Center-based care includes day care centers, nursery schools, preschools and Head Start programs. Home-based care or other nonrelative care includes family day care providers, babysitters, nannies, friends, neighbors, and other nonrelatives providing care in either the child's or provider's home. Other relatives include siblings and other relatives. Mother care includes care by the mother while she worked. To see trends in individual child care arrangement types refer to Overturf Johnson, J. (2005). Who's minding the kids? Child care arrangements: Winter 2002. *Current Population Reports*, U.S. Census Bureau, Washington, DC, 70–101.

[20] Schmidley, A.D. (2001). Profile of the foreign-born population in the United States: 2000. *Current Population Reports* (P23–206), U.S. Census Bureau. Washington, DC: U.S. Government Printing Office. Retrieved from http://www.census.gov/prod/2002pubs/p23-206.pdf.

[21] Schmidley, A.D. (2003). The foreign-born population in the United States: March 2002, *Current Population Reports* (P20–539). Washington, DC: U.S. Census Bureau. Retrieved from http://www.census.gov/prod/2003pubs/p20-539.pdf.

[22] Gibson, C.J., and Lennon, E. (1999). Historical Census Statistics on the Foreign-Born Population of the United States: 1850–1990, Population Division Working Paper No. 29. Washington, DC: U.S. Census Bureau. Retrieved from http://www.census.gov/population/www/documentation/twps0029/twps0029.html.

[23] If the child lived with two parents, the education reflected is that of the most educated parent.

[24] Adult respondents were asked if the children in the household spoke a language other than English at home and how well they could speak English. Categories used for reporting how well children could speak English were "Very well," "Well," "Not well," and "Not at all." All those who were reported to speak English less than "Very well" were considered to have difficulty speaking English based on an evaluation of the English-speaking ability of a sample of children in the 1980s.

[25] The percentage of White, non-Hispanic children ages 5–17 who spoke English less than "very well" (1.2 percent) was not statistically different from the percentage of Black, non-Hispanic children (1.2 percent).

[26] Klerman, L.V. (1993). Adolescent pregnancy and parenting: Controversies of the past and lessons for the future. *Journal of Adolescent Health, 14,* 553–561.

[27] Kiely, J.L., Brett, K.M., Yu, S., and Rowley, D.L. (1994). Low birthweight and intrauterine growth retardation. In L.S. Wilcox, and J.S. Marks, (Eds.), *From data to action: CDC's public health surveillance for women, infants, and children* (pp. 185–202). Atlanta, GA: Centers for Disease Control and Prevention.

[28] Maynard, R.A. (Ed.). (1997). *Kids having kids: Economic costs and social consequences of teen pregnancy.* Washington, DC: The Urban Institute Press.

[29] Office on Child Abuse and Neglect, Department of Health and Human Services. (2003). *A Coordinated Response to Child Abuse and Neglect: The Foundation for Practice.* Retrieved August 28, 2006, from the Child Welfare Information Gateway, http://www.childwelfare.gov/pubs/usermanuals/foundation/foundationf.cfm.

[30] Data from 2007 are not directly comparable with prior years as differences may be partially attributed to changes in one state's procedures for determination of maltreatment. Other reasons include the increase in children who received an "other" disposition, the decrease in the percentage of children who received a substantiated or indicated disposition, and the decrease in the number of children who received an investigation or assessment.

[31] Estimates based on the official definition of poverty include estimates for children in two ways. First, estimates for all children include anyone in the poverty universe under age 18. Second, estimates for related children under 18 include children related to the householder (or reference person of an unrelated subfamily) who are not themselves a householder or spouse of the householder (or family reference person).

[32] Duncan, G., and Brooks-Gunn, J. (Eds.). (1997). *Consequences of growing up poor.* New York, NY: Russell Sage Press.

[33] An, C., Haveman, R., and Wolfe, B. (1993). Teen out-of-wedlock births and welfare receipt: The role of childhood events and economic circumstances. *Review of Economics and Statistics, 75*(2), 195–208.

[34] The poverty calculations in this section use the official poverty measure based on the Office of Management and Budget Statistical Policy Directive 14. A child is living below poverty if the child lives in a family with before-tax cash income below a defined level of need, called a poverty threshold. The official poverty thresholds in use today were devised in the early 1960s based on the minimum cost of what was considered to be a nutritionally adequate diet. Since then, the poverty thresholds have been updated annually for inflation using the Consumer Price Index for all urban consumers. Poverty thresholds vary based on the size of the family and the number of children in the family.

[35] The percent of Black children in female-householder families that lived in poverty was not statistically different from that of children in Hispanic female-householder families.

[36] Mayer, S.E. (1997). Income, employment and the support of children. In R.M. Hauser, B.V. Brown, and W. Prosser. (Eds.), *Indicators of children's well-being.* New York, NY: Russell Sage Press.

[37] Smith, J.R., Brooks-Gunn, J., and Jackson, A.P. (1997). Parental employment and children. In R.M. Hauser, B.V. Brown, and W. Prosser. (Eds.), *Indicators of children's well-being.* New York, NY: Russell Sage Press.

[38] Anderson, S.A. (Ed.). (1990). Core indicators of nutritional state for difficult-to-sample populations. *Journal of Nutrition 120*(11S), 1557–1600.

[39] Nord, M. (2002). *Food insecurity in households with children* (Food Assistance and Nutrition Research Report FANRR34–13). Washington, DC: U.S. Department of Agriculture, Economic Research Service. Retrieved from http://www.ers.usda.gov/publications/fanrr34/fanrr34-13.

[40] In reports prior to 2006, households with "very low food security among children" were described as "food insecure with hunger among children." In 2006, USDA introduced new language to describe ranges of severity of food insecurity in response to recommendations by an expert panel convened by the Committee on National Statistics of the National Academies. The methods used to assess children's food security remained unchanged, so the statistics for 2005 and later years are directly comparable with those for 2004 and earlier years. For further information see the following reports:

> National Research Council, (2006). *Food insecurity and hunger in the United States: An assessment of the measure.* Committee on National Statistics, Panel to Review the U.S. Department of Agriculture's Measurement of Food Insecurity and Hunger, G.S. Wunderlich and J.L. Norwood. (Eds.). Washington, DC: The National Academies Press.

> Nord, M., Andrews, M., and Carlson, S. (2006). *Household food security in the United States 2005* (Economic Research Report 29). Washington, DC: U.S. Department of Agriculture, Economic Research Service. Retrieved from http://www.ers.usda.gov/publications/err29.

[41] Green, M. (Ed.). (1994). *Bright futures: Guidelines for health supervision of infants, children, and adolescents.* Arlington, VA: National Center for Education in Maternal and Child Health.

[42] Simpson, G., Bloom, B., Cohen, R.A., and Parsons, P.E. (1997). Access to health care. Part 1: Children. *Vital and Health Statistics, 10*(Series 196). Hyattsville, MD: National Center for Health Statistics.

[43] Bartman, B.A., Moy, E., and D'Angelo, L.J. (1997). Access to ambulatory care for adolescents: The role of a usual source of care. *Journal of Health Care for the Poor and Underserved, 8,* 214–226.

[44] Folton, G.L. (1995). Critical issues in urban emergency medical services for children. *Pediatrics, 96*(2), 174–179.

[45] For more information, refer to http://www.cdc.gov/vaccines/vac-gen/shortages/past/pneumo-2001.htm.

[46] U.S. Department of Health and Human Services. (2000). *Oral health in America: A report of the Surgeon General.* Rockville, MD: Health and Human Services, National Institutes of Health, National Institute of Dental and Craniofacial Research.

[47] American Academy of Pediatric Dentistry. (1999). *Handbook of pediatric dentistry.* Chicago, IL: The Academy.

[48] Institute of Medicine. (2001). *Crossing the quality chasm.* Washington, DC: National Academies Press.

[49] This measure does not differentiate between counties in which the Primary National Ambient Air Quality Standards are exceeded frequently or by a large margin and counties in which the standards are exceeded only rarely or by a small margin. It must also be noted that this analysis differs from the analysis utilized by the U.S. Environmental Protection Agency for the designation of "nonattainment areas" for regulatory compliance purposes.

[50] U.S. Environmental Protection Agency. (1994). *Supplement to the second addendum (1986) to air quality criteria for particulate matter and sulfur oxides (1982): Assessment of new findings on sulfur dioxide acute exposure health effects in asthmatic individuals* (EPA/600/FP-93/002). Research Triangle Park, NC: Author.

[51] U.S. Environmental Protection Agency. (2008). *Integrated Science Assessment for Oxides of Nitrogen—Health Criteria* (EPA/600/R-08/071). Research Triangle Park, NC: Author.

[52] U.S. Environmental Protection Agency. (2006). *Air quality criteria for ozone and related photochemical oxidants* (EPA/600/R-05/004aF). Research Triangle Park, NC: Author.

[53] U.S. Environmental Protection Agency. (2004). *Air quality criteria for particulate matter* (EPA/600/P-99/002aF, EPA/600/P-99/002bF). Research Triangle Park, NC: Author.

[54] U.S. Environmental Protection Agency. (2006). *Air quality criteria for lead: Volume I* (EPA/600/R-05/144aF). Research Triangle Park, NC: Author.

[55] U.S. Environmental Protection Agency. (2000). *Air quality criteria for carbon monoxide* (EPA 600/P-99/001F). Research Triangle Park, NC: Author.

[56] Burnett R.T., Cakmak, S., Brook, J.R., and Krewski, D. (1997). The role of particulate size and chemistry in the association between summertime ambient air pollution and hospitalization for cardiorespiratory diseases. *Environmental Health Perspectives, 105*(6), 614–620.

[57] Burnett, R.T., Smith-Doiron, M., Stieb, D., Cakmak, S., and Brook, J.R. (1999). Effects of particulate and gaseous air pollution on cardiorespiratory hospitalizations. *Archives of Environmental Health, 54*(2), 130–139.

[58] Gwynn, R.C., Burnett, R.T., and Thurston, G.D. (2000). A time-series analysis of acidic particulate matter and daily mortality and morbidity in the Buffalo, New York, region. *Environmental Health Perspectives, 108*(2), 125–133.

[59] Thurston, G., Kazuhiko, I., Hayes, C., Bates, D., and Lippmann, M. (1994). Respiratory hospital admissions and summertime haze air pollution in Toronto, Ontario: Consideration of the role of acidic aerosols. *Journal of Exposure Analysis and Environmental Epidemiology, 2,* 429–450.

[60] U.S. Department of Health and Human Services. (2006). *The health consequences of involuntary exposure to tobacco smoke: A report of the Surgeon General.* Atlanta, GA: Centers for Disease Control and Prevention, Coordinating Center for Health Promotion, National Center for Chronic Disease Prevention and Health Promotion, Office on Smoking and Health.

[61] Regular smoking is defined as smoking by a resident that occurs 4 or more days per week.

[62] U.S. Environmental Protection Agency. (2006). *Drinking water contaminants.* EPA Office of Water. Retrieved from http://www.epa.gov/safewater/hfacts.html.

[63] U.S. Environmental Protection Agency. (2006). *Current drinking water standards.* EPA Office of Water. Retrieved from http://www.epa.gov/safewater/mcl.html.

[64] Hutson, S.S., Barber, N.L., Kenny, J.F., Linsey, K.S., Lumia, D.S., and Maupin, M.A. (2004). Estimated use of water in the United States in 2000. U.S. Geological Survey Circular 1268. Reston, VA: U.S. Geological Survey. Available at http://pubs.usgs.gov/circ/2004/circ1268/pdf/circular1268.pdf.

[65] U.S. Environmental Protection Agency. (2005). Economic analysis for the final stage 2 disinfectants and disinfection byproducts rule (EPA/815/R-05/010). Washington, DC: Office of Water.

[66] Bellinger, D., Leviton, A., Waternaux, C., Needleman, H., and Rabinowitz, M. (1987). Longitudinal analyses of prenatal and postnatal lead exposure and early cognitive development. *New England Journal of Medicine, 316*(17), 1037–1043.

[67] Needleman, H.L., Schell, A., Bellinger, D., Leviton, A., and Allred, E.N. (1990). The long-term effects of exposure to low doses of lead in childhood: An 11-year follow-up report. *New England Journal of Medicine, 322*(2), 83–88.

[68] Mendelsohn, A.L., Dreyer, B.P., Fierman, A.H., Rosen, C.M., Legano, L.A., Kruger, H.A., Lim, S.W., and Courtlandt, C.D. (1998). Low-level lead exposure and behavior in early childhood. *Pediatrics, 101*(3), E10.

[69] Needleman, H.L., Riess, J.A., Tobin, M.J., Biesecker, G.E., and Greenhouse, J.B. (1996). Bone lead levels and delinquent behavior. *Journal of the American Medical Association, 275*(5), 363–369.

[70] Centers for Disease Control and Prevention. (2002). *Managing elevated blood lead levels among young children: Recommendations from the Advisory Committee on Childhood Lead Poisoning Prevention.* Retrieved from http://www.cdc.gov/nceh/lead/CaseManagement/caseManage_main.htm.

[71] Canfield, R.L., Henderson, C.R., Jr., Cory-Slechta, D.A., Cox, C., Jusko, T.A., and Lanphear, B.P. (2003). Intellectual impairment in children with blood lead concentrations below 10 micrograms per deciliter. *New England Journal of Medicine, 348*(16), 1517–1526.

[72] Lanphear, B.P., Hornung, R., Khoury, J., Yolton, K., Baghurst, P., Bellinger, D.C., Canfield, R.L., Dietrich, K.N., Bornschein, R., Greene, T., Rothenberg, S.J., Needleman, H.L., Schnaas, L., Wasserman, G., Graziano, J., and Roberts, R. (2005). Low-level environmental lead exposure and children's intellectual function: An international pooled analysis. *Environmental Health Perspectives, 113*(7), 894–899.

[73] Jacobs, D.E., Clickner, R.P., Zhou, J.Y., Viet, S.M., Marker, D.A., Rogers, J.W., Zeldin, D.C., Broene, P., and Friedman, W. (2002). The prevalence of lead-based paint hazards in U.S. housing. *Environmental Health Perspectives, 110*(10), A599–606.

[74] U.S. Environmental Protection Agency. (2008). America's children and the environment. Measure B1: Lead in the blood of children, available at http://www.epa.gov/envirohealth/children/body_burdens/b1-graph.htm.

[75] For 2003–2006, the revised 1997 OMB Standards for Data on Race and Ethnicity were used. Persons could select one or more of five racial groups: White, Black or African American, American Indian or Alaska Native, Asian, and Native Hawaiian or Other Pacific Islander. Included in the total but not shown separately are American Indian or Alaska Native, Asian, or Native Hawaiian or Other Pacific Islander due to the small sample size for each of these groups. Data on race and Hispanic origin are collected separately but combined for reporting. Persons of Mexican origin may be of any race. The National Health and Nutrition Examination Survey (NHANES) sample was designed to provide estimates specifically for persons of Mexican origin.

[76] Papers addressing specific housing-related health issues are available at http://www.hud.gov/offices/lead/researchers.cfm.

[77] Bridge, C., Flatau, P., Whelan, S., Wood, G., and Yates, J. (2003). *Housing assistance and non-shelter outcomes.* Sydney, AU: Australian Housing and Urban Research Institute.

[78] Physically inadequate units are defined as those with moderate or severe physical problems. Common types of problems include lack of complete plumbing for exclusive use, unvented room heaters as the primary heating equipment, and multiple upkeep problems such as water leakage, open cracks or holes, broken plaster, or signs of rats. See definition in Appendix A of the American Housing Survey summary volume, American Housing Survey for the United States: 2007, Current Housing Reports, Series H150, U.S. Census Bureau, 2008.

[79] Paying 30 percent or more of income for housing may leave insufficient resources for other basic needs. See National Academy of Sciences. (1995). *Measuring poverty: A new approach.* Washington, DC: National Academy Press.

[80] The U.S. Department of Housing and Urban Development considers renter households to have "priority" housing problems if they have eligible incomes for, but do not receive, rental assistance, and they report either severe housing cost burdens or severe physical problems with their housing units. Because of questionnaire changes, data after 1997 on assisted families, priority problems, and severe physical problems are not comparable to earlier data.

[81] The U.S. Department of Housing and Urban Development defines "very-low-income renters" as renter households with incomes at or below half the median family income, adjusted for family size, within their geographic area.

[82] Finkelhor, D., and Dziuba-Leatherman, J. (1994). Victimization of children. *American Psychologist, 49*(3), 173–183.

[83] Lauritsen, J.L., Laub, J.H., and Sampson, R.J. (1992). Conventional and delinquent activities: Implications for the prevention of violent victimization among adolescents. *Violence and Victims, 7*(2), 91–108.

[84] Snyder, H.N., and Sickmund, M. (1999). *Juvenile offenders and victims: 1999 national report* (Publication No. NCJ 178257, p. 26). Washington, DC: Office of Juvenile Justice and Delinquency Prevention.

[85] National Research Council and Institute of Medicine. (2004). *Children's health, the nation's wealth: Assessing and improving child health.* Committee on Evaluating Children's Health, Board on Children, Youth and Families, Division of Behavioral and Social Sciences and Education. Washington, DC: The National Academies Press.

[86] Corso, P., Finkelstein, E., Miller, T., Fiebelkorn, I., and Zaloshnja, E. (2006). Incidence and lifetime costs of injuries in the United States. *Injury Prevention, 12*(4), 212–218.

[87] Centers for Disease Control and Prevention, National Center for Health Statistics, National Hospital Discharge Survey (2006) unpublished tabulations.

[88] Centers for Disease Control and Prevention, National Center for Health Statistics, National Hospital Ambulatory Medical Care Survey (2005–2006) unpublished tabulations.

[89] Centers for Disease Control and Prevention, National Center for Health Statistics, National Vital Statistics System (2006) unpublished tabulations.

[90] Bergen, G., Chen, L.H., Warner, M., and Fingerhut, L.A. (2008) *Injury in the United States: 2007 chartbook.* Hyattsville, MD: National Center for Health Statistics.

[91] U.S. Department of Health and Human Services. (2004). *The health consequences of smoking: A report of the Surgeon General.* Washington, DC: Government Printing Office.

[92] Hahn, E.J., Rayens, M.K., Chaloupka, F.J., Okoli, C.T.C., and Yang, J. (2002). *Projected smoking-related deaths among U.S. youth: A 2000 update.* Robert Wood Johnson Foundation ImpacTeen Research Paper Series, No. 22.

[93] National Institute on Alcohol Abuse and Alcoholism. (2004/2005). Alcohol development in youth: A multidisciplinary overview. *Alcohol Research & Health, 28*(3).

[94] National Institute on Drug Abuse. (2006). *NIDA InfoFacts: Crack and cocaine.* Available at http://www.nida.nih.gov/infofacts/cocaine.html.

[95] National Institute on Drug Abuse. (2004). *Marijuana: Facts parents need to know* (NIH Publication No. 04-4036). Washington, DC: U.S. Department of Health and Human Services.

[96] Pope Jr., H.G., and Yurgelun-Todd, D. (1996). The residual cognitive effects of heavy marijuana use in college students. *Journal of the American Medical Association, 275*(7).

[97] National Institute on Drug Abuse. (2001). *Research Report Series: Hallucinogens and dissociative drugs* (NIH Publication No. 01-4209). Washington, DC: U.S. Department of Health and Human Services.

[98] Hallfors, D., Waller, M., Bauer, D., Ford C., and Halpern, C. (2005). Which comes first in adolescence—sex and drugs or depression? *American Journal of Preventive Medicine, 29*(3), 163–170.

[99] Chandra, A., Martinez, G.M., Mosher, W.D., Abma, J.C., and Jones, J. (2005). Fertility, family planning, and reproductive health of U.S. women: Data from the 2002 National Survey of Family Growth. *Vital and Health Statistics, 23*(25). Hyattsville, MD: National Center for Health Statistics.

[100] Institute of Medicine. (1997). *The hidden epidemic: Confronting sexually transmitted disease* (T.R. Eng and W.T. Butler, Eds.). Washington, DC: National Academy Press.

[101] Fleming, D., McQuillan, G.M., Johnson, R.E., Nahmias, A.J., Aral, S.O., Lee, F.K., and St. Louis, M.E. (1997). Herpes Simplex Virus Type 2 in the United States, 1976–1994. *New England Journal of Medicine, 337*(16), 1105–1111.

[102] Centers for Disease Control and Prevention. 2007 Youth Risk Behavior Survey data. Available at http://apps.nccd.cdc.gov/yrbss/.

[103] Wells, C.G. (1985). Preschool literacy-related activities and success in school. In D. Olson, N. Torrance, and A. Hildyard. (Eds.), *Literacy, language, and learning: The nature and consequences of literacy* (pp. 229–255). Cambridge, England: Cambridge University Press.

[104] Among other changes, the framework was revised by merging the measurement and geometry content areas into one and by adding additional questions on algebra, data analysis, and probability. For more details, see Grigg, W., Donahue, P., and Dion, G. (2007). *The Nation's Report Card: 12th-grade reading and mathematics 2005* (NCES 2007-468). U.S. Department of Education, National Center for Education Statistics, Washington, DC: U.S. Government Printing Office.

[105] The achievement levels define what students should know and be able to do at each grade. They are set by the National Assessment Governing Board (NAGB) and have undergone several evaluations but remain developmental in nature and continue to be used on a trial basis. Until the Commissioner of the National Center for Education Statistics determines that the levels are reasonable, valid, and informative to the public, they should be interpreted and used with caution. For more information, see http://nces.ed.gov/nationsreportcard/.

[106] Parents' education is the highest educational attainment of either parent. Data on parents' level of education are not reliable for 4th-graders.

[107] Dalton, B., Ingels, S.J., Downing, J., and Bozick, R. (2007). *Advanced mathematics and science coursetaking in the spring high school senior classes of 1982, 1992, and 2004.* National Center for Education Statistics, Institute of Education Sciences, U.S. Department of Education. Washington, DC.

[108] Leow, C., Marcus, S., Zanutto, E., and Boruch, R. (2004). Effects of advanced course-taking on math and science achievement: Addressing selection bias using propensity scores. *American Journal of Evaluation, 25,* 461–478.

[109] Shettle, C., Roey, S., Mordica, J., Perkins, R., Nord, C., Teodorovic, J., Brown, J., Lyons, M., Averett, C., and Kastberg, D. (2007). *The Nation's Report Card: America's high school graduates* (NCES 2007-467). U.S. Department of Education. Washington, DC: National Center for Education Statistics.

[110] Brown, B. (1996). *Who are America's disconnected youth?* Report prepared for the American Enterprise Institute. Washington, DC: Child Trends, Inc.

[111] For more information, refer to table ED5.C at http://childstats.gov (available on the Web only).

[112] American Council on Education. (1994). *Higher education today: Facts in brief.* Washington, DC: Author.

[113] "High school completer" refers to those who completed 12 years of school for survey years 1980–1991 and to those who earned a high school diploma or equivalent (e.g., a General Educational Development [GED] certificate) for all years since 1992.

[114] Institute of Medicine, Committee on Understanding Premature Birth and Assuring Healthy Outcomes and Board on Health Sciences Policy. (2005). *Preterm birth: Causes, consequences, and prevention.* R.E. Behrman and A.S. Butler. (Eds). Washington, DC: The National Academies Press.

[115] Hack, M., Taylor, H.G., Droter, D., Schluchter, M., Cartar, L., Andreias, L., Wilson-Costello, D., and Klein, N. (2005). Chronic conditions, functional limitations, and special health care needs of school-aged children born with extremely low birthweight in the 1990s. *Journal of the American Medical Association 294:* 318–325.

[116] U.S. Department of Health and Human Services. (1999). *Mental health: A report of the Surgeon General.* Rockville, MD: U.S. Department of Health and Human Services, Substance Abuse and Mental Health Services Administration, Center for Mental Health Services, National Institutes of Health, National Institute of Mental Health, Retrieved from http://www.surgeongeneral.gov/library/mentalhealth/home.html.

[117] New Freedom Commission on Mental Health. (2003). *Achieving the promise: Transforming mental health care in America.* Final Report (DHHS Pub. No. SMA-03-3832). Rockville, MD: Department of Health and Human Services.

[118] Dulcan, M.K., Costello, E.J., Costello, A.J., Edelbrock, C., Brent, D., and Janiszewski, B.S. (1990). The pediatrician as gatekeeper to mental health care for children: Do parents' concerns open the gate? *Journal of the American Academy of Child and Adolescent Psychiatry, 29,* 453–458.

[119] Goodman, R. (1999). The extended version of the Strengths and Difficulties Questionnaire as a guide to child psychiatric caseness and consequent burden. *Journal of Child Psychology and Psychiatry, 40,* 791–799.

[120] Data for service contact and type of service or treatment for emotional or behavioral difficulties are from new service questions asked directly after the Strengths and Difficulties Questionnaire (SDQ) questions, first used in the 2005 National Health Interview Survey (NHIS).

[121] Birmaher, B., Brent, D.A., and Benson, R.S. (1998). Child and adolescent depression: A review of the past 10 years. *Journal of the American Academy of Child and Adolescent Psychiatry, 35,* 1427–1439.

[122] Bhatia, S.K., and Bhatia, S.C. (2007). Childhood and adolescent depression. *American Family Physician, 75,* 73–80.

[123] Substance Abuse and Mental Health Services Administration, Office of Applied Studies. (2008). *The NSDUH report: Major depressive episode among youths aged 12 to 17 in the United States: 2004 to 2006.* Rockville, MD: Author.

[124] Van Lieshout, R.J., and MacQueen, G. (2008). Psychological factors in asthma. *Allergy, Asthma and Clinical Immunology, 4*(1), 12–28.

[125] Goodman, E., and Whitaker, R.C. (2007) A prospective study of the role of depression in the development and persistence of adolescent obesity. *Pediatrics, 110*(3), 497–504.

[126] Weissman, M.M., Wolk, S., Goldstein, R. B., Moreau, D., Adams, P., Greenwald, S., Klier, C. M., Ryan, N. D., Dahl, R. E., and Wickramaratne, P. (1999). Depressed adolescents grown up. *Journal of the American Medical Association, 282,* 1701–1713.

[127] Shaffer, D., Gould, M.S., Fisher, P., Trautman, P., Moreau, D., Kleinman, M., and Flory, M. (1996). Psychiatric diagnosis in child and adolescent suicide. *Archives of General Psychiatry, 53,* 339–348.

[128] Substance Abuse and Mental Health Services Administration, Office of Applied Studies. (2007). *The NSDUH report: Depression and the initiation of alcohol and other drug use among youths aged 12 to 17.* Rockville, MD: Author.

[129] Substance Abuse and Mental Health Services Administration. (2008). *Results from the 2007 National Survey on Drug Use and Health: National Findings* (Office of Applied Studies, NSDUH Series H-32, DHHS Publication No. SMA 08-4343). Rockville, MD: Author.

[130] American Psychiatric Association. (1994). *Diagnostic and statistical manual of mental disorders (DSM-IV)* (4th ed.). Washington, DC: Author.

[131] National Center for Health Statistics. (2007) *Chartbook on trends in the health of Americans.* Limitation of activity: Children (pp. 42–43). Hyattsville, MD: Author.

[132] U.S. Health and Human Services and U.S. Department of Agriculture. (2005). Dietary Guidelines for Americans (6th ed.). Washington, DC: U.S. Government Printing Office.

[133] Guenther, P.M., Reedy, J., and Krebs-Smith, S.M. (2008). Development of the Healthy Eating Index-2005. *Journal of the American Dietetic Association, 108,* 1896–1901.

[134] Guenther, P.M., Reedy, J., Krebs-Smith, S.M., and Reeve, B.B. (2008). Evaluation of the Healthy Eating Index-2005. *Journal of the American Dietetic Association, 108,* 1854–1864.

[135] Freedman, L.S., Guenther, P.M., Krebs-Smith, S.M., and Kott, P.S. (2008). A population's mean Healthy Eating Index-2005 scores are best estimated by the score of the population ratio when one 24-hour recall is available. *Journal of Nutrition, 138,* 1725–1729.

[136] Oils include the oils found in fish, nuts, seeds, and soft margarines, as well as liquid vegetable oils, such as olive, canola, corn, and soybean.

[137] Serdula, M.K., Ivery, D., Coates, R.J., Freedman, D.S., Williamson, D.F., and Byers, T. (1993). Do obese children become obese adults? A review of the literature. *Preventive Medicine, 22,* 167–177.

[138] Pi-Sunyer, F.X. (1991). Health complications of obesity. *American Journal of Clinical Nutrition, 53,* 15955–16035.

[139] Dietz, W.H. (1998). Health consequences of obesity in youth: Childhood predictors of adult disease. *Pediatrics, 105,* 518–525.

[140] Ogden, C.L., Flegal, K.M., Carroll, M.D., and Johnson, C.L. (2002). Prevalence and trends in overweight among U.S. children and adolescents, 1999–2000. *Journal of the American Medical Association, 288*(14), 1728–1732.

[141] Ogden, C.L., Carroll, M.D., and Flegal, K.M. (2008) High body mass index for age among U.S. children and adolescents, 2003–2006. *Journal of the American Medical Association, 299*(20), 2401–2405.

[142] Eaton, D.K., Kann, L., Kinchen, S., Shanklin, S., Ross, J., Hawkins, J., Harris, W.A., Lowry, R., McManus, T., Chyen, D., Lim, C., Brener, N.D., and Wechsler, H. (2008). Centers for Disease Control and Prevention (CDC). Youth risk behavior surveillance—United States, 2007. Surveillance Summaries [June 6]. *Morbidity and Mortality Weekly Report 2008, 57*(4), 1–131.

[143] National Academy of Sciences. (2000). *Clearing the air: Asthma and indoor air exposures.* Washington, DC: National Academy Press. Retrieved from http://books.nap.edu/catalog/9610.html.

[144] Gern, J.E. (2004). Viral respiratory infection and the link to asthma. *Pediatric Infectious Disease Journal, 23*(1 Suppl.), S78–86.

[145] Lemanske, R.F., Jr., and Busse, W.W. (2003). Asthma. *Journal of Allergy and Clinical Immunology, 111*(2 Suppl.), S502–519.

[146] World Health Organization (WHO). (2007). *International Classification of Functioning, Disability and Health Children and Youth Version (ICF-CY).* Geneva: Author.

[147] McPherson, M., Arango, P., Fox, H., Lauver, C., McManus, M., Newacheck, P. W., Perrin, J.M., Shonkoff, J.P., and Strickland, B. (1998). A new definition of children with special health care needs. *Pediatrics, 102,* 137–139.

[148] Children with special health care needs (CSHCN) were identified using the five-item CSHCN Screener. Children are considered to have a special health care need if they have a parent-reported medical, behavioral, or other health condition that has lasted or is expected to last 12 months or longer and that has resulted in functional limitations and/or elevated use of or need for medical care, mental health or educational services, specialized therapy, or prescription medications beyond what is usual for other children of the same age.

[149] Newacheck, P. W. and Kim, S.E. (2005). A national profile of health care utilization and expenditures for children with special health care needs. *Archives of Pediatrics and Adolescent Medicine, 159,* 10–17.

[150] Lotstein, D.S., McPherson, M., Strickland, B., and Newacheck, P. W. (2005). Transition planning for youth with special health care needs: Results from the National Survey of Children With Special Health Care Needs. *Pediatrics, 115,* 1562–1568.

[151] Estimates of the prevalence of children with special health care needs (CSHCN) using the CSHCN Screener have been found to vary between 4 percentage points and 6 percentage points, depending on survey methodology. Bethell, C., Read, D., Blumberg, S., and Newacheck, P. (2008). What is the prevalence of children with special health care needs? Toward an understanding of variations in findings and methods across three national surveys. *Maternal and Child Health Journal, 12,* 1–14.

[152] All reports were made by the parent or caregiver who was most familiar with the child's health status and needs.

[153] U.S. Department of Health and Human Services, Health Resources and Services Administration, Maternal Child and Health Bureau. (2008). *The National Survey of Children with Special Health Care Needs chartbook 2005–06.* Rockville, MD: U.S. Department of Health and Human Services.

[154] U.S. Department of Health and Human Services, Health Resources and Services Administration, Maternal Child and Health Bureau (2008) unpublished tabulations.

Appendices

Appendix A:
Detailed Tables

Tables include data from 1950–2008, when available. Due to space limitations in this printed publication, selected years of data are shown where applicable. Full tables, including data from intervening years, are available on the Forum's website at http://childstats.gov.

Detailed Tables

Child population: Number of children (in millions) ages 0–17 in the United States by age, selected years 1950–2008 and projected 2009–2021

Number (in millions)	Estimated												Projected	
	1950	1960	1970	1980	1990	2000	2003	2004	2005	2006	2007	2008	2011	2021
All Children	47.3	64.5	69.8	63.7	64.2	72.4	73.0	73.2	73.4	73.6	73.9	73.9	75.6	82.3
Age														
Ages 0–5	19.1	24.3	20.9	19.6	22.5	23.2	23.6	23.9	24.2	24.5	24.8	25.1	25.5	27.6
Ages 6–11	15.3	21.8	24.6	20.8	21.6	25.0	24.2	24.0	23.7	23.6	23.7	23.8	25.1	27.5
Ages 12–17	12.9	18.4	24.3	23.3	20.1	24.2	25.1	25.3	25.4	25.5	25.4	25.0	25.0	27.3

NOTE: Population projections are based on the Census 2000 counts.

SOURCE: U.S. Census Bureau, *Current Population Reports,* Estimates of the population of the United States by single years of age, color, and sex: 1900 to 1959 (Series P-25, No. 311); Estimates of the population of the United States, by age, sex, and race: April 1, 1960, to July 1, 1973 (Series P-25, No. 519); Preliminary estimates of the population of the United States by age, sex, and race: 1970 to 1981 (Series P-25, No. 917); intercensal estimates for 1980–1989; and intercensal estimates for 1990–1999. The data for 2000 to 2008 are based on the population estimates released for July 1, 2008. The data for 2009 and beyond are derived from the national population projections released in August 2008.

Table POP2	Children as a percentage of the population: Persons in selected age groups as a percentage of the total U.S. population, and children ages 0–17 as a percentage of the dependent population, selected years 1950–2008 and projected 2009–2021

Age	Estimated												Projected	
	1950	1960	1970	1980	1990	2000	2003	2004	2005	2006	2007	2008	2011	2021
Percentage of total population														
Ages 0–17	31	36	34	28	26	25.6	25.1	25.0	24.8	24.7	24.5	24.3	24.1	23.9
Ages 18–64	61	55	56	61	62	61.9	62.5	62.6	62.7	62.8	62.9	62.9	62.7	59.7
Ages 65 and older	8	9	10	11	13	12.4	12.4	12.4	12.4	12.5	12.6	12.8	13.1	16.4
Children ages 0–17 as a percentage of the dependent population[a]														
Ages 0–17	79	79	78	71	67	67.3	67.0	66.8	66.6	66.4	66.1	65.5	64.8	59.3

[a] The dependent population includes all persons ages 17 and under and all persons ages 65 and over.

NOTE: Population projections are based on the Census 2000 counts.

SOURCE: U.S. Census Bureau, *Current Population Reports,* Estimates of the population of the United States by single years of age, color, and sex: 1900 to 1959 (Series P-25, No. 311); Estimates of the population of the United States, by age, sex, and race: April 1, 1960, to July 1, 1973 (Series P-25, No. 519); Preliminary estimates of the population of the United States by age, sex, and race: 1970 to 1981 (Series P-25, No. 917); and intercensal estimates for 1980–1989 and for 1990–1999. The data for 2000 to 2008 are based on the population estimates released for July 1, 2008. The data for 2009 and beyond are derived from the national population projections released in August 2008.

Racial and ethnic composition: Percentage of U.S. children ages 0–17 by race and Hispanic origin, selected years 1980–2008 and projected 2009–2021

Race and Hispanic origin[a]	Estimated											Projected	
	1980	1985	1990	1995	2000	2003	2004	2005	2006	2007	2008	2011	2021
White	—	—	—	—	76.8	76.5	76.4	76.3	76.1	76.0	75.9	75.9	75.2
White, non-Hispanic[b]	74	72	69	66	61.2	59.4	58.8	58.2	57.5	56.8	56.2	54.8	50.5
Black	—	—	—	—	15.6	15.5	15.4	15.3	15.3	15.2	15.2	14.6	14.1
Black, non-Hispanic[b]	15	15	15	15	—	—	—	—	—	—	—	—	—
American Indian or Alaskan Native[b]	1	1	1	1	—	—	—	—	—	—	—	—	—
Asian	—	—	—	—	3.6	3.8	3.9	4.0	4.0	4.1	4.2	4.5	4.9
Asian or Pacific Islander[b]	2	3	3	4	—	—	—	—	—	—	—	—	—
All other races[c]	—	—	—	—	4.0	4.3	4.3	4.4	4.5	4.7	4.8	5.0	5.8
Hispanic[d]	9	10	12	14	17.2	18.7	19.3	19.9	20.5	21.2	21.8	23.3	27.3

— Not available.

[a] For race and Hispanic-origin data in this table: In 1980 and 1990, following the 1977 OMB standards for collecting and presenting data on race, the decennial census asked respondents to choose one race from the following: White, Black, American Indian or Alaskan Native, or Asian or Pacific Islander. The Census Bureau also offered an "Other" category. Beginning in 2000, following the 1997 OMB standards for collecting and presenting data on race, the decennial census asked respondents to choose one or more races from the following: White, Black or African American, Asian, American Indian or Alaska Native, or Native Hawaiian or Other Pacific Islander. In addition, a "Some other race" category was included with OMB approval. Those who chose more than one race were classified as "Two or more races." Except for the "All other races" category, all race groups discussed in this table from 2000 onward refer to people who indicated only one racial identity within the racial categories presented. (Those who were "Two or more races" were included in the "All other races" category, along with American Indians or Alaska Natives and Native Hawaiians or Other Pacific Islanders.) People who responded to the question on race by indicating only one race are referred to as the race-alone population. The use of the race-alone population in this table does not imply that it is the preferred method of presenting or analyzing data. Data from 2000 onward are not directly comparable with data from earlier years. Data on race and Hispanic origin are collected separately; Hispanics may be of any race.

[b] Excludes persons in this race group who are of Hispanic origin.

[c] Includes American Indian, Eskimo and Aleut, Native Hawaiian and Other Pacific Islander, and all multiple race ("Two or more races").

[d] Persons of Hispanic origin may be of any race.

SOURCE: These data are available on the Census Bureau website at the Population Estimates or Projections site. The data for 1980 to 1989 are intercensal estimates and incorporate the 1980 and 1990 censuses as benchmarks. The 1990 to 1999 data are also intercensal estimates and incorporate the 1990 and 2000 censuses as benchmarks. The data for 2000 to 2008 are based on the population estimates released for July 1, 2008. The data for 2009 and beyond are derived from the national population projections released in August 2008.

Family structure and children's living arrangements: Percentage of children ages 0–17 by presence of parents in household and race and Hispanic origin, selected years 1980–2008

Race and Hispanic origin,[a] and family structure	1980	1985	1990	1995	2000	2003[b]	2004[b]	2005[b]	2006[b]	2007[b]	2008[b]
Total											
Two parents	—	—	—	—	—	—	—	—	—	70.7	69.9
Two married parents	77	74	73	69	69	68.4	67.8	67.3	67.4	67.8	66.7
Mother only	18	21	22	23	22	23.0	23.3	23.4	23.3	22.6	22.8
Father only	2	2	3	4	4	4.6	4.6	4.8	4.7	3.2	3.5
No parent	4	3	3	4	4	4.1	4.3	4.5	4.6	3.5	3.8
White, non-Hispanic											
Two married parents	—	—	81	78	77	—	—	—	—	—	—
Mother only	—	—	15	16	16	—	—	—	—	—	—
Father only	—	—	3	3	4	—	—	—	—	—	—
No parent	—	—	2	3	3	—	—	—	—	—	—
White-alone, non-Hispanic											
Two parents	—	—	—	—	—	—	—	—	—	78.6	77.8
Two married parents	—	—	—	—	—	76.9	76.9	75.9	75.9	76.2	75.4
Mother only	—	—	—	—	—	15.9	15.9	16.4	16.0	15.3	15.5
Father only	—	—	—	—	—	4.3	4.3	4.8	4.8	3.6	4.1
No parent	—	—	—	—	—	2.9	2.9	2.9	3.2	2.5	2.6
Black											
Two married parents	42	39	38	33	38	—	—	—	—	—	—
Mother only	44	51	51	52	49	—	—	—	—	—	—
Father only	2	3	4	4	4	—	—	—	—	—	—
No parent	12	7	8	11	9	—	—	—	—	—	—
Black-alone											
Two parents	—	—	—	—	—	—	—	—	—	39.8	37.5
Two married parents	—	—	—	—	—	36.0	35.0	35.0	34.6	36.8	34.5
Mother only	—	—	—	—	—	51.0	50.0	50.2	51.2	49.8	51.1
Father only	—	—	—	—	—	5.0	6.0	5.0	4.8	3.5	3.3
No parent	—	—	—	—	—	9.0	9.0	9.8	9.4	6.8	8.1
Hispanic[c]											
Two parents	—	—	—	—	—	—	—	—	—	69.8	69.7
Two married parents	75	68	67	63	65	64.6	64.6	64.7	65.9	65.5	64.2
Mother only	20	27	27	28	25	24.5	25.4	25.4	25.0	24.5	24.1
Father only	2	2	3	4	4	5.5	5.3	4.8	4.1	2.1	2.4
No parent	3	3	3	4	5	5.3	4.7	5.1	5.0	3.6	3.9

— Not available.

[a] For race and Hispanic-origin data in this table: From 1980 to 2002, following the 1977 OMB standards for collecting and presenting data on race, the Current Population Survey (CPS) asked respondents to choose one race from the following: White, Black, American Indian or Alaskan Native, or Asian or Pacific Islander. The Census Bureau also offered an "Other" category. Beginning in 2003, following the 1997 OMB standards for collecting and presenting data on race, the CPS asked respondents to choose one or more races from the following: White, Black or African American, Asian, American Indian or Alaska Native, or Native Hawaiian or Other Pacific Islander. All race groups discussed in this table from 2003 onward refer to people who indicated only one racial identity within the racial categories presented. People who responded to the question on race by indicating only one race are referred to as the race-alone population. The use of the race-alone population in this table does not imply that it is the preferred method of presenting or analyzing data. Data from 2003 onward are not directly comparable with data from earlier years. Data on race and Hispanic origin are collected separately. Persons of Hispanic origin may be of any race.

[b] Beginning with March 2001, data are from the expanded CPS sample and use population controls based on Census 2000.

[c] Persons of Hispanic origin may be of any race.

NOTE: Prior to 2007, CPS data identified only one parent on the child's record. This meant that a second parent could only be identified if they were married to the first parent. In 2007, a second parent identifier was added to CPS. This permits identification of two coresident parents, even if the parents are not married to each other. In this table, "two parents" reflects all children who have both a mother and father identified in the household, including biological, step, and adoptive parents. Before 2007, "mother only" and "father only" included some children who lived with a parent who was living with the other parent of the child, but was not married to them. Beginning in 2007, "mother only" and "father only" refer to children for whom only one parent has been identified, whether biological, step, or adoptive.

SOURCE: U.S. Census Bureau, Current Population Survey, Annual Social and Economic Supplements. U.S. Census Bureau, Families and Living Arrangements reports and detailed tables (from 1994) are available on the U.S. Census Bureau website at http://www.census.gov/population/www/socdemo/hh-fam.html.

Family structure and children's living arrangements: Detailed living arrangements of children by gender, race and Hispanic origin, age, parent's education, and poverty status, 2008

| Characteristic | Total | Two parents[a] | | | |
| | | Two biological/adoptive parents | | Biological/adoptive parent and stepparent | |
		Married	Cohabiting	Married	Cohabiting
Total (in thousands)	74,104	45,397	2,062	4,028	297
Percent					
Gender					
Male	51.1	51.5	52.0	50.8	41.8
Female	48.9	48.5	48.1	49.2	58.2
Race and Hispanic origin[b]					
White	78.2	84.9	79.8	82.4	78.8
White, non-Hispanic	56.7	64.2	40.7	64.0	57.6
Black	15.6	7.7	14.9	13.2	15.2
Black, non-Hispanic	14.6	7.2	12.8	12.0	14.8
Asian	1.1	0.8	1.6	1.2	2.7
All other races[b]	5.1	6.6	3.7	3.2	3.7
Hispanic (of any race)	21.1	20.5	38.3	18.3	22.6
Age					
Ages 0–5	33.7	36.0	69.2	10.4	31.3
Ages 6–14	48.6	48.3	26.2	58.4	47.8
Ages 15–17	17.8	15.7	4.7	31.3	21.2
Father's education					
Father not present	26.6	—	—	—	—
Less than high school	9.9	12.7	30.9	12.8	19.2
High school graduate	20.8	26.1	40.6	38.2	43.8
Some college	18.4	24.8	21.0	29.5	29.6
Bachelor's degree or more	24.2	36.4	7.5	19.5	7.7
Mother's education					
Mother not present	7.3	—	—	—	—
Less than high school	13.1	11.7	31.1	10.8	17.2
High school graduate	25.1	23.6	34.6	32.7	42.1
Some college	27.2	27.5	26.5	36.9	35.4
Bachelor's degree or more	27.3	37.2	7.8	19.6	5.7
Poverty status					
Below 100% poverty	18.4	8.3	45.0	9.1	33.0
100–199% poverty	21.0	17.5	30.3	19.4	34.3
200% poverty and above	60.6	74.2	24.8	71.6	32.7

See notes at end of table.

Family structure and children's living arrangements: Detailed living arrangements of children by gender, race and Hispanic origin, age, parent's education, and poverty status, 2008

Characteristic	One parent			
	Mother		Father	
	Not cohabiting	Cohabiting	Not cohabiting	Cohabiting
Total (in thousands)	15,181	1,706	2,106	507
Percent				
Gender				
Male	49.7	49.2	58.1	50.9
Female	50.3	50.8	41.9	49.3
Race and Hispanic origin[b]				
White	59.5	79.2	79.7	82.1
White, non-Hispanic	36.5	57.3	67.4	58.6
Black	36.8	15.9	14.7	14.2
Black, non-Hispanic	34.9	14.8	14.2	13.2
Asian	1.3	2.9	1.5	2.4
All other races[b]	2.5	2.0	4.1	1.4
Hispanic (of any race)	22.4	20.9	12.5	20.7
Age				
Ages 0–5	31.9	25.6	21.2	37.7
Ages 6–14	49.4	54.4	50.9	46.0
Ages 15–17	18.7	20.0	27.8	16.4
Father's education				
Father not present	100.0	100.0	—	—
Less than high school	—	—	14.7	12.8
High school graduate	—	—	38.3	45.0
Some college	—	—	26.8	28.8
Bachelor's degree or more	—	—	20.3	13.4
Mother's education				
Mother not present	—	—	100.0	100.0
Less than high school	19.6	17.5	—	—
High school graduate	33.1	40.7	—	—
Some college	33.0	31.4	—	—
Bachelor's degree or more	14.3	10.4	—	—
Poverty status				
Below 100% poverty	39.8	44.4	15.8	22.3
100–199% poverty	29.1	28.8	23.1	29.4
200% poverty and above	31.2	26.7	61.2	48.5

See notes at end of table.

Family structure and children's living arrangements: Detailed living arrangements of children by gender, race and Hispanic origin, age, parent's education, and poverty status, 2008

		No parents			
Characteristic	Grandparent	Other relatives only— no grandparent	Nonrelative only— not foster	Foster parent(s)	All other[c]
Total (in thousands)	1,510	705	252	228	124
Percent					
Gender					
Male	50.2	49.1	50.4	47.8	56.5
Female	49.8	50.9	49.6	51.8	43.5
Race and Hispanic origin[b]					
White	56.8	63.1	70.2	60.5	83.9
White, non-Hispanic	40.9	31.6	46.0	41.7	40.3
Black	38.7	28.1	21.0	36.8	12.1
Black, non-Hispanic	36.3	27.0	20.2	32.5	12.1
Asian	2.8	2.6	1.2	1.8	0.8
All other races[b]	1.7	6.2	7.5	0.9	4.0
Hispanic (of any race)	15.6	31.8	22.2	19.7	41.1
Age					
Ages 0–5	29.5	13.0	24.6	34.2	32.3
Ages 6–14	50.5	46.1	36.5	47.8	35.5
Ages 15–17	20.0	40.7	38.9	18.0	32.3
Father's education					
Father not present	100.0	100.0	100.0	100.0	100.0
Less than high school	—	—	—	—	—
High school graduate	—	—	—	—	—
Some college	—	—	—	—	—
Bachelor's degree or more	—	—	—	—	—
Mother's education					
Mother not present	100.0	100.0	100.0	100.0	100.0
Less than high school	—	—	—	—	—
High school graduate	—	—	—	—	—
Some college	—	—	—	—	—
Bachelor's degree or more	—	—	—	—	—
Poverty status					
Below 100% poverty	32.3	38.3	96.4	99.6	33.9
100–199% poverty	25.9	22.6	2.0	0.4	26.6
200% poverty and above	41.9	39.1	1.2	*	38.7

— Not available.

* Represents or rounds to zero.

[a] This category also includes children living with two stepparents.

[b] For race and Hispanic-origin data in this table: Following the 1997 OMB standards for collecting and presenting data on race, the Survey of Income and Program Participation (SIPP) asked respondents to choose one or more races from the following: White, Black or African American, Asian, American Indian or Alaska Native, or Native Hawaiian or Other Pacific Islander. The Census Bureau also offered an "Other" category. Those who chose more than one race were classified as "Two or more races." Except for the "All other races" category, all race groups discussed in this table refer to people who indicated only one racial identity within the racial categories presented. (Those who were "Two or more races" were included in the "All other races" category, along with American Indians or Alaska Natives, Native Hawaiians or Other Pacific Islanders, and those who chose "Other".) People who responded to the question on race by indicating only one race are referred to as the race-alone population. The use of the race-alone population in this table does not imply that it is the preferred method of presenting or analyzing data. Data on race and Hispanic origin are collected separately. Persons of Hispanic origin may be of any race.

[c] The category "All other" includes children who live with other relatives and nonrelatives (no grandparents).

NOTE: "Cohabiting" means the parent is cohabiting with an unmarried partner. Relatives are anyone who is reported as related to the householder by blood, marriage, or adoption.

SOURCE: U.S. Census Bureau, Current Population Survey, Annual Social and Economic Supplement.

Births to unmarried women: Birth rates for unmarried women by age of mother, selected years 1980–2007

(Live births to unmarried women per 1,000 in specified age group)

Age of mother	1980	1985	1990	1995	2000	2003	2004	2005	2006	2007
Total ages 15–44	29.4	32.8	43.8	44.3	44.1	44.9	46.1	47.5	50.6	52.9
Age										
Ages 15–17	20.6	22.4	29.6	30.1	23.9	20.3	20.1	19.7	20.4	—
Ages 18–19	39.0	45.9	60.7	66.5	62.2	57.6	57.7	58.4	61.8	—
Ages 20–24	40.9	46.5	65.1	68.7	72.2	71.2	72.5	74.9	79.5	—
Ages 25–29	34.0	39.9	56.0	54.3	58.5	65.7	68.6	71.1	74.9	—
Ages 30–34	21.1	25.2	37.6	38.9	39.3	44.0	47.0	50.0	54.8	—
Ages 35–39	9.7	11.6	17.3	19.3	19.7	22.3	23.5	24.5	26.8	—
Ages 40–44	2.6	2.5	3.6	4.7	5.0	5.8	6.0	6.2	6.5	—

— Not available.

NOTE: The 2007 rate for total ages 15-44 is preliminary. 2007 data for specific age groups are not yet available. Births to unmarried women were somewhat underreported in Michigan and Texas during the years 1989–1993; data since 1994 have been reported on a complete basis.

SOURCE: National Center for Health Statistics, National Vital Statistics System. Hamilton, B.E., Martin, J.A., and Ventura, S.J. (2009). Births: Preliminary data for 2007. *National Vital Statistics Reports, 57*(12). Hyattsville, MD: National Center for Health Statistics. Martin, J.A., Hamilton, B.E., Sutton, P.D., Ventura, S.J., Menacker, F. Kirmeyer, S., and Mathews, T.J. (2009). Births: Final data for 2006. *National Vital Statistics Reports, 57*(7). Hyattsville, MD: National Center for Health Statistics. Hamilton, B.E., Sutton, P.D., and Ventura, S.J. (2003). Revised birth and fertility rates for the 1990s: United States, and new rates for Hispanic populations, 2000 and 2001. *National Vital Statistics Reports, 51*(12). Hyattsville, MD: National Center for Health Statistics. Ventura, S.J., and Bachrach, C.A. (2000). Nonmarital childbearing in the United States, 1940–99. *National Vital Statistics Reports, 48*(16). Hyattsville, MD: National Center for Health Statistics.

Table FAM2.B	Births to unmarried women: Percentage of all births that are to unmarried women by age of mother, selected years 1980–2007									
Age of mother	1980	1985	1990	1995	2000	2003	2004	2005	2006	2007
All ages	18.4	22.0	28.0	32.2	33.2	34.6	35.8	36.9	38.5	39.7
Age										
Under age 15	88.7	91.8	91.6	93.5	96.5	97.1	97.4	98.0	98.3	98.8
Ages 15–17	61.5	70.9	77.7	83.7	87.7	89.7	90.3	90.9	91.9	92.8
Ages 18–19	39.8	50.7	61.3	69.8	74.3	77.3	78.7	79.7	80.6	82.1
Ages 20–24	19.3	26.3	36.9	44.7	49.5	53.2	54.7	56.2	57.9	59.5
Ages 25–29	9.0	12.7	18.0	21.5	23.5	26.4	27.8	29.3	31.0	32.2
Ages 30–34	7.4	9.7	13.3	14.7	14.0	15.1	16.1	17.0	18.3	19.3
Ages 35–39	9.4	11.2	13.9	15.7	14.3	14.8	15.2	15.7	16.4	17.3
Ages 40 and older	12.1	14.0	17.0	18.1	16.8	17.9	18.2	18.8	19.4	19.9

NOTE: Data for 2007 are preliminary.

SOURCE: National Center for Health Statistics, National Vital Statistics System. Ventura, S.J., and Bachrach, C.A. (2000). Nonmarital childbearing in the United States, 1940–99. *National Vital Statistics Reports, 48*(16). Martin, J.A., Hamilton, B.E., Ventura, S.J., Menacker, F., and Park, M.M. (2002). Births: Final data for 2000. *National Vital Statistics Reports, 50*(5). Hyattsville, MD: National Center for Health Statistics. Martin, J.A., Hamilton, B.E., Ventura, S.J., Menaker, F., Park, M.M., and Sutton, P.D. (2002). Births: Final data for 2001. *National Vital Statistics Reports, 51*(2). Hyattsville, MD: National Center for Health Statistics. Martin, J.A., Hamilton, B.E., Sutton, P.D., Ventura, S.J., Menacker, F., and Munson, M.L. (2003). Births: Final data for 2002. *National Vital Statistics Reports, 52*(10). Hyattsville, MD: National Center for Health Statistics. Martin, J.A., Hamilton, B.E., Sutton, P.D., Ventura, S.J., Menacker, F., and Munson, M.L. (2005). Births: Final Data for 2003. National Vital Statistics Reports 54(2). Hyattsville, MD: National Center for Health Statistics. Martin, J.A., Hamilton, B.E., Sutton, P.D., Ventura, S.J., Menacker, F., and Kirmeyer, S. (2006). Births: Final data for 2004. National Vital Statistics Reports 55(1). Hyattsville, MD: National Center for Health Statistics. Martin, J.A., Hamilton, B.E., Sutton, P.D., Ventura, S.J., Menacker, F., Kirmeyer, S., and Munson, M.L. (2007). Births: Final data for 2005. *National Vital Statistics Reports 56*(6). Hyattsville, MD: National Center for Health Statistics. Martin, J.A., Hamilton, B.E., Sutton, P.D., Ventura, S.J., Menacker, F., Kirmeyer, S., and Mathews, T.J. (2009). Births: Final data for 2006. *National Vital Statistics Reports 57*(7). Hyattsville, MD: National Center for Health Statistics. Hamilton, B.E., Martin, J.A., Ventura, S.J. (2009). Births: Preliminary data for 2007. *National Vital Statistics Reports 57*(12). Hyattsville, MD: National Center for Health Statistics.

Child care: Primary child care arrangements for children ages 0–4 with employed mothers by selected characteristics, selected years 1985–2005 and summer 2006

Type of child care (during mother's work hours)	1985	1988	1990	1991	1993	1995	1999	2002	2005	2006[a]
Percent										
Total										
Mother care[b]	8.1	7.6	6.4	8.7	6.2	5.4	3.0	3.2	4.4	2.5
Father care[b]	15.7	15.1	16.5	20.0	15.9	16.6	17.1	17.5	17.3	12.8
Grandparent care	15.9	13.9	14.3	15.8	17.0	15.9	19.7	18.6	19.6	13.4
Other relative care[c]	8.2	7.2	8.8	7.7	9.0	5.5	8.0	6.2	6.6	3.8
Center-based care[d]	23.1	25.8	27.5	23.1	29.9	25.1	21.0	24.3	23.8	15.8
Other nonrelative care[e]	28.2	28.9	25.1	23.3	21.6	28.4	18.8	17.2	16.0	9.6
Other[f]	0.8	1.6	1.3	1.6	1.1	2.9	12.4	13.0	12.0	42.0
Poverty status										
Below 100% poverty										
Mother care[b]	—	11.3	—	9.5	8.1	4.5	2.9	4.1	7.8	1.2
Father care[b]	—	15.0	—	26.7	16.2	20.1	14.5	19.9	19.8	13.6
Grandparent care	—	19.4	—	16.3	20.0	22.4	23.8	19.7	19.8	16.2
Other relative care[c]	—	11.3	—	11.4	15.8	7.0	13.5	10.0	8.8	4.8
Center-based care[d]	—	21.6	—	21.1	21.0	25.8	18.3	15.9	18.2	12.2
Other nonrelative care[e]	—	21.1	—	15.1	18.8	16.5	18.0	12.6	11.8	4.6
Other[f]	—	0.8	—	2.7	1.2	3.5	8.8	17.6	13.7	47.3
100% poverty and above										
Mother care[b]	—	7.3	—	8.5	5.9	5.5	2.9	3.1	3.8	2.5
Father care[b]	—	15.1	—	19.4	16.0	16.4	17.6	17.3	17.1	12.7
Grandparent care	—	13.4	—	15.6	16.0	15.1	19.3	18.7	19.7	13.2
Other relative care[c]	—	6.8	—	7.3	8.0	5.3	7.3	5.7	6.2	3.7
Center-based care[d]	—	27.8	—	25.1	32.3	24.8	21.1	25.1	24.8	16.4
Other nonrelative care[e]	—	29.6	—	24.2	21.8	29.9	19.4	18.4	16.7	10.3
Other[f]	—	1.6	—	1.5	1.1	2.8	12.2	11.7	11.4	41.2
Region[g]										
Northeast										
Mother care[b]	—	—	—	—	—	5.3	2.3	2.9	3.5	1.2
Father care[b]	—	—	—	—	—	22.4	21.5	21.4	19.3	15.7
Grandparent care	—	—	—	—	—	12.9	18.7	18.8	20.6	15.1
Other relative care[c]	—	—	—	—	—	8.0	7.3	4.4	5.0	3.2
Center-based care[d]	—	—	—	—	—	24.4	18.4	24.5	23.2	15.6
Other nonrelative care[e]	—	—	—	—	—	23.9	17.9	14.7	15.9	8.5
Other[f]	—	—	—	—	—	3.0	13.7	13.1	12.3	40.4
South										
Mother care[b]	—	—	—	—	—	4.3	3.3	2.1	4.2	2.5
Father care[b]	—	—	—	—	—	9.3	12.9	13.4	14.1	10.0
Grandparent care	—	—	—	—	—	17.1	21.8	20.9	20.9	12.5
Other relative care[c]	—	—	—	—	—	5.3	7.6	7.8	6.5	3.3
Center-based care[d]	—	—	—	—	—	30.7	26.8	28.0	28.0	17.4
Other nonrelative care[e]	—	—	—	—	—	30.0	18.1	15.9	13.0	8.3
Other[f]	—	—	—	—	—	3.1	9.3	11.8	13.1	45.9
Midwest										
Mother care[b]	—	—	—	—	—	6.3	2.0	3.5	5.4	2.9
Father care[b]	—	—	—	—	—	19.1	20.3	21.6	18.7	14.8
Grandparent care	—	—	—	—	—	15.4	16.3	15.9	17.1	12.2
Other relative care[c]	—	—	—	—	—	5.0	6.6	3.6	6.5	4.8
Center-based care[d]	—	—	—	—	—	21.1	19.9	20.7	21.7	16.3
Other nonrelative care[e]	—	—	—	—	—	30.9	24.0	22.6	19.4	11.7
Other[f]	—	—	—	—	—	2.0	10.9	11.9	11.0	37.1

See notes at end of table.

Child care: Primary child care arrangements for children ages 0–4 with employed mothers by selected characteristics, selected years 1985–2005 and summer 2006

Type of child care (during mother's work hours)	1985	1988	1990	1991	1993	1995	1999	2002	2005	2006[a]
Region[g]—continued										
West										
Mother care[b]	—	—	—	—	—	5.6	3.9	4.9	4.3	2.9
Father care[b]	—	—	—	—	—	18.5	17.0	17.8	19.9	13.1
Grandparent care	—	—	—	—	—	17.5	21.4	18.3	19.5	14.9
Other relative care[c]	—	—	—	—	—	4.1	10.5	8.1	8.1	4.0
Center-based care[d]	—	—	—	—	—	23.1	15.5	19.9	19.7	13.0
Other nonrelative care[e]	—	—	—	—	—	27.2	16.7	17.1	17.5	10.2
Other[f]	—	—	—	—	—	3.8	14.8	14.0	10.9	41.6
Race and Hispanic origin of mother[h]										
White										
Mother care[b]	—	—	—	—	—	5.8	3.2	3.5	4.8	2.8
Father care[b]	—	—	—	—	—	17.8	18.1	18.4	18.4	13.8
Grandparent care	—	—	—	—	—	15.5	17.7	17.9	19.2	13.6
Other relative care[c]	—	—	—	—	—	4.5	7.6	4.9	5.5	3.5
Center-based care[d]	—	—	—	—	—	24.3	20.1	23.2	22.4	15.5
Other nonrelative care[e]	—	—	—	—	—	29.0	20.9	18.4	17.1	10.5
Other[f]	—	—	—	—	—	2.9	12.1	13.5	12.4	40.3
White, non-Hispanic										
Mother care[b]	—	—	—	—	—	6.1	3.2	3.7	4.9	3.1
Father care[b]	—	—	—	—	—	17.6	18.1	19.1	19.3	14.0
Grandparent care	—	—	—	—	—	15.4	17.0	16.5	17.5	13.7
Other relative care[c]	—	—	—	—	—	4.0	6.2	3.6	3.8	2.7
Center-based care[d]	—	—	—	—	—	24.8	22.2	24.3	24.5	16.4
Other nonrelative care[e]	—	—	—	—	—	29.4	21.3	19.6	17.7	11.0
Other[f]	—	—	—	—	—	2.7	12.0	13.3	12.0	38.9
Black										
Mother care[b]	—	—	—	—	—	2.1	1.8	1.2	3.1	0.7
Father care[b]	—	—	—	—	—	8.8	12.9	13.5	12.3	7.2
Grandparent care	—	—	—	—	—	16.0	25.1	21.6	19.5	10.3
Other relative care[c]	—	—	—	—	—	9.9	10.6	12.6	10.9	5.8
Center-based care[d]	—	—	—	—	—	32.5	27.0	27.4	29.6	17.9
Other nonrelative care[e]	—	—	—	—	—	28.3	13.1	14.3	13.3	6.4
Other[f]	—	—	—	—	—	2.3	9.4	9.2	11.1	51.4
Black, non-Hispanic										
Mother care[b]	—	—	—	—	—	2.2	1.9	1.2	3.3	0.7
Father care[b]	—	—	—	—	—	8.9	12.4	13.2	11.9	6.9
Grandparent care	—	—	—	—	—	15.7	24.4	22.9	19.5	10.1
Other relative care[c]	—	—	—	—	—	10.1	10.9	12.0	11.3	6.0
Center-based care[d]	—	—	—	—	—	33.2	27.5	27.0	29.5	18.3
Other nonrelative care[e]	—	—	—	—	—	27.9	13.5	13.7	13.2	6.6
Other[f]	—	—	—	—	—	1.9	9.3	9.9	11.2	51.0
Hispanic										
Mother care[b]	—	—	—	—	—	3.6	2.6	2.7	3.4	1.6
Father care[b]	—	—	—	—	—	19.0	18.6	15.1	14.7	12.6
Grandparent care	—	—	—	—	—	17.0	21.9	23.9	27.0	14.5
Other relative care[c]	—	—	—	—	—	8.7	14.0	12.0	12.8	5.8
Center-based care[d]	—	—	—	—	—	20.8	10.9	19.8	14.2	12.3
Other nonrelative care[e]	—	—	—	—	—	25.0	18.2	13.9	14.2	7.8
Other[f]	—	—	—	—	—	5.8	13.6	12.6	13.7	45.4

See notes at end of table.

Child care: Primary child care arrangements for children ages 0–4 with employed mothers by selected characteristics, selected years 1985–2005 and summer 2006

Type of child care (during mother's work hours)	1985	1988	1990	1991	1993	1995	1999	2002	2005	2006[a]
Educational attainment of mother										
Less than high school										
Mother care[b]	—	—	—	—	—	6.3	1.7	4.1	5.4	2.1
Father care[b]	—	—	—	—	—	18.2	14.4	19.2	22.3	10.7
Grandparent care	—	—	—	—	—	21.2	23.4	15.5	16.7	19.1
Other relative care[c]	—	—	—	—	—	10.8	20.7	12.0	15.4	9.4
Center-based care[d]	—	—	—	—	—	16.9	16.3	17.5	12.0	6.0
Other nonrelative care[e]	—	—	—	—	—	20.8	13.5	17.4	11.7	7.1
Other[f]	—	—	—	—	—	4.8	9.9	14.2	16.2	45.3
High school diploma or equivalent										
Mother care[b]	—	—	—	—	—	5.6	3.5	2.5	4.1	2.4
Father care[b]	—	—	—	—	—	16.6	20.3	19.7	16.6	12.1
Grandparent care	—	—	—	—	—	20.5	23.5	23.2	25.7	16.2
Other relative care[c]	—	—	—	—	—	5.4	7.9	6.0	9.4	4.9
Center-based care[d]	—	—	—	—	—	25.7	18.8	20.0	18.4	11.5
Other nonrelative care[e]	—	—	—	—	—	23.2	14.2	14.5	13.0	6.9
Other[f]	—	—	—	—	—	2.6	11.7	13.9	12.7	45.8
Some college, including vocational/technical/ associate's degree										
Mother care[b]	—	—	—	—	—	4.9	1.9	3.2	4.3	1.6
Father care[b]	—	—	—	—	—	18.4	16.7	19.3	17.7	12.8
Grandparent care	—	—	—	—	—	14.2	20.1	20.8	21.9	13.2
Other relative care[c]	—	—	—	—	—	5.8	7.4	7.5	6.6	4.3
Center-based care[d]	—	—	—	—	—	25.6	18.6	23.2	23.8	13.7
Other nonrelative care[e]	—	—	—	—	—	27.7	21.1	15.3	15.5	9.3
Other[f]	—	—	—	—	—	3.1	14.1	10.6	10.1	44.9
Bachelor's degree or higher										
Mother care[b]	—	—	—	—	—	5.2	4.0	3.5	4.6	3.4
Father care[b]	—	—	—	—	—	14.4	15.7	13.7	16.6	13.6
Grandparent care	—	—	—	—	—	11.4	14.4	13.9	13.1	10.9
Other relative care[c]	—	—	—	—	—	3.4	4.0	3.4	2.7	1.5
Center-based care[d]	—	—	—	—	—	26.0	27.5	29.9	30.5	22.4
Other nonrelative care[e]	—	—	—	—	—	36.9	24.4	22.6	19.9	12.1
Other[f]	—	—	—	—	—	2.3	9.9	13.0	12.7	35.9

See notes at end of table.

Child care: Primary child care arrangements for children ages 0–4 with employed mothers by selected characteristics, selected years 1985–2005 and summer 2006

Type of child care (during mother's work hours)	1985	1988	1990	1991	1993	1995	1999	2002	2005	2006[a]
Family structure										
Two married parents										
Mother care[b]	—	—	—	—	—	6.2	3.4	3.5	4.9	2.9
Father care[b]	—	—	—	—	—	18.7	19.9	20.6	19.5	13.5
Grandparent care	—	—	—	—	—	14.4	16.4	17.3	17.6	11.6
Other relative care[c]	—	—	—	—	—	4.8	6.4	4.7	4.8	2.4
Center-based care[d]	—	—	—	—	—	23.0	20.7	22.7	24.0	16.8
Other nonrelative care[e]	—	—	—	—	—	29.4	19.7	17.2	16.3	10.1
Other[f]	—	—	—	—	—	3.1	13.4	13.8	12.7	42.5
Mother only										
Mother care[b]	—	—	—	—	—	2.8	1.9	2.5	3.0	1.4
Father care[b]	—	—	—	—	—	10.4	10.1	9.8	12.1	11.0
Grandparent care	—	—	—	—	—	20.5	29.1	22.7	24.5	18.1
Other relative care[c]	—	—	—	—	—	7.2	12.2	10.2	11.0	7.5
Center-based care[d]	—	—	—	—	—	30.3	21.5	27.0	23.4	13.0
Other nonrelative care[e]	—	—	—	—	—	26.1	17.6	18.4	15.6	8.4
Other[f]	—	—	—	—	—	2.4	7.4	9.2	10.2	40.3

— Not available.

[a] SIPP child care data collected in 2006 cannot be compared directly with SIPP child care data from previous years due to seasonality differences such as preschool closings, seasonal variations in school activities, and availability of child care arrangements. The 2006 child care data was collected during summer months, whereas previous survey years typically collected data during spring or fall months.

[b] Mother and father care includes care while the mother worked.

[c] Other relatives include siblings and other relatives.

[d] Center-based care includes day care centers, nursery schools, preschools, and Head Start programs.

[e] Other nonrelative care includes family day care providers, in-home babysitters, and other nonrelatives providing care in either the child's or provider's home.

[f] Other for 1985–1993 includes children in kindergarten or grade school, in a school-based activity, or in self care. In 1995, it also includes children with no regular arrangement. Beginning in 1997, other includes children in kindergarten or grade school, self-care, and with no regular arrangement, but does not include school-based activities, as they were deleted as categorical choices for preschoolers.

[g] Regions: Northeast includes CT, MA, ME, NH, NJ, NY, PA, RI, and VT. South includes AL, AR, DC, DE, FL, GA, KY, LA, MD, MS, NC, OK, SC, TN, TX, VA, and WV. Midwest includes IA, IL, IN, KS, MI, MN, MO, ND, NE, OH, SD, and WI. West includes AK, AZ, CA, CO, HI, ID, MT, NM, NV, OR, UT, WA, and WY.

[h] For race and Hispanic-origin data in this table: From 1995 to 2002, following the 1977 OMB standards for collecting and presenting data on race, the Survey of Income and Program Participation (SIPP) asked respondents to choose one race from the following: White, Black, American Indian or Alaskan Native, or Asian or Pacific Islander. The Census Bureau also offered an "Other" category. Beginning in 2004, following the 1997 OMB standards for collecting and presenting data on race, the SIPP asked respondents to choose one or more races from the following: White, Black or African American, Asian, American Indian or Alaska Native, or Native Hawaiian or Other Pacific Islander. The Census Bureau also offered an "Other" category. All race groups discussed in this table from 2004 onward refer to people who indicated only one racial identity within the racial categories presented. People who responded to the question on race by indicating only one race are referred to as the race-alone population. The use of the race-alone population in this table does not imply that it is the preferred method of presenting or analyzing data. Data from 2004 onward are not directly comparable with data from earlier years. Data on race and Hispanic origin are collected separately. Persons of Hispanic origin may be of any race.

NOTE: Employed mothers are those with wage and salary employment or other employment arrangements including contingent work and self-employment. Data for years 1995 to 2005 were proportionately redistributed to account for tied responses for the primary arrangement so that they total to 100 percent and are comparable to earlier years. Data for 2006 was also proportionately redistributed, but is not comparable to earlier years due to seasonality differences.

SOURCE: U.S. Census Bureau, Survey of Income and Program Participation.

Child care: Percentage of children ages 0–6 not yet in kindergarten by type of care arrangement and child and family characteristics, 2001 and 2005

Characteristic	Parental care only		Type of nonparental care arrangement							
			Total in nonparental care[b]		Care in a home[a]				Center-based program[c]	
					By a relative		By a nonrelative			
	2001	2005	2001	2005	2001	2005	2001	2005	2001	2005
Total	38.8	39.2	61.2	60.8	23.1	22.3	16.3	13.9	33.4	36.1
Age										
Ages 0–2	48.0	49.3	52.0	50.7	23.3	22.0	18.0	15.6	16.5	19.6
Ages 3–6, not yet in kindergarten	26.3	23.6	73.7	73.7	22.7	22.7	14.0	11.7	56.3	57.1
Race and Hispanic origin[d]										
White, non-Hispanic	38.4	37.2	61.6	62.8	20.3	21.0	18.7	17.0	35.1	37.8
Black, non-Hispanic	26.1	30.1	73.9	69.9	34.6	27.7	12.9	10.2	40.2	43.9
Asian	43.2	43.5	56.8	56.5	22.9	21.3	8.7	9.0	34.1	37.0
Hispanic	52.0	50.5	48.0	49.5	22.9	21.2	11.8	10.4	20.7	25.2
Poverty status										
Below 100% poverty	45.3	49.2	54.7	50.8	27.4	23.3	10.6	8.0	26.9	28.3
100–199% poverty	46.3	47.2	53.7	52.8	22.5	23.5	12.6	9.3	27.8	29.4
200% poverty and above	32.7	31.6	67.3	68.4	21.4	21.4	20.5	18.3	38.7	42.2
Family type										
Two parents[e]	42.7	42.9	57.3	57.1	19.0	18.8	16.2	14.1	32.3	34.4
Two parents, married	42.2	41.8	57.8	58.2	18.4	18.6	16.6	14.2	33.1	35.8
Two parents, unmarried	47.3	53.0	52.7	47.0	24.4	20.4	12.4	13.0	25.0	21.7
One parent	26.5	24.9	73.5	75.1	36.6	36.0	17.3	13.4	36.1	42.3
No parents	17.9	33.1	82.1	66.9	38.5	28.3	9.2	10.0	47.9	43.6
Mother's highest level of education[f]										
Less than high school	55.5	63.7	44.5	36.3	21.7	16.1	8.3	5.5	20.8	18.9
High school diploma or equivalent	42.3	44.4	57.7	55.6	26.2	24.1	13.3	9.9	28.1	30.7
Some college, including vocational/ technical/associate's degree	36.7	36.5	63.3	63.5	25.3	25.8	15.4	14.5	35.3	35.2
Bachelor's degree or higher	31.3	30.5	68.7	69.5	16.9	19.1	23.6	19.2	42.1	45.8
Mother's employment status[f]										
35 hours or more per week	14.8	14.7	85.2	85.3	34.0	31.8	26.2	23.3	42.1	47.6
Less than 35 hours per week	29.0	30.3	71.0	69.7	31.6	30.5	19.9	18.0	35.6	37.8
Looking for work	57.3	53.3	42.7	46.7	16.7	20.7	9.6	7.5	24.5	23.3
Not in the labor force	67.6	66.1	32.4	33.9	7.0	7.8	4.8	3.6	24.1	25.8
Region[g]										
Northeast	35.8	38.3	64.2	61.7	27.0	21.0	15.9	15.1	35.5	37.9
South	37.0	38.0	63.0	62.0	22.9	22.3	14.1	11.1	36.4	38.8
Midwest	37.0	36.7	63.0	63.3	22.0	23.8	21.1	18.8	33.8	33.5
West	45.5	43.9	54.5	56.1	21.4	21.8	14.9	12.6	27.1	33.1

[a] Relative and nonrelative care can take place in either the child's own home or another home.

[b] Some children participate in more than one type of nonparental care arrangement. Thus, details do not sum to the total percentage of children in nonparental care.

[c] Center-based programs include day care centers, prekindergartens, nursery schools, Head Start programs, and other early childhood education programs.

[d] In 2001, the 1977 OMB Standards for Data on Race and Ethnicity were used to classify persons into one of the following four racial groups: White, Black, American Indian or Alaskan Native, or Asian or Pacific Islander. For data from 2005, the revised 1997 OMB standards were used. Persons could select one or more of five racial groups: White, Black or African American, American Indian or Alaska Native, Asian, or Native Hawaiian or Other Pacific Islander. Included in the total but not shown separately are American Indian or Alaska Native and respondents with "Two or more races." For continuity purposes, in 2005, respondents who reported the child being Asian or Native Hawaiian or Other Pacific Islander were combined. Data on race and Hispanic origin are collected separately. Persons of Hispanic origin may be of any race.

[e] Refers to adults' relationship to child and does not indicate marital status.

[f] Children without a mother in the home are excluded from estimates of mother's highest level of education and mother's employment status.

[g] Regions: Northeast includes CT, MA, ME, NH, NJ, NY, PA, RI, and VT. South includes AL, AR, DC, DE, FL, GA, KY, LA, MD, MS, NC, OK, SC, TN, TX, VA, and WV. Midwest includes IA, IL, IN, KS, MI, MN, MO, ND, NE, OH, SD, and WI. West includes AK, AZ, CA, CO, HI, ID, MT, NM, NV, OR, UT, WA, and WY.

SOURCE: U.S. Department of Education, National Center for Education Statistics, National Household Education Surveys Program.

Child care: Percentage of children in kindergarten through 8th grade in weekday care and activities by poverty status, race and Hispanic origin, and grade level, 2005

Grade level, care arrangement, and activity	Total	Poverty status			Race and Hispanic origin[a]			
		Below 100% poverty	100–199% poverty	200% poverty and above	White, non-Hispanic	Black, non-Hispanic	Asian	Hispanic
Kindergarten–3rd grade								
Care arrangements								
Parental care only	53.1	52.0	54.5	53.0	58.3	34.6	49.9	55.3
Nonparental care[b]	46.9	48.0	45.5	47.0	41.7	65.4	50.1	44.7
Home-based care[c]	23.6	25.2	24.5	22.6	22.0	32.2	26.5	20.4
Center-based care	24.4	25.0	21.6	25.2	20.5	39.8	21.4	23.4
Activities used for supervision	5.2	3.1	5.3	6.0	4.8	5.8	13.4	3.2
Self care	2.6	5.1	3.6	1.3	1.6	4.1	3.6	4.2
Activities								
Any activity[b]	46.2	24.3	34.0	59.5	56.2	30.4	45.8	30.4
Sports	31.8	12.1	19.5	44.3	40.2	16.8	29.3	20.8
Religious activities	19.4	13.5	14.8	23.4	24.0	14.6	11.5	11.9
Arts[d]	17.2	6.0	10.8	24.1	21.8	8.3	27.1	8.2
Scouts	12.9	5.3	8.0	17.8	18.2	4.9	11.1	3.8
Academic activities[e]	4.7	3.8	3.8	5.3	5.1	4.4	7.4	3.5
Community services	4.2	1.9	3.0	5.5	5.3	3.3	2.6	1.7
Clubs	3.2	1.3	2.4	4.3	4.3	1.1	4.2	1.8
4th–8th grade								
Care arrangements								
Parental care only	46.9	46.7	45.2	47.6	51.2	34.5	44.2	45.0
Nonparental care[b]	53.1	53.3	54.8	52.4	48.8	65.5	55.8	55.0
Home-based care[c]	18.1	15.0	20.0	18.4	16.4	24.1	17.5	18.6
Center-based care	19.0	21.3	21.3	17.4	14.2	28.9	21.9	25.4
Activities used for supervision	9.0	7.8	6.9	10.2	8.9	10.5	11.9	7.5
Self care	22.2	23.5	23.8	21.2	21.1	27.1	21.0	19.6
Activities								
Any activity[b]	53.7	30.4	40.5	65.9	63.3	39.7	51.2	35.4
Sports	39.3	18.6	26.1	50.8	47.8	24.2	37.2	26.7
Religious activities	24.9	12.5	20.0	30.7	29.7	20.9	18.3	14.8
Arts[d]	21.5	9.7	12.5	28.5	25.8	13.3	25.5	13.2
Scouts	10.1	4.8	6.4	13.2	13.3	5.6	7.7	5.4
Academic activities[e]	9.7	6.6	7.1	11.6	10.0	12.0	13.0	5.9
Community services	12.7	5.0	10.6	15.9	15.6	8.2	13.1	7.1
Clubs	8.7	3.7	4.6	11.8	11.0	4.9	8.9	4.1

[a] The 1997 OMB Standards for Data on Race and Ethnicity were used, allowing persons to select one or more of five racial groups: White, Black or African American, American Indian or Alaska Native, Asian, or Native Hawaiian or Other Pacific Islander. Included in the total but not shown separately are American Indian or Alaska Native and respondents with "Two or more races." Respondents who reported the child being Asian or Native Hawaiian or Other Pacific Islander were combined. Data on race and Hispanic origin are collected separately. Persons of Hispanic origin may be of any race.

[b] Children may have multiple nonparental child care arrangements, in addition to being involved in more than one activity; thus, the total of the four kinds of nonparental arrangements may not sum to the category "Nonparental care." Likewise, the seven activities listed may not sum to the category "Any activity." Activities include organized programs a child participates in outside of school hours that are not part of a before- or after-school program.

[c] Home-based care includes care that takes place in a relative's or nonrelative's private home.

[d] Arts include activities such as music, dance, and painting.

[e] Academic activities include activities such as tutoring or math lab.

SOURCE: U.S. Department of Education, National Center for Education Statistics, National Household Education Surveys Program.

Children of at least one foreign-born parent: Percentage of children ages 0–17 by nativity of child and parents,[a] parent's education, poverty status, and other characteristics, selected years 1994–2008[b]

Characteristic	1994			1998			2002		
	Native child and parents	Foreign-born parent		Native child and parents	Foreign-born parent		Native child and parents	Foreign-born parent	
		Native child	Foreign-born child		Native child	Foreign-born child		Native child	Foreign-born child
Number of children ages 0–17 living with one or both parents (in thousands)	56,338	8,176	2,160	56,237	9,883	2,298	55,264	11,518	2,654
Percent of all children[c]	82	12	3	80	14	3	76	16	4
Gender of child									
Male	—	—	—	—	—	—	51	51	52
Female	—	—	—	—	—	—	49	49	48
Age of child									
Under 1 year	—	—	—	—	—	—	6	7	1
Ages 1–2	—	—	—	—	—	—	11	14	3
Ages 3–5	—	—	—	—	—	—	16	19	10
Ages 6–8	—	—	—	—	—	—	17	17	14
Ages 9–11	—	—	—	—	—	—	18	17	20
Ages 12–14	—	—	—	—	—	—	18	14	25
Ages 15–17	—	—	—	—	—	—	17	11	28
Race and Hispanic origin of child[d]									
White	—	—	—	—	—	—	80	72	70
White, non-Hispanic	—	—	—	—	—	—	73	21	17
Black	—	—	—	—	—	—	17	9	9
Asian	—	—	—	—	—	—	1	17	20
Hispanic[e]	—	—	—	—	—	—	8	55	55
Education of parent[f]									
Less than high school	14	38	48	12	37	45	10	36	41
High school graduate	35	21	20	34	23	22	31	23	21
Some college or associate's degree	28	19	11	30	18	11	32	18	12
Bachelor's degree or greater	23	22	21	23	23	22	27	23	27
Poverty status[g]									
Below 100% poverty	20	28	41	17	25	39	14	20	27
100% poverty and above	80	72	59	83	75	61	—	—	—
100–199% poverty	—	—	—	—	—	—	20	29	33
200% poverty and above	—	—	—	—	—	—	66	51	40
Area of residence									
Central city of MSA[h]	27	43	48	26	43	49	26	41	42
Outside central city, in MSA[h]	48	51	47	51	50	45	54	52	51
Outside metropolitan area	25	6	6	22	7	6	21	7	7
Presence of parents									
Two married parents present[i]	70	82	78	69	82	78	69	81	81
Living with mother only	26	16	19	26	15	20	26	16	16
Living with father only	4	2	3	5	3	3	5	3	4
Presence of adults other than parents									
Other relatives only	17	25	36	17	26	29	17	26	31
Nonrelatives only	5	5	5	6	4	4	6	5	5
Both relatives and nonrelatives	1	1	3	1	1	2	1	2	3
No other relatives or nonrelatives	78	68	56	77	68	65	77	68	61

See notes at end of table.

Children of at least one foreign-born parent: Percentage of children ages 0–17 by nativity of child and parents,[a] parent's education, poverty status, and other characteristics, selected years 1994–2008[b]

Characteristic	2006			2008		
		Foreign-born parent			Foreign-born parent	
	Native child and parents	Native child	Foreign-born child	Native child and parents	Native child	Foreign-born child
Number of children ages 0–17 living with one or both parents (in thousands)	54,976	12,706	2,599	54,993	13,755	2,538
Percent of all children[c]	75	17	4	74	19	3
Gender of child						
Male	51	52	52	51	51	52
Female	49	49	49	49	49	48
Age of child						
Under 1 year	6	7	1	6	8	1
Ages 1–2	11	15	4	11	14	4
Ages 3–5	16	19	10	16	19	10
Ages 6–8	16	16	15	16	17	14
Ages 9–11	16	16	20	16	15	20
Ages 12–14	17	15	22	17	14	24
Ages 15–17	18	12	28	18	13	27
Race and Hispanic origin of child[d]						
White-alone	79	72	68	79	72	66
White-alone, non-Hispanic	70	18	16	69	18	15
White-alone or in combination with one or more races	82	75	69	82	75	66
Black-alone	16	9	10	16	9	10
Black-alone or in combination with one or more races	18	9	11	18	10	10
Asian-alone	1	15	19	1	14	22
Asian-alone or in combination with one or more races	1	17	19	1	16	22
Hispanic[e]	10	57	55	10	58	53
All remaining single races and all race combinations	4	5	3	5	5	2
Education of parent[f]						
Less than high school	10	33	39	7	26	29
High school graduate	30	24	24	24	25	25
Some college or associate's degree	32	19	11	32	19	12
Bachelor's degree or greater	29	25	27	38	30	34

See notes at end of table.

Children of at least one foreign-born parent: Percentage of children ages 0–17 by nativity of child and parents,[a] parent's education, poverty status, and other characteristics, selected years 1994–2008[b]

Characteristic	2006			2008		
		Foreign-born parent			Foreign-born parent	
	Native child and parents	Native child	Foreign-born child	Native child and parents	Native child	Foreign-born child
Poverty status[g]						
Below 100% poverty	15	20	30	16	21	30
100–199% poverty	19	28	31	19	29	28
200% poverty and above	65	52	39	66	50	42
Presence of parents						
Two married parents present[i]	68	82	80	70	84	79
Living with mother only	27	15	16	26	14	19
Living with father only	5	3	3	4	2	2
Presence of adults other than parents						
Other relatives only	17	25	31	19	25	27
Nonrelatives only	6	4	3	4	3	3
Both relatives and nonrelatives	1	2	1	1	1	1
No other relatives or nonrelatives	75	70	64	76	72	68

— Not available.

[a] Native parents means that all of the parents that the child lives with are native-born, while foreign-born means that at least one of the child's parents is foreign-born. Anyone with U.S. citizenship at birth is considered native, which includes persons born in the United States and in U.S. outlying areas, and persons born abroad with at least one American parent.

[b] Beginning with March 2001, data are from the Expanded Current Population Survey Sample and use population controls based on Census 2000.

[c] The percent of all children is of all children under 18, including those living with no parents and excluding children in group quarters.

[d] For race and Hispanic-origin data in this table: From 1994 to 2002, following the 1977 OMB standards for collecting and presenting data on race, the Current Population Survey (CPS) asked respondents to choose one race from the following: White, Black, American Indian or Alaskan Native, or Asian or Pacific Islander. The Census Bureau also offered an "Other" category. Beginning in 2003, following the 1997 OMB standards for collecting and presenting data on race, the CPS asked respondents to choose one or more races from the following: White, Black or African American, Asian, American Indian or Alaska Native, or Native Hawaiian or Other Pacific Islander. People who responded to the question on race by indicating only one race are referred to as the race-alone population. The use of the race-alone population in this table does not imply that it is the preferred method of presenting or analyzing data. Prior to 2004, "Asian" refers to Asians and Pacific Islanders; beginning in 2004, "Asian" refers to Asians alone. Data from 2004 onward are not directly comparable with data from earlier years. Data on race and Hispanic origin are collected separately. Persons of Hispanic origin may be of any race.

[e] Persons of Hispanic origin may be of any race.

[f] Prior to 2007, this category reflected the education of the parent identified by the parent pointer. Beginning in 2007, it shows the education of the parent with the highest educational attainment if the child lives with two parents.

[g] The poverty status groups are derived from the ratio of the family's income to the family's poverty threshold. Below 100 percent of poverty refers to children living below the poverty line, 100–199 percent of poverty refers to children living in low-income households, and 200 percent of poverty and above refers to children living in medium- and high-income households. See ECON1.B for the income levels.

[h] An MSA is a Metropolitan Statistical Area. The U.S. Office of Management and Budget (OMB) defines metropolitan areas (MAs) according to published standards that are applied to Census Bureau data. The 1990 standards provide that each newly qualifying MSA must include at least: (1) one city with 50,000 or more inhabitants, or (2) a Census Bureau-defined urbanized area (of at least 50,000 inhabitants) and a total metropolitan population of at least 100,000 (75,000 in New England). MSA information is discontinued for 2003 and later due to discontinuity in the metro definitions in the Current Population Survey.

[i] Prior to 2007, this category included only married parents. Beginning in 2007, all children with two parents are included, regardless of whether the parents are married. Prior to 2007, Current Population Survey (CPS) data identified only one parent on the child's record. This meant that a second parent could only be identified if they were married to the first parent. In 2007, a second parent identifier was added to CPS. This permits identification of two coresident parents, even if the parents are not married to each other. In this table, "two parents" reflects all children who have both a mother and father identified in the household, including biological, step, and adoptive parents. Before 2007, "mother only" and "father only" included some children who lived with a parent who was living with the other parent of the child, but was not married to them. Beginning in 2007, "mother only" and "father only" refer to children for whom only one parent has been identified, whether biological, step, or adoptive.

SOURCE: U.S. Census Bureau. Current Population Survey, Annual Social and Economic Supplements.

Language spoken at home and difficulty speaking English: Number of children ages 5–17 who speak a language other than English at home by language spoken and ability to speak English, and the percentages of those speaking a language other than English at home and those with difficulty speaking English[a] by selected characteristics, selected years 1979–2007

Characteristic	Current Population Survey					American Community Survey							
	1979	1989	1992	1995[b]	1999[b]	2000	2001	2002	2003	2004	2005	2006	2007
Children who speak another language at home													
Number (in thousands)	3,826	5,177	6,264	6,657	8,815	9,526	9,764	9,793	9,854	9,977	10,507	10,862	10,918
Language spoken[c] (in thousands)													
Spanish	2,529	3,550	4,314	5,037	6,339	6,533	6,794	6,859	7,021	7,103	7,530	7,805	7,872
Other Indo-European	622	727	505	514	433	1,535	1,489	1,480	1,398	1,440	1,462	1,458	1,479
Asian or Pacific Island languages	160	551	978	504	1,177	1,147	1,152	1,127	1,110	1,116	1,140	1,177	1,173
Other languages	515	349	467	602	865	311	329	327	324	318	375	422	394
Ability to speak English (in thousands)													
Very well	2,576	3,369	4,104	4,226	6,185	6,640	6,920	7,012	6,973	7,202	7,701	8,095	8,170
Well	783	1,144	1,436	1,538	1,743	1,754	1,723	1,709	1,852	1,774	1,818	1,792	1,841
Not well	362	568	627	749	758	926	923	906	869	828	819	817	760
Not at all	105	96	97	143	130	206	198	166	159	173	169	158	147
Percentage of school-aged children	8.5	12.3	13.2	14.1	16.7	18.1	18.5	18.5	18.6	18.9	19.9	20.3	20.5
Poverty status[d]													
Below 100% poverty	—	—	—	—	—	28.4	28.9	29.1	28.4	28.2	30.2	30.2	30.5
100% poverty and above	—	—	—	—	—	16.1	16.5	16.4	16.7	16.9	17.7	18.4	18.6
Nativity status[e]													
Native child and parents	—	—	—	—	—	5.0	5.1	4.8	4.7	4.6	5.0	5.1	4.9
Foreign-born parent	—	—	—	—	—	72.0	71.7	71.0	71.0	71.0	71.8	72.1	72.1
Native child	—	—	—	—	—	66.9	66.4	65.7	66.2	66.4	67.1	67.8	68.0
Foreign-born child	—	—	—	—	—	87.9	88.7	88.6	87.5	87.5	88.6	88.2	88.2
Family structure													
Two married parents	—	—	—	—	—	18.5	19.0	19.1	19.5	19.8	20.4	21.2	21.4
Mother only	—	—	—	—	—	15.8	16.5	16.5	16.2	16.4	17.9	18.0	18.2
Father only	—	—	—	—	—	19.3	18.7	17.6	18.1	18.5	21.1	20.9	20.7
No parent	—	—	—	—	—	20.1	19.9	20.1	18.3	18.4	20.4	20.1	19.7
Education of parent[f]													
Less than high school graduate	—	—	—	—	—	47.4	48.1	51.0	53.5	53.2	55.3	56.1	57.7
High school graduate	—	—	—	—	—	15.5	16.6	17.2	18.0	18.8	20.4	22.0	22.6
Some college	—	—	—	—	—	12.4	12.8	12.4	12.6	12.6	13.4	13.7	13.5
Bachelor's degree or higher	—	—	—	—	—	12.9	12.8	12.6	12.6	12.8	13.2	13.6	13.6

See notes at end of table.

Language spoken at home and difficulty speaking English: Number of children ages 5–17 who speak a language other than English at home by language spoken and ability to speak English, and the percentages of those speaking a language other than English at home and those with difficulty speaking English[a] by selected characteristics, selected years 1979–2007

Characteristic	Current Population Survey					American Community Survey							
	1979	1989	1992	1995[b]	1999[b]	2000	2001	2002	2003	2004	2005	2006	2007
Children who speak another language at home—continued													
Race and Hispanic origin[g]													
White	8.7	12.0	12.6	13.3	16.4	—	—	—	—	—	—	—	—
White-alone	—	—	—	—	—	14.4	14.4	14.1	14.5	14.5	14.7	14.8	15.2
White, non-Hispanic	3.2	3.3	3.3	3.6	3.9	—	—	—	—	—	—	—	—
White-alone, non-Hispanic	—	—	—	—	—	5.7	5.7	5.6	5.1	5.3	5.6	5.7	5.7
Black	1.9	3.1	4.3	4.2	5.8	—	—	—	—	—	—	—	—
Black-alone	—	—	—	—	—	5.1	5.1	5.1	5.8	5.4	6.0	6.1	6.0
Black, non-Hispanic	1.3	2.3	3.7	3.0	4.5	—	—	—	—	—	—	—	—
Black-alone, non-Hispanic	—	—	—	—	—	4.4	4.5	4.5	5.0	4.7	5.3	5.5	5.3
American Indian or Alaskan Native	—	16.6	13.6	17.8	20.4	—	—	—	—	—	—	—	—
American Indian or Alaska Native-alone	—	—	—	—	—	20.5	24.2	22.3	20.7	17.0	20.0	22.4	20.0
Asian or Pacific Islander[h]	—	62.2	65.2	60.2	60.4	—	—	—	—	—	—	—	—
Asian-alone	—	—	—	—	—	67.1	66.6	64.4	63.5	63.4	64.0	63.6	63.7
Native Hawaiian or Other Pacific Islander-alone	—	—	—	—	—	29.8	36.9	31.5	26.0	32.6	29.8	32.9	34.7
Other	44.5	43.6	51.7	64.0	—	—	—	—	—	—	—	—	—
Some other race alone	—	—	—	—	—	75.4	72.6	73.6	73.0	74.1	74.5	74.8	74.6
Two or more races	—	—	—	—	—	17.6	17.5	16.8	14.8	13.4	14.4	14.3	14.0
Hispanic (of any race)[i]	75.1	69.4	71.5	73.8	70.9	68.6	68.7	67.8	67.6	67.4	68.9	68.9	68.4
Region[j]													
Northeast	10.5	12.8	14.9	15.2	17.7	19.1	18.7	18.4	19.0	19.0	19.7	20.1	20.3
South	6.8	10.6	10.5	11.7	14.3	14.6	15.1	15.4	15.7	15.6	16.8	17.3	17.6
Midwest	3.7	4.7	5.3	5.9	7.5	9.5	9.9	10.0	9.9	10.5	10.8	11.1	11.4
West	17.0	23.6	25.3	26.4	28.8	31.0	31.1	31.3	31.0	31.4	33.0	33.6	33.6
Living in linguistically isolated household[k]													
Number (in thousands)	—	—	—	—	—	2,576	2,749	2,748	2,950	2,926	2,952	2,976	3,046
Percentage of school-aged children	—	—	—	—	—	4.9	5.2	5.2	5.6	5.5	5.6	5.6	5.7

See notes at end of table.

Language spoken at home and difficulty speaking English: Number of children ages 5–17 who speak a language other than English at home by language spoken and ability to speak English, and the percentages of those speaking a language other than English at home and those with difficulty speaking English[a] by selected characteristics, selected years 1979–2007

Characteristic	Current Population Survey					American Community Survey							
	1979	1989	1992	1995[b]	1999[b]	2000	2001	2002	2003	2004	2005	2006	2007
Children who speak another language at home and have difficulty speaking English													
Number (in thousands)	1,250	1,808	2,160	2,431	2,630	2,886	2,844	2,780	2,881	2,774	2,806	2,767	2,748
Percentage of school-aged children	2.8	4.3	4.6	5.2	5.0	5.5	5.4	5.3	5.4	5.2	5.3	5.2	5.2
Language spoken[c]													
Spanish	2.1	3.1	3.3	4.3	4.3	4.0	3.9	3.8	4.1	3.9	4.0	3.9	3.9
Other Indo-European	0.2	0.4	0.2	0.2	0.2	0.6	0.6	0.6	0.6	0.6	0.6	0.5	0.5
Asian or Pacific Island languages	0.1	0.6	0.8	0.4	0.6	0.7	0.7	0.6	0.6	0.6	0.6	0.6	0.6
Other languages	0.4	0.2	0.3	0.3	0.5	0.1	0.1	0.1	0.1	0.1	0.1	0.1	0.1
Poverty status[d]													
Below 100% poverty	—	—	—	—	—	11.3	11.1	10.4	10.8	10.0	10.2	9.8	9.7
100% poverty and above	—	—	—	—	—	4.3	4.3	4.2	4.4	4.2	4.3	4.2	4.2
Nativity status[e]													
Native child and parents	—	—	—	—	—	1.3	1.2	1.0	1.1	1.2	1.1	1.0	1.0
Foreign-born parent	—	—	—	—	—	21.8	21.6	20.8	21.2	19.4	19.4	18.7	18.4
Native child	—	—	—	—	—	17.2	16.7	16.1	16.5	15.1	15.1	14.6	14.6
Foreign-born child	—	—	—	—	—	36.0	36.7	36.3	37.1	34.6	34.6	34.0	33.1
Family structure													
Two married parents	—	—	—	—	—	5.4	5.5	5.4	5.6	5.4	5.4	5.3	5.3
Mother only	—	—	—	—	—	4.3	4.2	4.1	4.4	4.2	4.2	4.0	4.0
Father only	—	—	—	—	—	6.8	6.4	6.4	6.0	6.1	6.6	6.3	6.1
No parent	—	—	—	—	—	8.6	7.5	7.5	6.9	7.2	7.5	7.0	7.0
Education of parent[f]													
Less than high school graduate	—	—	—	—	—	17.8	17.0	18.2	20.3	18.6	18.7	18.4	18.7
High school graduate	—	—	—	—	—	4.4	4.6	4.5	5.1	4.9	5.2	5.4	5.5
Some college	—	—	—	—	—	3.0	3.1	2.9	2.8	2.8	2.9	2.6	2.6
Bachelor's degree or higher	—	—	—	—	—	2.8	2.9	2.7	2.8	2.8	2.6	2.6	2.5
Race and Hispanic origin[g]													
White	2.8	4.2	4.3	4.9	5.2	—	—	—	—	—	—	—	—
White-alone	—	—	—	—	—	4.4	4.2	3.8	4.3	4.0	3.9	3.9	3.9
White, non-Hispanic	0.5	0.7	0.6	0.7	1.0	—	—	—	—	—	—	—	—
White-alone, non-Hispanic	—	—	—	—	—	1.3	1.4	1.3	1.4	1.3	1.3	1.2	1.2
Black	0.5	0.7	1.5	1.5	1.3	—	—	—	—	—	—	—	—
Black-alone	—	—	—	—	—	1.4	1.2	1.3	1.6	1.4	1.4	1.5	1.4
Black, non-Hispanic	0.3	0.5	1.2	0.9	1.0	—	—	—	—	—	—	—	—
Black-alone, non-Hispanic	—	—	—	—	—	1.2	1.0	1.2	1.3	1.2	1.3	1.3	1.2
American Indian or Alaskan Native	—	4.5	1.4	3.8	8.2	—	—	—	—	—	—	—	—
American Indian or Alaska Native-alone	—	—	—	—	—	4.6	4.4	4.4	3.8	3.1	4.1	4.0	4.2
Asian or Pacific Islander[h]	—	24.5	25	19.4	13.9	—	—	—	—	—	—	—	—
Asian-alone	—	—	—	—	—	19.8	20.5	18.7	17.5	16.9	17.2	16.5	16.4
Native Hawaiian or Other Pacific Islander-alone	—	—	—	—	—	10.3	8.4	6.3	6.2	7.1	7.3	6.9	6.9
Other	19.5	9.0	18.1	27.1	—	—	—	—	—	—	—	—	—
Some other race alone	—	—	—	—	—	24.7	22.1	23.8	22.0	22.2	20.7	18.9	18.7
Two or more races	—	—	—	—	—	4.2	3.9	3.9	3.2	2.5	2.6	2.7	2.6
Hispanic (of any race)[i]	28.7	26.7	27.9	30.9	23.4	22.8	21.3	20.5	20.9	19.7	19.4	18.5	18.1

See notes at end of table.

Language spoken at home and difficulty speaking English: Number of children ages 5–17 who speak a language other than English at home by language spoken and ability to speak English, and the percentages of those speaking a language other than English at home and those with difficulty speaking English[a] by selected characteristics, selected years 1979–2007

Characteristic	Current Population Survey					American Community Survey							
	1979	1989	1992	1995[b]	1999[b]	2000	2001	2002	2003	2004	2005	2006	2007
Children who speak another language at home and have difficulty speaking English—continued													
Region[j]													
Northeast	2.9	4.5	4.8	5.0	4.4	5.0	5.1	5.0	5.5	4.8	4.5	4.4	4.3
South	2.2	3.8	3.3	3.4	3.6	4.4	4.1	4.3	4.7	4.4	4.6	4.6	4.7
Midwest	1.1	1.2	1.5	2.3	2.0	2.8	2.9	3.0	3.2	3.2	3.1	3.0	3.0
West	6.5	8.6	9.8	11.4	10.5	10.0	9.7	9.0	8.7	8.8	8.9	8.6	8.5

— Not available.

[a] Respondents were asked if the children in the household spoke a language other than English at home and how well they could speak English. Categories used for reporting were "Very well," "Well," "Not well," and "Not at all." All those reported to speak English less than "Very well" were considered to have difficulty speaking English based on an evaluation of the English-speaking ability of a sample of the children in the 1980s.

[b] Numbers from the Current Population Survey (CPS) in 1995 and after may reflect changes in the survey because of newly instituted computer-assisted interviewing techniques and/or because of the change in the population controls to the 1990 Census-based estimates, with adjustments.

[c] In the 1979 CPS questionnaire, the language spoken at home variable had 10 specific categories: Chinese, Filipino, French, German, Greek, Italian, Polish, Portuguese, Spanish, and Other. In the 1989 CPS questionnaire, the language spoken at home variable had 34 specific categories. In the 1992 to 1999 CPS questionnaires, the language spoken at home variable had 4 categories: Spanish, Asian, Other European, and Other. In the American Community Survey (ACS), respondents are asked the question, and their response is recorded in an open-ended format.

[d] Limited to the population for whom poverty status is determined.

[e] Native parents means that all of the parents that the child lives with are native-born, while foreign-born means that at least one of the child's parents is foreign-born. Anyone with U.S. citizenship at birth is considered native, which includes persons born in the United States and in U.S. outlying areas, and persons born abroad with at least one American parent.

[f] Highest level of educational attainment is shown for either parent.

[g] For race and Hispanic-origin data in this table: From 1979 to 1999, following the 1977 OMB standards for collecting and presenting data on race, the CPS asked respondents to choose one race from the following: White, Black, American Indian or Alaskan Native, or Asian or Pacific Islander. The Census Bureau also offered an "Other" category. Beginning in 2000, following the 1997 OMB standards for collecting and presenting data on race, the ACS asked respondents to choose one or more races from the following: White, Black or African American, Asian, American Indian or Alaska Native, or Native Hawaiian or Other Pacific Islander. In addition, a "Some other race" category was included with OMB approval. Those who chose more than one race were classified as "Two or more races." Except for those who were "Two or more races," all race groups discussed in this table from 2000 onward refer to people who indicated only one racial identity within the racial categories presented. People who responded to the question on race by indicating only one race are referred to as the race-alone population. The use of the race-alone population in this table does not imply that it is the preferred method of presenting or analyzing data. Prior to 2000, "Asian" refers to Asians and Pacific Islanders; beginning in 2000, "Asian" refers to Asians alone. Data from 2000 onward are not directly comparable with data from earlier years. Data on race and Hispanic origin are collected separately. Persons of Hispanic origin may be of any race.

[h] In 2000, the "Asian or Pacific Islander" category was separated into two categories, "Asian" and "Native Hawaiian or Other Pacific Islander." Because of this change, race data from 2000 to the present are not directly comparable with data from earlier years.

[i] Persons of Hispanic origin may be of any race.

[j] Regions: Northeast includes CT, MA, ME, NH, NJ, NY, PA, RI, and VT. South includes AL, AR, DC, DE, FL, GA, KY, LA, MD, MS, NC, OK, SC, TN, TX, VA, and WV. Midwest includes IA, IL, IN, KS, MI, MN, MO, ND, NE, OH, SD, and WI. West includes AK, AZ, CA, CO, HI, ID, MT, NM, NV, OR, UT, WA, and WY.

[k] A linguistically isolated household is one in which no person age 14 or over speaks English at least "Very well." That is, no person age 14 or over speaks only English at home, or speaks another language at home and speaks English "Very well."

NOTE: All nonresponses to the CPS language questions are excluded from the tabulations, except in 1999. In 1999, imputations were instituted for nonresponse on the language items.

SOURCE: U.S. Census Bureau, October (1992, 1995, and 1999) and November (1979 and 1989) Current Population Surveys, and 2000–2007 American Community Survey.

Adolescent births: Birth rates by mother's age and race and Hispanic origin,ª selected years 1980–2007

(Live births per 1,000 females in specified age group)

Characteristic	1980	1985	1990	1995	2000	2003	2004	2005	2006	2007
All races										
Ages 10–14	1.1	1.2	1.4	1.3	0.9	0.6	0.7	0.7	0.6	0.6
Ages 15–17	32.5	31.0	37.5	35.5	26.9	22.4	22.1	21.4	22.0	22.2
Ages 18–19	82.1	79.6	88.6	87.7	78.1	70.7	70.0	69.9	73.0	73.9
Ages 15–19	53.0	51.0	59.9	56.0	47.7	41.6	41.2	40.5	41.9	42.5
White, total										
Ages 10–14	0.6	0.6	0.7	0.8	0.6	0.5	0.5	0.5	0.5	—
Ages 15–17	25.5	24.4	29.5	29.6	23.3	19.8	19.5	18.9	19.4	—
Ages 18–19	73.2	70.4	78.0	80.2	72.3	66.2	65.0	64.7	67.5	—
Ages 15–19	45.4	43.3	50.8	49.5	43.2	38.3	37.7	37.0	38.2	—
White, non-Hispanic										
Ages 10–14	0.4	—	0.5	0.4	0.3	0.2	0.2	0.2	0.2	0.2
Ages 15–17	22.4	—	23.2	22.0	15.8	12.4	12.0	11.5	11.8	11.8
Ages 18–19	67.7	—	66.6	66.2	57.5	50.0	48.7	48.0	49.3	50.5
Ages 15–19	41.2	—	42.5	39.3	32.6	27.4	26.7	25.9	26.6	27.2
Black, total										
Ages 10–14	4.3	4.5	4.9	4.1	2.3	1.6	1.6	1.7	1.5	—
Ages 15–17	72.5	69.3	82.3	68.5	49.0	38.2	37.2	35.5	36.6	—
Ages 18–19	135.1	132.4	152.9	135.0	118.8	103.7	104.4	104.9	110.2	—
Ages 15–19	97.8	95.4	112.8	94.4	77.4	63.8	63.3	62.0	64.6	—
Black, non-Hispanic										
Ages 10–14	4.6	—	5.0	4.2	2.4	1.6	1.6	1.7	1.6	1.5
Ages 15–17	77.2	—	84.9	70.4	50.1	38.7	37.1	34.9	36.2	35.8
Ages 18–19	146.5	—	157.5	139.2	121.9	105.3	103.9	103.0	108.4	109.3
Ages 15–19	105.1	—	116.2	97.2	79.2	64.7	63.1	60.9	63.7	64.3
American Indian or Alaskan Native										
Ages 10–14	1.9	1.7	1.6	1.6	1.1	1.0	0.9	0.9	0.9	0.9
Ages 15–17	51.5	47.7	48.5	44.6	34.1	30.6	30.0	30.5	30.7	31.7
Ages 18–19	129.5	124.1	129.3	122.2	97.1	87.3	87.0	87.6	93.0	101.3
Ages 15–19	82.2	79.2	81.1	72.9	58.3	53.1	52.5	52.7	55.0	59.0
Asian or Pacific Islander										
Ages 10–14	0.3	0.4	0.7	0.7	0.3	0.2	0.2	0.2	0.2	0.2
Ages 15–17	12.0	12.5	16.0	15.6	11.6	8.8	8.9	8.2	8.8	8.4
Ages 18–19	46.2	40.8	40.2	40.1	32.6	29.8	29.6	30.1	29.5	30.7
Ages 15–19	26.2	23.8	26.4	25.5	20.5	17.4	17.3	17.0	17.0	17.3

See notes at end of table.

Adolescent births: Birth rates by mother's age and race and Hispanic origin,[a] selected years 1980–2007

(Live births per 1,000 females in specified age group)

Characteristic	1980	1985	1990	1995	2000	2003	2004	2005	2006	2007
Hispanic[b]										
Ages 10–14	1.7	—	2.4	2.6	1.7	1.3	1.3	1.3	1.3	1.2
Ages 15–17	52.1	—	65.9	68.3	55.5	49.7	49.7	48.5	47.9	47.8
Ages 18–19	126.9	—	147.7	145.4	132.6	132.0	133.5	134.6	139.7	137.1
Ages 15–19	82.2	—	100.3	99.3	87.3	82.3	82.6	81.7	83.0	81.7

— Not available.

[a] The 1977 OMB Standards for Data on Race and Ethnicity were used to classify persons into one of the following four racial groups: White, Black, American Indian or Alaskan Native, or Asian or Pacific Islander. The following states reported multiple-race data in 2003, following the revised 1997 OMB standards: CT, HI, OH (for December only), PA, UT, and WA. In 2004, the following states began to report multiple-race data: FL, ID, KY, MI, MN, NH, NY State (excluding New York City), SC, and TN. Multiple-race data were reported by 19 states in 2005: FL, ID, KS, KY, NE, NH, NY State (excluding New York City), PA, SC, TN, TX, VT (beginning July 1), WA, CA, HI, MI (for births at selected facilities only), MN, OH, and UT. In 2006, 23 states reported multiple-race data: CA, DE, FL, ID, KS, KY, NE, NH, NY State (excluding New York City), ND, OH, PA, SC, SD, TN, TX, VT, WA, WY, HI, MI (for births at selected facilities only), MN, and UT. In 2007, 27 states reported multiple-race data: CA, CO, DE, FL, GA (partial year only), ID, IN, IA, KS, KY, MI (for births at most facilities), NE, NH, NY State (excluding New York City), ND, OH, PA, SC, SD, TN, TX, VT, WA, WY, HI, MN, and UT. The multiple-race data for these states were bridged to the single-race categories of the 1977 OMB standards for comparability with other states. In addition, note that data on race and Hispanic origin are collected and reported separately.

[b] Persons of Hispanic origin may be of any race. Trends for the Hispanic population are affected by an expansion in the number of registration areas that included an item on Hispanic origin on the birth certificate. The number of states in the reporting area increased from 22 in 1980 to 23 and the District of Columbia (DC) in 1983–1987, 30 and DC in 1988, 47 and DC in 1989, 48 and DC in 1990, 49 and DC in 1991–1992, and 50 and DC in 1993. Rates in 1981–1988 were not calculated for Hispanics, Black, non-Hispanics, and White, non-Hispanics because estimates for these populations were not available. Recent declines in teenage birth rates parallel but outpace the reductions in birth rates for unmarried teenagers (FAM2.A). Birth rates for married teenagers fell sharply between 1990 and 2004, but relatively few teenagers are married.

NOTE: Data for 2007 are preliminary.

SOURCE: National Center for Health Statistics, National Vital Statistics System. Martin, J.A., Hamilton, B.E., Sutton, P.D., Ventura, S.J., Menacker, F., Kirmeyer S., and Mathews, T.J. (2009). Births: Final data for 2006. *National Vital Statistics Reports, 57*(7). Hyattsville, MD: National Center for Health Statistics. Hamilton, B.E., Martin, J.A., and Ventura, S.J. (2009). Births: Preliminary Data for 2007. *National Vital Statistics Reports 57*(12). Hyattsville, MD: National Center for Health Statistics.

| Table FAM7.A | Child maltreatment: Rate of substantiated maltreatment reports of children ages 0–17 by selected characteristics, selected years 1998–2007 |

(Substantiated maltreatment reports per 1,000 children ages 0–17)

Characteristic	1998	2000	2002	2003	2004	2005	2006	2007[a]
Total	12.9	12.2	12.3	12.2	12.0	12.1	12.1	10.6
Gender								
Male	—	11.4	11.5	11.5	11.3	11.3	11.4	10.0
Female	—	12.9	13.0	12.9	12.7	12.7	12.7	11.2
Race and Hispanic origin[b]								
White, non-Hispanic	—	10.7	10.9	11.0	10.9	10.8	10.7	9.1
Black, non-Hispanic	—	21.5	20.8	20.7	20.1	19.5	19.8	16.7
American Indian or Alaska Native	—	20.5	21.8	21.5	16.5	16.5	15.9	14.1
Asian	—	2.0	3.2	3.0	2.9	2.5	2.5	2.4
Native Hawaiian or Other Pacific Islander	—	21.7	18.6	18.6	18.0	16.1	14.3	13.6
Two or more races	—	12.3	13	12.9	14.5	15.0	15.4	14.0
Hispanic	—	10.2	8.2	10.2	10.1	10.7	10.8	10.3
Age								
Ages 0–3	—	15.7	16.1	16.1	16.0	16.5	16.8	15.0
Age <1	—	—	21.6	21.7	22.0	23.4	23.9	22.0
Ages 1–3	—	—	14.2	14.2	13.9	14.1	14.2	12.6
Ages 4–7	—	13.4	13.6	13.7	13.5	13.5	13.5	11.6
Ages 8–11	—	11.8	11.9	11.6	11.1	10.9	10.8	9.4
Ages 12–15	—	10.4	10.7	10.6	10.3	10.2	10.2	8.7
Ages 16–17	—	5.8	6.0	6.0	6.1	6.2	6.3	5.4

— Not available.

[a] Data from 2007 are not directly comparable with prior years as differences may be partially attributed to changes in one state's procedures for determination of maltreatment. Other reasons include the increase in children who received an "other" disposition, the decrease in the percentage of children who received a substantiated or indicated disposition, and the decrease in the number of children who received an investigation or assessment.

[b] The revised 1997 OMB standards were used for Race and Hispanic origin, where respondents could choose one or more of five racial groups: White, Black or African American, Asian, Native Hawaiian or Other Pacific Islander, or American Indian or Alaska Native. Those reporting more than one race were classified as "Two or more races." In addition, note that data on race and Hispanic origin are collected separately, but are combined for reporting. Persons of Hispanic origin may be of any race.

NOTE: The count of child victims is based on the number of investigations by Child Protective Services that found the child to be a victim of one or more types of maltreatment. The count of victims is, therefore, a report-based count and is a "duplicated count," since an individual child may have been maltreated more than once. Substantiated maltreatment includes the dispositions of substantiated, indicated, or alternative response-victim. Rates are based on the number of states submitting data to National Child Abuse and Neglect Data System (NCANDS) each year; states include the District of Columbia and Puerto Rico. The overall rate of maltreatment is based on the following number of states for each year: 51 in 1998, 50 in 1999, 50 in 2000, 51 in 2001, 51 in 2002, 51 in 2003, 50 in 2004, 52 in 2005, 51 in 2006, and 50 in 2007. The number of states reporting on gender for the years of 2000–2007 was 50 in 2000, 51 in 2001, 51 in 2002, 51 in 2003, 50 in 2004, 51 in 2005, 51 in 2006, and 50 in 2007. The number of states reporting on race and Hispanic origin for the years 2000–2007 was 48 in 2000, 49 in 2001, 50 in 2002, 50 in 2003, 49 in 2004, 50 in 2005, 49 in 2006, and 46 in 2007. The number of states reporting on age for the years of 2000–2007 was 50 in 2000, 51 in 2001, 51 in 2002, 51 in 2003, 50 in 2004, 51 in 2005, 51 in 2006, and 50 in 2007. Rates from 1998–1999 are based on aggregated data submitted by states; rates from 2000–2007 are based on case-level data submitted by the states. The reporting year changed in 2003 from the calendar year to the Federal fiscal year. Additional technical notes are available in the annual reports entitled *Child Maltreatment*. These reports are available on the Internet at http://www.acf.hhs.gov/programs/cb/stats_research/index.htm#can.

SOURCE: Administration for Children and Families, National Child Abuse and Neglect Data System.

| | Table FAM7.B | Child maltreatment: Percentage of substantiated maltreatment reports of children ages 0–17 by maltreatment type and age, 2007 |

Characteristic	Physical abuse	Neglect	Medical neglect	Sexual abuse	Psychological abuse	Other abuse	Unknown
Overall	16.2	71.0	2.1	9.5	6.6	8.3	0.1
Age							
Ages 0–3	13.3	79.3	2.6	1.9	5.4	9.3	0.1
Age <1	16.2	78.0	3.2	0.5	4.0	9.9	0.1
Ages 1–3	11.5	80.0	2.2	2.8	6.2	8.9	0.1
Ages 4–7	15.5	71.7	1.8	9.0	6.8	8.0	0.1
Ages 8–11	16.7	68.0	2.0	11.7	7.8	7.9	0.1
Ages 12–15	19.7	61.9	2.0	18.0	7.2	7.5	0.1
Ages 16–17	21.4	62.0	1.9	17.4	6.5	7.7	0.1
Unknown or missing	24.3	59.7	1.0	11.5	6.0	5.1	0.1

NOTE: Based on data from 47 states. The count of child victims is based on the number of investigations by Child Protective Services that found the child to be a victim of one or more types of maltreatment. The count of victims is, therefore, a report-based count and is a "duplicated count," since an individual child may have been maltreated more than once. Substantiated maltreatment includes the dispositions of substantiated, indicated, or alternative response-victim. States vary in their definition of abuse and neglect. Rows total more than 100 percent since a single child may be the victim of multiple kinds of maltreatment. The category of unknown includes missing children and children older than 17 years.

SOURCE: Administration for Children and Families, National Child Abuse and Neglect Data System.

Child poverty: Percentage of all children and related children[a] ages 0–17 living below selected poverty levels by selected characteristics, selected years 1980–2007

Characteristic	1980	1985	1990	1995	2000	2003	2004	2005	2006	2007
All children[b]	18.3	20.7	20.6	20.8	16.2	17.6	17.8	17.6	17.4	18.0
Gender										
Male	18.1	20.3	20.5	20.4	16.0	17.7	17.8	17.4	17.2	17.9
Female	18.6	21.1	20.8	21.2	16.3	17.6	17.8	17.8	17.6	18.1
Age										
Ages 0–5	20.7	23.0	23.6	24.1	18.3	20.1	20.3	20.2	20.3	21.1
Ages 6–17	17.3	19.5	19.0	19.1	15.2	16.4	16.6	16.3	16.0	16.5
Race and Hispanic origin[c]										
White, non-Hispanic	11.8	12.8	12.3	11.2	9.1	—	—	—	—	—
White-alone, non-Hispanic	—	—	—	—	—	9.8	10.5	10.0	10.0	10.1
Black	42.3	43.6	44.8	41.9	31.2	—	—	—	—	—
Black-alone	—	—	—	—	—	34.1	33.7	34.5	33.4	34.5
Hispanic[d]	33.2	40.3	38.4	40.0	28.4	29.7	28.9	28.3	26.9	28.6
Region[e]										
Northeast	16.3	18.5	18.4	19.0	14.5	15.3	15.7	15.5	15.7	16.1
South	22.5	22.8	23.8	23.5	18.4	20.3	19.6	19.7	19.4	20.8
Midwest	16.3	20.7	18.8	16.9	13.1	14.9	16.8	15.9	16.3	16.6
West	16.1	19.3	19.8	22.1	16.9	17.8	17.5	17.5	16.6	16.3
Related children[a]										
Children in all families, total	17.9	20.1	19.9	20.2	15.6	17.2	17.3	17.1	16.9	17.6
Related children ages 0–5	20.3	22.6	23.0	23.7	17.8	19.8	20.0	20.0	20.0	20.8
Related children ages 6–17	16.8	18.8	18.2	18.3	14.5	15.9	16.0	15.7	15.4	16.0
White, non-Hispanic	11.3	12.3	11.6	10.6	8.5	—	—	—	—	—
White-alone, non-Hispanic	—	—	—	—	—	9.3	9.9	9.5	9.5	9.7
Black	42.1	43.1	44.2	41.5	30.9	—	—	—	—	—
Black-alone	—	—	—	—	—	33.6	33.4	34.2	33.0	34.3
Hispanic[d]	33.0	39.6	37.7	39.3	27.6	29.5	28.6	27.7	26.6	28.3
Children in married-couple families, total	—	—	10.2	10.0	8.0	8.6	9.0	8.5	8.1	8.5
Related children ages 0–5	—	—	11.6	11.1	8.7	9.6	10.1	9.9	9.4	9.5
Related children ages 6–17	—	—	9.5	9.4	7.6	8.1	8.4	7.7	7.5	8.0
White, non-Hispanic	—	—	6.8	5.9	4.7	—	—	—	—	—
White-alone, non-Hispanic	—	—	—	—	—	4.8	5.2	4.5	4.3	4.7
Black	—	—	18.1	12.8	8.8	—	—	—	—	—
Black-alone	—	—	—	—	—	11.2	12.6	12.5	12.0	11.0
Hispanic[d]	—	—	26.5	28.4	20.7	21.4	20.6	20.1	18.5	19.2
Children in female-householder families, no husband present, total	50.8	53.6	53.4	50.3	40.1	41.8	41.9	42.8	42.1	43.0
Related children ages 0–5	65.2	65.8	65.5	61.8	50.3	52.9	52.5	52.9	52.7	54.0
Related children ages 6–17	45.5	48.3	47.3	44.6	35.7	37.1	37.3	38.3	37.4	37.8
White, non-Hispanic	—	—	39.6	33.5	28.0	—	—	—	—	—
White-alone, non-Hispanic	—	—	—	—	—	30.7	31.5	33.1	32.9	32.4
Black	64.8	66.9	64.7	61.6	49.3	—	—	—	—	—
Black-alone	—	—	—	—	—	49.7	49.2	50.2	49.7	50.4
Hispanic[d]	65.0	72.4	68.4	65.7	49.8	50.6	51.9	50.2	47.2	51.6

See notes at end of table.

Characteristic	1980	1985	1990	1995	2000	2003	2004	2005	2006	2007
Below 50% poverty										
All children[b]	6.9	8.6	8.8	8.5	6.7	7.7	7.6	7.7	7.5	7.8
Gender										
Male	6.9	8.6	8.8	8.4	6.6	7.8	7.6	7.3	7.5	7.8
Female	6.9	8.6	8.8	8.5	6.8	7.7	7.7	8.1	7.5	7.8
Age										
Ages 0–5	8.3	10.0	10.7	10.8	8.1	9.7	9.3	9.1	9.4	9.8
Ages 6–17	6.2	7.8	7.8	7.2	6.0	6.7	6.8	7.0	6.5	6.8
Race and Hispanic origin[c]										
White, non-Hispanic	—	—	5.0	3.9	3.7	—	—	—	—	—
White-alone, non-Hispanic	—	—	—	—	—	4.1	4.5	4.1	4.3	4.3
Black	—	—	22.8	20.6	15.2	—	—	—	—	—
Black-alone	—	—	—	—	—	17.9	17.1	17.3	16.0	17.3
Hispanic[d]	—	—	14.2	16.3	10.2	10.9	10.3	11.5	10.3	11.0
Region[e]										
Northeast	4.7	6.5	7.6	8.6	6.4	6.9	7.7	7.5	6.4	7.4
South	9.7	10.9	11.3	10.1	7.9	8.6	8.6	9.0	8.5	8.9
Midwest	6.3	9.5	8.9	6.6	5.5	7.0	7.0	6.5	7.3	7.4
West	5.1	5.6	6.1	7.8	6.2	7.5	6.8	7.0	6.8	6.7
Related children[a]										
Children in all families, total	—	—	8.3	7.9	6.3	7.3	7.2	7.2	7.1	7.4
Related children ages 0–5	—	—	10.3	10.4	7.9	9.5	9.1	8.9	9.2	9.6
Related children ages 6–17	—	—	7.2	6.6	5.5	6.2	6.3	6.4	6.0	6.3
White, non-Hispanic	—	—	4.4	3.4	3.3	—	—	—	—	—
White-alone, non-Hispanic	—	—	—	—	—	3.7	4.0	3.6	3.9	3.9
Black	—	—	22.3	20.1	14.8	—	—	—	—	—
Black-alone	—	—	—	—	—	17.4	16.8	16.9	15.7	17.1
Hispanic[d]	—	—	13.5	15.6	9.4	10.6	9.9	10.8	10.0	10.5
Children in married-couple families, total	—	—	2.7	2.6	2.2	2.4	2.5	2.4	2.2	2.6
Related children ages 0–5	—	—	3.1	2.9	2.2	2.8	2.8	2.8	2.8	2.8
Related children ages 6–17	—	—	2.4	2.5	2.2	2.2	2.3	2.1	1.9	2.5
White, non-Hispanic	—	—	1.9	1.4	1.5	—	—	—	—	—
White-alone, non-Hispanic	—	—	—	—	—	1.4	1.8	1.2	1.2	1.4
Black	—	—	3.9	2.9	3.1	—	—	—	—	—
Black-alone	—	—	—	—	—	4.0	3.6	4.5	2.9	4.4
Hispanic[d]	—	—	6.7	8.6	4.4	5.3	3.8	5.2	4.7	5.4
Children in female-householder families, no husband present, total	—	—	27.7	23.8	18.9	21.5	21.7	21.8	21.1	21.2
Related children ages 0–5	—	—	37.0	33.7	27.9	31.4	30.6	29.1	29.5	30.2
Related children ages 6–17	—	—	23.0	18.9	15.2	17.3	17.9	18.5	17.4	17.0
White, non-Hispanic	—	—	19.1	13.1	12.0	—	—	—	—	—
White-alone, non-Hispanic	—	—	—	—	—	14.6	14.6	15.2	16.1	15.9
Black	—	—	36.8	32.2	24.2	—	—	—	—	—
Black-alone	—	—	—	—	—	27.1	27.2	26.1	26.0	25.9
Hispanic[d]	—	—	31.9	32.5	24.8	25.3	27.7	27.7	22.9	24.4

See notes at end of table.

Child poverty: Percentage of all children and related children[a] ages 0–17 living below selected poverty levels by selected characteristics, selected years 1980–2007

Characteristic	1980	1985	1990	1995	2000	2003	2004	2005	2006	2007
Below 150% poverty										
All children[b]	29.9	32.3	31.4	32.2	26.7	28.6	28.2	28.2	28.6	29.3
Gender										
Male	29.6	32.2	31.3	31.7	26.6	28.5	28.1	28.0	28.4	29.2
Female	30.3	32.3	31.6	32.7	26.8	28.8	28.4	28.3	28.8	29.5
Age										
Ages 0–5	33.2	35.6	34.6	35.5	29.3	31.6	31.6	31.5	32.2	33.2
Ages 6–17	28.4	30.5	29.7	30.5	25.4	27.2	26.6	26.5	26.8	27.4
Race and Hispanic origin[c]										
White, non-Hispanic	—	—	21.4	20.1	16.4	—	—	—	—	—
White-alone, non-Hispanic	—	—	—	—	—	17.6	17.5	17.2	17.7	17.8
Black	—	—	57.9	56.8	45.7	—	—	—	—	—
Black-alone	—	—	—	—	—	48.5	48.0	48.8	48.1	49.0
Hispanic[d]	—	—	56.0	59.4	47.3	48.4	47.0	45.9	45.9	47.8
Region[e]										
Northeast	27.0	28.1	26.7	28.8	23.4	24.5	23.4	24.9	24.6	26.0
South	35.8	36.7	36.0	35.8	29.5	32.3	31.3	31.2	31.6	32.8
Midwest	26.0	31.0	28.7	26.8	21.8	24.5	25.6	25.0	26.5	26.3
West	27.9	30.4	31.4	35.0	29.3	29.8	29.5	28.8	28.7	29.0
Related children[a]										
Children in all families, total	—	—	30.6	31.5	26.1	28.1	27.7	27.6	28.1	28.8
Related children ages 0–5	—	—	33.9	35.1	28.9	31.3	31.3	31.2	31.7	32.9
Related children ages 6–17	—	—	28.8	29.6	24.7	26.5	26.0	25.8	26.2	26.8
White, non-Hispanic	—	—	20.5	19.3	15.8	—	—	—	—	—
White-alone, non-Hispanic	—	—	—	—	—	17.0	16.8	16.5	17.1	17.3
Black	—	—	57.4	56.3	45.4	—	—	—	—	—
Black-alone	—	—	—	—	—	48.1	47.7	48.5	47.8	48.9
Hispanic[d]	—	—	55.4	59.0	46.6	48.0	46.8	45.5	45.6	47.4
Children in married-couple families, total	—	—	19.9	19.9	16.2	17.6	17.3	17.0	17.1	17.4
Related children ages 0–5	—	—	22.1	21.3	17.8	19.9	20.0	19.7	19.6	19.5
Related children ages 6–17	—	—	18.7	19.1	15.4	16.5	16.0	15.6	15.8	16.3
White, non-Hispanic	—	—	14.6	13.4	10.0	—	—	—	—	—
White-alone, non-Hispanic	—	—	—	—	—	10.9	10.4	10.0	10.2	10.3
Black	—	—	31.7	26.2	20.7	—	—	—	—	—
Black-alone	—	—	—	—	—	22.0	22.7	23.3	23.1	21.2
Hispanic[d]	—	—	46.5	49.8	39.4	40.9	39.6	38.5	37.4	38.7
Children in female-householder families, no husband present, total	—	—	66.9	65.2	57.2	58.0	57.6	58.6	59.4	60.5
Related children ages 0–5	—	—	76.7	75.1	66.8	68.1	67.9	68.6	69.2	71.3
Related children ages 6–17	—	—	62.0	60.3	53.2	53.7	53.3	54.3	55.0	55.4
White, non-Hispanic	—	—	54.4	48.6	44.1	—	—	—	—	—
White-alone, non-Hispanic	—	—	—	—	—	45.6	46.0	46.8	48.3	49.1
Black	—	—	77.1	76.2	66.2	—	—	—	—	—
Black-alone	—	—	—	—	—	66.8	66.4	67.1	67.6	68.0
Hispanic[d]	—	—	80.3	81.6	70.1	68.2	68.0	66.9	67.1	69.7

See notes at end of table.

Child poverty: Percentage of all children and related children[a] ages 0–17 living below selected poverty levels by selected characteristics, selected years 1980–2007

Characteristic	1980	1985	1990	1995	2000	2003	2004	2005	2006	2007
Below 200% poverty										
All children[b]	42.3	43.5	42.4	43.3	37.5	39.1	39.3	38.9	39.0	39.2
Gender										
Male	42.3	43.2	42.5	43.1	37.5	38.8	39.0	38.6	38.8	39.1
Female	42.4	43.7	42.3	43.5	37.6	39.5	39.6	39.3	39.2	39.3
Age										
Ages 0–5	46.8	47.1	46.0	46.7	41.0	42.2	42.6	42.4	42.9	42.9
Ages 6–17	40.3	41.6	40.5	41.5	35.9	37.6	37.6	37.3	37.1	37.3
Race and Hispanic origin[c]										
White, non-Hispanic	—	—	32.3	30.5	25.5	—	—	—	—	—
White-alone, non-Hispanic	—	—	—	—	—	26.4	26.8	26.2	26.3	26.2
Black	—	—	68.3	68.1	59.2	—	—	—	—	—
Black-alone	—	—	—	—	—	61.3	60.6	61.3	60.2	60.6
Hispanic[d]	—	—	69.5	72.9	62.6	62.6	62.2	60.7	61.0	60.8
Region[e]										
Northeast	39.1	37.5	36.3	38.2	33.0	34.3	32.6	33.9	34.1	35.1
South	47.8	48.6	47.7	48.4	41.6	43.5	42.7	42.5	42.4	42.6
Midwest	39.1	42.5	39.6	36.9	31.2	34.2	36.3	35.3	35.9	36.4
West	40.5	41.7	42.7	46.1	40.5	40.6	41.6	40.5	40.1	39.4
Related children[a]										
Children in all families, total	—	—	41.7	42.6	36.9	38.6	38.7	38.4	38.5	38.7
Related children ages 0–5	—	—	45.4	46.3	40.5	42.0	42.3	42.1	42.5	42.6
Related children ages 6–17	—	—	39.6	40.7	35.2	37.0	36.9	36.6	36.5	36.7
White, non-Hispanic	—	—	31.4	29.8	24.8	—	—	—	—	—
White-alone, non-Hispanic	—	—	—	—	—	25.9	26.1	25.6	25.6	25.5
Black	—	—	67.9	67.8	58.9	—	—	—	—	—
Black-alone	—	—	—	—	—	60.9	60.3	61.1	60.0	60.5
Hispanic[d]	—	—	69.1	72.5	62.1	62.3	62.1	60.3	60.7	60.4
Children in married-couple families, total	—	—	31.2	31.0	26.4	27.2	27.4	27.0	26.6	26.3
Related children ages 0–5	—	—	34.3	33.2	29.1	30.3	30.5	30.1	30.1	28.9
Related children ages 6–17	—	—	29.5	29.9	25.1	25.7	25.8	25.4	24.8	24.9
White, non-Hispanic	—	—	25.2	23.3	18.2	—	—	—	—	—
White-alone, non-Hispanic	—	—	—	—	—	18.6	18.4	18.1	17.7	17.4
Black	—	—	44.6	39.1	35.9	—	—	—	—	—
Black-alone	—	—	—	—	—	35.9	35.6	35.7	34.9	33.2
Hispanic[d]	—	—	62.0	65.9	55.4	55.7	55.6	54.1	53.3	52.1

See notes at end of table.

Child poverty: Percentage of all children and related children[a] ages 0–17 living below selected poverty levels by selected characteristics, selected years 1980–2007

Characteristic	1980	1985	1990	1995	2000	2003	2004	2005	2006	2007
Children in female-householder families, no husband present, total	—	—	77.0	76.0	69.4	70.2	70.5	71.0	71.6	72.1
Related children ages 0–5	—	—	85.1	84.1	78.3	78.4	78.8	79.9	79.9	80.7
Related children ages 6–17	—	—	72.9	72.0	65.6	66.8	67.0	67.1	67.8	68.1
White, non-Hispanic	—	—	66.5	61.3	56.0	—	—	—	—	—
White-alone, non-Hispanic	—	—	—	—	—	58.8	59.6	59.3	60.8	61.0
Black	—	—	85.6	86.8	78.6	—	—	—	—	—
Black-alone	—	—	—	—	—	78.4	78.9	78.8	79.0	79.5
Hispanic[d]	—	—	88.9	88.3	82.4	80.3	80.1	80.3	79.7	81.0

— Not available.

[a] A related child is a person ages 0–17 who is related to the householder by birth, marriage, or adoption, but is not the householder or the householder's spouse.

[b] Includes children not related to the householder.

[c] For race and Hispanic-origin data in this table: From 1980 to 2002, following the 1977 OMB standards for collecting and presenting data on race, the Current Population Survey (CPS) asked respondents to choose one race from the following: White, Black, American Indian or Alaskan Native, or Asian or Pacific Islander. The Census Bureau also offered an "Other" category. Beginning in 2003, following the 1997 OMB standards for collecting and presenting data on race, the CPS asked respondents to choose one or more races from the following: White, Black or African American, Asian, American Indian or Alaska Native, or Native Hawaiian or Other Pacific Islander. All race groups discussed in this table from 2002 onward refer to people who indicated only one racial identity within the racial categories presented. People who responded to the question on race by indicating only one race are referred to as the race-alone population. The use of the race-alone population in this table does not imply that it is the preferred method of presenting or analyzing data. Data from 2002 onward are not directly comparable with data from earlier years. Data on race and Hispanic origin are collected separately. Persons of Hispanic origin may be of any race.

[d] Persons of Hispanic origin may be of any race.

[e] Regions: Northeast includes CT, MA, ME, NH, NJ, NY, PA, RI, and VT. South includes AL, AR, DC, DE, FL, GA, KY, LA, MD, MS, NC, OK, SC, TN, TX, VA, and WV. Midwest includes IA, IL, IN, KS, MI, MN, MO, ND, NE, OH, SD, and WI. West includes AK, AZ, CA, CO, HI, ID, MT, NM, NV, OR, UT, WA, and WY.

NOTE: The 2004 data have been revised to reflect a correction to the weights in the 2005 Annual Social and Economic Supplement. Data for 1999, 2000, and 2001 use Census 2000 population controls. Data for 2000 onward are from the expanded Current Population Survey sample. The poverty level is based on money income and does not include noncash benefits, such as food stamps. Poverty thresholds reflect family size and composition and are adjusted each year using the annual average Consumer Price Index level. The average poverty threshold for a family of four was $21,203 in 2007. The levels shown here are derived from the ratio of the family's income to the family's poverty threshold. For more detail, see U.S. Census Bureau, Series P–60, no. 235.

SOURCE: U.S. Census Bureau, Current Population Survey, Annual Social and Economic Supplements.

Poverty level	1980	1985	1990	1995	2000	2001	2002	2003	2004	2005	2006	2007
Table ECON1.B				**Income distribution: Percentage of related children ages 0–17 by family income relative to the poverty line, selected years 1980–2007**								

Poverty level	1980	1985	1990	1995	2000	2001	2002	2003	2004	2005	2006	2007
Extreme poverty	6.6	8.1	8.3	7.9	6.3	6.6	6.6	7.3	7.2	7.2	7.1	7.4
Below poverty, but above extreme poverty	11.3	12.0	11.6	12.2	9.4	9.1	9.7	9.9	10.1	9.9	9.9	10.2
Low income	24.0	22.8	21.8	22.5	21.3	21.9	21.5	21.5	21.4	21.3	21.5	21.1
Medium income	41.4	37.7	37.0	34.5	34.0	33.2	32.7	32.0	32.3	32.1	31.6	31.8
High income	16.8	19.4	21.3	22.9	29.0	29.2	29.6	29.4	28.9	29.5	29.9	29.5
Very high income	4.3	6.1	7.4	8.9	12.6	12.9	12.9	13.1	12.9	13.5	13.8	13.4

NOTE: The 2004 data have been revised to reflect a correction to the weights in the 2005 Annual Social and Economic Supplement (ASEC). Data for 1999, 2000, and 2001 use Census 2000 population controls. Data for 2000 onward are from the expanded Current Population Survey sample. Estimates refer to children who are related to the householder and who are ages 0–17. The income classes are derived from the ratio of the family's income to the family's poverty threshold. Extreme poverty is less than 50 percent of the poverty threshold (i.e., $10,513 for a family of four with 2 related children in 2007). Below poverty, but above extreme poverty is between 50 and 99 percent of the poverty threshold (i.e., between $10,514 and $21,026 for a family of four with 2 related children in 2007). Low income is between 100 and 199 percent of the poverty threshold (i.e., between $21,027 and $42,053 for a family of four with 2 related children in 2007). Medium income is between 200 and 399 percent of the poverty threshold (i.e., between $42,054 and $84,107 for a family of four with 2 related children in 2007). High income is 400 percent of the poverty threshold or more (i.e., $84,108 or more for a family of four with 2 related children in 2007). Very high income is 600 percent of the poverty threshold and over (i.e., $126,162 or more for a family of four with 2 related children in 2007). [These income categories are similar to those used in the Economic report for the President (1998). A similar approach is found in Hernandez, Donald J. (1993). *America's children: Resources from family, government, and the economy.* New York: Russell Sage Foundation for the National Committee for Research on the 1980 Census, except that Hernandez uses the relationship to median income to define his categories. The medium- and high-income categories are similar for either method.]

SOURCE: U.S. Census Bureau, Current Population Survey, Annual Social and Economic Supplements.

Characteristic	1980	1985	1990	1995	2000	2003	2004	2005	2006	2007
All children living with parent(s)[b]										
Total	70	70	72	74	80	77	78	78	78	77
Race and Hispanic origin[c]										
White, non-Hispanic	75	77	79	81	85	82	82	84	83	82
Black, non-Hispanic	50	48	50	54	66	61	62	62	64	64
Hispanic	59	55	60	61	72	71	73	74	74	72
Poverty status										
Below 100% poverty	21	20	22	25	34	30	33	32	33	32
100% poverty and above	81	82	85	86	88	86	87	88	88	87
Age										
Ages 0–5	67	67	68	69	76	73	74	75	75	73
Ages 6–17	72	72	74	76	81	79	79	80	80	79
Children living in families maintained by two married parents										
Total	80	81	85	87	90	88	88	89	89	89
Race and Hispanic origin[c]										
White, non-Hispanic	81	83	86	89	92	90	90	91	91	90
Black, non-Hispanic	73	76	84	85	90	85	86	85	86	87
Hispanic	71	70	74	77	85	82	84	85	85	84
Poverty status										
Below 100% poverty	38	37	44	46	58	52	55	57	58	54
100% poverty and above	84	87	89	91	93	91	92	92	92	92
Age										
Ages 0–5	76	79	83	86	89	86	86	87	87	87
Ages 6–17	81	82	85	87	91	88	89	90	90	90
With both parents working year round, full time	17	20	25	28	33	29	30	31	32	32
Children living in families maintained by single mothers[d]										
Total	33	32	33	38	49	47	47	48	48	47
Race and Hispanic origin[c]										
White, non-Hispanic	39	39	40	46	53	52	49	52	51	49
Black, non-Hispanic	28	25	27	33	49	44	45	45	46	48
Hispanic	22	22	24	27	38	43	45	45	46	44
Poverty status										
Below 100% poverty	7	7	9	14	20	17	19	17	19	20
100% poverty and above	59	59	60	61	67	69	67	70	70	68
Age										
Ages 0–5	20	20	21	24	36	34	34	37	37	36
Ages 6–17	38	37	40	45	55	53	52	53	54	53

Table ECON2   Secure parental employment: Percentage of children ages 0–17 living with at least one parent employed year round, full time[a] by family structure, race and Hispanic origin, poverty status, and age, selected years 1980–2007

See notes at end of table.

Secure parental employment: Percentage of children ages 0–17 living with at least one parent employed year round, full time[a] by family structure, race and Hispanic origin, poverty status, and age, selected years 1980–2007

Characteristic	1980	1985	1990	1995	2000	2003	2004	2005	2006	2007
Children living in families maintained by single fathers[d]										
Total	57	60	64	67	69	63	68	71	67	66
Race and Hispanic origin[c]										
White, non-Hispanic	61	62	68	72	74	66	70	74	70	68
Black, non-Hispanic	41	59	53	64	52	54	61	65	64	62
Hispanic	53	53	59	58	68	63	69	67	64	61
Poverty status										
Below 100% poverty	15	23	21	24	21	27	26	32	26	28
100% poverty and above	68	69	74	79	79	73	78	80	78	76
Age										
Ages 0–5	48	57	58	54	65	56	62	66	61	61
Ages 6–17	59	62	67	74	70	65	71	73	70	69

[a] Year round, full-time employment is defined as usually working full time (35 hours or more per week) for 50 to 52 weeks.

[b] Total children living with parent(s) (in thousands)	60,683	61,264	63,351	68,090	69,126	70,089	70,210	70,292	71,229	71,285
Total living with relatives but not with parent(s) (in thousands)	1,954	1,379	1,455	2,160	2,212	2,380	2,528	2,419	2,017	2,256

[c] For data from 1980 to 2002, the 1977 OMB Standards for Data on Race and Ethnicity were used to classify persons into one of the following four racial groups: White, Black, American Indian or Alaskan Native, or Asian or Pacific Islander. The revised 1997 OMB standards were used for data for 2003 and later years. Persons could select one or more of five racial groups: White, Black or African American, American Indian or Alaska Native, Asian, or Native Hawaiian or Other Pacific Islander. Included in the total, but not shown separately, are American Indian or Alaska Native, Asian, Native Hawaiian or Other Pacific Islander, and "Two or more races." Beginning in 2003, those in each racial category represent those reporting only one race. Data from 2003 onward are not directly comparable with data from earlier years. Data on race and Hispanic origin are collected separately. Persons of Hispanic origin may be of any race.

[d] Includes some families where both parents are present in the household, but living as unmarried partners.

SOURCE: U.S. Bureau of Labor Statistics, Current Population Survey, Annual Social and Economic Supplements.

Characteristic	1995[a]	1999	2001	2002	2003	2004	2005	2006	2007
All children									
In food-insecure households[b]	19.4	16.9	17.6	18.1	18.2	19.0	16.9	17.2	16.9
In households with very low food security among children[c]	1.3	0.7	0.6	0.8	0.6	0.7	0.8	0.6	0.9
Poverty status									
Below 100% poverty									
In food-insecure households[b]	44.4	44.0	45.9	45.6	45.2	47.1	42.5	43.6	42.9
In households with very low food security among children[c]	3.4	2.2	2.6	2.4	2.0	2.5	2.9	2.1	3.0
100–199% poverty									
In food-insecure households[b]	25.4	23.4	27.1	28.4	29.6	28.0	26.4	26.7	27.5
In households with very low food security among children[c]	1.4	0.9	0.8	1.2	0.9	1.1	0.8	0.8	1.2
200% poverty and above									
In food-insecure households[b]	4.8	5.2	5.5	6.0	6.2	6.2	6.0	6.1	6.1
In households with very low food security among children[c]	0.2	0.2	0.1	0.1	0.1	0.1	0.3	0.1	0.2
Race and Hispanic origin[d]									
White, non-Hispanic									
In food-insecure households[b]	14.0	11.0	11.9	12.6	12.0	13.0	12.2	11.8	11.9
In households with very low food security among children[c]	0.8	0.4	0.2	0.4	0.2	0.4	0.5	0.3	0.5
Black, non-Hispanic									
In food-insecure households[b]	30.6	28.6	29.6	29.4	30.8	31.2	29.2	29.3	26.1
In households with very low food security among children[c]	2.3	1.0	1.4	1.3	1.0	1.3	1.9	1.5	1.8
Hispanic									
In food-insecure households[b]	33.9	29.2	28.6	29.2	30.8	29.6	23.7	26.0	26.7
In households with very low food security among children[c]	2.6	1.3	1.3	1.6	1.6	1.2	1.2	0.7	1.9
Region[e]									
Northeast									
In food-insecure households[b]	16.8	13.9	13.2	15.2	15.9	14.7	14.1	14.3	14.6
In households with very low food security among children[c]	0.8	0.3	0.8	0.7	0.5	0.5	1.0	0.5	0.7
South									
In food-insecure households[b]	20.5	17.9	19.9	20.2	19.3	20.2	18.0	19.3	18.3
In households with very low food security among children[c]	1.3	0.7	0.6	0.9	0.7	0.9	0.7	0.6	0.9
Midwest									
In food-insecure households[b]	16.2	14.2	14.0	15.8	16.5	17.6	15.8	16.5	15.4
In households with very low food security among children[c]	0.8	0.6	0.5	0.3	0.3	0.7	0.6	0.6	0.9
West									
In food-insecure households[b]	23.2	20.3	20.9	19.5	19.8	21.7	18.1	16.7	17.7
In households with very low food security among children[c]	2.1	1.2	0.7	1.1	0.6	0.8	1.1	0.6	1.2
Parental education									
Parent or guardian with highest education less than high school or GED									
In food-insecure households[b]	41.8	40.5	37.6	41.4	37.7	39.8	37.3	39.2	38.2
In households with very low food security among children[c]	3.0	2.0	1.1	1.8	1.4	1.2	1.4	2.3	2.4

See notes at end of table.

Food security: Percentage of children ages 0–17 in food-insecure households by severity of food insecurity and selected characteristics, selected years 1995–2007

Characteristic	1995[a]	1999	2001	2002	2003	2004	2005	2006	2007
Parental education—continued									
Parent or guardian with highest education high school or GED									
In food-insecure households[b]	24.9	24.2	25.9	25.1	26.7	27.7	25.1	25.2	23.7
In households with very low food security among children[c]	1.2	0.7	1.1	1.2	0.8	1.3	0.9	0.8	1.6
Parent or guardian with highest education some college, including vocational/technical or associate's degree									
In food-insecure households[b]	18.9	15.6	17.5	18.8	19.2	20.7	18.3	19.3	18.7
In households with very low food security among children[c]	1.5	0.9	0.5	0.8	0.7	0.9	1.1	0.5	1.0
Parent or guardian with highest education bachelor's degree or higher									
In food-insecure households[b]	5.1	4.4	5.3	5.6	6.1	5.5	4.9	4.7	5.8
In households with very low food security among children[c]	0.4	0.2	0.2	0.2	0.1	0.1	0.3	0.1	0.1
Family structure									
Married-couple household									
In food-insecure households[b]	13.3	11.5	12.6	12.0	12.3	13.0	11.3	11.5	11.8
In households with very low food security among children[c]	0.8	0.4	0.3	0.4	0.2	0.5	0.5	0.2	0.6
Female-headed household, no spouse									
In food-insecure households[b]	38.6	33.4	33.5	35.5	34.5	35.8	32.8	33.3	31.8
In households with very low food security among children[c]	2.8	1.6	1.7	1.8	1.8	1.5	1.7	1.6	2.0
Male-headed household, no spouse									
In food-insecure households[b]	21.0	18.8	17.1	23.0	24.3	24.0	18.4	19.5	20.5
In households with very low food security among children[c]	1.1	0.8	0.9	1.1	0.7	1.0	0.7	0.6	0.6

[a] Statistics for 1995 are not precisely comparable with those for more recent years, due to a change in the method of screening Current Population Survey (CPS) sample households into the food security questions. The effect on 1995 statistics (a slight downward bias) is perceptible only for the category "In food-insecure households." Statistics for 1996, 1997, 1998, and 2000 are omitted because they are not directly comparable with those for the other years.

[b] Either adults or children or both were food insecure. At times they were unable to acquire adequate food for active, healthy living for all household members because they had insufficient money and other resources for food.

[c] In these households, eating patterns of one or more children were disrupted and their food intake was reduced below a level considered adequate by their caregiver. Prior to 2006, the category "with very low food security among children" was labeled "food insecure with hunger among children." USDA introduced the new label based on recommendations by the Committee on National Statistics.

[d] Race and Hispanic origin are those of the household reference person. From 1995 to 2002, the 1977 OMB Standards for Data on Race and Ethnicity were used to classify persons into one of the following four racial groups: White, Black, American Indian or Alaskan Native, or Asian or Pacific Islander. Beginning in 2003, the revised 1997 OMB standards were used. Persons could select one or more of five racial groups: White, Black or African American, American Indian or Alaska Native, Asian, or Native Hawaiian or Other Pacific Islander. Included in the total, but not shown separately, are American Indian or Alaska Native, Asian, and Native Hawaiian or Other Pacific Islander, and "Two or more races." From 2003 onward, statistics for White non-Hispanics and Black non-Hispanics exclude persons who indicated "Two or more races." Statistics by race and ethnicity from 2003 onward are not directly comparable with statistics for earlier years, although examination of the size and food security prevalence rates of the multiple-race categories suggests that effects of the reclassification on food security prevalence statistics were small. Data on race and Hispanic origin are collected separately. Persons of Hispanic origin may be of any race.

[e] Regions: Northeast includes CT, MA, ME, NH, NJ, NY, PA, RI, and VT. South includes AL, AR, DC, DE, FL, GA, KY, LA, MD, MS, NC, OK, SC, TN, TX, VA, and WV. Midwest includes IA, IL, IN, KS, MI, MN, MO, ND, NE, OH, SD, and WI. West includes AK, AZ, CA, CO, HI, ID, MT, NM, NV, OR, UT, WA, and WY.

NOTE: The food security measure is based on data collected annually in the Food Security Supplement to the Current Population Survey (CPS). The criteria for classifying households as food insecure reflect a consensus judgment of an expert working group on food security measurement. For detailed explanations, see *Guide to Measuring Household Food Security,* Revised 2000, Alexandria, VA: Food and Nutrition Service (2000); and *Household Food Security in the United States,* 2007, Economic Research Report No. 66, Washington, DC: Economic Research Service (2008).

SOURCE: U.S. Census Bureau, Current Population Survey Food Security Supplement; tabulated by U.S. Department of Agriculture, Economic Research Service and Food and Nutrition Service.

| Table HC1 | | | | Health insurance coverage: Percentage of children ages 0–17 covered by health insurance at some time during the year[a] by type of health insurance and selected characteristics, selected years 1987–2007 | | | | | | | |

Characteristic	1987	1990	1995	2000	2001	2002	2003	2004	2005	2006	2007
Any health insurance											
Total	87.1	87.0	86.2	88.4	88.7	88.8	89.0	89.5	89.1	88.3	89.0
Gender											
Male	87.1	86.9	86.3	88.4	88.8	88.6	89.0	89.6	88.9	87.9	89.1
Female	87.1	87.0	86.2	88.4	88.6	89.0	88.9	89.5	89.3	88.7	89.0
Age											
Ages 0–5	87.6	88.5	86.7	88.8	89.6	89.5	89.9	90.7	89.6	88.7	89.5
Ages 6–11	87.3	87.0	86.5	88.7	89.1	89.4	89.3	89.8	90.1	88.9	89.7
Ages 12–17	86.4	85.2	85.5	87.7	87.4	87.5	87.8	88.2	87.8	87.4	88.0
Race and Hispanic origin[b]											
White, non-Hispanic	90.3	90.0	89.5	92.8	93.0	—	—	—	—	—	—
White-alone, non-Hispanic	—	—	—	—	—	92.6	92.9	93.0	93.0	92.7	92.7
Black	83.1	85.4	84.7	86.3	86.8	—	—	—	—	—	—
Black-alone	—	—	—	—	—	86.5	86.1	88.2	88.2	85.9	87.8
Hispanic	71.5	71.6	73.2	75.1	76.2	77.8	79.3	79.7	78.5	77.9	80.0
Region[c]											
Northeast	92.4	92.0	89.4	91.8	91.8	91.3	91.4	92.2	92.4	91.5	91.8
South	82.1	82.9	82.9	86.0	86.7	86.3	86.4	87.2	87.0	85.2	85.6
Midwest	92.3	91.1	90.5	91.9	92.7	92.7	92.5	92.4	92.5	92.8	92.9
West	84.6	84.3	84.3	86.3	86.1	86.9	87.8	88.4	86.9	86.9	89.0
Private health insurance											
Total	73.6	71.1	66.1	70.2	68.8	67.9	66.3	66.4	65.8	64.7	64.2
Gender											
Male	73.4	71.1	66.4	70.1	69.1	67.8	66.3	66.2	65.7	64.5	64.4
Female	73.9	71.2	65.8	70.3	68.5	68.1	66.3	66.7	66.0	64.8	63.9
Age											
Ages 0–5	71.7	68.2	60.4	66.5	64.9	63.9	62.3	62.3	61.4	60.5	59.3
Ages 6–11	74.3	72.5	67.2	70.4	69.0	68.5	66.6	67.3	66.6	65.4	65.4
Ages 12–17	75.1	73.0	71.0	73.5	72.4	71.2	69.7	69.5	69.2	67.9	67.8
Race and Hispanic origin[b]											
White, non-Hispanic	83.2	80.8	78.0	81.4	80.2	—	—	—	—	—	—
White-alone, non-Hispanic	—	—	—	—	—	79.6	78.6	77.9	78.1	76.9	76.9
Black	49.2	48.5	43.9	53.9	53.1	—	—	—	—	—	—
Black-alone	—	—	—	—	—	50.8	48.0	49.3	48.7	49.0	48.1
Hispanic	47.9	44.9	38.3	45.2	43.9	43.5	42.4	43.8	42.0	40.9	40.4
Region[c]											
Northeast	79.4	76.7	71.2	73.7	72.7	71.2	71.6	72.0	71.2	70.3	69.4
South	68.1	66.4	61.0	66.5	64.9	62.9	61.2	61.9	61.2	59.6	58.6
Midwest	79.4	76.0	74.4	78.6	77.5	76.6	74.3	73.1	72.8	71.7	70.4
West	71.2	68.3	61.2	65.4	64.5	64.9	62.7	63.1	62.6	62.0	63.5

See notes at end of table.

| Table HC1 (cont.) | Health insurance coverage: Percentage of children ages 0–17 covered by health insurance at some time during the year[a] by type of health insurance and selected characteristics, selected years 1987–2007 |

Characteristic	1987	1990	1995	2000	2001	2002	2003	2004	2005	2006	2007
Public health insurance[d]											
Total	19.0	21.9	26.4	24.4	25.9	26.8	29.1	29.9	29.7	29.8	31.0
Gender											
Male	19.2	22.1	26.2	24.7	25.8	26.8	29.2	30.1	29.6	29.6	31.0
Female	18.8	21.7	26.6	24.2	26.1	26.8	29.0	29.6	29.7	30.1	31.0
Age											
Ages 0–5	22.1	27.6	32.6	29.2	31.3	32.1	34.4	35.5	34.7	34.7	36.4
Ages 6–11	18.6	20.0	25.6	24.5	26.4	26.8	28.8	29.5	29.8	29.5	30.4
Ages 12–17	16.1	17.5	20.5	19.8	20.3	21.9	24.4	25.0	24.7	25.5	26.2
Race and Hispanic origin[b]											
White, non-Hispanic	12.1	14.7	17.5	17.2	18.7	—	—	—	—	—	—
White-alone, non-Hispanic	—	—	—	—	—	18.5	20.5	21.2	21.2	22.0	22.0
Black	42.1	45.5	48.8	41.9	41.6	—	—	—	—	—	—
Black-alone	—	—	—	—	—	44.2	46.5	48.4	48.0	44.0	47.7
Hispanic	28.2	31.9	39.0	34.6	37.0	39.6	42.0	42.2	41.4	42.3	44.2
Region[c]											
Northeast	17.9	20.9	23.4	24.3	24.8	25.0	25.8	26.4	27.2	27.0	27.9
South	19.7	23.0	28.2	25.8	28.5	30.0	31.8	32.3	32.8	31.9	33.4
Midwest	18.2	20.0	22.7	19.1	21.1	22.0	24.9	26.2	26.0	27.5	29.2
West	19.9	23.2	29.8	27.3	27.1	27.9	31.2	32.0	30.1	30.8	30.9

— Not available.

[a] Children are considered to be covered by health insurance if they had public or private coverage at any time during the year. Some children are covered by both types of insurance; hence, the sum of public and private is greater than the total.

[b] For race and Hispanic-origin data in this table: From 1987 to 2002, following the 1977 OMB standards for collecting and presenting data on race, the Current Population Survey (CPS) asked respondents to choose one race from the following: White, Black, American Indian or Alaskan Native, or Asian or Pacific Islander. The Census Bureau also offered an "Other" category. Beginning in 2003, following the 1997 OMB standards for collecting and presenting data on race, the CPS asked respondents to choose one or more races from the following: White, Black or African American, Asian, American Indian or Alaska Native, or Native Hawaiian or Other Pacific Islander. All race groups discussed in this table from 2002 onward refer to people who indicated only one racial identity within the racial categories presented. People who responded to the question on race by indicating only one race are referred to as the race-alone population. The use of the race-alone population in this table does not imply that it is the preferred method of presenting or analyzing data. Data from 2002 onward are not directly comparable with data from earlier years. Data on race and Hispanic origin are collected separately. Persons of Hispanic origin may be of any race.

[c] Regions: Northeast includes CT, MA, ME, NH, NJ, NY, PA, RI, and VT. South includes AL, AR, DC, DE, FL, GA, KY, LA, MD, MS, NC, OK, SC, TN, TX, VA, and WV. Midwest includes IA, IL, IN, KS, MI, MN, MO, ND, NE, OH, SD, and WI. West includes AK, AZ, CA, CO, HI, ID, MT, NM, NV, OR, UT, WA, and WY.

[d] Public health insurance for children consists mostly of Medicaid, but also includes Medicare, the State Children's Health Insurance Programs (SCHIP), and the Civilian Health and Medical Care Program of the Uniformed Services (CHAMPUS/Tricare).

NOTE: The data from 1996 to 2004 have been revised since initially published. For more information see user note at: http://www.census.gov/hhes/www/hlthins/usernote/schedule.html. Estimates beginning in 1999 include follow-up questions to verify health insurance status and use the Census 2000-based weights.

SOURCE: U.S. Census Bureau, unpublished tables based on analyses from the Current Population Survey, Annual Social and Economic Supplements.

| Table HC2 | Usual source of health care: Percentage of children ages 0–17 with no usual source of health care[a] by age, type of health insurance, and poverty status, selected years 1993–2007 |

Characteristic	1993	1995	2000[b]	2001[b]	2002[b]	2003[b]	2004[b]	2005[b]	2006[b,c]	2007[b,c]
Ages 0–17										
Total	8.0	6.5	7.0	5.8	6.1	5.4	5.4	5.3	5.6	6.0
Type of insurance										
Private insurance[d]	3.9	3.2	3.4	2.4	2.6	2.2	2.5	2.0	2.2	2.9
Public insurance[d,e]	10.8	6.8	4.8	5.4	5.6	4.4	4.7	3.8	4.1	4.6
No insurance	24.3	22.5	29.7	28.0	29.6	28.8	28.9	31.6	29.7	32.2
Poverty status										
Below 100% poverty	15.7	10.9	12.4	12.3	11.0	10.3	10.9	8.6	8.6	9.6
100–199% poverty	9.1	8.6	10.9	8.6	9.0	7.9	7.6	7.8	8.4	8.9
200% poverty and above	3.8	3.6	4.0	2.9	3.6	2.9	3.0	3.4	3.3	3.7
Ages 0–5										
Total	5.5	4.4	4.6	4.1	4.6	3.5	3.3	3.3	3.9	3.5
Type of insurance										
Private insurance[d]	2.0	1.7	2.3	1.5	1.3	1.3	1.4	0.9	1.3	1.8
Public insurance[d,e]	7.6	5.1	3.2	4.4	3.6	3.0	3.6	2.9	3.3	2.7
No insurance	19.4	17.3	19.6	22.2	27.8	22.6	17.1	22.8	23.5	22.2
Poverty status										
Below 100% poverty	11.2	7.9	6.9	8.4	8.1	6.2	6.4	5.0	6.1	4.9
100–199% poverty	6.2	6.0	7.9	6.5	7.4	5.8	4.0	4.4	5.9	5.3
200% poverty and above	1.8	1.9	2.6	1.8	2.3	1.5	1.8	2.2	2.0	2.0
Ages 6–17										
Total	9.4	7.5	8.1	6.6	6.8	6.3	6.5	6.3	6.4	7.3
Type of insurance										
Private insurance[d]	4.9	3.9	3.9	2.9	3.1	2.5	2.9	2.4	2.6	3.4
Public insurance[d,e]	13.8	8.4	6.0	6.0	6.9	5.4	5.5	4.4	4.6	5.9
No insurance	26.5	24.8	34.5	30.3	30.3	30.9	33.5	34.7	31.9	35.5
Poverty status										
Below 100% poverty	18.7	12.8	15.6	14.4	12.6	12.6	13.5	10.8	10.1	12.8
100–199% poverty	10.8	10.0	12.5	9.7	9.8	9.1	9.4	9.4	9.7	10.9
200% poverty and above	4.8	4.4	4.6	3.4	4.2	3.5	3.5	3.9	3.9	4.4

[a] Excludes emergency rooms as a usual source of health care.

[b] In 1997, the National Health Interview Survey (NHIS) was redesigned. Data for 1997–2007 are not strictly comparable with earlier data.

[c] In 2006, the NHIS underwent a sample redesign. The impact of the new sample design on estimates is expected to be minimal.

[d] Children with both public and private insurance coverage are placed in the private insurance category.

[e] As defined here, public health insurance for children consists mostly of Medicaid or other public assistance programs, including state plans. Beginning in 1999, the public health insurance category also includes the State Children's Health Insurance Program (SCHIP). It does not include children with only Medicare, Tricare, or CHAMP-VA.

SOURCE: National Center for Health Statistics, National Health Interview Survey.

Childhood immunization: Percentage of children ages 19–35 months vaccinated for selected diseases by poverty status,[a] and race and Hispanic origin,[b] selected years 1996–2007

Characteristic	Total					Below 100% poverty					100% poverty and above				
	1996	1999	2002	2005	2007	1996	1999	2002	2005	2007	1996	1999	2002	2005	2007
Total															
Combined series (4:3:1:3:3:1)[c]	—	—	65.5	76.1	77.4	—	—	61.6	73.9	75.0	—	—	66.3	77.2	78.2
Combined series (4:3:1:3:3)[d]	67.7	73.2	74.8	80.8	80.1	61.4	68.3	69.3	77.4	76.9	69.9	75.3	76.2	82.5	81.4
Combined series (4:3:1:3)[e]	76.4	78.4	77.5	82.4	81.8	68.9	73.3	71.8	79.2	78.8	79.2	80.7	79.0	84.1	82.9
Combined series (4:3:1)[f]	78.4	79.9	78.5	83.1	82.8	71.6	75.2	72.8	79.6	79.8	80.8	82.0	80.0	84.8	84.0
DTP (4 doses or more)[g]	81.1	83.3	81.6	85.7	84.5	73.9	78.5	75.4	81.8	81.1	83.6	85.4	83.5	87.4	85.9
Polio (3 doses or more)[h]	91.0	89.6	90.2	91.7	92.6	87.7	87.4	88.3	89.7	91.9	92.0	90.5	90.6	92.4	92.8
MMR (1 dose or more)[i]	90.6	91.5	91.6	91.5	92.3	87.2	90.0	90.2	89.3	91.3	91.9	92.4	91.9	92.1	92.6
Hib (3 doses or more)[j]	91.4	93.5	93.1	93.9	92.6	86.9	90.8	90.1	91.9	91.0	93.1	95.0	93.9	94.6	93.1
Hepatitis B (3 doses or more)[k]	81.8	88.1	89.9	92.9	92.7	78.0	86.5	87.7	91.4	92.1	83.2	89.0	90.3	93.5	92.9
Varicella (1 dose or more)[l]	12.2	57.5	80.6	87.9	90.0	5.4	55.4	78.9	87.3	89.2	15.3	58.2	80.9	87.7	90.1
PCV (3 doses or more)[m]	—	—	40.8	82.8	90.0	—	—	33.2	78.3	89.0	—	—	43.4	84.4	90.3
PCV (4 doses or more)[m]	—	—	—	53.7	75.3	—	—	—	44.6	72.8	—	—	—	57.1	76.3
White, non-Hispanic															
Combined series (4:3:1:3:3:1)[c]	—	—	66.2	76.0	77.5	—	—	58.9	70.3	69.8	—	—	67.0	77.2	78.5
Combined series (4:3:1:3:3)[d]	68.9	75.6	77.7	82.1	81.0	59.3	70.9	70.0	76.3	73.0	70.5	76.3	78.4	83.4	82.0
Combined series (4:3:1:3)[e]	78.5	81.0	80.2	83.6	82.6	68.0	75.7	71.8	77.5	74.9	80.4	81.8	81.0	84.8	83.5
Combined series (4:3:1)[f]	80.1	82.0	81.2	84.0	83.3	70.3	77.1	73.0	77.7	75.2	81.9	82.8	82.0	85.3	84.3
DTP (4 doses or more)[g]	82.7	85.5	84.4	87.1	85.3	72.4	81.0	74.6	81.4	77.0	84.7	86.3	85.5	88.1	86.3
Polio (3 doses or more)[h]	91.9	90.3	91.2	91.4	92.6	88.2	87.7	88.0	87.4	86.1	92.5	90.8	91.5	92.3	93.5
MMR (1 dose or more)[i]	91.4	92.4	92.6	91.4	92.1	85.1	90.3	90.4	86.7	88.3	92.5	92.8	92.9	92.1	92.4
Hib (3 doses or more)[j]	92.8	94.8	94.1	94.2	92.9	87.4	92.5	88.4	89.4	86.7	93.7	95.2	94.7	95.1	93.8
Hepatitis B (3 doses or more)[k]	82.1	88.9	90.9	93.1	92.5	76.4	87.8	85.9	90.2	87.8	83.3	89.0	91.5	93.6	93.2
Varicella (1 dose or more)[l]	14.5	56.0	79.4	86.1	89.2	6.4	50.7	75.0	82.3	85.1	16.3	56.6	80.2	86.6	89.8
PCV (3 doses or more)[m]	—	—	43.5	83.2	89.8	—	—	31.3	76.4	84.9	—	—	45.6	84.3	90.4
PCV (4 doses or more)[m]	—	—	—	57.3	76.6	—	—	—	46.6	69.4	—	—	—	59.3	77.6
Black, non-Hispanic															
Combined series (4:3:1:3:3:1)[c]	—	—	61.7	76.3	75.3	—	—	59.3	73.5	74.4	—	—	62.1	80.1	76.5
Combined series (4:3:1:3:3)[d]	66.8	69.4	67.7	79.3	77.5	61.3	66.9	65.9	75.8	75.9	71.9	72.9	68.3	83.0	79.6
Combined series (4:3:1:3)[e]	74.2	73.8	70.7	80.5	79.5	69.3	72.4	68.4	76.8	77.9	79.1	76.7	71.7	83.8	82.0
Combined series (4:3:1)[f]	76.6	75.1	71.6	81.4	81.0	72.5	73.8	69.3	77.8	79.7	80.9	77.9	72.6	84.2	83.4
DTP (4 doses or more)[g]	79.0	79.0	75.8	84.0	82.3	74.3	77.9	73.5	79.7	81.0	83.3	82.5	77.3	87.5	84.2
Polio (3 doses or more)[h]	90.1	87.0	87.4	91.0	91.1	86.8	86.2	87.0	89.0	91.2	92.6	88.4	87.1	92.6	91.3
MMR (1 dose or more)[i]	89.7	89.8	90.3	91.9	91.5	88.3	90.2	89.8	91.3	90.2	90.8	90.9	90.2	92.8	93.4
Hib (3 doses or more)[j]	89.4	91.8	91.6	92.9	90.8	85.9	90.7	88.3	91.6	89.4	92.8	94.1	93.9	94.8	92.2
Hepatitis B (3 doses or more)[k]	81.9	86.5	88.0	92.7	91.2	77.8	85.6	88.6	92.7	91.6	85.0	89.9	87.7	94.1	91.0
Varicella (1 dose or more)[l]	8.6	57.6	82.7	90.6	89.8	—	57.1	79.7	91.0	89.3	12.9	60.4	83.6	90.8	90.8
PCV (3 doses or more)[m]	—	—	33.9	79.6	89.5	—	—	30.2	76.8	87.8	—	—	37.5	82.2	91.4
PCV (4 doses or more)[m]	—	—	—	46.2	70.3	—	—	—	42.7	66.1	—	—	—	48.1	74.4

See notes at end of table.

Childhood immunization: Percentage of children ages 19–35 months vaccinated for selected diseases by poverty status,[a] and race and Hispanic origin,[b] selected years 1996–2007

Characteristic	Total					Below 100% poverty					100% poverty and above				
	1996	1999	2002	2005	2007	1996	1999	2002	2005	2007	1996	1999	2002	2005	2007
Hispanic															
Combined series (4:3:1:3:3:1)[c]	—	—	66.0	75.6	78.0	—	—	66.0	75.6	77.7	—	—	65.5	74.8	78.5
Combined series (4:3:1:3:3)[d]	63.7	69.6	72.7	78.8	79.8	62.4	68.0	71.8	78.3	79.0	64.1	72.9	72.9	79.1	80.9
Combined series (4:3:1:3)[e]	71.1	74.9	75.5	81.2	81.5	68.2	73.3	74.8	80.9	80.9	72.7	78.4	75.6	81.9	82.5
Combined series (4:3:1)[f]	74.1	77.3	76.5	81.8	82.4	70.9	75.6	75.6	81.0	81.9	74.6	80.1	76.6	82.7	83.5
DTP (4 doses or more)[g]	77.2	80.2	79.2	83.6	83.8	74.0	77.9	77.9	82.5	82.9	77.5	82.4	79.7	84.9	85.2
Polio (3 doses or more)[h]	89.4	89.4	90.4	92.3	93.0	88.0	88.8	89.3	91.5	95.3	89.8	89.9	90.7	92.3	90.4
MMR (1 dose or more)[i]	88.2	90.2	90.5	91.1	92.6	87.4	89.9	90.8	89.5	92.9	89.0	91.3	89.0	91.4	92.1
Hib (3 doses or more)[j]	88.5	92.0	92.4	94.2	93.5	87.1	90.7	93.1	93.6	93.9	90.3	95.1	92.2	93.9	92.9
Hepatitis B (3 doses or more)[k]	80.8	87.3	89.5	92.7	93.6	79.9	86.5	89.0	91.5	94.5	81.1	88.9	88.9	92.8	92.6
Varicella (1 dose or more)[l]	7.6	60.5	81.8	89.2	90.6	6.3	58.6	82.4	88.4	91.2	11.2	61.7	80.6	88.8	89.3
PCV (3 doses or more)[m]	—	—	37.4	83.5	91.0	—	—	35.1	80.0	91.6	—	—	37.6	86.0	90.3
PCV (4 doses or more)[m]	—	—	—	50.5	75.4	—	—	—	44.7	77.5	—	—	—	53.8	73.3

— Not available.

[a] Based on family income and household size using U.S. Bureau of Census poverty thresholds for the year of data collection.

[b] From 1996 to 2001, the 1977 OMB Standards for Data on Race and Ethnicity were used to classify persons into one of the following racial groups: White, Black, American Indian or Alaskan Native, or Asian or Pacific Islander. Beginning in 2002, the revised 1997 OMB Standards for Data on Race and Ethnicity were used. Persons could select one or more from the following racial groups: White, Black or African American, American Indian or Alaska Native, Asian, or Native Hawaiian or Other Pacific Islander. Persons of Hispanic origin may be of any race. Included in the total but not shown separately are American Indian or Alaska Native, Asian, Native Hawaiian or Other Pacific Islander and "Two or more races" due to the small sample size. Data on race and Hispanic origin are collected separately but combined for reporting.

[c] The 4:3:1:3:3:1 series consists of 4 doses (or more) of diphtheria, tetanus toxoids, and pertussis (DTP) vaccines, diphtheria and tetanus toxoids (DT), or diphtheria, tetanus toxoids, and any acellular pertussis (DTaP) vaccines; 3 doses (or more) of poliovirus vaccines; 1 dose (or more) of any measles-containing vaccine; 3 doses (or more) of *Haemophilus influenzae* type b (Hib) vaccines; 3 doses (or more) of hepatitis B vaccines; and 1 dose (or more) of varicella vaccine. The collection of coverage rate estimates for this series began in 2002.

[d] The 4:3:1:3:3 series consists of 4 doses (or more) of diphtheria, tetanus toxoids, and pertussis (DTP) vaccines, diphtheria and tetanus toxoids (DT), or diphtheria, tetanus toxoids, and any acellular pertussis (DTaP) vaccines; 3 doses (or more) of poliovirus vaccines; 1 dose (or more) of any measles-containing vaccine; 3 doses (or more) of *Haemophilus influenzae* type b (Hib) vaccines; and 3 doses (or more) of hepatitis B vaccines.

[e] The 4:3:1:3 series consists of 4 doses (or more) of diphtheria, tetanus toxoids, and pertussis (DTP) vaccines, diphtheria and tetanus toxoids (DT), or diphtheria, tetanus toxoids, and any acellular pertussis (DTaP) vaccines; 3 doses (or more) of poliovirus vaccines; 1 dose (or more) of any measles-containing vaccine; and 3 doses (or more) of *Haemophilus influenzae* type b (Hib) vaccines.

[f] The 4:3:1 series consists of 4 doses (or more) of diphtheria, tetanus toxoids, and pertussis (DTP) vaccines, diphtheria and tetanus toxoids (DT), or diphtheria, tetanus toxoids, and any acellular pertussis (DTaP) vaccines, 3 doses (or more) of poliovirus vaccines; and 1 dose (or more) of any measles-containing vaccine.

[g] Diphtheria, tetanus toxoids, and pertussis vaccine (4 doses or more of any diphtheria, tetanus toxoids, and pertussis vaccines, including diphtheria and tetanus toxoids and any acellular pertussis vaccine).

[h] Poliovirus vaccine (3 doses or more).

[i] Measles-mumps-rubella (MMR) vaccine (1 dose or more) was used beginning in 2005. The previous coverage years reported measles-containing vaccines.

[j] *Haemophilus influenzae* type b (Hib) vaccine (3 doses or more).

[k] Hepatitis B vaccine (3 doses or more).

[l] Varicella vaccine (1 dose or more) is recommended at any visit at or after age 12 months for susceptible children (i.e., those who lack a reliable history of chickenpox).

[m] The heptavalent pneumococcal conjugate vaccine (PCV) is recommended for all children aged less than 5 years. The series consists of doses at ages 2, 4, and 6 months, and a booster dose at ages 12–15 months.

SOURCE: Centers for Disease Control and Prevention, National Center for Immunization and Respiratory Diseases and National Center for Health Statistics, National Immunization Survey.

Oral health: Percentage of children ages 2–17 with a dental visit in the past year by selected characteristics, 1997–2007

Characteristic	1997	1998	1999	2000	2001	2002	2003	2004	2005	2006	2007
Ages 2–17											
Total	72.7	73.5	72.6	74.1	73.3	74.2	75.0	76.4	76.2	75.7	76.7
Poverty status[a]											
Below 100% poverty	62.0	63.5	58.4	62.4	61.3	64.4	65.8	65.5	66.2	67.5	67.3
100–199% poverty	62.5	62.2	62.9	66.1	64.1	66.9	66.6	69.0	68.6	68.4	70.2
200% poverty and above	80.1	80.6	79.8	80.2	79.7	79.6	80.8	82.2	82.0	81.5	82.0
Type of insurance[b]											
Private insurance[c]	78.5	78.7	78.4	79.8	79.1	80.0	80.1	82.2	82.1	82.4	82.2
Public insurance[c,d]	69.6	68.5	65.3	68.6	66.3	68.6	71.0	71.1	71.4	71.2	72.7
No insurance	46.7	49.2	46.9	50.6	49.2	50.2	51.0	49.0	49.5	48.8	51.9
Race and Hispanic origin[e]											
White, non-Hispanic	76.4	77.1	77.0	78.9	78.0	79.4	79.4	80.9	80.4	79.6	79.5
Black, non-Hispanic	68.8	69.8	67.7	70.0	68.0	68.6	70.6	72.9	72.7	72.4	75.0
American Indian or Alaska Native	66.8	72.6	58.2	71.3	73.1	66.6	69.9	70.3	74.8	72.0	85.4
Asian	69.9	67.9	69.6	72.8	74.6	66.8	72.9	73.8	70.1	75.5	70.7
Two or more races	—	—	73.0	71.4	69.3	71.4	74.5	78.0	78.1	78.1	75.3
Hispanic	61.0	62.4	59.3	60.6	60.7	62.5	64.5	65.3	66.5	66.3	71.2
Ages 2–5											
Total	52.5	51.0	48.4	51.9	51.9	49.3	54.1	53.7	55.1	52.8	55.8
Poverty status[a]											
Below 100% poverty	51.7	51.3	40.8	53.1	47.6	47.5	51.5	49.7	50.0	49.7	51.9
100–199% poverty	46.7	41.6	46.9	48.7	45.0	42.4	49.1	50.1	48.9	47.5	54.0
200% poverty and above	55.2	54.6	51.5	52.7	55.9	52.6	57.2	56.5	59.2	56.3	58.2
Type of insurance[b]											
Private insurance[c]	55.3	53.5	51.3	54.0	55.0	52.9	54.2	57.4	59.2	57.2	57.6
Public insurance[c,d]	54.6	52.3	49.0	53.1	49.6	49.6	54.9	53.1	52.0	52.2	56.6
No insurance	35.1	34.0	31.5	39.9	37.3	27.2	48.1	29.3	36.3	28.3	40.0
Race and Hispanic origin[e]											
White, non-Hispanic	53.3	51.5	50.1	54.0	55.0	51.4	55.7	55.6	56.8	53.5	55.3
Black, non-Hispanic	55.2	54.0	49.7	50.6	50.4	47.4	53.9	47.8	55.8	46.9	59.3
American Indian or Alaska Native	56.3	47.8	49.8	65.9	42.5	42.5	56.5	53.2	65.9	*	65.0
Asian	51.5	50.6	40.4	46.9	48.3	41.5	44.6	51.9	45.5	54.4	45.3
Two or more races	—	—	56.6	60.4	46.9	58.9	59.5	60.4	57.9	63.3	59.6
Hispanic	48.1	48.9	41.2	44.9	44.9	44.6	49.2	51.8	50.3	52.4	56.6
Ages 6–11											
Total	81.7	81.8	81.7	82.2	80.6	83.7	82.3	85.2	84.6	83.9	85.2
Poverty status[a]											
Below 100% poverty	71.0	71.0	67.4	68.6	67.6	73.4	73.0	74.4	74.7	74.4	78.2
100–199% poverty	72.2	70.0	70.2	74.7	71.4	78.1	74.2	77.6	76.9	76.5	79.2
200% poverty and above	89.2	89.4	89.5	88.9	87.5	88.9	88.4	91.2	90.4	90.4	89.6
Type of insurance[b]											
Private insurance[c]	87.2	86.6	87.9	87.8	86.5	89.1	87.5	90.3	89.5	90.6	90.1
Public insurance[c,d]	79.5	77.7	71.4	76.0	75.3	78.2	79.3	81.6	81.3	79.1	82.2
No insurance	56.4	59.0	57.3	60.1	52.2	61.6	57.2	58.4	60.6	56.9	60.0
Race and Hispanic origin[e]											
White, non-Hispanic	85.2	85.5	86.8	87.0	84.9	89.1	86.6	89.8	88.0	88.4	87.3
Black, non-Hispanic	78.7	77.8	75.0	79.0	73.4	79.5	77.4	83.0	80.8	79.8	85.0
American Indian or Alaska Native	73.7	88.3	71.2	78.4	80.5	73.0	70.0	85.0	80.4	83.1	96.3
Asian	77.8	76.8	77.8	88.1	87.0	78.2	83.3	86.7	81.9	85.3	83.2
Two or more races	—	—	79.8	80.7	84.2	76.2	87.1	84.6	87.2	83.1	77.6
Hispanic	70.3	70.3	67.2	67.2	70.2	71.8	72.6	72.2	76.3	74.2	80.2

See notes at end of table.

Oral health: Percentage of children ages 2–17 with a dental visit in the past year by selected characteristics, 1997–2007

Characteristic	1997	1998	1999	2000	2001	2002	2003	2004	2005	2006	2007
Ages 12–17											
Total	77.4	79.8	78.6	80.2	79.7	80.7	81.4	82.4	81.6	82.8	82.5
Poverty status[a]											
Below 100% poverty	61.0	65.9	62.5	62.7	64.4	66.7	68.7	69.0	70.1	75.7	69.4
100–199% poverty	62.9	68.1	66.3	68.3	70.6	72.0	72.3	73.3	73.1	74.0	73.1
200% poverty and above	86.6	87.4	86.7	88.2	86.4	86.8	87.4	88.9	87.4	88.1	89.2
Type of insurance[b]											
Private insurance[c]	84.0	86.0	84.9	87.2	86.4	86.8	88.3	89.0	87.8	89.5	89.7
Public insurance[c,d]	74.6	74.7	74.1	74.1	70.4	73.5	76.6	75.7	78.3	80.0	77.2
No insurance	44.6	49.1	45.6	47.3	53.2	53.5	46.9	50.6	47.4	51.2	50.3
Race and Hispanic origin[e]											
White, non-Hispanic	82.6	84.9	83.5	85.8	85.2	86.6	87.1	87.7	87.1	87.5	87.2
Black, non-Hispanic	67.6	71.5	70.7	72.4	73.0	70.9	73.6	78.1	76.3	80.6	76.5
American Indian or Alaska Native	68.7	70.2	55.4	69.0	81.0	78.1	77.1	67.0	76.1	72.5	87.4
Asian	74.6	72.5	78.9	78.6	81.5	74.5	81.7	75.8	71.7	81.8	78.8
Two or more races	—	—	81.2	71.5	74.8	82.1	76.5	86.4	82.2	85.5	84.2
Hispanic	62.3	65.3	65.1	65.5	63.2	65.7	67.7	68.9	69.1	69.1	72.9

— Not available.

* Estimates are considered unreliable (relative standard error greater than 30 percent).

[a] Family income was imputed for data years 1997 and beyond. Missing family income data were imputed for 22–31 percent of children ages 2–17 in 1997–2007.

[b] Children with health insurance may or may not have dental coverage.

[c] Children with both public and private insurance coverage are placed in the private insurance category.

[d] As defined here, public health insurance for children consists mostly of Medicaid or other public assistance programs, including state plans. Beginning in 1999, the public health insurance category also includes the State Children's Health Insurance Program (SCHIP). It does not include children with only Medicare, Tricare, or CHAMP-VA.

[e] For the 1997–1998 race-specific estimates, the 1977 OMB Standards for Data on Race and Ethnicity were used to classify persons into one of the following four racial groups: White, Black, American Indian or Alaskan Native, or Asian or Pacific Islander. The revised 1997 OMB standards for race were used for the 1999–2007 race-specific estimates and classified persons into one or more of five racial groups: White, Black or African American, American Indian or Alaska Native, Asian, or Native Hawaiian or Other Pacific Islander. From 1999 onward, respondents could choose more than one race. Those reporting more than one race were classified as "Two or more races." Data on race and Hispanic origin are collected separately but are combined for reporting. Persons of Hispanic origin may be of any race. Included in the total but not shown separately are persons of Native Hawaiian or other Pacific Islander origin. Data from 1999 onward are not directly comparable with data from earlier years.

NOTE: From 1997–2000, children were identified as having a dental visit in the past year by asking parents "About how long has it been since your child last saw or talked to a dentist?" In 2001 and later years, the question was "About how long has it been since your child last saw a dentist?" Parents were directed to include all types of dentists, such as orthodontists, oral surgeons, and all other dental specialists, as well as dental hygienists.

SOURCE: National Center for Health Statistics, National Health Interview Survey.

Table HC4.B	Oral health: Percentage of children ages 2–17 with untreated dental caries (cavities) by age, poverty status, and race and Hispanic origin, 1999–2002 and 2003–2004

Characteristic	1999–2002	2003–2004
Ages 2–17		
Total	21.3	25.0
Poverty status		
Below 100% poverty	32.4	32.4
100–199% poverty	27.0	36.3
200% poverty and above	12.7	16.6
Race and Hispanic origin[a]		
White, non-Hispanic	17.8	21.3
Black, non-Hispanic	27.4	26.7
Mexican American	32.2	34.1
Ages 2–5		
Total	19.3	23.4
Poverty status		
Below 100% poverty	31.8	29.1
100–199% poverty	20.1	29.2
200% poverty and above	11.0	17.6
Race and Hispanic origin[a]		
White, non-Hispanic	16.9	17.1
Black, non-Hispanic	24.1	25.0
Mexican American	31.4	30.8
Ages 6–17		
Total	12.1	14.0
Poverty status		
Below 100% poverty	18.2	21.4
100–199% poverty	16.8	19.8
200% poverty and above	6.8	8.2
Race and Hispanic origin[a]		
White, non-Hispanic	9.2	11.7
Black, non-Hispanic	15.8	15.8
Mexican American	18.7	19.5

[a] From 1999 to 2004, the revised 1997 OMB Standards for Data on Race and Ethnicity were used. Persons could select one or more of five racial groups: White, Black or African American, American Indian or Alaska Native, Asian, or Native Hawaiian or Other Pacific Islander. Included in the total, but not shown separately are American Indian or Alaska Native, Native Hawaiian or other Pacific Islander, Asian, and "Two or more races." Data on race and Hispanic origin are collected separately, but are combined for reporting. Persons of Hispanic origin may be of any race. The National Health and Nutrition Examination Survey (NHANES) sample was designed to provide estimates specifically for persons of Mexican origin and not for all persons of Hispanic origin.

NOTE: Children ages 2–5 had at least one primary tooth with untreated decay. Children ages 6–17 had at least one permanent tooth with untreated decay. Children ages 2–17 had at least one primary or permanent tooth with untreated decay. Thus, estimates for children ages 2–17 may be higher than estimates for children ages 2–5 and ages 6–17 combined.

SOURCE: National Center for Health Statistics, National Health and Nutrition Examination Survey.

| Table PHY1.A | Outdoor air quality: Percentage of children ages 0–17 living in counties in which levels of one or more air pollutants were above allowable levels, 1999–2007 | | | | | | | | |

Characteristic	1999	2000	2001	2002	2003	2004	2005	2006	2007
One or more pollutants	67.15	68.94	68.76	67.25	69.56	63.71	69.99	66.46	65.89
Pollutant									
Ozone	65.24	64.96	66.29	66.19	67.90	61.70	66.37	65.53	64.25
Carbon monoxide	5.68	0.72	0.71	4.12	1.03	0.07	0.18	0.49	0.11
Particulate matter (PM_{10})	11.26	5.81	5.88	9.43	7.57	6.68	6.06	8.52	15.82
Particulate matter ($PM_{2.5}$)	23.57	29.21	25.42	21.45	19.38	15.68	24.46	12.54	16.00
Lead	0.69	1.02	1.03	0.08	0.01	0.00	0.07	0.07	0.47
Nitrogen dioxide	0.00	0.00	0.00	0.00	0.00	0.00	0.00	0.00	0.00
Sulfur dioxide	0.00	0.00	0.00	0.00	0.00	0.00	0.00	0.00	0.00

NOTE: Percentages are based on the number of children living in counties where air pollution levels were higher than the allowable level of the Primary National Ambient Air Quality Standards. This analysis differs from the analysis utilized by the U.S. Environmental Protection Agency for the designation of "nonattainment areas" for regulatory compliance purposes. This analysis incorporates a new Primary National Ambient Air Quality Standard for ozone that was promulgated in 2008. For more information on the air quality standards that are used in calculating these percentages, please see http://www.epa.gov/air/criteria.html.

SOURCE: U.S. Environmental Protection Agency, Office of Air and Radiation, Air Quality System.

| Table PHY1.B | Indoor air quality: Percentage of children ages 4–17 with specified blood cotinine levels by age, selected years 1988–2006 | | | | |

Characteristic	1988–1994	1999–2000	2001–2002	2003–2004	2005–2006
Ages 4–17					
Total					
Any detectable cotinine	87.4	64.2	52.6	61.1	48.9
Blood cotinine more than 1.0 ng/mL	23.7	16.9	16.1	17.1	11.6
Ages 4–11					
Total					
Any detectable cotinine	87.7	64.4	55.1	63.7	51.4
Blood cotinine more than 1.0 ng/mL	25.7	17.7	18.1	18.7	12.3
Ages 12–17					
Total					
Any detectable cotinine	87.0	63.9	49.6	57.9	46.0
Blood cotinine more than 1.0 ng/mL	21.1	16.0	13.6	15.0	10.8

NOTE: "Any detectable cotinine" indicates blood cotinine levels at or above 0.05 nanograms per milliliter (ng/mL), the detectable level of cotinine in the blood in 1988–1994. Cotinine levels are reported for nonsmoking children only. The average (geometric mean) blood cotinine level in children living in homes where someone smokes was 1.0 ng/mL in 1988–1994.[1]

SOURCE: National Center for Health Statistics, National Health and Nutrition Examination Survey.

[1] Mannino, D.M., Caraballo, R., Benowitz, N., and Repace, J. (2001). Predictors of cotinine levels in U.S. children: Data from the Third National Health and Nutrition Examination Survey. CHEST, 120, 718–724.

Table PHY1.C	Indoor air quality: Percentage of children ages 0–6 living in homes where someone smoked regularly[a] by race and Hispanic origin and poverty status, 1994 and 2005	
Characteristic	1994	2005
All		
Total	27.3	8.4
Race and Hispanic origin[b]		
White, non-Hispanic	29.4	9.1
Black, non-Hispanic	27.6	12.0
Hispanic	19.9	4.3
Mexican	19.2	3.9
Puerto Rican	*	9.3
Poverty status		
Below 100% poverty	37.1	14.6
100–199% poverty	32.7	11.7
200% poverty and above	18.5	4.7

* Estimate is considered unreliable (relative standard error is greater than 40 percent).

[a] Regular smoking is defined as smoking by a resident that occurs 4 or more days per week.

[b] For the 1994 race-specific estimates, the 1977 OMB Standards for Data on Race and Ethnicity were used to classify persons into one of the following four racial groups: White, Black, American Indian or Alaskan Native, or Asian or Pacific Islander. The revised 1997 OMB standards for race were used for the 2005 race-specific estimates and classified persons into one or more of five racial groups: White, Black or African American, American Indian or Alaska Native, Asian, or Native Hawaiian or Other Pacific Islander. Included in the total, but not shown separately are American Indian or Alaska Native, Native Hawaiian or Other Pacific Islander, Asian, and "Two or more races." Data on race and Hispanic origin are collected separately but are combined for reporting. Persons of Hispanic origin may be of any race.

SOURCE: National Center for Health Statistics, National Health Interview Survey.

| Table PHY2 | Drinking water quality: Percentage of children served by community water systems that did not meet all applicable health-based drinking water standards, 1993–2007 |

Characteristic	1993	1994	1995	1996	1997	1998	1999	2000
Type of standard violated								
All health-based standards	19.7	15.2	11.5	10.4	10.0	8.6	8.0	8.5
Lead and copper	2.8	1.7	2.0	1.8	1.9	1.6	1.5	1.2
Coliforms	8.6	7.3	4.2	4.4	3.7	3.1	3.2	3.0
Chemical and radionuclide	1.8	1.3	1.8	1.2	1.6	1.7	1.2	1.5
Surface water treatment and filtration	7.9	6.0	4.4	4.0	3.6	2.9	2.5	3.2
Nitrate/nitrite	0.3	0.1	0.2	0.2	0.4	0.6	0.3	0.5
Disinfection byproducts	—	—	—	—	—	—	—	—

Characteristic	2001	2002	2003	2004	2005	2006	2007
Type of standard violated							
All health-based standards	5.3	11.0	8.3	10.5	11.2	9.5	7.8
Lead and copper	1.1	0.8	0.6	0.9	0.8	0.5	0.4
Coliforms	2.1	2.6	3.0	3.5	3.3	2.7	2.4
Chemical and radionuclide	1.0	2.1	2.0	2.2	2.8	2.6	2.2
Surface water treatment and filtration	1.2	5.0	1.4	3.3	3.8	3.5	2.5
Nitrate/nitrite	0.2	0.5	0.3	0.1	0.1	0.5	0.1
Disinfection byproducts	—	1.4	2.9	2.0	2.6	1.5	1.5

— Not available.

NOTE: A new standard for disinfection byproducts was implemented beginning in 2002 for larger drinking water systems and in 2004 for smaller systems. Revisions to the standard for surface water treatment took effect in 2002. A revised standard for radionuclides went into effect in 2003. A revised standard for arsenic (included in the Chemical and radionuclide category) went into effect in 2006. No other revisions to the standards have taken effect during the period of trend data (beginning with 1993). Data have been revised since previous publication in *America's Children*. Values for years prior to 2007 have been recalculated based on updated data in the Safe Drinking Water Information System.

SOURCE: U.S. Environmental Protection Agency, Office of Water, Safe Drinking Water Information System.

Table PHY3.A	Lead in the blood of children: Percentage of children ages 1–5 with specified blood lead levels, selected years 1988–2006		
Specified blood lead level	1988–1994	1999–2002	2003–2006
≥10 μg/dL	6.3	1.6	0.9[a]
≥ 5 μg/dL	25.6	8.7	4.1
≥ 2.5 μg/dL	61.2	34.0	20.9

[a] Estimate is unstable (relative standard error is greater than 30 percent but less than 40 percent).

NOTE: A blood lead level of 10 μg/dL or greater is considered elevated,[1] but adverse health effects have been shown to occur at lower concentrations.[2]

SOURCE: National Center for Health Statistics, National Health and Nutrition Examination Survey.

[1] Centers for Disease Control and Prevention. (2002). Managing elevated blood lead levels among young children: Recommendations from the Advisory Committee on Childhood Lead Poisoning Prevention. Atlanta, GA. Available at http://www.cdc.gov/nceh/lead/CaseManagement/caseManage_main.htm.

[2] Canfield, R.L., Henderson, C.R., Jr., Cory-Slechta, D.A., Cox, C., Jusko, T.A., and Lanphear, B.P. (2003). Intellectual impairment in children with blood lead concentrations below 10 micrograms per deciliter. *New England Journal of Medicine, 348*(16), 1517–1526.

Table PHY3.B	Lead in the blood of children: Percentage of children ages 1–5 with specified blood lead levels by race and Hispanic origin and poverty status, 2003–2006	
Characteristic	≥ 5 μg/dL	≥ 2.5 μg/dL
Total[a]	4.1	20.9
Race and Hispanic origin[b]		
White, non-Hispanic	2.3	14.3
Black, non-Hispanic	12.3	43.9
Mexican American	2.6[c]	21.3
Poverty status		
Below 100% poverty	9.0	35.5
100% poverty and above	2.2	15.0

[a] Totals include data for racial/ethnic groups not shown separately.

[b] For 2003–2006, the revised 1997 OMB Standards for Data on Race and Ethnicity were used. Persons could select one or more of five racial groups: White, Black or African American, American Indian or Alaska Native, Asian, and Native Hawaiian or Other Pacific Islander. Included in the total but not shown separately are American Indian or Alaska Native, Asian, and Native Hawaiian or Other Pacific Islander due to the small sample size for each of these groups. Data on race and Hispanic origin are collected separately but combined for reporting. Persons of Mexican origin may be of any race. The National Health and Nutrition Examination Survey (NHANES) sample was designed to provide estimates specifically for persons of Mexican origin.

[c] Estimate is unstable (relative standard error is greater than 30 percent but less than 40 percent).

NOTE: Data for 2003–2006 are combined. A blood lead level of 10 μg/dL or greater is considered elevated,[1] but adverse health effects have been shown to occur at lower concentrations.[2] Data for percentage of children with blood lead above 10 μg/dL are not shown because estimates by race and Hispanic origin and by poverty status are considered unreliable (relative standard error is greater than 40 percent).

SOURCE: National Center for Health Statistics, National Health and Nutrition Examination Survey.

[1] Centers for Disease Control and Prevention. (2002). Managing elevated blood lead levels among young children: Recommendations from the Advisory Committee on Childhood Lead Poisoning Prevention. Atlanta, GA. Available at http://www.cdc.gov/nceh/lead/CaseManagement/caseManage_main.htm.

[2] Canfield, R.L., Henderson, C.R., Jr., Cory-Slechta, D.A., Cox, C., Jusko, T.A., and Lanphear, B.P. (2003). Intellectual impairment in children with blood lead concentrations below 10 micrograms per deciliter. *New England Journal of Medicine, 348*(16), 1517–1526.

Housing problems: Percentage of households with children ages 0–17 that reported housing problems by type of problem, selected years 1978–2007[a]

Household type	1978	1983	1989	1993	1997	1999	2001	2003	2005	2007
All households with children										
Number of households (in millions)	32.3	33.6	35.4	35.4	37.0	37.5	38.6	38.4	38.7	38.1
Percent with										
Any problems	30	33	33	34	36	35	36.1	36.9	40.3	43.0
Inadequate housing[b]	9	8	9	7	7	7	6.7	5.8	5.4	5.1
Crowded housing	9	8	7	6	7	7	6.3	6.2	6.3	6.2
Cost burden greater than 30 percent[c]	15	21	24	26	28	28	28.5	30.1	34.2	37.2
Cost burden greater than 50 percent[c]	6	11	9	11	12	11	11.2	11.5	14.5	15.8
Severe problems[d]	8	12	10	11	11	11	11.1	11.3	13.8	15.1
Very-low-income renter households with children[e]										
Number of households (in millions)	4.2	5.1	5.9	6.6	6.4	6.2	6.0	6.4	6.5	6.3
Percent with										
Any problems	79	83	77	75	82	80	79.4	77.5	82.2	82.5
Inadequate housing[b]	18	18	18	14	16	15	15.4	12.8	12.2	11.4
Crowded housing	22	18	17	14	17	17	15.4	14.5	14.2	14.1
Cost burden greater than 30 percent[c]	59	68	67	67	73	70	69.5	70.4	75.9	75.9
Cost burden greater than 50 percent[c]	31	38	36	38	41	37	37.7	36.2	44.9	44.1
Severe problems[d]	33	42	31	33	32	29	30.2	29.0	35.9	34.6
Rental assistance[f]	23	23	33	33	31	31	30.3	28.1	27.7	27.7

[a] Data are available for 1978, 1983, 1989, and biennially since 1993. All data are weighted using the decennial Census that preceded the date of their collection. Because of questionnaire changes, data since 1997 on families with rental assistance, priority problems, and severe physical problems are not directly comparable with earlier data. See Office of Policy Development and Research, U.S. Department of Housing and Urban Development. (2003). *Trends in worst case needs for housing, 1978–1999: A report to Congress on worst case housing needs—Plus update on worst case needs in 2001.* Washington, DC: U.S. Department of Housing and Urban Development.

[b] Inadequate housing refers to housing with "moderate or severe physical problems." The most common problems meeting the definition are lacking complete plumbing for exclusive use, having unvented room heaters as the primary heating equipment, and multiple upkeep problems such as water leakage, open cracks or holes, broken plaster, or signs of rats. Problems appearing in public halls of multifamily structures are no longer counted beginning in 2007. See definition in Appendix A and changes in Appendix C of the American Housing Survey summary volume, *American Housing Survey for the United States: 2007,* Current Housing Reports, Series H150/07, U.S. Census Bureau, 2008.

[c] Cost burden refers to expenditures on housing and utilities that exceed the specified proportion, 30 percent or 50 percent, of reported income.

[d] Severe problems: For households not reporting housing assistance, cost burden is greater than 50 percent of income or severe physical problems are present.

[e] Very-low-income households are those with incomes at or below one-half the median income, adjusted for family size, in a geographic area.

[f] Renters are either in a public housing project or have a subsidy (i.e., pay a lower rent because a Federal, state, or local government program pays part of the cost of construction, mortgage, or operating expenses).

SOURCE: U.S. Census Bureau and the U.S. Department of Housing and Urban Development, American Housing Survey. Tabulated by U.S. Department of Housing and Urban Development.

Characteristic	1980	1985	1990	1995	2000	2002	2003[a]	2004[a]	2005[a]	2006[b]	2007
Rate per 1,000 youth ages 12–17											
Age											
Ages 12–17	37.6	34.3	43.2	28.3	16.4	11.2	17.7	11.3	13.6	15.6	9.9
Ages 12–14	33.4	28.1	41.2	26.7	13.7	8.0	13.6	10.9	9.9	14.1	8.9
Ages 15–17	41.4	40.3	45.2	30.0	19.0	14.4	22.1	11.7	17.2	17.2	10.7
Race and Hispanic origin[c]											
White	34.1	34.4	37.0	25.5	15.4	10.4	—	—	—	—	—
White, non-Hispanic[d]	—	—	—	—	—	—	17.9	11.2	10.9	15.7	10.6
Black	60.2	35.2	77.0	44.5	23.6	16.6	—	—	—	—	—
Black, non-Hispanic[d]	—	—	—	—	—	—	19.4	22.9	17.9	20.3	*
Hispanic[e]	—	—	—	—	—	—	7.9	4.6	17.7	13.2	12.8
Other	21.7	28.8	37.3	23.7	7.7	3.4	—	—	—	—	—
Gender											
Male	54.8	49.8	60.5	39.0	22.9	13.0	24.7	15.0	15.9	17.0	15.9
Female	19.7	18.2	24.9	17.0	9.6	9.2	10.4	7.3	11.2	14.3	*
Number of victimizations of youth ages 12–17											
Age											
Ages 12–17	877,104	742,815	866,272	633,301	394,107	276,686	446,445	285,674	346,031	399,204	248,871
Ages 12–14	364,437	295,972	412,125	303,287	166,212	101,811	176,959	140,190	126,425	175,431	110,621
Ages 15–17	512,667	446,843	454,147	330,014	227,895	174,875	269,486	145,484	219,606	223,773	138,250
Race and Hispanic origin[c]											
White	658,539	606,739	593,596	451,830	293,860	203,767	—	—	—	—	—
White, non-Hispanic[d]	—	—	—	—	—	—	275,924	170,779	169,292	237,841	157,916
Black	206,227	113,960	238,141	154,013	91,751	69,235	—	—	—	—	—
Black, non-Hispanic[d]	—	—	—	—	—	—	73,102	87,364	69,003	79,881	*
Hispanic[e]	—	—	—	—	—	—	35,852	21,655	79,631	60,399	63,583
Other	12,292	22,111	34,523	27,445	8,483	3,674	—	—	—	—	—
Gender											
Male	651,976	550,860	623,509	447,695	281,709	165,369	318,137	194,850	207,073	221,344	204,785
Female	225,127	191,955	242,763	185,606	112,398	111,317	128,307	90,825	138,688	177,860	*

— Not available.

* Reporting standards not met due to insufficient unweighted sample cases.

[a] Revised. Estimates corrected from previous publication in *America's Children*.

[b] Due to changes in methodology, the 2006 national crime victimization rates are not comparable to other years and cannot be used for yearly trend comparisons. See *Criminal Victimization, 2006,* http://www.ojp.usdoj.gov/bjs/abstract/cv06.htm.

[c] From 1980 to 2002, the 1977 OMB Standards for Data on Race and Ethnicity were used to classify persons into one of the following racial groups: White, Black, or Other. "Other" included American Indian or Alaskan Native, and Asian or Pacific Islander. Data from 2003 onward are collected under the 1997 OMB Standards. Persons could select one or more of five racial groups: White, Black or African American, American Indian or Alaska Native, Asian, or Native Hawaiian or Other Pacific Islander. Included in the total, but not shown separately are American Indian or Alaska Native, Asian, Native Hawaiian or Other Pacific Islander, and "Two or more races." Data from 2003 onward are not directly comparable with data from earlier years. Data on race and Hispanic origin are collected separately. Persons of Hispanic origin may be of any race.

[d] Homicide data is collected using the FBI's Supplementary Homicide Reports (SHR) for which Hispanic origin is not available. Homicide is included here, but the victim may have been Hispanic.

[e] Victimization estimates for Hispanics exclude homicides because homicide data are collected using the FBI's Supplementary Homicide Reports (SHR) for which Hispanic origin is not available.

NOTE: Serious violent crimes include aggravated assault, rape, robbery, and homicide. Aggravated assault is an attack with a weapon, regardless of whether or not an injury occurred, or an attack without a weapon when serious injury resulted. Robbery is stealing by force or threat of force. Because of changes made in the victimization survey, data prior to 1992 were adjusted to make them comparable with data collected under the redesigned methodology.

SOURCE: Bureau of Justice Statistics, National Crime Victimization Survey and Federal Bureau of Investigation, Uniform Crime Reporting Program, Supplementary Homicide Reports.

Table PHY6.A	Child injury and mortality: Emergency department visit rates for children ages 1–14 by leading causes of injury visits, 1995–2006					

(Emergency department visits per 1,000 children ages 1–4 and ages 5–14)

Characteristic	1995–1996	1997–1998	1999–2000	2001–2002	2003–2004	2005–2006
Ages 1–4						
All injury visits[a]	161.2	158.6	165.4	139.3	151.3	150.7
All initial injury visits[b]	—	—	—	129.0	142.7	142.6
Leading causes of injury visits[c]						
Cut or pierced from instrument or object	12.2	9.7	12.1	6.5	7.4	5.6
Fall	47.2	39.2	48.2	35.0	49.3	53.7
Motor vehicle traffic	6.2	8.1	6.9	6.5	7.4	7.1
Natural or environmental factors[d]	9.9	9.0	14.5	7.4	10.6	10.4
Overexertion	1.6	4.3	3.0	1.8	2.2	3.4
Poisoning	9.8	8.3	7.8	4.9	8.1	7.6
Struck by/against an object or person	24.9	38.2	29.4	28.2	20.5	14.7
Ages 5–14						
All injury visits[a]	126.8	119.8	122.9	118.1	120.5	112.1
All initial injury visits[b]	—	—	—	110.0	114.3	105.4
Leading causes of injury visits[c]						
Cut or pierced from instrument or object	10.9	10.7	8.4	7.8	7.6	6.5
Fall	31.3	27.0	27.0	27.6	28.0	28.1
Motor vehicle traffic	10.1	8.3	10.1	7.7	7.9	8.2
Natural or environmental factors[d]	8.5	6.2	5.7	5.5	8.1	6.2
Overexertion	2.4	2.3	2.8	3.6	3.8	3.8
Poisoning	1.6	1.1	1.6	1.4	1.7	1.5
Struck by/against an object or person	21.1	27.8	30.2	26.9	25.3	20.2

— Not available.

[a] Any emergency department visit where there is a valid first-listed injury diagnosis code or a valid first-listed external cause of injury code.

[b] In 2005–2006, 94 percent of injury-related emergency department visits for children ages 1–4 and for children ages 5–14 were for an initial visit.

[c] Data for 2001–2006 are for initial visits only. Initial visit status was imputed for 2005–2006.

[d] Insect or animal bites accounted for the majority of emergency department visits caused by natural or environmental factors.

SOURCE: National Center for Health Statistics, National Hospital Ambulatory Medical Care Survey.

Child injury and mortality: Death rates among children ages 1–14 by gender, race and Hispanic origin, and all causes and all injury causes, selected years 1980–2006

(Deaths per 100,000 children ages 1–4 and ages 5–14)

Characteristic	1980	1985	1990	1995	2000	2001	2002	2003	2004	2005	2006
Ages 1–4											
All causes[a]	63.9	51.8	46.8	40.4	32.4	33.3	31.2	31.5	29.9	29.4	28.4
Gender											
Male	72.6	58.5	52.4	44.5	35.9	37.0	35.2	35.1	32.4	33.4	30.5
Female	54.7	44.8	41.0	36.0	28.7	29.5	27.0	27.8	27.3	25.1	26.3
Race and Hispanic origin[b]											
White	57.9	46.6	41.1	35.2	29.2	30.7	28.1	28.5	27.0	27.0	25.5
White, non-Hispanic[c]	—	45.3	37.6	34.2	28.5	30.1	27.1	27.6	26.8	26.2	25.0
Black	97.6	80.7	76.8	66.4	49.9	47.5	47.1	46.8	44.8	41.8	43.3
Asian or Pacific Islander	43.2	40.1	38.6	26.5	21.6	22.3	23.4	22.5	21.3	19.2	19.6
Hispanic[c]	—	46.1	43.5	36.3	29.6	30.6	29.8	30.2	27.3	28.9	26.4
Leading causes of death[d]											
Unintentional injuries	25.9	20.2	17.3	14.4	11.9	11.2	10.5	10.9	10.3	10.3	9.9
Cancer	4.5	3.8	3.5	3.1	2.7	2.7	2.6	2.5	2.5	2.3	2.3
Birth defects	8.0	5.9	6.1	4.4	3.2	3.6	3.4	3.4	3.6	3.2	3.2
Homicide	2.5	2.5	2.6	2.9	2.3	2.7	2.7	2.4	2.4	2.3	2.2
Heart disease	2.6	2.2	1.9	1.6	1.2	1.5	1.1	1.2	1.2	0.9	1.0
Pneumonia/influenza	2.1	1.6	1.2	1.0	0.7	0.7	0.7	1.0	0.7	0.7	0.8
Injury-related causes of death[d]											
All injuries (intentional and unintentional)	28.9	23.0	19.9	17.3	14.5	14.2	13.6	13.4	12.9	13.0	12.5
Motor vehicle traffic-related	7.4	5.9	5.3	4.4	3.7	3.6	3.4	3.2	3.3	3.0	2.9
Drowning	5.7	4.4	3.9	3.5	3.3	3.1	3.1	3.0	2.8	3.2	2.9
Fire and burns	6.1	4.8	4.0	3.1	2.1	1.7	1.6	1.6	1.5	1.5	1.3
Firearms	0.7	0.7	0.6	0.6	0.3	0.5	0.4	0.3	0.3	0.4	0.3
Suffocation	1.9	1.4	1.3	1.3	1.2	1.1	1.1	1.1	1.0	0.9	1.0
Pedestrian (non-traffic)[e]	1.5	1.1	0.9	0.7	0.6	0.5	0.5	0.7	0.7	0.8	0.7
Fall	0.9	0.6	0.6	0.3	0.2	0.2	0.3	0.4	0.3	0.2	0.3

See notes at end of table.

Child injury and mortality: Death rates among children ages 1–14 by gender, race and Hispanic origin, and all causes and all injury causes, selected years 1980–2006

(Deaths per 100,000 children ages 1–4 and ages 5–14)

Characteristic	1980	1985	1990	1995	2000	2001	2002	2003	2004	2005	2006
Ages 5–14											
All causes[a]	30.6	26.5	24.0	22.2	18.0	17.3	17.4	17.0	16.8	16.3	15.2
Gender											
Male	36.7	31.8	28.5	26.4	20.9	19.8	20.0	19.8	19.2	18.6	17.6
Female	24.2	21.0	19.3	17.9	15.0	14.6	14.7	14.0	14.3	13.9	12.8
Race and Hispanic origin[b]											
White	29.1	25.0	22.3	20.5	17.0	16.2	16.1	15.8	15.5	15.0	14.2
White, non-Hispanic[c]	—	23.1	21.5	20.1	17.1	16.3	16.0	15.6	15.5	15.2	14.0
Black	39.0	35.5	34.4	32.0	24.2	23.3	24.5	22.9	23.6	23.3	21.2
Asian or Pacific Islander	24.2	20.8	16.9	17.5	12.3	12.2	12.4	13.1	12.2	12.9	11.1
Hispanic[c]	—	19.3	20.0	19.9	15.7	14.7	15.5	15.7	14.4	13.7	14.2
Leading causes of death[d]											
Unintentional injuries	15.0	12.6	10.4	9.2	7.3	6.9	6.6	6.4	6.5	6.0	5.6
Cancer	4.3	3.5	3.1	2.7	2.5	2.5	2.6	2.6	2.5	2.5	2.2
Birth defects	1.6	1.4	1.5	1.2	1.0	0.9	1.0	0.9	1.0	1.0	0.9
Homicide	1.2	1.2	1.3	1.5	0.9	0.8	0.9	0.8	0.8	0.8	1.0
Heart disease	0.9	1.0	0.9	0.8	0.7	0.7	0.6	0.6	0.6	0.6	0.6
Pneumonia/influenza	0.6	0.4	0.4	0.3	0.2	0.2	0.2	0.4	0.2	0.3	0.2
Injury-related causes of death[d]											
All injuries (intentional and unintentional)	16.7	14.7	12.7	11.5	9.1	8.5	8.3	7.9	8.2	7.7	7.3
Motor vehicle traffic-related	7.5	6.6	5.6	5.1	4.0	3.8	3.6	3.7	3.7	3.3	3.0
Drowning	2.5	1.8	1.5	1.2	0.9	0.8	0.8	0.7	0.7	0.7	0.7
Fire and burns	1.5	1.4	1.0	0.9	0.7	0.7	0.7	0.6	0.7	0.6	0.5
Firearms	1.6	1.8	1.9	1.9	0.9	0.8	0.9	0.8	0.7	0.8	0.9
Suffocation	0.9	0.9	0.8	0.8	0.8	0.8	0.8	0.7	0.9	0.8	0.8
Pedestrian (non-traffic)[e]	0.2	0.1	0.1	0.1	0.2	0.2	0.1	0.1	0.1	0.1	0.1
Fall	0.3	0.2	0.1	0.2	0.1	0.2	0.1	0.1	0.1	0.1	0.1

— Not available.

[a] Total includes American Indians/Alaskan Natives.

[b] The 1977 OMB Standards for Data on Race and Ethnicity were used to classify persons into one of the following three racial groups: White, Black, or Asian or Pacific Islander. Death rates for American Indian or Alaskan Natives are not shown separately because the numbers of deaths were too small for the calculation of reliable rates and American Indians are underreported on the death certificate. CA, HI, ID, ME, MT, NY, and WI reported multiple-race data in 2003. In 2004, the following states began to report multiple-race data: MI, MN, NH, NJ, OK, SD, WA, and WY. In 2005, the following states began to report multiple-race data: CT, FL, KS, NE, SC, UT, and DC (mid-year). In 2006, NM, OR, RI, and TX began to report multiple-race data. The multiple-race data for these states were bridged to the single-race categories of the 1977 OMB standards for comparability with other states rather than following the revised 1997 OMB standards for a select group of states. In addition, note that data on race and Hispanic origin are collected and reported separately. Persons of Hispanic origin may be of any race.

[c] Trends for the Hispanic population are affected by an expansion in the number of registration areas that included an item on Hispanic origin on the death certificate. Tabulations are restricted to a subset of the states that include the item on the death certificate and that meet a minimal quality standard. The quality of reporting has improved substantially over time, so that the minimal quality standard was relaxed in 1992 for those areas reporting Hispanic origin on at least 80 percent of records. The number of states in the reporting area increased from 15 states in 1984 to 17 states and the District of Columbia (DC) in 1985; 18 states and DC in 1986–1987; 26 states and DC in 1988; 44 states and DC in 1989; 45 states, New York State (excluding New York City), and DC in 1990; 47 states, New York State (excluding New York City), and DC in 1991; 48 states and DC in 1992; and 49 states and DC in 1993–1996. Complete reporting began in 1997. The population data in 1990 and 1991 do not exclude New York City.

[d] Cause-of-death information for 1980–1998 is classified according to the Ninth Revision of the International Classification of Diseases. Cause-of-death information for 1999–2006 is classified according to the Tenth Revision of the International Classification of Diseases.

[e] Includes deaths occurring on private property. Pedestrian deaths on public roads are included in the motor vehicle traffic-related category.

SOURCE: National Center for Health Statistics, National Vital Statistics System.

Adolescent injury and mortality: Emergency department visit rates for adolescents ages 15–19 by leading causes of injury visits, 1995–2006

(Emergency department visits per 1,000 adolescents ages 15–19)

Characteristic	1995–1996	1997–1998	1999–2000	2001–2002	2003–2004	2005–2006
All injury visits[a]	179.8	170.9	178.4	154.4	160.7	161.4
All initial injury visits[b]	—	—	—	141.5	148.2	147.5
Leading causes of injury visits[c]						
Cut or pierced from instrument or object	16.2	18.2	18.0	12.4	12.4	12.4
Unintentional	14.0	15.2	15.6	11.0	11.1	10.0
Fall[d]	24.8	20.6	21.1	16.0	20.4	22.3
Motor vehicle traffic[d]	32.9	32.3	32.7	26.0	24.6	24.1
Natural or environmental factors[d,e]	5.6	4.4	7.1	5.2	6.9	5.9
Overexertion[d]	7.4	4.8	7.3	5.9	7.0	8.1
Poisoning	4.3	5.9	4.3	5.7	6.4	5.4
Unintentional	2.9	3.0	1.8	3.3	2.3	2.9
Self-inflicted	1.4	2.0	2.2	2.0	3.4	1.7
Struck by/against an object or person	35.1	44.3	41.4	34.8	32.6	26.0
Unintentional	25.3	37.2	32.1	27.2	24.9	19.1
Assault	9.7	6.9	9.2	7.5	7.7	6.6

— Not available.

[a] Any emergency department visit where there is a valid first-listed injury diagnosis code or a valid first-listed external cause code on the emergency department discharge record.

[b] In 2005–2006, 91 percent of injury-related emergency department visits were an initial visit.

[c] Data for 2001–2006 included initial visits only. Initial visit status was imputed in 2005–2006.

[d] Falls, motor vehicle traffic, natural or environmental factors, and overexertion were unintentional for 99–100 percent of the visits.

[e] Insect or animal bites accounted for the majority of emergency department visits caused by natural or environmental factors.

SOURCE: National Center for Health Statistics, National Hospital Ambulatory Medical Care Survey.

Adolescent mortality: Death rates among adolescents ages 15–19 by gender, race and Hispanic origin,[a] and all causes and all injury causes,[b] selected years 1980–2006

(Deaths per 100,000 adolescents ages 15–19)

Characteristic	1980	1985	1990	1995	2000	2003	2004	2005	2006
Total (all races)									
All causes	97.9	80.5	88.4	82.1	67.1	66.4	66.1	65.1	64.4
All injuries	78.1	62.8	71.4	65.0	51.6	50.6	51.3	49.8	50.3
Unintentional injuries	57.8	43.7	42.4	36.0	33.4	33.0	32.9	31.4	31.2
Homicide	10.5	8.4	16.9	17.8	9.5	9.5	9.3	9.9	10.7
Suicide	8.5	9.9	11.1	10.3	8.0	7.3	8.2	7.7	7.3
Leading mechanisms of injury									
Motor vehicle traffic	42.3	33.1	33.0	27.8	25.3	25.2	24.7	23.0	22.6
All firearm	14.7	13.3	23.5	24.1	12.9	12.1	12.0	12.5	13.2
Firearm homicide	7.0	5.7	14.0	15.3	7.7	7.7	7.6	8.3	9.1
Firearm suicide	5.4	6.0	7.5	6.9	4.4	3.6	3.8	3.5	3.3
Male									
White, non-Hispanic									
All causes	—	105.1	105.7	96.3	86.1	84.3	83.4	82.0	79.0
All injuries	—	86.2	87.5	77.5	69.4	66.9	68.1	64.8	64.2
Unintentional injuries	—	64.1	62.6	51.8	50.0	48.4	49.2	46.1	45.8
Homicide	—	5.2	5.6	5.8	3.5	3.6	3.3	3.5	3.4
Suicide	—	16.0	20.4	18.6	14.8	13.3	14.2	14.0	13.3
Leading mechanisms of injury									
Motor vehicle traffic	—	47.6	46.9	38.6	36.7	35.1	34.4	31.4	30.7
All firearm	—	17.0	20.4	20.0	12.3	11.1	10.8	10.5	10.3
Firearm homicide	—	3.7	3.9	4.5	2.5	2.6	2.2	2.5	2.6
Firearm suicide	—	10.5	13.3	12.7	8.6	7.4	7.5	7.2	6.7
Black									
All causes	134.5	125.5	199.9	200.1	130.1	120.9	121.0	127.2	130.8
All injuries	105.3	96.7	174.1	169.4	103.0	96.8	94.7	101.3	107.6
Unintentional injuries	49.1	40.7	45.6	44.2	34.5	30.0	31.2	32.5	33.1
Homicide	47.7	45.9	114.9	108.4	57.2	58.9	54.8	60.0	66.3
Suicide	5.6	8.2	11.5	13.6	9.5	6.6	7.4	7.2	7.0
Leading mechanisms of injury									
Motor vehicle traffic	24.3	21.9	28.6	28.6	22.5	21.3	21.2	22.1	21.3
All firearm	46.7	46.5	119.8	118.9	61.5	59.3	55.2	61.5	68.2
Firearm homicide	38.4	36.6	105.2	101.4	51.7	53.2	49.8	54.9	60.8
Firearm suicide	3.4	5.4	8.8	10.5	6.9	3.9	3.7	4.3	4.2
American Indian or Alaskan Native									
All causes	248.3	167.5	183.7	147.8	122.2	129.9	112.5	117.5	126.1
All injuries	222.7	148.4	157.2	133.5	108.5	108.6	99.3	101.8	111.9
Unintentional injuries	161.2	89.9	96.6	75.3	70.0	68.0	51.3	63.3	62.7
Homicide	*	*	*	30.5	14.4	15.3	14.5	13.1	16.8
Suicide	40.6	36.0	36.6	37.0	23.3	24.6	32.2	24.2	30.4
Leading mechanisms of injury									
Motor vehicle traffic	107.9	66.3	63.3	52.9	47.4	48.6	38.1	37.2	47.9
All firearm	40.6	29.2	29.6	43.9	22.0	22.7	25.0	23.5	25.9
Firearm homicide	*	*	*	19.7	*	*	*	*	*
Firearm suicide	26.7	*	*	*	*	*	13.8	*	13.6

See notes at end of table.

Adolescent mortality: Death rates among adolescents ages 15–19 by gender, race and Hispanic origin,[a] and all causes and all injury causes,[b] selected years 1980–2006

(Deaths per 100,000 adolescents ages 15–19)

Characteristic	1980	1985	1990	1995	2000	2003	2004	2005	2006
Male—continued									
Asian or Pacific Islander									
All causes	69.1	57.8	73.1	65.2	51.0	49.7	47.2	45.7	50.4
All injuries	53.5	47.4	62.3	51.9	39.1	38.0	38.2	34.0	40.2
Unintentional injuries	38.6	31.0	35.1	20.0	23.3	23.7	21.6	20.8	20.1
Homicide	*	*	14.8	20.5	7.5	6.9	7.3	7.8	11.3
Suicide	*	10.1	12.0	9.4	8.1	6.7	8.5	4.8	8.4
Leading mechanisms of injury									
Motor vehicle traffic	25.5	21.0	24.1	14.4	14.7	18.2	13.9	13.4	13.3
All firearm	*	9.2	22.2	26.9	8.8	7.4	8.8	9.4	12.7
Firearm homicide	*	*	12.6	18.6	5.7	5.4	5.3	6.9	9.8
Firearm suicide	*	*	8.3	6.1	*	*	*	*	*
Hispanic									
All causes	—	121.3	131.4	125.6	90.5	98.5	96.5	98.6	98.0
All injuries	—	103.7	115.9	110.0	75.9	80.1	79.9	81.7	81.0
Unintentional injuries	—	59.4	54.7	41.4	40.8	44.9	43.0	43.4	43.8
Homicide	—	30.6	49.7	53.5	25.7	25.1	25.8	27.8	28.0
Suicide	—	11.9	11.0	13.6	8.5	9.2	9.9	9.5	7.0
Leading mechanisms of injury									
Motor vehicle traffic	—	42.8	40.7	29.2	29.4	33.4	33.3	32.0	33.0
All firearm	—	31.2	51.7	60.4	27.9	27.0	28.1	29.5	29.8
Firearm homicide	—	20.9	39.7	47.3	21.9	21.1	22.0	24.1	24.0
Firearm suicide	—	6.7	8.6	9.2	4.6	4.3	5.1	3.9	4.1
Female									
White, non-Hispanic									
All causes	—	46.4	44.2	44.2	41.0	40.4	42.4	37.6	38.1
All injuries	—	33.7	32.3	32.2	29.3	29.0	31.0	27.0	27.9
Unintentional injuries	—	25.9	25.8	25.5	24.0	24.0	24.8	21.8	22.6
Homicide	—	2.9	2.8	3.3	1.9	1.4	1.8	1.5	1.7
Suicide	—	4.4	4.0	3.2	3.0	3.0	3.9	3.3	3.0
Leading mechanisms of injury									
Motor vehicle traffic	—	22.5	22.6	22.9	20.8	20.4	21.0	18.0	18.3
All firearm	—	3.8	3.9	3.7	2.2	1.7	2.3	1.9	1.7
Firearm homicide	—	1.1	1.3	1.7	0.9	0.7	1.0	0.9	0.9
Firearm suicide	—	2.2	2.2	1.8	1.2	0.9	1.2	1.0	0.7
Black									
All causes	50.3	44.6	54.4	55.1	43.7	37.8	40.7	38.8	37.4
All injuries	25.5	22.9	30.8	31.9	22.5	18.9	21.7	20.7	19.4
Unintentional injuries	12.0	10.7	13.2	13.0	12.7	11.2	11.8	12.7	10.1
Homicide	11.0	10.3	15.6	16.1	8.4	6.7	7.8	6.3	7.9
Suicide	1.6	1.5	1.9	2.3	1.4	*	1.9	1.4	1.3
Leading mechanisms of injury									
Motor vehicle traffic	6.6	7.5	9.7	10.5	10.0	9.2	9.6	10.5	8.4
All firearm	7.5	6.1	12.1	13.9	5.7	4.2	5.9	5.0	6.0
Firearm homicide	6.2	5.0	10.4	12.1	4.9	4.0	5.1	4.4	5.5
Firearm suicide	*	*	*	1.6	*	*	*	*	*

See notes at end of table.

Adolescent mortality: Death rates among adolescents ages 15–19 by gender, race and Hispanic origin,[a] and all causes and all injury causes,[b] selected years 1980–2006

(Deaths per 100,000 adolescents ages 15–19)

Characteristic	1980	1985	1990	1995	2000	2003	2004	2005	2006
Female—continued									
American Indian or Alaskan Native									
All causes	77.4	69.9	73.1	56.3	52.8	62.8	60.7	68.9	63.9
All injuries	64.3	56.8	61.1	43.2	44.9	50.4	49.4	53.3	47.3
Unintentional injuries	53.6	40.3	44.5	33.8	34.0	35.2	30.0	30.4	34.0
Homicide	*	*	*	*	*	*	*	*	*
Suicide	*	*	*	*	*	*	13.6	14.9	*
Leading mechanisms of injury									
Motor vehicle traffic	41.7	29.6	34.9	27.2	26.8	29.7	24.5	25.7	28.6
All firearm	*	*	*	*	*	*	*	*	*
Firearm homicide	*	*	*	*	*	*	*	*	*
Firearm suicide	*	*	*	*	*	*	*	*	*
Asian or Pacific Islander									
All causes	26.7	32.1	25.8	28.1	20.6	26.6	21.5	21.4	23.5
All injuries	16.7	19.3	18.2	19.4	11.9	17.2	13.1	13.8	14.6
Unintentional injuries	*	11.0	11.2	13.3	7.3	12.6	9.1	8.9	9.6
Homicide	*	*	*	*	*	*	*	*	*
Suicide	*	*	*	*	*	*	*	*	*
Leading mechanisms of injury									
Motor vehicle traffic	*	*	10.9	12.5	5.5	11.5	8.4	6.9	8.7
All firearm	*	*	*	*	*	*	*	*	*
Firearm homicide	*	*	*	*	*	*	*	*	*
Firearm suicide	*	*	*	*	*	*	*	*	*
Hispanic									
All causes	—	33.6	35.2	35.5	28.7	33.5	29.7	33.6	30.5
All injuries	—	20.7	22.7	23.1	18.4	21.7	19.4	22.1	19.7
Unintentional injuries	—	14.4	12.2	13.9	13.1	15.9	13.4	16.6	13.7
Homicide	—	3.8	7.2	6.5	2.8	3.1	2.9	2.9	3.0
Suicide	—	*	3.2	2.6	2.4	2.4	2.7	2.4	2.9
Leading mechanisms of injury									
Motor vehicle traffic	—	10.7	10.4	12.1	10.7	14.1	11.2	14.3	11.6
All firearm	—	4.5	6.8	5.7	2.7	2.8	2.7	2.1	2.3
Firearm homicide	—	*	4.9	4.6	2.0	2.0	2.1	1.6	2.1
Firearm suicide	—	*	*	*	*	*	*	*	*

— Not available.

* Number of deaths too few to calculate a reliable rate.

[a] From 1980 to 2005, the 1977 OMB Standards for Data on Race and Ethnicity were used to classify persons into one of the following four racial groups: White, Black, American Indian or Alaskan Native, or Asian or Pacific Islander. CA, HI , ID, ME, MT, NY, and WI reported multiple-race data in 2003. In 2004, the following states began to report multiple-race data: MI, MN, NH, NJ, OK, SD, WA, and WY. In 2005, the following states began to report multiple-race data: CT, FL, KS, NE, SC, UT, and DC (mid-year). In 2006, NM, OR, RI, and TX began to report multiple-race data. The multiple-race data for these states were bridged to the single-race categories of the 1977 OMB standards for comparability with other states rather than following the revised 1997 OMB standards for a select group of states. In addition, note that data on race and Hispanic origin are collected and reported separately. Persons of Hispanic origin may be of any race.

[b] Cause-of-death information for 1980–1998 is classified according to the Ninth Revision of the International Classification of Diseases. Cause-of-death information for 1999–2006 is classified according to the Tenth Revision of the International Classification of Diseases.

SOURCE: National Center for Health Statistics, National Vital Statistics System.

Characteristic	1980	1985	1990	1995	2000	2003	2004	2005	2006	2007	2008
8th grade											
Total	—	—	—	9.3	7.4	4.5	4.4	4.0	4.0	3.0	3.1
Gender											
Male	—	—	—	9.2	7.0	4.4	4.3	3.9	4.0	3.4	3.2
Female	—	—	—	9.2	7.5	4.5	4.3	4.0	3.8	2.6	2.9
Race and Hispanic origin[a]											
White	—	—	—	10.5	9.0	5.3	4.7	4.6	4.6	3.9	3.3
Black	—	—	—	2.8	3.2	2.9	2.7	2.1	1.9	2.1	1.9
Hispanic	—	—	—	9.2	7.1	3.7	3.5	3.1	2.8	2.8	2.5
10th grade											
Total	—	—	—	16.3	14.0	8.9	8.3	7.5	7.6	7.2	5.9
Gender											
Male	—	—	—	16.3	13.7	8.6	8.2	7.2	6.9	7.7	6.2
Female	—	—	—	16.1	14.1	9.0	8.2	7.7	8.1	6.6	5.5
Race and Hispanic origin[a]											
White	—	—	—	17.6	17.7	11.4	10.0	9.1	8.7	8.8	8.0
Black	—	—	—	4.7	5.2	4.3	4.4	3.9	3.3	3.2	3.0
Hispanic	—	—	—	9.9	8.8	6.0	6.0	5.9	5.3	3.8	3.8
12th grade											
Total	21.3	19.5	19.1	21.6	20.6	15.8	15.6	13.6	12.2	12.3	11.4
Gender											
Male	18.5	17.8	18.6	21.7	20.9	17.0	15.4	14.6	12.0	13.0	12.0
Female	23.5	20.6	19.3	20.8	19.7	14.0	15.0	11.9	11.8	11.2	10.6
Race and Hispanic origin[a]											
White	23.9	20.4	21.8	23.9	25.7	19.5	18.3	17.1	15.3	14.5	14.3
Black	17.4	9.9	5.8	6.1	8.0	5.4	5.2	5.6	5.7	5.8	5.8
Hispanic	12.8	11.8	10.9	11.6	15.7	8.0	8.2	7.7	7.0	6.6	6.7

— Not available.

[a] A 2-year moving average is presented, based on data from the year indicated and the previous year. Prior to 2005 respondents were asked to select the one category that they thought best described them, making Hispanic identification one of the mutually exclusive categories that could be chosen. After 2005 respondents could select multiple categories, some of which are for Hispanic subgroups, but only respondents selecting a single answer are included in the data reported. Approximately 6 percent gave multiple choices and were excluded. In 2005 specifically, half of the sample received the earlier version of the question and half the later one, and their data were combined.

SOURCE: Johnston, L.D., O'Malley, P.M., Bachman, J.G., and Schulenberg, J.E. (2008). *Monitoring the Future national survey results on drug use, 1975–2007, Volume I: Secondary school students* (NIH Publication No. 08-6418A), tables D-92 through D-94. Bethesda, MD: National Institute on Drug Abuse. Data for 2008 are from a press release of December 11, 2008, and demographic disaggregations are from unpublished tabulations from Monitoring the Future, University of Michigan.

Table BEH2				Alcohol use: Percentage of 8th-, 10th-, and 12th-grade students who reported having five or more alcoholic beverages in a row in the past 2 weeks by grade, gender, and race and Hispanic origin, selected years 1980–2008								

Characteristic	1980	1985	1990	1995	2000	2003	2004	2005	2006	2007	2008
8th grade											
Total	—	—	—	12.3	11.7	9.8	9.4	8.4	8.7	8.3	8.1
Gender											
Male	—	—	—	12.5	11.7	10.2	8.8	8.2	8.6	8.2	8.1
Female	—	—	—	12.1	11.3	9.4	9.9	8.6	8.5	8.2	8.0
Race and Hispanic origin[a]											
White	—	—	—	12.1	13.0	10.0	9.6	9.0	8.4	8.0	7.8
Black	—	—	—	8.3	7.3	7.5	6.9	6.1	5.7	5.6	5.7
Hispanic	—	—	—	18.4	16.0	13.8	13.2	12.1	11.6	12.5	12.3
10th grade											
Total	—	—	—	22.0	24.1	20.0	19.9	19.0	19.9	19.6	16.0
Gender											
Male	—	—	—	24.1	27.6	21.1	21.6	19.9	21.0	20.9	16.6
Female	—	—	—	19.7	20.6	19.0	18.1	17.9	18.9	18.3	15.4
Race and Hispanic origin[a]											
White	—	—	—	23.8	26.2	22.5	22.2	21.8	21.7	21.8	19.7
Black	—	—	—	11.1	10.8	9.8	9.7	9.1	9.1	10.0	9.8
Hispanic	—	—	—	23.3	25.1	22.9	23.3	22.4	21.2	20.1	19.6
12th grade											
Total	41.2	36.7	32.2	29.8	30.0	27.9	29.2	27.1	25.4	25.9	24.6
Gender											
Male	52.1	45.3	39.1	36.9	36.7	34.2	34.3	32.6	28.9	30.7	28.4
Female	30.5	28.2	24.4	23.0	23.5	22.1	24.2	21.6	21.5	21.5	21.3
Race and Hispanic origin[a]											
White	44.3	41.5	36.6	32.3	34.6	32.4	32.5	32.5	30.4	29.7	29.9
Black	17.7	15.7	14.4	14.9	11.5	10.8	11.4	11.3	11.4	11.5	10.9
Hispanic	33.1	31.7	25.6	26.6	31.0	25.9	26.0	23.9	23.3	22.5	21.5

— Not available.

[a] A 2-year moving average is presented, based on data from the year indicated and the previous year. Prior to 2005 respondents were asked to select the one category that they thought best described them, making Hispanic identification one of the mutually exclusive categories that could be chosen. After 2005 respondents could select multiple categories, some of which are for Hispanic subgroups, but only respondents selecting a single answer are included in the data reported. Approximately 6 percent gave multiple choices and were excluded. In 2005 specifically, half of the sample received the earlier version of the question and half the later one, and their data were combined.

NOTE: Data for 8th- and 10th-graders for all years have been revised since previous publication in *America's Children* due to revisions in data processing methods.

SOURCE: Johnston, L.D., O'Malley, P.M., Bachman, J.G., and Schulenberg, J.E. (2008). *Monitoring the Future national survey results on drug use, 1975–2007, Volume I: Secondary school students* (NIH Publication No. 08-6418A), tables D-71 through D-73. Bethesda, MD: National Institute on Drug Abuse. Data for 2008 are from a press release of December 11, 2008, and demographic disaggregations are from unpublished tabulations from Monitoring the Future, University of Michigan.

Illicit drug use: Percentage of 8th-, 10th-, and 12th-grade students who reported using illicit drugs in the past 30 days by grade, gender, and race and Hispanic origin, selected years 1980–2008

Characteristic	1980[a]	1985	1990	1995	2000	2003	2004	2005	2006	2007	2008
8th grade											
Total	—	—	—	12.4	11.9	9.7	8.4	8.5	8.1	7.4	7.6
Gender											
Male	—	—	—	12.7	12.0	10.2	7.8	8.8	8.0	7.5	7.8
Female	—	—	—	11.9	11.3	8.9	8.8	8.1	8.0	7.1	7.3
Race and Hispanic origin[b]											
White	—	—	—	18.9	11.2	9.6	8.4	7.7	7.5	7.1	6.9
Black	—	—	—	9.1	10.8	8.9	9.1	9.3	8.6	7.3	7.2
Hispanic	—	—	—	16.7	15.2	13.1	12.1	11.0	10.2	9.5	8.9
10th grade											
Total	—	—	—	20.2	22.5	19.5	18.3	17.3	16.8	16.9	15.8
Gender											
Male	—	—	—	21.1	25.4	21.0	19.6	18.3	17.9	18.0	17.1
Female	—	—	—	19.0	19.5	18.0	16.9	16.1	15.4	15.7	14.4
Race and Hispanic origin[b]											
White	—	—	—	19.7	23.0	21.2	19.3	18.2	17.6	17.5	16.8
Black	—	—	—	15.5	17.0	16.0	17.5	16.4	15.0	14.0	12.5
Hispanic	—	—	—	20.6	23.7	20.0	20.0	19.3	17.0	15.5	17.6
12th grade											
Total	37.2	29.7	17.2	23.8	24.9	24.1	23.4	23.1	21.5	21.9	22.3
Gender											
Male	39.6	32.1	18.9	26.8	27.5	27.3	26.1	26.7	22.8	25.2	25.0
Female	34.3	26.7	15.2	20.4	22.1	20.6	20.3	19.3	19.7	18.4	19.4
Race and Hispanic origin[b]											
White	38.8	30.2	20.5	23.8	25.9	26.5	25.7	25.3	24.0	23.1	23.6
Black	28.8	22.9	9.0	18.3	20.3	17.9	16.8	16.1	17.2	17.1	17.8
Hispanic	33.1	27.2	13.9	21.4	27.4	21.2	19.9	19.6	19.4	18.5	18.1

— Not available.

[a] Beginning in 1982, the question about stimulant use (i.e., amphetamines) was revised to get respondents to exclude the inappropriate reporting of nonprescription stimulants. The prevalence rate dropped slightly as a result of this methodological change.

[b] A 2-year moving average is presented, based on data from the year indicated and the previous year. Prior to 2005 respondents were asked to select the one category that they thought best described them, making Hispanic identification one of the mutually exclusive categories that could be chosen. After 2005 respondents could select multiple categories, some of which are for Hispanic subgroups, but only respondents selecting a single answer are included in the data reported. Approximately 6 percent gave multiple choices and were excluded. In 2005 specifically, half of the sample received the earlier version of the question and half the later one, and their data were combined.

NOTE: Use of "any illicit drug" includes any use of marijuana, LSD, other hallucinogens, crack, other cocaine, or heroin, or any use of other narcotics, amphetamines, barbiturates, or tranquilizers not under a doctor's orders. For 8th- and 10th-graders, the use of other narcotics and barbiturates has been excluded because these younger respondents appear to over report use (perhaps because they include the use of nonprescription drugs in their responses).

SOURCE: Johnston, L.D., O'Malley, P.M., Bachman, J.G., and Schulenberg, J.E. (2008). *Monitoring the Future national survey results on drug use, 1975–2007, Volume I: Secondary school students* (NIH Publication No. 08-6418A), tables 2–3. Bethesda, MD: National Institute on Drug Abuse. Data for 2008 are from a press release of December 11, 2008, and demographic disaggregations are from unpublished tabulations from Monitoring the Future, University of Michigan.

Sexual activity: Percentage of high school students who reported ever having had sexual intercourse by gender, race and Hispanic origin, and grade, selected years 1991–2007

Characteristic	1991	1993	1995	1997	1999	2001	2003	2005	2007
Total	54.1	53.0	53.1	48.4	49.9	45.6	46.7	46.8	47.8
Gender									
Male	57.4	55.6	54.0	48.9	52.2	48.5	48.0	47.9	49.8
Female	50.8	50.2	52.1	47.7	47.7	42.9	45.3	45.7	45.9
Race and Hispanic origin[a]									
White, non-Hispanic	50.0	48.4	48.9	43.6	45.1	43.2	41.8	43.0	43.7
Black, non-Hispanic	81.5	79.7	73.4	72.7	71.2	60.8	67.3	67.6	66.5
Hispanic	53.1	56.0	57.6	52.2	54.1	48.4	51.4	51.0	52.0
Other[b]	43.8	43.4	45.9	45.3	45.6	40.1	41.6	36.4	35.2
Grade									
9th grade	39.0	37.7	36.9	38.0	38.6	34.4	32.8	34.3	32.8
10th grade	48.2	46.1	48.0	42.5	46.8	40.8	44.1	42.8	43.8
11th grade	62.4	57.5	58.6	49.7	52.5	51.9	53.2	51.4	55.5
12th grade	66.7	68.3	66.4	60.9	64.9	60.5	61.6	63.1	64.6

[a] From 1991 to 2003, the 1977 OMB Standards for Data on Race and Ethnicity were used to classify persons into one of the following four racial groups: White, Black, American Indian or Alaskan Native, or Asian or Pacific Islander. In each survey, a single question format (approved by OMB) was used to ask about both race and ethnicity. In 2005, the national Youth Risk Behavior Survey (YRBS) applied OMB's 1997 revision to the 1977 directive and began asking about race and ethnicity in a two-question format (a methodological study[1] has been conducted to confirm that trend analyses would not be affected by the change in format starting with the 2005 survey). In addition, note that data on race and Hispanic origin are collected separately, but are combined for reporting. Regardless of question format, the data have been combined to create the following standard categories—White, non-Hispanic, Black, non-Hispanic, and Hispanic. Estimates are not shown separately for American Indian or Alaska Native, Asian, and Native Hawaiian or Other Pacific Islander races due to the small sample size for each of these groups.

[b] Students were coded as "Other" if they (1) did not self-report as Hispanic, and (2) selected "American Indian or Alaska Native," "Asian," and/or "Native Hawaiian or Other Pacific Islander," or selected more than one response to a question on race.

NOTE: Data are based on the student's response to the question "Have you ever had sexual intercourse?"

SOURCE: Centers for Disease Control and Prevention, National Center for Chronic Disease Prevention and Health Promotion, Youth Risk Behavior Surveillance System.

[1] Brener, N.D., Kann, L., and McManus, T. (2003). A comparison of two survey questions on race and ethnicity among high school students. *Public Opinion Quarterly, 67*, 227–236.

Sexual activity: Among those who reported having had sexual intercourse during the past 3 months, the percentage of high school students who reported use of birth control pills to prevent pregnancy and the percentage who reported condom use during last sexual intercourse, selected years 1991–2007

Characteristic	1991	1993	1995	1997	1999	2001	2003	2005	2007
Used birth control pills to prevent pregnancy before last sexual intercourse									
Total	20.8	18.4	17.4	16.6	16.2	18.2	17.0	17.6	16.0
Used a condom during last sexual intercourse									
Total	46.2	52.8	54.4	56.8	58.0	57.9	63.0	62.8	61.5

NOTE: Data for birth control pill use are based on the student's response to the question, "The last time you had sexual intercourse, what one method did you or your partner use to prevent pregnancy?"; "birth control pills" was one option, in addition to "I have never had sexual intercourse," "No method was used to prevent pregnancy," "Condoms," "Depo-Provera (injectable birth control)," "Withdrawal," "Some other method," and "Not sure." Data for condom use are based on the student's response to the question, "The last time you had sexual intercourse, did you or your partner use a condom?"

SOURCE: Centers for Disease Control and Prevention, National Center for Chronic Disease Prevention and Health Promotion, Youth Risk Behavior Surveillance System.

| Table BEH5 | Youth perpetrators of serious violent crimes: Rate and number of serious violent crimes by youth ages 12–17, selected years 1980–2007 |

Characteristic	1980	1985	1990	1995	2000	2001	2002	2003	2004[a]	2005[a]	2006[b]	2007
Rate per 1,000 youth ages 12–17												
Total	34.9	30.2	39.1	36.3	17.1	19.3	11.2	14.9	13.6	17.1	17.4	10.9
Number of serious violent crimes												
Total (in millions)	3.8	3.4	3.5	3.3	2.2	2.0	1.7	1.8	1.6	1.8	2.3	1.6
Number involving youth ages 12–17 (in thousands)	812	652	785	812	412	467	278	375	345	435	443	277
Percentage involving youth ages 12–17	21.3	19.4	22.4	24.7	19.0	23.2	16.5	20.5	20.9	23.9	19.6	17.1
Percentage of juvenile crimes involving multiple offenders	61.4	61.4	61.1	54.5	58.7	47.0	56.6	56.6	42.8	50.0	44.4	56.0

[a] Revised. Estimates corrected from previous publication in *America's Children.*

[b] Due to changes in methodology, the 2006 national crime perpetration rates are not comparable to other years and cannot be used for yearly trend comparisons. See *Criminal Victimization, 2006,* http://www.ojp.usdoj.gov/bjs/abstract/cv06.htm.

NOTE: The offending rate is the ratio of the number of crimes (aggravated assault, rape, and robbery, i.e., stealing by force or threat of violence) reported to the National Crime Victimization Survey that involved at least one offender perceived by the victim to be 12–17 years of age, plus the number of homicides reported to the police that involved at least one juvenile offender, to the number of juveniles in the population. Because of changes made in the victimization survey, data prior to 1992 are adjusted to make them comparable with data collected under the redesigned methodology.

SOURCE: Bureau of Justice Statistics, National Crime Victimization Survey and Federal Bureau of Investigation, Uniform Crime Reporting Program, Supplementary Homicide Reports.

| Table ED1 | Family reading to young children: Percentage of children ages 3–5[a] who were read to every day in the last week by a family member by child and family characteristics, selected years 1993–2007 | | | | | | |

Characteristic	1993	1995	1996	1999	2001	2005	2007
Total	52.8	58.0	56.5	53.5	57.5	60.3	55.3
Gender							
Male	51.3	57.0	55.6	52.3	54.5	58.7	53.8
Female	54.4	59.0	57.4	54.8	60.5	62.1	56.9
Race and Hispanic origin[b]							
White, non-Hispanic	59.1	65.4	64.3	61.3	64.2	67.7	67.4
Black, non-Hispanic	38.7	42.5	43.7	41.2	47.3	49.7	34.6
Asian or Pacific Islander, non-Hispanic	45.7	37.3	62.2	53.8	51.4	65.6	60.4
Hispanic	37.3	38.3	39.1	33.0	41.8	44.7	37.3
Poverty status							
Below 100% poverty	43.6	46.6	46.8	38.7	48.3	50.0	39.7
100–199% poverty	49.1	55.7	52.0	51.4	51.8	59.5	49.6
200% poverty and above	60.9	65.2	65.5	61.8	64.1	65.0	63.9
Family type							
Two parents[c]	55.3	61.2	60.7	57.8	60.7	62.2	58.9
Two parents, married	—	—	—	—	61.1	63.3	61.9
Two parents, unmarried	—	—	—	—	56.8	49.8	24.4
One parent	46.0	49.2	45.6	42.4	47.2	53.0	42.7
No parents	45.9	51.6	47.9	50.6	52.8	64.2	38.0
Mother's highest level of education[d]							
Less than high school	36.9	39.9	37.4	38.7	41.2	41.3	30.8
High school diploma or equivalent	47.7	48.0	49.0	45.2	49.2	55.2	39.4
Some college, including vocational/ technical/associate's degree	56.5	63.6	61.8	53.0	59.8	59.8	54.6
Bachelor's degree or higher	70.7	75.7	76.5	70.8	72.8	72.4	73.7
Mother's employment status[d]							
Worked 35 hours or more per week	51.5	55.3	54.3	48.9	55.1	56.6	51.1
Worked less than 35 hours per week	55.9	63.1	58.7	55.6	62.6	60.6	63.0
Looking for work	43.7	46.3	53.0	46.5	53.8	62.7	40.2
Not in labor force	54.8	59.8	59.4	59.7	58.2	64.5	57.9
Region[e]							
Northeast	58.9	64.2	61.2	59.0	62.4	66.4	59.3
South	48.3	53.7	54.7	51.1	53.3	55.7	52.1
Midwest	54.1	61.0	56.6	57.3	58.0	62.3	59.4
West	52.8	54.8	54.0	47.5	58.6	61.4	53.5

— Not available.

[a] Estimates are based on children who have yet to enter kindergarten.

[b] From 1993 to 2001, the 1977 OMB Standards for Data on Race and Ethnicity were used to classify persons into one of the following four racial groups: White, Black, American Indian or Alaskan Native, or Asian or Pacific Islander. For data from 2005 onward, the revised 1997 OMB standards were used. Persons could select one or more of five racial groups: White, Black or African American, American Indian or Alaska Native, Asian, or Native Hawaiian or Other Pacific Islander. Included in the total but not shown separately are American Indian or Alaska Native and respondents with "Two or more races." For continuity purposes, in 2005 and 2007, respondents who reported the child being Asian or Native Hawaiian or Other Pacific Islander were combined. Data on race and Hispanic origin are collected separately. Persons of Hispanic origin may be of any race.

[c] Refers to adults' relationship to child and does not indicate marital status.

[d] Children without mothers in the home are not included in estimates dealing with mother's education or mother's employment status.

[e] Regions: Northeast includes CT, MA, ME, NH, NJ, NY, PA, RI, and VT. South includes AL, AR, DC, DE, FL, GA, KY, LA, MD, MS, NC, OK, SC, TN, TX, VA, and WV. Midwest includes IA, IL, IN, KS, MI, MN, MO, ND, NE, OH, SD, and WI. West includes AK, AZ, CA, CO, HI, ID, MT, NM, NV, OR, UT, WA, and WY.

SOURCE: U.S. Department of Education, National Center for Education Statistics, National Household Education Surveys Program.

Mathematics and reading achievement: Average mathematics scale scores of 4th-, 8th-, and 12th-graders by child and family characteristics, selected years 1990–2007

Characteristic	1990[a]	1992[a]	1996[a]	1996	2000	2003	2005	2007
4th-graders								
Total	213	220	224	224	226	235	238	240
Gender								
Male	214	221	226	224	227	236	239	241
Female	213	219	222	223	224	233	237	239
Race and Hispanic origin[b]								
White, non-Hispanic	220	227	231	232	234	243	246	248
Black, non-Hispanic	188	193	199	198	203	216	220	222
American Indian or Alaska Native, non-Hispanic	—	—	—	217	208	223	226	228
Asian or Pacific Islander, non-Hispanic	225	231	226	229	—	246	251	253
Hispanic	200	202	205	207	208	222	226	227
8th-graders								
Total	263	268	272	270	273	278	279	281
Gender								
Male	263	268	272	271	274	278	280	282
Female	262	269	272	269	272	277	278	280
Race and Hispanic origin[b]								
White, non-Hispanic	270	277	281	281	284	288	289	291
Black, non-Hispanic	237	237	242	240	244	252	255	260
American Indian or Alaska Native, non-Hispanic	—	—	—	—	259	263	264	264
Asian or Pacific Islander, non-Hispanic	275	290	—	—	288	291	295	297
Hispanic	246	249	251	251	253	259	262	265
Parents' education								
Less than high school	242	249	254	250	253	257	259	263
High school diploma or equivalent	255	257	261	260	261	267	267	270
Some education after high school	267	271	279	277	277	280	280	283
Bachelor's degree or higher	274	281	282	281	286	288	290	292

See notes at end of table.

Mathematics and reading achievement: Average mathematics scale scores of 4th-, 8th-, and 12th-graders by child and family characteristics, selected years 1990–2007

Characteristic	1990ᵃ	1992ᵃ	1996ᵃ	1996	2000	2003	2005	2007
12th-graders								
Total	294	299	304	302	300	—	150.0ᶜ	—
Gender								
Male	297	301	305	303	302	—	151.3ᶜ	—
Female	291	298	303	300	299	—	148.8ᶜ	—
Race and Hispanic originᵇ								
White, non-Hispanic	300	305	311	309	307	—	157.5ᶜ	—
Black, non-Hispanic	268	275	280	275	273	—	126.6ᶜ	—
American Indian or Alaska Native, non-Hispanic	—	—	284	—	294	—	134.2ᶜ	—
Asian or Pacific Islander, non-Hispanic	311	312	312	305	315	—	162.6ᶜ	—
Hispanic	276	286	287	284	282	—	133.5ᶜ	—
Parents' education								
Less than high school	272	278	282	280	278	—	130.3ᶜ	—
High school diploma or equivalent	283	288	294	290	287	—	137.9ᶜ	—
Some education after high school	297	299	302	302	299	—	148.2ᶜ	—
Bachelor's degree or higher	306	311	314	313	312	—	161.5ᶜ	—

— Not available.

ᵃ Testing accommodations (e.g., extended time, small group testing) for children with disabilities and limited-English-proficient students were not permitted.

ᵇ For data before 2003, the 1977 OMB Standards for Data on Race and Ethnicity were used to classify persons into one of the following four racial groups: White, Black, American Indian or Alaskan Native, or Asian or Pacific Islander. The revised 1997 OMB standards were used for data from 2003 onward. Persons could select one or more of five racial groups: White, Black or African American, American Indian or Alaska Native, Asian, or Native Hawaiian or Other Pacific Islander. Included in the total but not shown separately are respondents with "Two or more races." Beginning in 2003, those in each racial category represent those reporting only one race. Data from 2003 onward are not directly comparable with data from earlier years. For continuity purposes, respondents who reported being Asian or Native Hawaiian or Other Pacific Islander were combined. Data on race and Hispanic origin are collected separately. Persons of Hispanic origin may be of any race.

ᶜ The 12th-grade mathematics assessment in 2005 was based on a revised National Assessment of Educational Progress (NAEP) mathematics framework for grade 12. In addition, unlike previous assessment results which were placed on a scale of 0–500, the results of the revised assessment were placed on a scale of 0–300. As a result of both changes, the 12th-grade assessment results cannot be compared with those of previous assessments.

NOTE: In 2003 and 2007, the assessment was only conducted at grades 4 and 8. The assessment was conducted at grade 12 in 2005, but the National Assessment Governing Board (NAGB) introduced changes in the 2005 NAEP mathematics framework for grade 12 in both the assessment content and administration procedures. As a result, the 12th-grade assessment results cannot be compared with those of previous assessments. Parents' education is the highest educational attainment of either parent. Data on parents' education are not reliable for 4th-graders.

SOURCE: U.S. Department of Education, National Center for Education Statistics, National Assessment of Educational Progress.

Mathematics and reading achievement: Average reading scale scores of 4th-, 8th-, and 12th-graders by child and family characteristics, selected years 1992–2007

Characteristic	1992[a]	1994[a]	1998[a]	1998	2000	2002	2003	2005	2007
4th-graders									
Total	217	214	217	215	213	219	218	219	221
Gender									
Male	213	209	214	212	208	215	215	216	218
Female	221	220	220	217	219	222	222	222	224
Race and Hispanic origin[b]									
White, non-Hispanic	224	224	226	225	224	229	229	229	231
Black, non-Hispanic	192	185	193	193	190	199	198	200	203
American Indian or Alaska Native, non-Hispanic	—	211	—	—	214	207	202	204	203
Asian or Pacific Islander, non-Hispanic	216	220	221	215	225	224	226	229	232
Hispanic	197	188	195	193	190	201	200	203	205
8th-graders									
Total	260	260	264	263	—	264	263	262	263
Gender									
Male	254	252	257	256	—	260	258	257	258
Female	267	267	270	270	—	269	269	267	268
Race and Hispanic origin[b]									
White, non-Hispanic	267	267	271	270	—	272	272	271	272
Black, non-Hispanic	237	236	243	244	—	245	244	243	245
American Indian or Alaska Native, non-Hispanic	—	248	—	—	—	250	246	249	247
Asian or Pacific Islander, non-Hispanic	268	265	267	264	—	267	270	271	271
Hispanic	241	243	245	243	—	247	245	246	247
Parents' education									
Less than high school	243	238	243	242	—	248	245	244	245
High school diploma or equivalent	251	252	254	254	—	257	254	252	253
Some education after high school	265	266	269	268	—	268	267	265	266
Bachelor's degree or higher	271	270	274	273	—	274	273	272	273

See notes at end of table.

Mathematics and reading achievement: Average reading scale scores of 4th-, 8th-, and 12th-graders by child and family characteristics, selected years 1992–2007

Characteristic	1992[a]	1994[a]	1998[a]	1998	2000	2002	2003	2005	2007
12th-graders									
Total	292	287	291	290	—	287	—	286	—
Gender									
Male	287	280	283	282	—	279	—	279	—
Female	297	294	298	298	—	295	—	292	—
Race and Hispanic origin[b]									
White, non-Hispanic	297	293	297	297	—	292	—	293	—
Black, non-Hispanic	273	265	271	269	—	267	—	267	—
American Indian or Alaska Native, non-Hispanic	—	274	—	—	—	—	—	279	—
Asian or Pacific Islander, non-Hispanic	290	278	288	287	—	286	—	287	—
Hispanic	279	270	276	275	—	273	—	272	—
Parents' education									
Less than high school	275	266	268	268	—	268	—	268	—
High school diploma or equivalent	283	277	280	279	—	278	—	274	—
Some education after high school	294	289	292	291	—	289	—	287	—
Bachelor's degree or higher	301	298	301	300	—	296	—	297	—

— Not available.

[a] Testing accommodations (e.g., extended time, small group testing) for children with disabilities and limited-English-proficient students were not permitted.

[b] For data before 2003, the 1977 OMB Standards for Data on Race and Ethnicity were used to classify persons into one of the following four racial groups: White, Black, American Indian or Alaskan Native, or Asian or Pacific Islander. The revised 1997 OMB standards were used for data from 2003 onward. Persons could select one or more of five racial groups: White, Black or African American, American Indian or Alaska Native, Asian, or Native Hawaiian or Other Pacific Islander. Included in the total but not shown separately are respondents with "Two or more races." Beginning in 2003, those in each racial category represent those reporting only one race. Data from 2003 onward are not directly comparable with data from earlier years. For continuity purposes, respondents who reported being Asian or Native Hawaiian or Other Pacific Islander were combined. Data on race and Hispanic origin are collected separately. Persons of Hispanic origin may be of any race.

NOTE: In 2000, the assessment was only conducted at grade 4. In 2003 and 2007, the assessment was only conducted at grades 4 and 8. Parents' education is the highest educational attainment of either parent. Data on parents' education are not reliable for 4th-graders.

SOURCE: U.S. Department of Education, National Center for Education Statistics, National Assessment of Educational Progress.

| Table ED3.A | High school academic coursetaking: Percentage distribution of high school graduates by the highest level of mathematics courses taken, selected years 1982–2005 | | | | | | | |

Characteristic	1982	1987	1990	1992	1994	1998	2000	2005
Nonacademic or low academic								
Total	24.1	19.5	17.2	12.5	11.8	8.9	6.5	4.2
Middle academic								
Total	48.8	50.1	51.6	49.0	49.4	48.9	48.0	45.6
Algebra I/geometry	30.6	27.0	25.4	22.7	22.5	21.2	18.6	17.2
Algebra II	18.2	23.1	26.2	26.4	26.9	27.7	29.4	28.5
Advanced academic								
Total	26.3	29.5	30.6	38.1	38.1	41.4	44.6	48.8
Trigonometry/algebra III	15.6	12.9	12.9	16.4	16.3	14.4	14.1	15.5
Precalculus	4.8	9.0	10.4	10.9	11.6	15.2	18.0	18.8
Calculus	5.9	7.6	7.2	10.7	10.2	11.8	12.5	14.5

NOTE: Totals do not add to 100 because a small percentage of students completed no mathematics or only basic or remedial-level courses. The distribution of graduates among the various levels of mathematics courses was determined by the level of the most academically advanced course they had completed. Graduates may have completed advanced levels of courses without having taken courses at lower levels.

The courses classified at these mathematics academic levels are:

Nonacademic: General mathematics I or II; basic mathematics I, II, or III; consumer mathematics; technical or vocational mathematics; and mathematics review.

Low academic: Pre-algebra; algebra I (taught over 2 years); and geometry (informal).

Algebra I/geometry: Algebra I; plane geometry; plane and solid geometry; unified mathematics I and II; and pure mathematics.

Algebra II: Algebra II and unified mathematics III.

Trigonometry/algebra III: Algebra III; algebra/trigonometry; algebra/analytical geometry; trigonometry; trigonometry/solid geometry; analytical geometry; linear algebra; probability; probability/statistics; statistics (other); and independent study.

Precalculus: Precalculus and introduction to analysis.

Calculus: Advanced Placement calculus; calculus; and calculus/analytical geometry.

SOURCE: U.S. Department of Education, National Center for Education Statistics, High School Transcript Studies: High School and Beyond Study of 1980 Sophomores (1982), National Education Longitudinal Study of 1988 (1992), and National Assessment of Educational Progress Transcript Study (1987, 1990, 1994, 1998, 2000, and 2005).

Table ED3.B	High school academic coursetaking: Percentage distribution of high school graduates by the highest level of science courses taken, selected years 1982–2005							
Characteristic	1982	1987	1990	1992	1994	1998	2000	2005
Low academic								
Total	27.2	15.8	12.8	9.7	10.0	9.3	8.7	7.4
Primary physical science	12.2	6.7	4.2	2.8	1.9	3.0	2.8	1.9
Secondary physical science and basic biology	15.0	9.1	8.7	6.9	8.2	6.3	5.9	5.5
Middle academic								
General biology	35.2	41.5	37.0	36.4	34.1	28.6	27.5	28.9
Advanced academic								
Total	35.4	41.9	49.5	53.5	55.3	61.5	63.1	62.5
Chemistry I or physics I	14.9	21.4	25.8	27.1	29.4	30.2	30.5	30.1
Chemistry I and physics I	5.9	10.6	12.3	12.2	13.0	16.3	14.8	12.8
Chemistry II, physics II, and/or advanced biology	14.6	9.9	11.4	14.3	12.9	15.1	17.9	19.6

NOTE: Totals do not add to 100 because a small percentage of students completed no science or only basic or remedial-level courses.

The courses classified at these science academic levels are:

Primary physical science: Physical science; applied physical science; earth science; college preparatory earth science; and unified science.

Secondary physical science and basic biology: Astronomy; geology; environmental science; oceanography; general physics; and basic biology I.

General biology: General biology I; ecology; zoology; marine biology; human physiology; and general or honors biology II.

Chemistry I or physics I: Introductory chemistry; chemistry I; organic chemistry; physical chemistry; consumer chemistry; general physics; and physics I.

Chemistry I and physics I: 1 chemistry and 1 physics course from the list above.

Chemistry II, physics II, and/or advanced biology: International Baccalaureate (IB) biology II; IB biology III; AP biology; field biology; genetics; biopsychology; biology seminar; biochemistry and biophysics; biochemistry; botany; cell and molecular biology; cell biology; microbiology; anatomy; chemistry II; IB chemistry II; IB chemistry III; AP chemistry; physics II; IB physics; AP physics B; AP physics C: mechanics; AP physics C: electricity/magnetism; and physics II without calculus.

SOURCE: U.S. Department of Education, National Center for Education Statistics, High School Transcript Studies: High School and Beyond Study of 1980 Sophomores (1982), National Education Longitudinal Study of 1988 (1992), and National Assessment of Educational Progress Transcript Study (1987, 1990, 1994, 1998, 2000, and 2005).

Table ED3.C	High school academic coursetaking: Percentage distribution of high school graduates by the highest level of English courses taken, selected years 1982–2005							
Characteristic	1982	1987	1990	1992	1994	1998	2000	2005
Low academic								
Total	10.0	22.1	19.6	18.0	17.6	13.7	10.7	11.6
Middle academic								
Total	76.7	55.6	60.2	57.3	56.5	56.1	54.7	56.4
Advanced academic								
Total	13.3	21.5	19.6	24.4	25.1	29.3	33.9	30.9
Less than 50 percent in honors	6.1	7.9	7.0	7.6	7.7	9.1	11.6	9.1
50–74 percent in honors	3.3	5.0	3.6	5.8	5.4	7.7	7.2	7.4
75 percent or more in honors	3.8	8.7	9.1	11.1	12.0	12.4	15.1	14.3

NOTE: Totals do not add up to 100 because a small percentage of students completed no English courses or only English as a second language (ESL) courses.

The classification system for these English academic levels is:

Low academic: Graduates who have taken general English courses classified as "below grade level" as the majority of their English courses. Graduates may have taken a general English course classified as "honors" and be classified in the low academic level.

Middle academic: Graduates who completed English courses classified at grade level; no low academic level or honors courses.

Less than 50 percent honors: Graduates for whom the number of completed courses classified as honors level, when divided by the total number of completed low-, regular-, and honors-level academic courses, yields a percentage of less than 50.

50–74 percent in honors: Graduates for whom the number of completed courses classified as honors level, when divided by the total number of completed low-, regular-, and honors-level academic courses, yields a percentage of 50 or greater and less than 75.

75 percent or more in honors: Graduates for whom the number of completed courses classified as honors level, when divided by the total number of completed low-, regular-, and honors-level academic courses, yields a percentage between 75 and 100.

SOURCE: U.S. Department of Education, National Center for Education Statistics, High School Transcript Studies: High School and Beyond Study of 1980 Sophomores (1982), National Education Longitudinal Study of 1988 (1992), and National Assessment of Educational Progress Transcript Study (1987, 1990, 1994, 1998, 2000, and 2005).

| Table ED3.D | High school academic coursetaking: Percentage distribution of high school graduates by the highest level of foreign language courses taken, selected years 1982–2005 |

Characteristic	1982	1987	1990	1992	1994	1998	2000	2005[a]
No foreign language								
Total	45.6	33.3	26.9	22.5	22.3	19.4	17.4	16.4
Low academic								
Total	39.8	47.5	51.4	51.8	51.8	50.7	52.8	50.2
Year 1 or less	20.4	22.6	21.2	19.9	19.8	19.2	18.0	13.0
Year 2	19.5	24.9	30.2	32.0	32.1	31.5	34.9	37.1
Advanced academic								
Total	14.6	19.2	21.7	25.7	25.9	30.0	29.8	33.5
Year 3	8.9	11.9	12.9	14.8	15.0	17.4	16.5	18.6
Year 4	4.5	5.4	5.6	7.7	7.8	8.6	7.8	8.9
Advanced placement	1.2	1.9	3.2	3.2	3.1	4.1	5.4	5.9

[a] Expanded foreign language coursetaking based upon classes in Amharic (Ethiopian), Arabic, Chinese (Cantonese or Mandarin), Czech, Dutch, Finnish, French, German, Greek (Classical or Modern), Hawaiian, Hebrew, Italian, Japanese, Korean, Latin, Norse (Norwegian), Polish, Portuguese, Russian, Spanish, Swahili, Swedish, Turkish, Ukrainian, or Yiddish.

NOTE: Foreign language coursetaking based upon classes in Spanish, French, Latin, or German, unless noted otherwise. From 1982 to 2000, less than 1 percent of students studied only a foreign language other than Spanish, French, Latin, or German. The distribution of graduates among the various levels of foreign language courses was determined by the level of the most academically advanced course they completed. Graduates who had completed courses in different languages were counted according to the highest level course completed. Graduates may have completed advanced levels of courses without having taken courses at lower levels.

SOURCE: U.S. Department of Education, National Center for Education Statistics, High School Transcript Studies: High School and Beyond Study of 1980 Sophomores (1982), National Education Longitudinal Study of 1988 (1992), and National Assessment of Educational Progress Transcript Study (1987, 1990, 1994, 1998, 2000, and 2005).

| Table ED4 | High school completion: Percentage of young adults ages 18–24[a] who have completed high school by race and Hispanic origin and method of completion, selected years 1980–2007 |

Characteristic	1980	1985	1990	1995	2000	2003	2004	2005	2006	2007
Total										
Total completing high school[b]	83.9	85.4	85.6	85.3	86.5	87.1	86.9	87.6	87.8	88.9
Method of completion										
Diploma	—	—	80.6	77.5	—	—	—	—	—	—
Equivalent	—	—	4.9	7.7	—	—	—	—	—	—
White, non-Hispanic[c]										
Total completing high school[b]	87.5	88.2	89.6	89.8	91.8	91.9	91.7	92.3	92.6	93.5
Method of completion										
Diploma	—	—	85.0	83.0	—	—	—	—	—	—
Equivalent	—	—	5.0	7.0	—	—	—	—	—	—
Black, non-Hispanic[c]										
Total completing high school[b]	75.2	81.0	83.2	84.5	83.7	85.0	83.5	86.0	84.9	88.7
Method of completion										
Diploma	—	—	78.0	75.0	—	—	—	—	—	—
Equivalent	—	—	5.0	9.0	—	—	—	—	—	—
American Indian or Alaska Native[c]										
Total completing high school[b]	—	—	—	—	82.4	78.4	76.7	80.4	81.6	77.7
Method of completion										
Diploma	—	—	—	—	—	—	—	—	—	—
Equivalent	—	—	—	—	—	—	—	—	—	—
Asian or Pacific Islander[c]										
Total completing high school[b]	—	—	—	—	94.6	94.9	95.1	95.8	95.8	93.0
Method of completion										
Diploma	—	—	—	—	—	—	—	—	—	—
Equivalent	—	—	—	—	—	—	—	—	—	—
Two or more races[c]										
Total completing high school[b]	—	—	—	—	—	91.7	93.1	89.5	89.7	89.2
Method of completion										
Diploma	—	—	—	—	—	—	—	—	—	—
Equivalent	—	—	—	—	—	—	—	—	—	—
Hispanic[c]										
Total completing high school[b]	57.1	66.6	59.1	62.8	64.1	69.2	69.9	70.3	70.9	72.4
Method of completion										
Diploma	—	—	55.0	54.0	—	—	—	—	—	—
Equivalent	—	—	4.0	9.0	—	—	—	—	—	—

— Not available.

[a] Excludes those enrolled in high school or below.

[b] From 1980 to 1991, high school completion was measured as completing 4 years of high school rather than the actual attainment of a high school diploma or equivalent.

[c] For data before 2003, the 1977 OMB Standards for Data on Race and Ethnicity were used to classify persons into one of the following four racial groups: White, Black, American Indian or Alaskan Native, or Asian or Pacific Islander. The revised 1997 OMB standards were used for data for 2003 and later years. Persons could select one or more of five racial groups: White, Black or African American, American Indian or Alaska Native, Asian, or Native Hawaiian or Other Pacific Islander. Those reporting more than one race were classified as "Two or more races." For continuity purposes, respondents who reported being Asian or Native Hawaiian or Other Pacific Islander were combined. Beginning in 2003, those in each racial category represent those reporting only one race. Data from 2003 onward are not directly comparable with data from earlier years. Data on race and Hispanic origin are collected separately. Persons of Hispanic origin may be of any race.

NOTE: Data for 1994 and subsequent years are not strictly comparable with data for 1980–1993 because of revisions in the Current Population Survey (CPS) questionnaire and data collection methodology. Method of high school completion is not reported for 2000 and subsequent years because of changes in General Education Development (GED) items in the October 2001 CPS School Enrollment Supplement, making the 2001 data not comparable to previous years. Diploma equivalents include alternative credentials obtained by passing exams such as the GED test.

SOURCE: U.S. Census Bureau, Current Population Survey, School Enrollment Supplement.

Youth neither enrolled in school[a] nor working: Percentage of youth ages 16–19 who are neither enrolled in school nor working by age, gender, and race and Hispanic origin, selected years 1985–2008

Characteristic	1985	1990	1995[b]	2000[b]	2003[b]	2004[b]	2005[b]	2006[b]	2007[b]	2008[b]
Ages 16–19										
Total	11	10	9	8	8	8	8	8	8	8
Gender										
Male	9	8	8	7	8	7	7	7	8	8
Female	13	12	11	9	9	8	8	8	8	8
Race and Hispanic origin[c]										
White, non-Hispanic	9	8	7	6	6	6	6	6	6	7
Black, non-Hispanic	18	15	14	13	12	10	12	11	11	11
Hispanic	17	17	16	13	12	12	12	11	11	11
Ages 16–17										
Total	5	5	4	4	3	3	3	3	4	4
Gender										
Male	5	4	4	3	3	3	3	3	4	4
Female	6	5	5	4	4	4	3	3	4	4
Race and Hispanic origin[c]										
White, non-Hispanic	5	4	3	3	3	3	3	3	3	3
Black, non-Hispanic	6	6	6	5	4	4	4	4	4	5
Hispanic	10	10	9	7	6	5	5	6	6	5
Ages 18–19										
Total	17	15	15	12	14	13	13	13	13	14
Gender										
Male	13	12	12	11	14	12	13	12	13	13
Female	20	18	17	13	14	13	13	14	13	14
Race and Hispanic origin[c]										
White, non-Hispanic	14	12	11	9	10	10	10	10	10	11
Black, non-Hispanic	30	23	24	21	23	18	20	19	19	20
Hispanic	24	24	23	18	20	19	19	17	18	19

[a] School refers to both high school and college.

[b] Data for 1994 and subsequent years are not strictly comparable with data for prior years because of revisions to the questionnaire and data collection methodology for the Current Population Survey. Beginning in 2000, data incorporate population controls from Census 2000.

[c] For data before 2003, the 1977 OMB Standards for Data on Race and Ethnicity were used to classify persons into one of the following four racial groups: White, Black, American Indian or Alaskan Native, or Asian or Pacific Islander. The revised 1997 OMB standards were used for data for 2003 and later years. Persons could select one or more of five racial groups: White, Black or African American, American Indian or Alaska Native, Asian, or Native Hawaiian or Other Pacific Islander. Included in the total but not shown separately are American Indian or Alaska Native, Asian, Native Hawaiian or Other Pacific Islander, and "Two or more races." Beginning in 2003, those in each racial category represent those reporting only one race. Data from 2003 onward are not directly comparable with data from earlier years. Data on race and Hispanic origin are collected separately. Persons of Hispanic origin may be of any race.

NOTE: The information relates to the labor force and enrollment status of persons 16–19 years old in the civilian noninstitutionalized population during an "average" week of the school year. The percentages represent an average based on responses to the survey questions for the months that youth are usually in school (January through May and September through December). Results are based on uncomposited estimates and are not comparable to data from published tables.

SOURCE: U.S. Bureau of Labor Statistics, Current Population Survey.

| Table ED5.B | Youth enrolled in school[a] and working: Percentage of youth ages 16–19 who are enrolled in school and working by age, gender, and race and Hispanic origin, selected years 1985–2008 |

Characteristic	1985	1990	1995[b]	2000[b]	2003[b]	2004[b]	2005[b]	2006[b]	2007[b]	2008[b]
Ages 16–19										
Total	26	28	29	30	25	25	25	25	24	22
Gender										
Male	26	27	28	29	23	22	23	23	21	20
Female	26	28	30	32	27	27	27	27	26	25
Race and Hispanic origin[c]										
White, non-Hispanic	30	33	35	36	30	30	31	31	29	27
Black, non-Hispanic	12	15	16	19	14	14	13	15	13	12
Hispanic	15	17	16	19	15	16	17	17	17	16
Ages 16–17										
Total	29	29	30	31	24	23	23	23	21	19
Gender										
Male	28	29	29	29	22	21	20	21	20	17
Female	29	30	31	32	26	24	25	25	23	21
Race and Hispanic origin[c]										
White, non-Hispanic	34	36	37	37	29	28	29	29	27	24
Black, non-Hispanic	12	15	16	19	13	11	10	13	11	9
Hispanic	15	17	14	18	14	13	14	15	13	12
Ages 18–19										
Total	23	26	28	30	27	27	28	28	26	26
Gender										
Male	23	25	27	28	24	24	26	25	23	23
Female	23	26	30	31	30	30	30	30	29	28
Race and Hispanic origin[c]										
White, non-Hispanic	26	30	33	35	32	32	33	33	30	30
Black, non-Hispanic	12	15	17	18	16	17	16	18	16	16
Hispanic	15	16	19	20	17	20	21	19	20	20

[a] School refers to both high school and college.

[b] Data for 1994 and subsequent years are not strictly comparable with data for prior years because of revisions to the questionnaire and data collection methodology for the Current Population Survey. Beginning in 2000, data incorporate population controls from Census 2000.

[c] For data before 2003, the 1977 OMB Standards for Data on Race and Ethnicity were used to classify persons into one of the following four racial groups: White, Black, American Indian or Alaskan Native, or Asian or Pacific Islander. The revised 1997 OMB standards were used for data for 2003 and later years. Persons could select one or more of five racial groups: White, Black or African American, American Indian or Alaska Native, Asian, or Native Hawaiian or Other Pacific Islander. Included in the total but not shown separately are American Indian or Alaska Native, Asian, Native Hawaiian or Other Pacific Islander, and "Two or more races." Beginning in 2003, those in each racial category represent those reporting only one race. Data from 2003 onward are not directly comparable with data from earlier years. Data on race and Hispanic origin are collected separately. Persons of Hispanic origin may be of any race.

NOTE: The information relates to the labor force and enrollment status of persons ages 16–19 in the civilian noninstitutionalized population during an "average" week of the school year. The percentages represent an average based on responses to the survey questions for the months that youth are usually in school (January through May and September through December). Results are based on uncomposited estimates and are not comparable to data from published tables.

SOURCE: U.S. Bureau of Labor Statistics, Current Population Survey.

Table ED6		College enrollment: Percentage of high school completers who were enrolled in college the October immediately after completing high school by gender and race and Hispanic origin, selected years 1980–2007									

Characteristic	1980	1985	1990	1995	2000	2001	2004	2005	2006	2007
Total	49.3	57.7	60.1	61.9	63.3	61.8	66.7	68.6	66.0	67.2
Gender										
Male	46.7	58.6	58.0	62.6	59.9	60.1	61.4	66.5	65.8	66.1
Female	51.8	56.8	62.2	61.3	66.2	63.5	71.5	70.4	66.1	68.3
Race and Hispanic origin[a]										
White, non-Hispanic	49.8	60.1	63.0	64.3	65.7	64.3	68.8	73.2	68.5	69.5
Black, non-Hispanic[b]	42.7	42.2	46.8	51.2	54.9	55.0	62.5	55.7	55.5	55.7
Hispanic[b]										
Total	52.3	51.0	42.7	53.7	52.9	51.7	61.8	54.0	57.9	64.0
3-year moving average	49.8	46.5	51.7	51.2	49.0	52.7	58.1	57.9	58.6	—

— Not available.

[a] For data before 2003, the 1977 OMB Standards for Data on Race and Ethnicity were used to classify persons into one of the following four racial groups: White, Black, American Indian or Alaskan Native, or Asian or Pacific Islander. The revised 1997 OMB standards were used for data for 2003 and later years. Persons could select one or more of five racial groups: White, Black or African American, American Indian or Alaska Native, Asian, or Native Hawaiian or Other Pacific Islander. Included in the total but not shown separately are American Indian or Alaska Native, Asian, Native Hawaiian or Other Pacific Islander, and "Two or more races." Beginning in 2003, those in each racial category represent those reporting only one race. Data from 2003 onward are not directly comparable with data from earlier years. Data on race and Hispanic origin are collected separately. Persons of Hispanic origin may be of any race.

[b] Due to the small sample size, data are subject to relatively large sampling errors.

NOTE: Enrollment in college as of October of each year for individuals ages 16 to 24 who completed high school during the preceding 12 months. High school completion includes General Educational Development (GED) certificate recipients. Moving averages are used to produce more stable estimates. A 3-year moving average is the average of the estimates for the year prior to the reported year, the reported year, and the following year. Thus a moving average cannot be calculated for the most recent year.

SOURCE: U.S. Census Bureau, Current Population Survey, School Enrollment Supplement.

Table HEALTH1.A — Preterm birth: Percentage of infants born preterm by detailed race and Hispanic origin of mother, selected years 1990–2007

Characteristic	1990	1995	2000	2001	2002	2003	2004	2005	2006	2007[a]
Preterm (less than 37 completed weeks of gestation)										
Total	10.6	11.0	11.6	11.9	12.1	12.3	12.5	12.7	12.8	12.7
Race and Hispanic origin[b]										
White, non-Hispanic	8.5	9.4	10.4	10.8	11.0	11.3	11.5	11.7	11.7	11.5
Black, non-Hispanic	18.9	17.8	17.4	17.6	17.7	17.8	17.9	18.4	18.5	18.3
American Indian or Alaskan Native	11.8	12.4	12.7	13.2	13.1	13.5	13.7	14.1	14.2	13.9
Asian or Pacific Islander	10.1	9.9	9.9	10.3	10.4	10.5	10.5	10.8	10.9	10.9
Chinese	7.3	7.2	7.3	7.7	7.7	—	—	—	—	—
Japanese	7.7	8.3	8.3	8.8	9.2	—	—	—	—	—
Filipino	11.4	11.7	12.2	12.5	12.7	—	—	—	—	—
Hawaiian	11.3	11.0	11.7	14.2	13.5	—	—	—	—	—
Other Asian or Pacific Islander	10.6	10.3	10.1	10.3	10.5	—	—	—	—	—
Hispanic	11.0	10.9	11.2	11.4	11.6	11.9	12.0	12.1	12.2	12.3
Mexican American	10.6	10.6	11.0	11.2	11.4	11.7	11.8	11.8	11.9	—
Puerto Rican	13.4	13.4	13.5	13.7	14.0	13.8	14.0	14.3	14.4	—
Cuban	9.8	10.1	10.6	10.6	10.5	11.8	12.8	13.2	13.1	—
Central or South American	10.9	10.7	11.0	11.2	11.2	11.4	11.7	12.0	12.1	—
Other and unknown Hispanic	11.2	11.7	12.2	12.4	12.8	12.6	12.6	13.6	14.2	—
Late preterm (34–36 completed weeks of gestation)										
Total	7.3	7.7	8.2	8.5	8.6	8.8	8.9	9.1	9.1	9.0
Race and Hispanic origin[b]										
White, non-Hispanic	6.1	6.8	7.6	7.9	8.1	8.3	8.5	8.6	8.6	—
Black, non-Hispanic	11.5	10.9	10.9	11.2	11.2	11.4	11.4	11.8	11.9	—
American Indian or Alaskan Native	8.3	8.9	9.0	9.3	9.2	9.6	9.6	10.2	10.2	—
Asian or Pacific Islander	7.5	7.4	7.3	7.7	7.7	7.8	7.7	8.0	8.1	—
Chinese	5.7	5.5	5.5	6.0	5.9	—	—	—	—	—
Japanese	5.9	6.2	6.3	7.0	6.8	—	—	—	—	—
Filipino	8.3	8.7	8.9	9.3	9.4	—	—	—	—	—
Hawaiian	7.6	7.9	8.2	9.8	9.5	—	—	—	—	—
Other Asian or Pacific Islander	7.9	8.6	8.5	8.6	8.5	—	—	—	—	—
Hispanic	7.8	7.8	8.1	8.3	8.4	8.6	8.7	8.8	8.8	—
Mexican American	7.6	7.7	8.0	8.2	8.3	8.5	8.6	8.6	8.6	—
Puerto Rican	9.0	9.1	9.2	9.4	9.6	9.5	9.5	9.8	9.8	—
Cuban	6.9	7.1	7.6	7.6	7.7	8.7	9.5	9.5	9.6	—
Central or South American	7.7	7.6	7.8	8.1	8.0	8.3	8.5	8.7	8.8	—
Other and unknown Hispanic	8.0	8.3	8.6	8.9	9.2	9.0	9.2	9.8	10.2	—

— Not available.

[a] Data for 2007 are preliminary.

[b] The 1977 OMB Standards for Data on Race and Ethnicity were used to classify persons into one of the following four racial groups: White, Black, American Indian or Alaskan Native, or Asian or Pacific Islander. The following states reported multiple-race data in 2003, following the revised 1997 OMB standards: CT, HI, OH (for December only), PA, UT, and WA. In 2004, the following states began to report multiple-race data: FL, ID, KY, MI, MN, NH, NY State (excluding New York City), SC, and TN. Multiple-race data were reported by 19 states in 2005: FL, ID, KS, KY, NE, NH, NY State (excluding New York City), PA, SC, TN, TX, VT (beginning July 1), WA, CA, HI, MI (for births at selected facilities only), MN, OH, and UT. In 2006, 23 states reported multiple-race data: CA, DE, FL, ID, KS, KY, NE, NH, NY State (excluding New York City), ND, OH, PA, SC, SD, TN, TX, VT, WA, WY, HI, MI (for births at selected facilities only), MN, and UT. In 2007, 27 states reported multiple-race data: CA, CO, DE, FL, GA (partial year only), ID, IN, IA, KS, KY, MI (for births at most facilities), NE, NH, NY State (excluding New York City), ND, OH, PA, SC, SD, TN, TX, VT, WA, WY, HI, MN, and UT. The multiple-race data for these states were bridged to the single-race categories of the 1977 OMB standards for comparability with other states. In addition, note that data on race and Hispanic origin are collected and reported separately.

NOTE: Excludes live births with unknown gestational age. Trend data for births to Hispanic and to White, non-Hispanic and Black, non-Hispanic women are affected by expansion of the reporting area in which an item on Hispanic origin is included on the birth certificate. The number of states in the reporting area was 48 states and DC in 1990, 49 states and DC in 1991–92, and all 50 states and DC from 1993 onward. Trend data for births to Asian or Pacific Islander and Hispanic women are also affected by immigration. Beginning in 2003, data are no longer available for Asian or Pacific Islander subgroups.

SOURCE: National Center for Health Statistics, National Vital Statistics System. Martin, J.A., Hamilton, B.E., Sutton, P.D., Ventura, S.J., Menacker, F., Kirmeyer, S., and Mathews, T.J. (2009). Births: Final data for 2006. *National Vital Statistics Reports, 57*(7). Hyattsville, MD: National Center for Health Statistics. Hamilton, B.E., Martin, J.A., and Ventura, S.J. (2009). Births: Preliminary data for 2007. *National Vital Statistics Reports, 57*(12). Hyattsville, MD: National Center for Health Statistics.

Low birthweight: Percentage of infants born with low birthweight by detailed race and Hispanic origin of mother, selected years 1980–2007

Characteristic	1980	1985	1990	1995	2000	2003	2004	2005	2006	2007[a]
Low birthweight (less than 2,500 grams, or 5 lb. 8 oz.)										
Total	6.8	6.8	7.0	7.3	7.6	7.9	8.1	8.2	8.3	8.2
Race and Hispanic origin[b]										
White, non-Hispanic	5.7	5.6	5.6	6.2	6.6	7.0	7.2	7.3	7.3	7.2
Black, non-Hispanic	12.7	12.6	13.3	13.2	13.1	13.6	13.7	14.0	14.0	13.8
American Indian or Alaskan Native	6.4	5.9	6.1	6.6	6.8	7.4	7.5	7.4	7.5	7.5
Asian or Pacific Islander	6.7	6.2	6.5	6.9	7.3	7.8	7.9	8.0	8.1	8.1
Chinese	5.2	5.0	4.7	5.3	5.1	—	—	—	—	—
Japanese	6.6	6.2	6.2	7.3	7.1	—	—	—	—	—
Filipino	7.4	6.9	7.3	7.8	8.5	—	—	—	—	—
Hawaiian	7.2	6.5	7.2	6.8	6.8	—	—	—	—	—
Other Asian or Pacific Islander	6.8	6.2	6.6	7.1	7.7	—	—	—	—	—
Hispanic	6.1	6.2	6.1	6.3	6.4	6.7	6.8	6.9	7.0	6.9
Mexican American	5.6	5.8	5.5	5.8	6.0	6.3	6.4	6.5	6.6	—
Puerto Rican	9.0	8.7	9.0	9.4	9.3	10.0	9.8	9.9	10.1	—
Cuban	5.6	6.0	5.7	6.5	6.5	7.0	7.7	7.6	7.1	—
Central or South American	5.8	5.7	5.8	6.2	6.3	6.7	6.7	6.8	6.8	—
Other and unknown Hispanic	7.0	6.8	6.9	7.5	7.8	8.0	7.8	8.3	8.5	—
Very low birthweight (less than 1,500 grams, or 3 lb. 4 oz.)										
Total	1.15	1.21	1.27	1.35	1.43	1.45	1.48	1.49	1.49	1.48
Race and Hispanic origin[b]										
White, non-Hispanic	0.86	0.90	0.93	1.04	1.14	1.18	1.20	1.21	1.20	1.19
Black, non-Hispanic	2.46	2.66	2.93	2.98	3.10	3.12	3.15	3.27	3.15	3.19
American Indian or Alaskan Native	0.92	1.01	1.01	1.10	1.16	1.30	1.28	1.17	1.28	1.27
Asian or Pacific Islander	0.92	0.85	0.87	0.91	1.05	1.09	1.14	1.14	1.12	1.14
Chinese	0.66	0.57	0.51	0.67	0.77	—	—	—	—	—
Japanese	0.94	0.84	0.73	0.87	0.75	—	—	—	—	—
Filipino	0.99	0.86	1.05	1.13	1.38	—	—	—	—	—
Hawaiian	1.05	1.03	0.97	0.94	1.39	—	—	—	—	—
Other Asian or Pacific Islander	0.96	0.91	0.92	0.91	1.04	—	—	—	—	—
Hispanic	0.98	1.01	1.03	1.11	1.14	1.16	1.20	1.20	1.19	1.21
Mexican American	0.92	0.97	0.92	1.01	1.03	1.06	1.13	1.12	1.12	—
Puerto Rican	1.29	1.30	1.62	1.79	1.93	2.00	1.96	1.87	1.91	—
Cuban	1.02	1.18	1.20	1.19	1.21	1.37	1.30	1.50	1.28	—
Central or South American	0.99	1.01	1.05	1.13	1.20	1.17	1.19	1.19	1.13	—
Other and unknown Hispanic	1.01	0.96	1.09	1.28	1.42	1.28	1.27	1.36	1.36	—

— Not available.

[a] Data for 2007 are preliminary.

[b] The 1977 OMB Standards for Data on Race and Ethnicity were used to classify persons into one of the following four racial groups: White, Black, American Indian or Alaskan Native, or Asian or Pacific Islander. The following states reported multiple-race data in 2003, following the revised 1997 OMB standards: CT, HI, OH (for December only), PA, UT, and WA. In 2004, the following states began to report multiple-race data: FL, ID, KY, MI, MN, NH, NY State (excluding New York City), SC, and TN. Multiple-race data were reported by 19 states in 2005: FL, ID, KS, KY, NE, NH, NY State (excluding New York City), PA, SC, TN, TX, VT (beginning July 1), WA, CA, HI, MI (for births at selected facilities only), MN, OH, and UT. In 2006, 23 states reported multiple-race data: CA, DE, FL, ID, KS, KY, NE, NH, NY State (excluding New York City), ND, OH, PA, SC, SD, TN, TX, VT, WA, WY, HI, MI (for births at selected facilities only), MN, and UT. In 2007, 27 states reported multiple-race data: CA, CO, DE, FL, GA (partial year only), ID, IN, IA, KS, KY, MI (for births at most facilities), NE, NH, NY State (excluding New York City), ND, OH, PA, SC, SD, TN, TX, VT, WA, WY, HI, MN, and UT. The multiple-race data for these states were bridged to the single-race categories of the 1977 OMB standards for comparability with other states. In addition, note that data on race and Hispanic origin are collected and reported separately.

NOTE: Excludes live births with unknown birthweight. Low birthweight infants weigh less than 2,500 grams, or 5 lb. 8 oz., at birth. Very low birthweight infants weigh less than 1,500 grams, or 3 lb. 4 oz. Trend data for births to Hispanic and to White, non-Hispanic and Black, non-Hispanic women are affected by expansion of the reporting area in which an item on Hispanic origin is included on the birth certificate. The number of states in the reporting area increased from 22 states in 1980 to 23 states and the District of Columbia (DC) in 1983–1987, 30 states and DC in 1988, 47 states and DC in 1989, 48 states and DC in 1990, 49 states and DC in 1991–92, and all 50 states and DC from 1993 onward. Trend data for births to Asian or Pacific Islander and Hispanic women are also affected by immigration. Beginning in 2003, data are no longer available for Asian or Pacific Islander subgroups.

SOURCE: National Center for Health Statistics, National Vital Statistics System. Martin, J.A., Hamilton, B.E., Sutton, P.D., Ventura, S.J., Menacker, F., Kirmeyer, S., and Mathews, T.J. (2009). Births: Final data for 2006. *National Vital Statistics Reports, 57*(7). Hyattsville, MD: National Center for Health Statistics. Hamilton, B.E., Martin, J.A., and Ventura, S.J. (2009). Births: Preliminary data for 2007. *National Vital Statistics Reports, 57*(12). Hyattsville, MD: National Center for Health Statistics.

Infant mortality: Death rates among infants by detailed race and Hispanic origin of mother, selected years 1983–2006

(Infant deaths per 1,000 live births)

Characteristic	1983	1985	1990	1995[a]	2000[a]	2001[a]	2002[a]	2003[a,b]	2004[a,b]	2005[a,b]	2006[b,c]
Total	10.9	10.4	8.9	7.6	6.9	6.8	7.0	6.8	6.8	6.9	6.7
Race and Hispanic origin[d]											
White, non-Hispanic	9.2	8.6	7.2	6.3	5.7	5.7	5.8	5.7	5.7	5.8	—
Black, non-Hispanic	19.1	18.3	16.9	14.7	13.6	13.5	13.9	13.6	13.6	13.6	—
American Indian or Alaskan Native	15.2	13.1	13.1	9.0	8.3	9.7	8.6	8.7	8.4	8.1	—
Asian or Pacific Islander	8.3	7.8	6.6	5.3	4.9	4.7	4.8	4.8	4.7	4.9	—
Chinese	9.5	5.8	4.3	3.8	3.5	3.2	3.0	—	—	—	—
Japanese	*	6.0	5.5	5.3	4.6	4.0	4.9	—	—	—	—
Filipino	8.4	7.7	6.0	5.6	5.7	5.5	5.7	—	—	—	—
Hawaiian	11.2	9.9	8.0	6.6	9.1	7.3	9.6	—	—	—	—
Other Asian or Pacific Islander	8.1	8.5	7.4	5.5	4.8	4.8	4.7	—	—	—	—
Hispanic[e]	9.5	8.8	7.5	6.3	5.6	5.4	5.6	5.6	5.5	5.6	—
Mexican American	9.1	8.5	7.2	6.0	5.4	5.2	5.4	5.5	5.5	5.5	—
Puerto Rican	12.9	11.2	9.9	8.9	8.2	8.5	8.2	8.2	7.8	8.3	—
Cuban	7.5	8.5	7.2	5.3	4.5	4.2	3.7	4.6	4.6	4.4	—
Central or South American	8.5	8.0	6.8	5.5	4.6	5.0	5.1	5.0	4.6	4.7	—
Other and unknown Hispanic	10.6	9.5	8.0	7.4	6.9	6.0	7.1	6.7	6.7	6.4	—

— Not available.

* Number too small to calculate a reliable rate.

[a] Beginning with data for 1995, rates are on a period basis. Earlier rates are on a cohort basis. Data for 1995–2005 are weighted to account for unmatched records.

[b] Beginning in 2003, infant mortality rates are being reported to two decimal places in National Center for Health Statistics (NCHS) reports, so the rates reported here will vary from those in other reports. This difference in reporting could affect significance testing.

[c] The infant mortality rate for 2006 was obtained from unlinked death records from the National Vital Statistics System because data for 2006 are not currently available from the National Linked Files of Live Births and Infant Deaths.

[d] The 1977 OMB Standards for Data on Race and Ethnicity were used to classify persons into one of the following four racial groups: White, Black, American Indian or Alaskan Native, or Asian or Pacific Islander. CA, HI, OH (for December only), PA, UT, and WA reported multiple-race data in 2003, following the revised 1997 OMB standards. In 2004, the following states began to report multiple-race data: FL, ID, KY, MI, MN, NH, NY State (excluding New York City), SC, and TN. The multiple-race data for these states were bridged to the single-race categories of the 1977 OMB standards for comparability with other states. In addition, note that data on race and Hispanic origin are collected and reported separately. Persons of Hispanic origin may be of any race.

[e] Trends for the Hispanic population are affected by an expansion in the number of registration areas that included an item on Hispanic origin on the birth certificate. The number of states in the reporting area increased from 22 states in 1980 to 23 states and the District of Columbia (DC) in 1983–1987, 30 states and DC in 1988, 47 states and DC in 1989, 48 states and DC in 1990, 49 states and DC in 1991, and all 50 states and DC from 1993 onward

NOTE: Infant deaths are deaths before an infant's first birthday. Rates for race groups from the National Linked Files of Live Births and Infant Deaths vary slightly from those obtained via unlinked infant death records using the National Vital Statistics System because the race reported on the death certificate sometimes does not match the race on the infant's birth certificate. Rates obtained from linked data (where race is obtained from the birth, rather than the death, certificate) are considered more reliable, but linked data are not available before 1983 and are also not available for 1992–1995 nor 2006.

SOURCE: National Center for Health Statistics, National Vital Statistics System.

| Table HEALTH3.A | Emotional and behavioral difficulties: Percentage of children ages 4–17 reported by a parent to have serious, minor, or no difficulties with emotions, concentration, behavior, or getting along with other people by selected characteristics, 2007 |

Characteristic	Serious difficulties	Minor difficulties	No difficulties
Age and gender			
Total ages 4–17	5.2	14.4	80.4
Ages 4–7	3.8	12.5	83.8
Ages 8–10	4.4	16.4	79.2
Ages 11–14	6.0	15.8	78.2
Ages 15–17	6.8	13.1	80.1
Males ages 4–17	6.4	16.1	77.5
Ages 4–7	5.1	13.3	81.6
Ages 8–10	6.3	18.1	75.6
Ages 11–14	7.5	19.1	73.4
Ages 15–17	6.9	14.0	79.1
Females ages 4–17	3.9	12.6	83.5
Ages 4–7	2.4	11.6	86.0
Ages 8–10	2.3	14.6	83.2
Ages 11–14	4.5	12.3	83.2
Ages 15–17	6.6	12.2	81.2
Poverty status			
Below 100% poverty	7.0	17.7	75.3
100–199% poverty	7.3	16.3	76.5
200% poverty and above	3.9	12.7	83.4
Race and Hispanic origin[a]			
White, non-Hispanic	5.6	15.2	79.3
Black, non-Hispanic	5.9	16.5	77.6
Other, non-Hispanic and multiple races	4.7	8.1	87.2
Hispanic	3.7	12.1	84.2
Family structure[b]			
Two parents	4.2	12.2	83.6
Mother only	7.1	19.5	73.3
Father only	5.5	18.2	76.2
No parents	11.5	19.9	68.6

[a] The revised 1997 OMB standards for race were used for the 2007 race-specific estimates. A person's race is described by one or more of five racial groups: White, Black or African American, American Indian or Alaska Native, Asian, and Native Hawaiian or Other Pacific Islander. Data on race and Hispanic origin are collected separately, but are combined for reporting. Estimates are not shown separately for the race categories American Indian or Alaska Native, Asian, Native Hawaiian or Other Pacific Islander, or multiple races due to the small sample size for each of these groups. Persons of Hispanic origin may be of any race.

[b] "Two parents" includes two married or unmarried parents. The terms "mother" and "father" can include biological, adoptive, step, or foster relationships. "No parents" can include children cared for by other relatives or a legal guardian.

NOTE: Emotional or behavioral difficulties of children were based on parental responses to the following question on the Strengths and Difficulties Questionnaire (SDQ):[1] "Overall, do you think that (child) has any difficulties in one or more of the following areas: emotions, concentration, behavior, or being able to get along with other people?" Response choices were: (1) no; (2) yes, minor difficulties; (3) yes, definite difficulties; and (4) yes, severe difficulties. Children with serious emotional or behavioral difficulties are defined as those whose parent responded "yes, definite" or "yes, severe." These difficulties may be similar to but do not equate with the Federal definition of serious emotional disturbances (SED), used by the Federal government for planning purposes.

SOURCE: National Center for Health Statistics, National Health Interview Survey.

[1] Goodman, R. (1999). The extended version of the Strengths and Difficulties Questionnaire as a guide to child psychiatric caseness and consequent burden. *Journal of Child Psychology and Psychiatry, 40,* 791–799.

| Table HEALTH3.B | Emotional and behavioral difficulties: Percentage of children ages 4–17 whose parent had contact[a] with a health care provider or school staff, who were prescribed medication, or who received treatment other than medication by level of emotional and behavioral difficulty, 2007 |

Level of difficulty	Contact with health care provider or school staff	Prescribed medication[b]	Treatment[b] other than medication
Serious difficulties	85.5	46.1	50.5
Minor difficulties	51.0	14.4	16.4
No difficulties	3.6	1.0	1.0

[a] Data on service contact and type of service for an emotional or behavioral difficulty are from new service questions added in 2005 and asked directly after the Strengths and Difficulties Questionnaire. A child who had more than one type of service or contact was included in more than one column.

[b] Prescribed medication or treatment for emotional or behavioral difficulties.

NOTE: Emotional or behavioral difficulties of children were based on parental responses to the following question on the Strengths and Difficulties Questionnaire (SDQ):[1] "Overall, do you think that (child) has any difficulties in one or more of the following areas: emotions, concentration, behavior, or being able to get along with other people?" Response choices were: (1) no; (2) yes, minor difficulties; (3) yes, definite difficulties; and (4) yes, severe difficulties. Children with serious emotional or behavioral difficulties are defined as those whose parent responded "yes, definite" or "yes, severe." These difficulties may be similar to but do not equate with the Federal definition of serious emotional disturbances (SED), used by the Federal government for planning purposes.

SOURCE: National Center for Health Statistics, National Health Interview Survey.

[1] Goodman, R. (1999). The extended version of the Strengths and Difficulties Questionnaire as a guide to child psychiatric caseness and consequent burden. *Journal of Child Psychology and Psychiatry, 40,* 791–799.

| Table HEALTH4.A | Adolescent depression: Percentage of youth ages 12–17 who had at least one Major Depressive Episode (MDE) in the past year by age, gender, race and Hispanic origin, and poverty status, 2004–2007 |

Characteristic	2004	2005	2006	2007
Total	9.0	8.8	7.9	8.2
Age				
Ages 12–13	5.4	5.2	4.9	4.3
Ages 14–15	9.2	9.5	7.9	8.4
Ages 16–17	12.3	11.5	10.7	11.5
Gender				
Male	5.0	4.5	4.2	4.6
Female	13.1	13.3	11.8	11.9
Race and Hispanic origin[a]				
White, non-Hispanic	9.2	9.1	8.1	8.7
Black, non-Hispanic	7.7	7.6	6.4	7.8
American Indian or Alaska Native	7.8	6.1	9.3	4.6
Asian	8.3	6.0	7.6	6.8
Two or more races	11.7	10.5	13.0	10.0
Hispanic	9.1	9.1	8.0	7.1
Poverty status				
Below 100% poverty	—	8.1	7.6	7.6
100–199% poverty	—	9.6	9.0	8.9
200% poverty and above	—	8.7	7.6	8.0

— Not available.

[a] 1997 OMB standards were used to collect race and ethnicity data. Persons could select one or more of five racial groups: White, Black or African American, American Indian or Alaska Native, Native Hawaiian or other Pacific Islander, or Asian. Respondents could choose more than one race. Those reporting more than one race were classified as "Two or more races." Data on Hispanic origin are collected separately. Persons of Hispanic origin may be of any race. Included in the total but not shown separately are persons of Native Hawaiian or Other Pacific Islander origin.

NOTE: Major Depressive Episode (MDE) is defined as a period of at least 2 weeks when a person experienced a depressed mood or loss of interest or pleasure in daily activities and had at least four additional symptoms (such as problems with sleep, eating, energy, concentration and feelings of worth) as described in the 4th edition of the *Diagnostic and Statistical Manual of Mental Disorders (DSM-IV)*.[1]

SOURCE: Substance Abuse and Mental Health Services Administration, National Survey on Drug Use and Health.

[1] American Psychiatric Association. (1994). *Diagnostic and Statistical Manual of Mental Disorders (DSM-IV)* (4th ed.). Washington, DC: Author.

| Table HEALTH4.B | Adolescent depression: Percentage of youth ages 12–17 with at least one Major Depressive Episode (MDE) in the past year who received treatment for depression[a] by age, gender, race and Hispanic origin, and poverty status, 2004–2007 |

Characteristic	2004	2005	2006	2007
Total	40.3	37.8	38.9	38.9
Age				
Ages 12–13	38.2	32.9	35.1	41.4
Ages 14–15	35.5	41.1	38.7	36.9
Ages 16–17	45.0	37.1	40.8	39.6
Gender				
Male	37.7	34.1	35.4	36.7
Female	41.3	39.0	40.3	39.9
Race and Hispanic origin[b]				
White, non-Hispanic	44.9	39.3	41.4	42.6
Black, non-Hispanic	28.9	39.3	29.0	39.9
Hispanic	36.8	31.8	36.0	28.1
Poverty status				
Below 100% poverty	—	37.3	33.2	39.4
100–199% poverty	—	32.1	40.9	36.9
200% poverty and above	—	40.1	39.9	36.9

— Not available.

[a] Treatment is defined as seeing or talking to a medical doctor or other professional or using prescription medication in the past year for depression. Respondents with unknown treatment data were excluded.

[b] 1997 OMB standards were used to collect race and ethnicity data. Persons could select one or more of five racial groups: White, Black or African American, American Indian or Alaska Native, Native Hawaiian or other Pacific Islander, or Asian. Respondents could choose more than one race. Those reporting more than one race were classified as "Two or more races." Data on Hispanic origin are collected separately. Persons of Hispanic origin may be of any race. Included in the total but not shown separately are American Indian or Alaska Native, Native Hawaiian or Other Pacific Islander, Asian, and "Two or more races."

NOTE: Major Depressive Episode (MDE) is defined as a period of at least 2 weeks when a person experienced a depressed mood or loss of interest or pleasure in daily activities and had at least four additional symptoms (such as problems with sleep, eating, energy, concentration and feelings of worth) as described in the 4th edition of the *Diagnostic and Statistical Manual of Mental Disorders (DSM-IV)*.[1]

SOURCE: Substance Abuse and Mental Health Services Administration, National Survey on Drug Use and Health.

[1] American Psychiatric Association. (1994). *Diagnostic and Statistical Manual of Mental Disorders (DSM-IV)* (4th ed.). Washington, DC: Author.

| Table HEALTH4.C | Adolescent depression: Percentage of youth ages 12–17 who had at least one Major Depressive Episode (MDE) with severe impairment in the past year by age, gender, race and Hispanic origin, and poverty status, 2004–2007 |

Characteristic	2004	2005	2006	2007
Total	6.2	6.0	5.5	5.5
Age				
Ages 12–13	3.5	3.3	2.7	2.5
Ages 14–15	6.3	6.6	6.0	6.0
Ages 16–17	8.8	8.1	7.5	7.9
Gender				
Male	3.3	2.9	2.6	3.0
Female	9.2	9.4	8.4	8.2
Race and Hispanic origin[a]				
White, non-Hispanic	6.5	6.3	5.8	5.9
Black, non-Hispanic	5.0	5.1	3.9	5.1
American Indian or Alaska Native	4.9	4.1	6.6	2.6
Asian	4.4	3.7	5.3	4.0
Two or more races	9.3	7.7	8.0	7.8
Hispanic	6.1	6.2	5.4	5.0
Poverty status				
Below 100% poverty	—	5.2	5.4	5.1
100–199% poverty	—	6.7	6.3	6.0
200% poverty and above	—	6.0	5.2	5.5

— Not available.

[a] 1997 OMB standards were used to collect race and ethnicity data. Persons could select one or more of five racial groups: White, Black or African American, American Indian or Alaska Native, Native Hawaiian or other Pacific Islander, or Asian. Respondents could choose more than one race. Those reporting more than one race were classified as "Two or more races." Data on Hispanic origin are collected separately. Persons of Hispanic origin may be of any race. Included in the total but not shown separately are persons of Native Hawaiian or Other Pacific Islander origin.

NOTE: Major Depressive Episode (MDE) is defined as a period of at least 2 weeks when a person experienced a depressed mood or loss of interest or pleasure in daily activities and had at least four additional symptoms (such as problems with sleep, eating, energy, concentration and feelings of worth) as described in the 4th edition of the *Diagnostic and Statistical Manual of Mental Disorders (DSM-IV)*.[1] Impairment is identified using the Sheehan Disability Scale (SDS)[2] items that measure the impact of MDE across four role domains: (1) chores at home, (2) school or work, (3) close relationships with family, and (4) social life. Ratings are made on a 0 to 10 scale with ratings greater than or equal to 7 considered severe impairment.

SOURCE: Substance Abuse and Mental Health Services Administration, National Survey on Drug Use and Health.

[1] American Psychiatric Association. (1994). *Diagnostic and Statistical Manual of Mental Disorders (DSM-IV)* (4th ed.). Washington, DC: Author.

[2] Leon, A.C., Olfson, M., Portera, L., Farber, L., and Sheehan, D.V. (1997). Assessing psychiatric impairment in primary care with the Sheehan Disability Scale. *International Journal of Methods in Psychiatric Research. 27*(2), 93–105.

Table HEALTH5	Activity limitation: Percentage of children ages 5–17 with activity limitation resulting from one or more chronic health conditions[a] by gender, poverty status, and race and Hispanic origin, selected years 1997–2007									

Characteristic	1997	1999	2000	2001	2002	2003	2004	2005	2006	2007
Ages 5–17										
Total	7.8	7.0	7.0	8.0	8.5	8.1	8.4	8.0	8.6	8.3
Special education only[b]	5.4	5.3	5.0	6.2	6.3	6.3	6.3	6.1	6.7	6.5
Other limitations[c]	2.4	1.7	2.0	1.8	2.1	1.8	2.1	1.8	1.9	1.8
Gender										
Male	10.0	8.8	8.8	10.4	10.7	10.1	10.6	10.2	11.0	10.8
Special education only[b]	7.2	6.8	6.5	8.2	8.2	8.1	8.0	8.1	8.8	8.7
Other limitations[c]	2.8	2.0	2.4	2.2	2.5	2.0	2.5	2.1	2.2	2.1
Female	5.5	5.2	5.1	5.5	6.2	6.0	6.1	5.7	6.1	5.6
Special education only[b]	3.5	3.8	3.6	4.0	4.4	4.4	4.5	4.1	4.4	4.2
Other limitations[c]	2.0	1.4	1.5	1.5	1.8	1.6	1.6	1.6	1.6	1.5
Poverty status[d]										
Below 100% poverty	10.6	9.8	9.9	10.8	11.6	10.3	11.7	10.8	11.4	11.6
Special education only[b]	7.2	7.0	7.2	8.3	8.1	7.7	8.7	7.7	8.9	8.7
Other limitations[c]	3.4	2.8	2.7	2.5	3.5	2.6	3.0	3.0	2.5	2.9
100–199% poverty	9.3	8.4	8.0	8.9	10.5	10.0	9.7	9.1	9.8	10.1
Special education only[b]	7.0	6.5	5.6	6.7	7.9	7.3	7.1	7.3	7.7	7.9
Other limitations[c]	2.3	1.9	2.4	2.2	2.6	2.7	2.6	1.8	2.1	2.2
200% poverty and above	6.3	5.8	5.8	6.9	6.9	6.8	7.0	6.8	7.2	6.7
Special education only[b]	4.2	4.4	4.3	5.4	5.3	5.5	5.4	5.3	5.6	5.3
Other limitations[c]	2.2	1.3	1.6	1.5	1.6	1.3	1.6	1.5	1.6	1.3
Race and Hispanic origin[e]										
White, non-Hispanic	8.3	7.5	7.5	8.5	8.8	8.6	8.8	8.3	9.5	9.0
Special education only[b]	5.8	5.7	5.4	6.5	6.6	6.8	6.7	6.2	7.7	7.1
Other limitations[c]	2.5	1.8	2.1	2.0	2.2	1.8	2.1	2.1	1.8	1.9
Black, non-Hispanic	8.2	7.0	7.5	9.0	10.2	8.3	10.3	8.7	8.3	8.9
Special education only[b]	5.3	4.9	5.6	7.0	7.8	6.5	7.7	6.9	5.9	7.2
Other limitations[c]	2.9	2.1	1.9	1.9	2.5	1.8	2.6	1.8	2.4	1.7
Hispanic	5.9	5.7	5.3	5.6	6.7	6.6	6.0	7.0	6.6	6.1
Special education only[b]	4.0	4.5	3.7	4.3	5.0	4.9	4.4	5.6	4.9	4.7
Other limitations[c]	1.9	1.2	1.6	1.2	1.7	1.8	1.7	1.4	1.7	1.4

[a] Chronic health conditions are conditions that once acquired are not cured or have a duration of 3 months or more.

[b] Special education, as mandated by Federal legislation known as the Individuals with Disabilities Education Act (IDEA), is designed to meet the individual needs of the child, and may take place in a regular classroom setting, a separate classroom, a special school, a private school, at home, or at a hospital. To qualify for special education services, a child must have a condition covered by the IDEA which adversely affects educational performance. Children in this category include children identified solely by their use of special education services.

[c] Other limitations include limitations in children's ability to walk, care for themselves, or perform any other activities. Children in this category may also receive special education services.

[d] Starting with *America's Children, 2005*, a new methodology for imputing family income was used for data years 1997 and beyond. Missing family income data were imputed for 22–31 percent of children ages 5–17 in 1997–2007. Therefore, estimates by poverty for 1997–2001 may differ from those in previous editions.

[e] The revised 1997 OMB standards for race were used for the 1997–2007 race-specific estimates. A person's race is described by one or more of five racial groups: White, Black or African American, American Indian or Alaska Native, Asian, or Native Hawaiian or Other Pacific Islander. Data on race and Hispanic origin are collected separately but are combined for reporting. Persons of Hispanic origin may be of any race. Included in the total but not shown separately are American Indian or Alaska Native, Asian, Native Hawaiian or Other Pacific Islander, and "Two or more races" due to the small sample size for each of these groups.

NOTE: The prevalence of activity limitation among children ages 5–17 is based on household responses in the National Health Interview Survey family core questionnaire. The child was considered to have an activity limitation if the parent gave a positive response to any of the following questions about the child: (1) "Does (child's name) receive Special Education Services?" (2) "Because of a physical, mental, or emotional problem, does (child's name) need the help of other persons with personal care needs, such as eating, bathing, dressing, or getting around inside the home?" (3) "Because of a health problem does (child's name) have difficulty walking without using any special equipment?" (4) "Is (child's name) limited in any way because of difficulty remembering or because of periods of confusion?" (5) "Is (child's name) limited in any activities because of physical, mental, or emotional problems?"

SOURCE: National Center for Health Statistics, National Health Interview Survey.

Dietary component	Ages 2–17	Ages 2–5	Ages 6–11	Ages 12–17
Table HEALTH6 — Diet quality: Average diet scores for children ages 2–17 as a percentage of Federal diet quality standards by age and dietary component, 2003–2004				
Total Healthy Eating Index-2005 score	56	60	55	55
Dietary adequacy components[a]				
Total fruit	64	100	58	50
Whole fruit	56	86	55	44
Total vegetables	47	44	46	49
Dark green and orange vegetables and legumes	12	13	11	12
Total grains	100	100	100	100
Whole grains	15	17	18	13
Milk	87	100	87	77
Meat and beans	81	73	78	88
Oils	67	55	66	75
Dietary moderation components[b]				
Saturated fat	52	47	52	54
Sodium	44	48	45	42
Extra calories[c]	41	47	38	39

[a] Higher scores reflect higher intakes.

[b] Higher scores reflect lower intakes.

[c] Extra calories from other sources, such as solid fats and added sugars.

NOTE: The Healthy Eating Index-2005 (HEI-2005) is a dietary assessment tool comprised of 12 components designed to measure quality in terms of how well diets meet the recommendations of the 2005 Dietary Guidelines for Americans and MyPyramid, USDA's food guidance system (http://www.MyPyramid.gov).[1–3] The HEI-2005 component scores are averages across all children which reflect usual dietary intakes.[4] These scores are expressed as percentages of recommended dietary intake levels. A score corresponding to 100 percent indicates that the recommendation was met or exceeded, on average. A score below 100 percent indicates that average intake does not meet the recommendations for that component. Nine components of the HEI-2005 address nutrient adequacy. The remaining three components assess saturated fat, sodium, and extra calories, all of which should be consumed in moderation. For the adequacy components, higher scores reflect higher intakes; for the moderation components, higher scores reflect lower intakes because lower intakes are more desirable. For all components, a higher percentage indicates a higher quality diet.

SOURCE: National Center for Health Statistics, National Health and Nutrition Examination Survey, 2003–2004 and U.S. Department of Agriculture, Center for Nutrition Policy and Promotion, Healthy Eating Index-2005.

[1] U.S. Health and Human Services and U.S. Department of Agriculture. (2005). *Dietary Guidelines for Americans* (6th ed.). Washington, DC: U.S. Government Printing Office.

[2] Guenther, P.M., Reedy, J., and Krebs-Smith, S.M. (2008). Development of the Healthy Eating Index-2005. *Journal of the American Dietetic Association, 108,* 1896–1901.

[3] Guenther, P.M., Reedy, J., Krebs-Smith, S.M., and Reeve, B.B. (2008). Evaluation of the Healthy Eating Index-2005. *Journal of the American Dietetic Association, 108,* 1854–1864.

[4] Freedman, L.S., Guenther, P.M., Krebs-Smith, S.M., and Kott, P.S. (2008). A population's mean Healthy Eating Index-2005 scores are best estimated by the score of the population ratio when one 24-hour recall is available. *Journal of Nutrition, 138,* 1725–1729.

Table HEALTH7	Overweight: Percentage of children ages 6–17 who are overweight by age and gender, selected years 1976–2006					
Characteristic	1976–1980	1988–1994	1999–2000	2001–2002	2003–2004	2005–2006
Ages 6–17						
Total	5.7	11.2	15.0	16.5	18.0	16.5
Gender						
Male	5.5	11.8	15.7	18.0	19.1	17.2
Female	5.8	10.6	14.3	15.1	16.8	15.9
Ages 6–11						
Total	6.5	11.3	15.1	16.3	18.8	15.1
Gender						
Male	6.7	11.6	15.7	17.5	19.9	16.2
Female	6.4	11.0	14.3	14.9	17.6	14.1
Ages 12–17						
Total	5.0	11.1	14.9	16.8	17.2	17.8
Gender						
Male	4.5	12.0	15.6	18.4	18.3	18.1
Female	5.4	10.2	14.2	15.2	16.0	17.5

NOTE: Overweight is defined as body mass index (BMI) at or above the 95th percentile of the 2000 Centers for Disease Control and Prevention sex-specific BMI-for-age growth charts (http://www.cdc.gov/growthcharts).

SOURCE: National Center for Health Statistics, National Health and Nutrition Examination Survey.

Table HEALTH8.A	Asthma: Percentage of children ages 0–17 with asthma, selected years 1980–2007												
Characteristic	1980	1985	1990	1995	1997[a]	2000[a]	2001[a]	2002[a]	2003[a]	2004[a]	2005[a]	2006[a]	2007[a]
Asthma in past 12 months[b]	3.6	4.8	5.8	7.5	—	—	—	—	—	—	—	—	—
Ever diagnosed with asthma[c]	—	—	—	—	11.4	12.3	12.7	12.3	12.5	12.2	12.7	13.5	13.1
Currently have asthma[d]	—	—	—	—	—	—	8.8	8.4	8.5	8.5	8.9	9.3	9.1
Having at least one asthma attack[e]	—	—	—	—	5.4	5.5	5.7	5.8	5.5	5.6	5.2	5.6	5.2

— Not available.

[a] In 1997, the National Health Interview Survey was redesigned. Data for 1997–2007 are not strictly comparable to earlier data.

[b] Children with asthma in the past 12 months.

[c] Children ever diagnosed with asthma by doctor or other health care professional.

[d] Children ever diagnosed with asthma who currently have asthma.

[e] Children having had an episode of asthma or asthma attack in the past 12 months.

NOTE: From 1997 to 2007, children are identified as ever diagnosed with asthma by asking parents "Has a doctor or other health professional EVER told you that your child has asthma?" If the parent answered YES to this question, they were then asked (1) "Does your child still have asthma?" and (2) "During the past twelve months, has your child had an episode of asthma or an asthma attack?" The question "Does your child still have asthma?" was introduced in 2001 and identifies children who currently have asthma.

SOURCE: National Center for Health Statistics, National Health Interview Survey.

Table HEALTH8.B	Asthma: Percentage of children ages 0–17 who currently have asthma[a] by age, poverty status, race and Hispanic origin, and area of residence, 2001–2007						
Characteristic	2001	2002	2003	2004	2005	2006	2007
Age							
Ages 0–5	6.2	6.4	6.3	6.4	7.2	6.9	7.1
Ages 6–10	9.8	8.6	9.4	8.3	10.0	11.4	9.1
Ages 11–17	10.1	9.7	9.8	10.3	9.6	9.9	10.9
Poverty status[b]							
Below 100% poverty	10.8	11.6	10.9	9.6	10.6	12.2	11.4
100–199% poverty	8.6	7.8	8.3	9.3	8.3	9.6	9.8
200% poverty and above	8.2	7.6	7.9	7.9	8.6	8.1	8.1
Race and Hispanic origin[c]							
White, non-Hispanic	8.5	8.0	7.5	8.2	7.9	8.6	7.3
Black, non-Hispanic	11.3	12.7	13.4	12.4	13.1	12.8	15.4
American Indian or Alaska Native	8.9*	12.0	16.2	6.4*	13.6*	**	7.7*
Asian	7.3	5.3	4.4*	3.4	6.5	6.3	7.4
Hispanic	7.2	6.3	7.4	6.9	8.6	9.0	9.3
Mexican	5.1	4.4	4.9	5.4	7.4	6.6	8.5
Puerto Rican	18.2	17.3	20.6	18.4	19.9	25.7	14.8
Area of residence[d]							
Central city	8.8	8.4	9.1	8.7	10.3	10.5	9.9
Non-central city	8.8	8.4	8.3	8.4	8.4	8.8	8.8

* Estimate is considered unstable (relative standard error is greater than 30 percent).

** Estimate is considered unreliable (relative standard error greater than 40 percent).

[a] Children ever diagnosed with asthma that still have asthma.

[b] Missing family income data were imputed for 28–30 percent of children ages 0–17 in 2001–2007.

[c] The revised 1997 OMB standards for race were used for the 2001–2007 race-specific estimates. A person's race is described by one or more of five racial groups: White, Black or African American, American Indian or Alaska Native, Asian, or Native Hawaiian or Other Pacific Islander. Data on race and Hispanic origin are collected separately, but are combined for reporting. Included in other categories but not shown separately under race and Hispanic origin are Native Hawaiians or Other Pacific Islanders and respondents with "Two or more races." Persons of Hispanic origin may be of any race.

[d] "Central city" is defined as the central city of a Metropolitan Statistical Area (MSA), while "Non-central city" is defined as an area in an MSA outside of the central city or in an area outside of an MSA. For more information on MSA's, see National Center for Health Statistics. *Health, United States, 2008.* Appendix II, p. 555. Retrieved from http://www.cdc.gov/nchs/data/hus/hus08.pdf.

SOURCE: National Center for Health Statistics, National Health Interview Survey.

Children with special health care needs: Percentage of children ages 0–17 with special health care needs by age, gender, race and Hispanic origin, and poverty status, 2005–2006

Characteristic	Percentage
Age and gender	
Total ages 0–17	13.9
Ages 0–5	8.8
Ages 6–11	16.0
Ages 12–17	16.8
Males ages 0–17	16.1
Ages 0–5	10.5
Ages 6–11	19.2
Ages 12–17	18.7
Females ages 0–17	11.6
Ages 0–5	7.0
Ages 6–11	12.7
Ages 12–17	14.8
Race and Hispanic origin[a]	
White, non-Hispanic	15.5
Black, non-Hispanic	15.0
American Indian or Alaska Native	14.5
Asian	6.3
Native Hawaiian or Other Pacific Islander	11.5
Two or more races	17.9
Hispanic	8.3
Poverty status	
Below 100% poverty	13.9
100–199% poverty	14.0
200–399% poverty	13.6
400% poverty and above	14.0

[a] Data on race and ethnicity are reported using the revised 1997 OMB standards which identify five racial groups: White, Black or African American, American Indian or Alaska Native, Asian, or Native Hawaiian or Other Pacific Islander. Data on race and Hispanic origin are collected separately but combined for reporting. Persons of Hispanic origin may be of any race. Respondents were given the opportunity to self-report their race. If a race other than one of the OMB categories was indicated, the verbatim response was captured. Those who chose more than one race were classified as "Two or more races."

NOTE: Children with special health care needs (CSHCN) were identified using the five-item CSHCN Screener. Children are considered to have a special health care need if they have a parent-reported physical, developmental, behavioral, or emotional condition that has lasted or is expected to last 12 months or longer and that requires health and related services of a type or amount beyond that required generally by children of the same age.

SOURCE: Maternal and Child Health Bureau and National Center for Health Statistics, State and Local Area Integrated Telephone Survey, National Survey of Children with Special Health Care Needs, 2005–2006.

Table SPECIAL1.B	Children with special health care needs: Percentage of children with special health care needs (CSHCN) ages 0–17 by insurance type, number of conditions, effect on daily activities, and criteria met to determine CSHCN status, 2005–2006

Characteristic	Percentage
Insurance type	
Private	59.3
Public[a]	28.1
Private and public[a]	7.4
Other comprehensive[b]	1.7
Uninsured	3.5
Number of parent-reported health conditions	
No conditions[c]	8.9
One condition	33.9
Two conditions	32.2
Three conditions	14.1
Four or more conditions	10.9
Effect on daily activities	
Never affected[d]	37.5
Moderately affected	38.5
Usually or always affected	24.0
Criteria met to determine CSHCN status[e]	
Prescription medication	78.4
Elevated service use	38.8
Emotional, behavioral, or developmental problem	28.6
Limitations in activities	21.5
Use of or need for therapies	17.7

[a] Public health insurance includes Medicaid, State Children's Health Insurance Program (SCHIP), and Medicare coverage.

[b] Comprehensive coverage includes any insurance coverage or health plan that pays for both doctor visits and hospital stays but could not be conclusively determined to be public or private coverage

[c] No survey could include a complete list of all conditions that CSHCN may have. This survey included 16 conditions. Nine percent of CSHCN did not have one of these 16 conditions.

[d] Children whose conditions never affected their daily activities reflect either the effects of treatment used to manage the condition or the nature of the condition.

[e] Percentages do not equal 100% because CSHCN may have met more than one criterion.

NOTE: Children with special health care needs (CSHCN) were identified using the five-item CSHCN Screener. Children are considered to have a special health care need if they have a parent-reported physical, developmental, behavioral, or emotional condition that has lasted or is expected to last 12 months or longer and that requires health and related services of a type or amount beyond that required generally by children of the same age.

SOURCE: Maternal and Child Health Bureau and National Center for Health Statistics, State and Local Area Integrated Telephone Survey, National Survey of Children with Special Health Care Needs, 2005–2006

**Appendix B:
Data Source Descriptions**

Data Source Descriptions

Data Source Descriptions

Air Quality System

The Air Quality System (AQS) contains ambient air pollution data collected by the U.S. Environmental Protection Agency (EPA) and by state, local, and tribal air pollution control agencies. Data on criteria pollutants (particulate matter, ozone, carbon monoxide, nitrogen dioxide, sulfur dioxide, and lead) consist of air quality measurements collected by sensitive equipment at thousands of monitoring stations in all 50 states, plus the District of Columbia, Puerto Rico, and the U.S. Virgin Islands. Each monitor measures the concentration of a particular pollutant in the air. Monitoring data indicate the average pollutant concentration during a specified time interval, usually 1 hour or 24 hours. AQS also contains meteorological data, descriptive information about each monitoring station (including its geographic location and its operator), and data quality assurance/quality control information. The system is administered by the EPA's Office of Air Quality Planning and Standards (OAQPS), Information Transfer and Program Integration Division (ITPID), located in Research Triangle Park, North Carolina.

Information about the AQS is available online at http://www.epa.gov/air/data/aqsdb.html.

Agency Contact:
David Mintz
U.S. Environmental Protection Agency
Phone: (919) 541-5224

American Community Survey

The American Community Survey (ACS) is an annual nationwide survey that will replace the decennial long form in future censuses. The objective of the ACS is to provide data users with timely housing, social, and economic data that is updated every year and can be compared across states, communities, and population groups.

The ACS has been implemented in three parts:
(1) Demonstration period, 1996–1998, beginning at 4 sites; (2) Comparison site period, 1999–2004, comparing 31 sites continuously over this period as well as adding other counties to the survey in preparation for full implementation; and (3) Full implementation nationwide in 2005. (Sampling of group quarters was added in 2006.)

Starting in January 2005, the U.S. Census Bureau implemented the American Community Survey in every county of the United States with an annual sample of 3 million housing units. Once the survey is in full operation, American Community Survey data will be available every year for areas and population groups of 65,000 or more.

For small areas and population groups of 20,000 or less, it will take 5 years to accumulate a large enough sample to provide estimates with accuracy similar to the decennial census. Each month, a systematic sample of addresses will be selected from the most current Master Address File (MAF). The sample will represent the entire United States. Data are collected by mail, and sample addresses that do not respond by mail may be contacted using computer-assisted telephone interviewing (CATI), computer-assisted personal interviewing (CAPI), or both of these follow-up procedures.

Information about the American Community Survey is available online at http://www.census.gov/acs/www/index.html.

Agency Contact:
Hyon Shin
U.S. Census Bureau
Phone: (301) 763-2464

American Housing Survey

This survey provides data necessary for evaluating progress toward "a decent home and a suitable living environment for every American family," a goal affirmed in 1949 and 1968 legislation. National data come from a sample survey conducted by the U.S. Census Bureau in odd numbered years. Supplemental surveys are conducted in 47 metropolitan statistical areas over a multiyear cycle. These data detail the types, size, conditions, characteristics, costs and values, equipment, utilities, and dynamics of the housing inventory; describe the demographic, financial, and mobility characteristics of the occupants; and give some information on neighborhood conditions. In 1997, the survey was conducted using computer-assisted personal interviewing (CAPI) for the first time, and questions on rental assistance and physical problems also were changed. Therefore, data collected since 1997 on assisted families, priority problems, and severe physical problems are not comparable with earlier data.

Information about the American Housing Survey is available online at http://www.census.gov/hhes/www/ahs.html.

Agency Contact:
Barry Steffen
U.S. Department of Housing and Urban Development
Phone: (202) 402-5926

Current Population Survey

Core survey and supplements. The Current Population Survey (CPS) is a nationwide survey of about 60,000 households conducted monthly for the U.S. Bureau of Labor Statistics by the U.S. Census Bureau. It represents the civilian noninstitutionalized population nationally and for every state and the District of Columbia.

The CPS core survey is the primary source of information on the employment characteristics of the noninstitutionalized civilian population, ages 15 and older, including estimates of unemployment released every month by the U.S. Bureau of Labor Statistics.

In addition to the core survey, monthly CPS supplements provide additional demographic and social data. The Annual Social and Economic Supplement (ASEC)—formerly called the March Supplement—and the October school enrollment supplement provide information used to estimate the status and well-being of children. The ASEC and school enrollment supplement have been administered every year since 1947. The October supplement to the CPS asks questions on school enrollment by grade and on other school characteristics about each member of the household age 3 or older. In this report, data on poverty status, health insurance, and the highest level of school completed or degree attained are derived from the ASEC. The food security supplement, introduced in April 1995 and administered in December since 2001, is described in detail below.

The CPS sample is selected from a complete address list of geographically delineated primary sampling units, which are based on census addresses and updated using recent construction and other data. It is administered through field representatives, either in person or by telephone using computer-assisted personal interviewing (CAPI). Some CPS data is also collected through a centralized telephone operation, computer-assisted telephone interviewing (CATI). For more information regarding the CPS, its sampling structure, and estimation methodology, see *Current Population Survey Design and Methodology Technical Paper 66*, Bureau of Labor Statistics, October 2006, available online at http://www.census.gov/prod/2006pubs/tp-66.pdf.

Effective with the release of July 2001 data, official labor force estimates from the CPS reflect the expansion of the monthly CPS sample from about 50,000 to about 60,000 eligible households. This expansion of the monthly CPS sample was one part of the U.S. Census Bureau's plan to meet the requirements of the State Children's Health Insurance Program (SCHIP) legislation. The SCHIP legislation requires the U.S. Census Bureau to improve state estimates of the number of children who live in low-income families and lack health insurance. These estimates are obtained from the ASEC supplement to the CPS. The ASEC reflects interviews based on a sample of about 100,000 households. The ASEC (formerly the March Supplement) now includes data collected in February, March, and April. In September 2000, the U.S. Census Bureau began expanding the monthly CPS sample in 31 states and the District of Columbia. States were identified for sample supplementation based on the

standard error of their March estimate of low-income children without health insurance.

Food security supplement. The food security supplement collects information on households' economic access to enough food, actual food spending, and use of Federal and community food assistance programs. The survey contains a systematic set of questions validated as measures of severity of food insecurity on a 12-month and a 30-day basis. Statistics presented in this report are based on 12-month data from the CPS food security supplements. The food security questions are based on material reported in prior research on hunger and food security and reflect the consensus of nearly 100 experts at the 1994 Food Security and Measurement Conference, convened jointly by the National Center for Health Statistics (NCHS) and the Food and Nutrition Service of the U.S. Department of Agriculture. The supplement was developed, tested, and refined further by the conferees, members of a Federal interagency working group, and survey methods specialists for the U.S. Census Bureau's Center for Survey Methods Research. All households interviewed in the CPS in December are eligible for the supplement. Special supplement sample weights were computed to adjust for the demographic characteristics of supplement noninterviews.

Information about food security is available online at the Economic Research Service, Food Security Briefing Room at http://www.ers.usda.gov/briefing/foodsecurity.

Information about the CPS is available online at http://www.census.gov/cps.

Agency Contacts:
For more information on:

Difficulty speaking English, contact:
Hyon Shin
U.S. Census Bureau
Phone: (301) 763-2464

Early childhood education, contact:
Chris Chapman
National Center for Education Statistics
Phone: (202) 502-7414
E-mail: Chris.Chapman@ed.gov

Family structure, contact:
Fertility and Family Statistics Branch
U.S. Census Bureau
Phone: (301) 763-2416

Food security, contact:
Mark Nord
Economic Research Service
U.S. Department of Agriculture
E-mail: marknord@ers.usda.gov

High school completion, contact:
Chris Chapman
National Center for Education Statistics
Phone: (202) 502-7414
E-mail: Chris.Chapman@ed.gov

Higher education, contact:
Tom Snyder
National Center for Education Statistics
Phone: (202) 502-7452
E-mail: Tom.Snyder@ed.gov

Poverty, family income, and access to health care, contact:
Housing and Household Economic Statistics (HHES)/
Statistical Information Staff
U.S. Census Bureau
Phone: (301) 763-3242

Secure parental employment and youth neither enrolled in school nor working, contact:
Teri Morisi
U.S. Bureau of Labor Statistics
Phone: (202) 691-6378

Decennial Census Data

Every 10 years, beginning with the first census in 1790, the U.S. government conducts a census, or count, of the entire population as mandated by the U.S. Constitution. In 2000, as in several previous censuses, two forms were used—a short form and a long form.

The Census 2000 short form questionnaire included seven basic questions for each household: name, sex, age, relationship, Hispanic origin, race, and whether the housing unit was owned or rented. The long form, in addition to the basic items, asked for more detailed information on subjects such as education, employment, income, ancestry, homeowner costs, units in a structure, number of rooms, plumbing facilities, etc. In 2000, the short form questions were asked of every household, and the long form was sent to approximately 1 in every 6 households. Decennial censuses not only count the population but also sample the socioeconomic status of the population, providing a tool for the government, educators, business owners, and others to get a snapshot of the state of the Nation. A more comprehensive description of Census 2000 is available online at http://www.census.gov/mso/www/c2000basics.

While it is impossible to completely eliminate error from an operation as large and complex as the decennial census, the U.S. Census Bureau attempts to control the sources of such error during the data collection and processing operations. The primary sources of error and the programs instituted to control error in Census 2000 are described

in detail in Summary File 1 Technical Documentation in Chapter 8, "Accuracy of the Data," located at http://www.census.gov/prod/cen2000/doc/sf1.pdf.

For further information on the computation and use of standard errors, contact:
Decennial Statistical Studies Division
U.S. Census Bureau
Phone: (301) 763-4242

High School Transcript Studies

High school transcript studies have been conducted since 1982 and are associated with a major National Center for Education Statistics (NCES) data collection. The studies collect information that is contained in a student's high school record—courses taken while attending secondary school, information on credits earned, when specific courses were taken, and final grades. Similar studies were conducted of the coursetaking patterns of 1982, 1987, 1990, 1992, 1994, 1998, 2000, and 2005 high school graduates. The 1982 data are based on approximately 12,000 transcripts collected by the High School and Beyond Longitudinal study (HS&B). The 1987 data are based on approximately 22,799 transcripts from 433 schools obtained as part of the 1987 National Assessment of Educational Progress (NAEP) High School Transcript Study (HSTS), a scope comparable to that of the NAEP transcript studies conducted in 1990, 1994, 1998, 2000, and 2005. The 1992 data are based on approximately 7,600 transcripts collected by the National Education Longitudinal Study of 1988 (NELS:88/92).

Conducted in association with NAEP, the HSTS provides coursetaking and demographic information for a nationally representative, stratified sample of high school seniors. Sample sizes have ranged from approximately 21,000 to 25,000 students in approximately 300 schools. The HSTS provides the U.S. Department of Education and other education policymakers with information regarding current course offerings and coursetaking patterns in the Nation's secondary schools. In addition, it provides information on the relationship of student coursetaking patterns to achievement as measured by NAEP. The study excluded students who did not graduate from high school, had not received a "regular" or "honors" diploma, or did not have complete transcript data. For all transcripts and samples, a course identification code number, based on the Classification of Secondary School Courses (CSSC), was assigned to each course taken by a student. Courses were further classified into subject (e.g., mathematics) and program (e.g., academic) areas using a 1998 revision of the CSSC (Bradby, D., and Hoachlander, E.G. (1999). *1998 Revision of the secondary school taxonomy*. Washington, DC: National Center for Education Statistics.).

For more information about the NAEP HSTS, see:

U.S. Department of Education. National Center for Education Statistics (NCES). The 1998 High School Transcript Study Tabulation: Comparative data on credits earned and demographics for 1998, 1994, 1990, 1987, and 1982 high school graduates (NCES 2001-498), by Stephen Roey, Nancy Caldwell, Keith Rust, Eyal Blumstein, Tom Krenzke, Stan Legum, Judy Kuhn, Mark Waksberg, and Jacqueline Haynes.

Information about the NAEP High School Transcript Study is available online at http://nces.ed.gov/nationsreportcard/hsts.

Agency Contact:
Janis Brown
National Center for Education Statistics
Phone: (202) 502-7482
E-mail: Janis.Brown@ed.gov

Information about other high school transcript studies is available online at http://nces.ed.gov/surveys/hst.

Agency Contact:
Carl Schmitt
National Center for Education Statistics
Phone: (202) 502-7350
E-mail: Carl.Schmitt@ed.gov

Monitoring the Future

The Monitoring the Future (MTF) Study is a continuing series of surveys intended to assess the changing lifestyles, values, and preferences of American youth. Each year since 1975, high school seniors from a representative sample of public and private high schools have participated in this study. The 2008 survey is the 18th survey to include comparable samples of 8th- and 10th-graders in addition to seniors. The study is conducted by the University of Michigan's Institute for Social Research (ISR) under a grant from the National Institute on Drug Abuse. The survey design consists of a multistage random sample where the stages include selection of geographic areas, selection of one or more schools in each area, and selection of a sample of students within each school. Data are collected in the spring of each year using questionnaires administered in the classroom by representatives from ISR. The 2008 survey included 14,577 12th-graders from 120 schools, 15,518 10th-graders from 122 schools, and 16,253 8th-graders from 144 schools (a total of 46,348 students from 386 schools).

Information about MTF is available online at http://www.nida.nih.gov/DrugPages/MTF.html and http://monitoringthefuture.org.

Agency Contact:
Marsha F. Lopez
National Institute on Drug Abuse
Phone: (301) 402-1846

National Assessment of Educational Progress

The National Assessment of Educational Progress (NAEP) is mandated by Congress to continuously monitor the knowledge, skills, and performance of the Nation's children and youth. To measure trends in educational performance, NAEP has periodically assessed students in grades 4, 8, and 12 since 1990 in reading and mathematics, as well as in other subjects such as science, writing, and U.S. history. The assessments use the curriculum frameworks developed by the National Assessment Governing Board (NAGB) and the latest advances in assessment methodology. The frameworks use standards developed within the field, using a consensus process involving educators, subject-matter experts, and other interested citizens.

The content and nature of the main NAEP evolves periodically to reflect changes in curriculum and instructional practices. NAEP includes students in public and nonpublic schools. A charter school could be sampled, since such schools are within the universe of public schools, but homeschoolers are not included. Before 2002, the NAEP national sample was an independently selected national sample. However, beginning in 2002, the NAEP national sample was obtained by aggregating the samples from each state. As a result, the size of the national sample increased in 2002, which means that smaller differences between estimates from different administrations and different types of students may now be found to be statistically significant than could have been detected in assessment results reported before 2002.

Until 1996, NAEP assessments excluded certain subgroups of students identified as "special needs students," including students with disabilities and students with limited English proficiency. For the 1996 and 2000 mathematics assessments and the 1998 and 2000 reading assessments, NAEP included separate assessments with provisions for accommodating these students (e.g., extended time, small group testing, mathematics questions read aloud, and so on). For these years, results are reported for both the unaccommodated and accommodated assessments. After 2000, only a single accommodated assessment was administered.

Information about NAEP is available online at http://nces.ed.gov/nationsreportcard.

Agency Contact:
Suzanne Triplett
National Center for Education Statistics
Phone: (202) 502-7465
E-mail: Suzanne.Triplett@ed.gov

National Child Abuse and Neglect Data System

The National Child Abuse and Neglect Data System (NCANDS) annually collects case-level data on reports alleging child abuse and neglect, as well as the results of these reports, from state child protective services (CPS) agencies. The mandate for NCANDS is based on the Child Abuse Prevention and Treatment Act (CAPTA), as amended in 1988, which directed the Secretary of the U.S. Department of Health and Human Services (HHS) to establish a national data collection and analysis program that would make available state child abuse and neglect reporting information. HHS responded by establishing NCANDS as a voluntary, national reporting system. In 1992, HHS produced its first NCANDS report based on data from 1990. The annual data report *Child Maltreatment* evolved from that initial report.

During the early years, states provided aggregated data on key indicators of reporting of alleged child maltreatment. Starting with the 1993 data year, states voluntarily began to submit case-level data. For a number of years, states provided both data sets, but starting with data year 2000, the case-level data set became the primary source of data for the annual report. In 1996, CAPTA was amended to require all states that receive funds from the Basic State Grant program to work with the Secretary of HHS to provide specific data, to the extent practicable, on children who had been maltreated. The NCANDS data elements were revised to meet these requirements beginning with the submission of 1998 data.

States that submit case-level data construct a child-specific record for each report of alleged child abuse or neglect that received a disposition as a result of an investigation or an assessment during the reporting period. The reporting period for 2007 was from October 1, 2006 through September 30, 2007. The case-level data are reported in the Child File. Data fields include the demographics of the children and their perpetrators, types of maltreatment, investigation or assessment dispositions, risk factors, and services provided as a result of the investigation or assessment. In 2007, forty-eight states submitted the Child File; almost all of them also reported aggregate-level data in the Agency File for items that were not obtainable at the child level, such as the number of CPS workers. Two states reported only aggregate statistics on key indicators; these states are in the process of developing the Child File. Two states were not able to submit data to NCANDS.

The count of child victims is based on the number of investigations that found a child to be a victim of one or more types of maltreatment. The count of victims is, therefore, a report-based count and is a "duplicated count," since an individual child may have been the subject of a report more than once. Children are considered to be "victims of maltreatment" if the allegation is either "substantiated" or "indicated" by the investigation process. Substantiation is a case determination that concludes that the allegation of maltreatment or risk of maltreatment is supported by state law or policy. "Indicated" is a case determination that concludes that maltreatment cannot be substantiated by state law or policy, but there is reason to suspect that the child may have been maltreated or was at risk of maltreatment.

Data collected by NCANDS are a critical source of information for many publications, reports, and activities of the Federal government and other groups. An annual report on child welfare outcomes includes context and outcome data on safety based on state submissions to NCANDS. NCANDS data have been incorporated into the Child and Family Services Reviews (CFSR), which ensures conformity with state plan requirements in titles IV–B and IV–E of the Social Security Act. The NCANDS data also are used in the Program Assessment Rating Tool (PART), which is "a systematic method of assessing the performance of program activities across the Federal government." Children's Bureau programs funded under the CAPTA Basic State Grant and the Community-Based Child Abuse Prevention (CBCAP) State Grants use data from NCANDS as a component of their PART assessments.

Rates are based on the number of states submitting data to NCANDS each year; states include the District of Columbia and Puerto Rico. The overall rate of maltreatment is based on the following number of states for each year: 51 in 1998, 50 in 1999, 50 in 2000, 51 in 2001, 51 in 2002, 51 in 2003, 50 in 2004, 52 in 2005, 51 in 2006, and 50 in 2007. The number of states reporting on sex for the years 2000–2007 was 50 in 2000, 51 in 2001, 51 in 2002, 51 in 2003, 50 in 2004, 51 in 2005, 51 in 2006, and 50 in 2007. The number of states reporting on race and Hispanic origin for the years 2000–2007 was 48 in 2000, 49 in 2001, 50 in 2002, 50 in 2003, 49 in 2004, 50 in 2005, 49 in 2006, and 46 in 2007. The number of states reporting on age for the years 2000–2007 was 50 in 2000, 51 in 2001, 51 in 2002, 51 in 2003, 50 in 2004, 51 in 2005, 51 in 2006, and 50 in 2007. Rates from 1998–1999 are based on aggregated data submitted by states; rates from 2000–2007 are based on case-level data submitted by states. The reporting year changed in 2003 from the calendar year to the Federal fiscal year.

Information about NCANDS is available online at http://www.acf.hhs.gov/programs/cb/stats_research/index.htm#can.

Agency Contact:
John A. Gaudiosi
Children's Bureau
Administration on Children, Youth, and Families
Administration for Children and Families
Phone: (202) 205-8625
E-mail: john.gaudiosi@acf.hhs.gov

National Crime Victimization Survey

The National Crime Victimization Survey (NCVS) is the Nation's primary source of information on criminal victimization. In earlier years, researchers obtained data from interviews with a nationally representative sample of roughly 49,000 households that included more than 100,000 persons ages 12 and older. The sample for the most recent year, 2007, was 46,000 households and 85,000 persons ages 12 and older. Sample households are chosen using a multistage stratified sample design. All household members ages 12 and older in selected households are interviewed to obtain information on the frequency, characteristics, and consequences of criminal victimization in the United States. The survey measures the likelihood of victimization by rape, sexual assault, robbery, assault, theft, household burglary, and motor vehicle theft for the population as a whole, as well as for segments of the population such as adolescents and members of various racial and gender groups. Either in person or by telephone, victims are also asked whether they reported the incident to the police. In instances of personal violent crimes, they are asked about the characteristics of the perpetrator. The response rate for 2007 was 90.3 percent of eligible households and 86.2 percent of eligible individuals. The NCVS provides the largest national forum for victims to describe the impact of crime and their characteristics and those of violent offenders. It has been ongoing since 1973 and was redesigned in 1992.

Due to changes in survey methodology in 2006 that mainly affected rural areas, national-level estimates were not comparable to estimates based on NCVS data from previous years. The U.S. Census Bureau, the Bureau of Justice Statistics (BJS), and a panel of outside experts extensively reviewed the 2006 NCVS data and determined that there was a break in series between 2006 and previous years that prevented annual comparison of criminal victimization at the national level. This was mainly the result of three major changes in the survey methodology: (1) introducing a new sample to account for shifts in population and location of households that occur over time; (2) incorporating responses from households that were in the survey for the first time; and (3) using computer-assisted personal interviewing (CAPI). These effects were reversed in 2007, suggesting that the 2006 findings represent a temporary anomaly in the data.

Information about the NCVS is available online at http://www.ojp.usdoj.gov/bjs/cvict.htm#Programs.

Agency Contact:
Katrina Baum
Bureau of Justice Statistics
Phone: (202) 307-5889

National Health and Nutrition Examination Survey

The National Health and Nutrition Examination Survey (NHANES) is conducted by the National Center for Health Statistics (NCHS) of the Centers for Disease Control and Prevention (CDC). The survey is designed to assess the health and nutritional status of the noninstitutionalized civilian population through direct physical examinations and interviews, using a complex stratified, multistage, probability sampling design. Interviewers obtain information on personal and demographic characteristics, including age, household income, and race and ethnicity, through self-reports or reports from an informant. The first survey, NHANES I, was conducted during the period 1971–1974; NHANES II covered the period 1976–1980; and NHANES III covered the period 1988–1994. Only NHANES III (in its first phase, conducted 1988–91), however, collected data on serum cotinine levels. NHANES III provided cotinine data for children ages 4–17.

For descriptions of the survey design, the methods used in estimation, and the general qualifications of the data, see:

Plan and Operation of the Third National Health and Nutrition Examination Survey, 1988–94: Series 1: Programs and collection procedures, No. 32. Vital and Health Statistics, Hyattsville, MD: National Center for Health Statistics.

Starting in 1999, NHANES changed to a continuous survey, visiting 15 U.S. locations per year and surveying and reporting for approximately 5,000 people annually. However, 2 or more years of data are necessary for adequate sample sizes for subgroup analyses.

Continuous NHANES 1999–2006 is a complex, multistage probability sample of the civilian noninstitutionalized population of the United States. Individuals of all ages were sampled. The NHANES 1999–2006 samples include expanded samples of Mexican Americans, African Americans, adolescents 12 to 19 years, and adults 60 years and older. In 2000, the sample individual selection probabilities were modified to increase the number of sampled persons in low-income, non-Hispanic White population domains. Additionally, screening and sampling rates were adjusted for women of childbearing age to increase the number of pregnant women included in the sample. Statistical weights were used to make the sample representative of the U.S. population. For more information on the NHANES data, see http://www.cdc.gov/nchs/data/nhanes/guidelines1.pdf.

NHANES data used to calculate Healthy Eating Index-2005 scores. Participants in NHANES provide information on their dietary intake via an interviewer-administered 24-hour recall of all foods and beverages consumed. Data from the 2003–2004 survey cycle were used to calculate the Healthy Eating Index-2005 (HEI-2005) component scores shown in this report. The HEI-2005 has been computed for all individuals age 2 years and older because the Dietary Guidelines for Americans are not applicable to younger children nor infants. Breast-fed children were excluded because breast milk intake was not quantified.

Information about NHANES is available online at http://www.cdc.gov/nchs/nhanes.htm, and information about the Healthy Eating Index-2005 is available at http://www.cnpp.usda.gov/HealthyEatingIndex.htm.

Agency Contacts:
For more information on:

The Healthy Eating Index, contact:
Thomas Fungwe
Center for Nutrition Policy and Promotion
U.S. Department of Agriculture
Phone: (703) 305-2309

Lead and cotinine, contact:
Debra Brody
National Center for Health Statistics
Phone: (301) 458-4116

Oral health, contact:
Bruce Dye
National Center for Health Statistics
Phone: (301) 458-4199

Overweight, contact:
Cynthia Ogden
National Center for Health Statistics
Phone: (301) 458-4405

National Health Interview Survey

The National Health Interview Survey (NHIS) is a continuing nationwide sample survey of the noninstitutionalized civilian population for which data are collected during personal household interviews. Interviewers obtain information on personal and demographic characteristics, including race and ethnicity, through self-reports or reports by a member of the household. Interviewers also collect data on illnesses, injuries, impairments, chronic conditions, activity limitation caused by chronic conditions, utilization of health services, and other health topics. Each year the survey is reviewed and special topics are added or deleted. For most health topics, the survey collects data over an entire year.

The NHIS sample is designed to estimate the national prevalence of health conditions, health service utilization, and health problems of the noninstitutionalized civilian population of the United States, and includes an oversample of Black, Hispanic, and Asian persons. The household response rate for the ongoing part of the survey has been between 87 and 98 percent over the years. In 1997, the NHIS was redesigned; estimates beginning in 1997 are likely to vary slightly from those for previous years. Interviewers collected information for the basic questionnaire on 75,764 persons in 2007, including 9,417 children under 18 years of age.

For background and health data for children, see:

Bloom, B., Cohen, R.A. (2009). Summary health statistics for U.S. children: National Health Interview Survey, 2007. *Vital and Health Statistics, 10*(239). Hyattsville, MD: National Center for Health Statistics.

Information about NHIS is available online at http://www.cdc.gov/nchs/nhis.htm.

Agency Contacts:
For more information on:

Activity limitation, contact:
Patricia Pastor
National Center for Health Statistics
Phone: (301) 458-4422

Asthma, contact:
Lara Akinbami
National Center for Health Statistics
Phone: (301) 458-4306

Emotional and behavioral difficulties, contact:
Shelli Avenevoli
National Institute of Mental Health
Phone: (301) 443-8316

Patricia Pastor
National Center for Health Statistics
Phone: (301) 458-4422

Oral health, contact:
Bruce Dye
National Center for Health Statistics
Phone: (301) 458-4199

Usual source of health care, contact:
Robin Cohen
National Center for Health Statistics
Phone: (301) 458-4152

National Hospital Ambulatory Medical Care Survey

The National Hospital Ambulatory Medical Care Survey (NHAMCS) collects data on the utilization and provision of medical care services provided in hospital emergency and outpatient departments. Data are collected from medical records on type of health care provider seen; reason for visit; diagnoses; drugs ordered, provided, or continued; and selected procedures and tests performed during the visit. Patient data include age, sex, race, and expected source of payment. Data are also collected on selected characteristics of hospitals included in the survey. Annual data collection began in 1992.

The survey is a representative sample of visits to emergency departments (EDs) and outpatient departments (OPDs) of non-Federal, short-stay, or general hospitals. Telephone contacts are excluded. A four-stage probability sample design is used in NHAMCS, involving samples of primary sampling units (PSUs), hospitals within PSUs, clinics within OPDs, and patient visits within clinics.

The hospital sample consists of approximately 500 hospitals. In 2005, 33,605 ED patient record forms (PRFs) were completed, and in 2006, 35,849 PRFs were completed. The ED hospital response rate was 90 percent in 2005 and 91 percent in 2006.

For background information, see:

McCaig, L.F., and McLemore, T. (1994). Plan and operation of the National Hospital Ambulatory Medical Care Survey. *Vital and Health Statistics 1*(34). Hyattsville MD: National Center for Health Statistics. Available online at: http://www.cdc.gov/nchs/data/series/sr_01/sr01_034acc.pdf.

Information about NHAMCS is available on the National Health Care Survey (NHCS) website at http://www.cdc.gov/nchs/nhcs.htm or the Ambulatory Health Care website at http://www.cdc.gov/nchs/about/major/ahcd/ahcd1.htm.

Agency Contact:
Margaret Warner
National Center for Health Statistics
Phone: (301) 458-4556

National Household Education Survey

The National Household Education Surveys Program (NHES), conducted by the National Center for Education Statistics (NCES), collects detailed information about education issues through a household-based survey that uses telephone interviews. The sample for the NHES is drawn from the noninstitutionalized civilian population in households with a telephone in the 50 states and the District of Columbia. In each survey, between 44,000 and 60,000 households are screened to identify persons eligible for one of the topics. Generally, each collection covers two topical surveys, and researchers conduct between 2,500 and 25,000 interviews for each survey. The data are weighted to permit nationally representative estimates of the population of interest. In addition, the NHES design samples minorities at a higher rate than nonminorities to increase the reliability of estimates for smaller groups.

The 1991 NHES included a survey on early childhood program participation. Investigators screened approximately 60,000 households to identify a sample of about 14,000 children, ages 3–8. They interviewed parents in order to collect information about these children's educational activities and the role of the family in the children's learning. In 1993, NCES fielded a school readiness survey in which parents of approximately 11,000 children age 3 through 2nd grade were asked about their children's experiences in early childhood programs, developmental level, school adjustment and related problems, early primary school experiences, general health and nutrition status, home activities, and family characteristics, including family stability and economic risk factors. In 1995, NCES also fielded an early childhood program participation survey, similar to that of 1991. It entailed screening approximately 44,000 households and interviewing 14,000 parents of children from birth through 3rd grade. In 1996, NCES fielded a survey of parent and family involvement in education, interviewing nearly 21,000 parents of children from age 3 through 12th grade. About 8,000 youth in grades 6 through 12 were also interviewed about their community service and civic involvement. The 1999 NHES was designed to collect end-of-the-decade estimates of key indicators collected in previous NHES surveys and to collect data from children and their parents about plans for the child's education after high school. Interviews were conducted with 24,000 parents of children ranging from newborns through 12th-graders, approximately 8,000 students in 6th through 12th grade in the youth interview, and nearly 7,000 adults.

Three surveys were fielded as part of the 2001 NHES. The Early Childhood Program Participation survey was similar in content to the 1995 collection and collected data about the education of 7,000 prekindergarten children ranging in age from birth to age 6. The Before and After-School Programs and Activities survey collected data about nonparental care arrangements and educational and noneducational activities in which children participate before and after school. Data were collected for approximately 10,000 kindergartners through 8th-graders. The third survey fielded in 2001 was the Adult Education and Lifelong Learning survey, which gathered data about the formal and informal educational activities of 11,000 adults.

The 2005 NHES included surveys that covered early childhood program participation and after-school programs and activities. Data were collected from parents of about 7,200 children for the Early Childhood Program Participation Survey and from parents of nearly 11,700 children for the After-School Programs and Activities Survey. These surveys were substantially similar to the surveys conducted in 2001, with the exceptions that the Early Childhood Program Participation Survey and After-School Programs and Activities Survey did not collect information about before-school care for school-age children.

The 2007 NHES fielded the Parent and Family Involvement in Education Survey. This survey was similar in design and content to the 2003 collection. New features added to the Parent and Family Involvement Survey were questions about supplemental education services provided by schools and school districts (including use of and satisfaction with such services), as well as questions to efficiently identify the school attended by the sampled students. For the Parent and Family Involvement Survey, interviews were completed with parents of 10,681 sampled children in kindergarten through 12th grade, including 10,370 students enrolled in public or private schools and 311 homeschooled children.

Information about the NHES is available online at http://nces.ed.gov/nhes.

Agency Contact:
Chris Chapman
National Center for Education Statistics
Phone: (202) 502-7414
E-mail: Chris.Chapman@ed.gov

National Immunization Survey

The National Immunization Survey (NIS) is a continuing nationwide telephone sample survey of families with children ages 19 to 35 months. Estimates of vaccine-specific coverage are available for the Nation, states, and selected urban areas.

The NIS uses a two-stage sample design that includes household data collection and provider record check. First, a random-digit-dialing sample of telephone numbers is drawn. When households with children ages 19 to 35 months are contacted, the interviewer collects information on the vaccinations received by all age-eligible children. The interviewer also collects information on the vaccination providers. In the second phase, all vaccination providers are contacted by mail. Providers' responses are combined with information obtained from the households to render estimates of vaccination coverage levels more accurately. Final estimates are adjusted for noncoverage of households without telephones.

Information about the NIS is available online at http://www.cdc.gov/vaccines/stats-surv/imz-coverage.htm#nis.

Agency Contact:
James Singleton
Centers for Disease Control and Prevention
Phone: (404) 639-8560

National Survey of Children with Special Health Care Needs

The 2005–2006 National Survey of Children with Special Health Care Needs (NS-CSHCN) was conducted as a module of the State and Local Area Integrated Telephone Survey (SLAITS). Similar to the first NS-CSHCN in 2001, it was funded by the Health Resources and Services Administration's (HRSA) Maternal and Child Health Bureau (MCHB) and conducted by the Centers for Disease Control and Prevention's (CDC) National Center for Health Statistics (NCHS). The primary goals of the survey were to assess the prevalence and impact of special health care needs among children in all 50 states and the District of Columbia and evaluate change since 2001. The survey explored the extent to which children with special health care needs (CSHCN) have medical homes, adequate health insurance, and access to needed services. Other topics included functional difficulties, care coordination, satisfaction with care, and transition services.

SLAITS is a broad-based, ongoing survey system available at national, state, and local levels to track and monitor the health and well-being of children and adults. Surveys conducted as part of the SLAITS system, like the 2005–2006 NS-CSHCN, use the same sampling frame as the CDC's National Immunization Study (NIS) and immediately follow the NIS in selected households. For the 2005–2006 NS-CSHCN, a random-digit-dial sample of households with children younger than 18 years of age was constructed for each of the 50 states and the District of Columbia. All children in each identified household were screened for special health care needs. If CSHCN were identified in the household, a detailed interview was conducted for one randomly selected child with special health care needs. Detailed interviews were also conducted for a separate national sample of children to generate estimates for children without special health care needs and permit comparisons with CSHCN on all study measures.

A total of 191,640 households were screened for the presence of CSHCN between April 2005 and February 2007; these households included 363,183 children. Screening identified 55,767 CSHCN in 44,795 households. One child with special health care needs was randomly selected from each of these households to be the subject of the interview, yielding 40,465 completed special health care need interviews. The response rate for the completion of the special needs interviews was 61.2 percent. The respondents were parents or guardians who knew about the children's health and health care.

Information about the NS-CSHCN is available online at http://www.cdc.gov/nchs/about/major/slaits/nscshcn_05_06.htm.

Agency Contact:
Stephen J. Blumberg
National Center for Health Statistics
Phone: (301) 458-4107

National Survey on Drug Use and Health

The National Survey on Drug Use and Health (NSDUH) is sponsored by the Substance Abuse and Mental Health Services Administration (SAMHSA). The survey has been conducted on a periodic basis from 1971 to 1988 and annually since 1990 and serves as the primary source of information on the prevalence and incidence of illicit drug, alcohol, and tobacco use in the civilian, noninstitutionalized population age 12 or older in the United States. Information about substance abuse and dependence, Major Depressive Episode, mental health problems, and receipt of substance abuse and mental health treatment is also included. Over 67,000 interviews are conducted each year using audio computer assisted self-interviewing (A-CASI) methodology. In 2007, weighted response rates for household screening and for interviewing were 89.5 and 73.9 percent, respectively.

The NSDUH collects information from residents of households, noninstitutional group quarters (e.g., shelters, rooming houses, dormitories), and civilians living on military bases. Persons excluded from the survey include homeless persons who do not use shelters, active-duty military personnel, and residents of institutional group quarters such as prisons and long-term hospitals. The survey design includes an independent, multistage area probability sample for each state and the District of Columbia to accommodate state estimates of substance use and mental health; the survey design also oversamples youths and young adults so that each state's sample is distributed equally among three age groups (12 to 17 years, 18 to 25 years, and 26 and older).

For additional background and data, see:

Substance Abuse and Mental Health Services Administration, Office of Applied Studies. (2008). Results from the 2007 National Survey on Drug Use and Health: National Findings (NSDUH Series H-34, DHHS Publication No. SMA 08-4343). Rockville, MD: Author.

Information about the NSDUH is available online at http://oas.samhsa.gov/nsduh.htm.

Agency Contact:
Lisa Colpe
Office of Applied Studies
Substance Abuse and Mental Health Services Administration
Phone: (240) 276-1245

National Vital Statistics System

Through the National Vital Statistics System, the National Center for Health Statistics (NCHS) collects and publishes data on births and deaths in the United States. NCHS obtains information on births and deaths from the registration offices of all states, New York City, and the District of Columbia.

Demographic information on birth certificates, such as race and ethnicity, is provided by the mother at the time of birth. Hospital records provide the base for information on birthweight, while funeral directors and family members provide demographic information on death certificates. Medical certification of cause of death is provided by a physician, medical examiner, or coroner.

Information on Hispanic origin. The number of states gathering information on births to parents of Hispanic origin has increased gradually since 1980–1981, when 22 states included this information on birth certificates. By 1993, the Hispanic origin of the mother was reported on birth certificates in all 50 states and the District of Columbia. Similarly, mortality data by Hispanic origin of decedent have become more complete over time. In 1997, Hispanic origin was reported on death certificates in all 50 states and the District of Columbia.

Population denominators. The natality and mortality rates shown in this report for 1991–2001 have been revised, based on populations consistent with the census conducted on April 1, 2000. Prior to *America's Children, 2003,* rates were based on populations projected from the 1990 Census. The population estimates for 2000–2007 can be found online at http://www.cdc.gov/nchs/about/major/dvs/popbridge/popbridge.htm. It was necessary to create population estimates for 2000–2007 that were consistent with the race categories used in the 1990 Census.

The revised intercensal population estimates for 5-year age groups for 1991–1999 can also be found online at http://www.cdc.gov/nchs/about/major/dvs/popbridge/popbridge.htm.

Detailed information on the methodologies used to develop the revised populations, including the populations for birth rates for teenagers and birth rates for unmarried teenagers, is presented in several publications.

For more information about these methodologies, see:

Ventura, S.J., Hamilton, B.E., Sutton, P.D. (2003). Revised birth and fertility rates for the United States, 2000 and 2001. *National Vital Statistics Reports, 51*(4). Hyattsville, MD: National Center for Health Statistics.

Hamilton, B.E., Sutton, P.D., and Ventura, S.J. (2003). Revised birth and fertility rates for the 1990s: United States, and new rates for Hispanic populations, 2000 and 2001. *National Vital Statistics Reports, 51*(12). Hyattsville, MD: National Center for Health Statistics.

National Center for Health Statistics. (2002). Unpublished estimates of the April 1, 2000, United States population by age, sex, race, and Hispanic origin, prepared under a collaborative arrangement with the U.S. Census Bureau. Available online at http://www.cdc.gov/nchs/about/major/dvs/popbridge/popbridge.htm.

Ingram, D.D., Weed, J.A., Parker, J.D., Hamilton, B.E., Schenker, N., Arias, E., and Madans, J. (2003). U.S. Census 2000 population with bridged race categories. National Center for Health Statistics. *Vital Health Statistics, 2*(135).

Anderson, R.N., and Arias, E. (2003). The effect of revised populations on mortality statistics for the United States, 2000. *National Vital Statistics Reports, 51*(9). Hyattsville, MD: National Center for Health Statistics.

Preliminary data. NCHS continuously receives statistical records from the states' vital registration systems, providing preliminary data. Investigators weight individual records of births and deaths to independent counts of vital events registered in each state and reported to NCHS. These independent counts, aggregated for a 12-month period, serve as control totals and are the basis for the individual unit record weights in the preliminary file. For selected variables, unknown or not-stated values are imputed. The percentage not stated is generally 1 percent or less.

For more information on national natality and mortality data, see:

National Center for Health Statistics. (2001). Technical appendix. *Vital Statistics of the United States, 1999,* natality. Hyattsville, Maryland: National Center for Health Statistics. Available online at http://www.cdc.gov/data/techap99.pdf.

National Center for Health Statistics. (2008). Detailed technical notes. United States, 2006, natality. Hyattsville, Maryland: National Center for Health Statistics. Available online at ftp://ftp.cdc.gov/pub/Health_Statistics/NCHS/Dataset_Documentation/DVS/natality/UserGuide2006.pdf.

National Center for Health Statistics. (2004). Technical appendix. *Vital Statistics of the United States, 1999,* vol. II, mortality, part A. Hyattsville, Maryland: National Center for Health Statistics. Available online at http://www.cdc.gov/nchs/data/statab/techap99.pdf.

Information about the National Vital Statistics System is available online at http://www.cdc.gov/nchs/nvss.htm.

Agency Contacts:
For more information on:

Adolescent mortality, contact:
Margaret Warner
National Center for Health Statistics
Phone: (301) 458-4556

Births to unmarried women, low birthweight, and adolescent births, contact:
Stephanie Ventura
National Center for Health Statistics
Phone: (301) 458-4547

Child mortality, contact:
Donna Hoyert
National Center for Health Statistics
Phone: (301) 458-4279

National Linked Files of Live Births and Infant Deaths

The National Linked File of Live Births and Infant Deaths is a data file for research on infant mortality. Beginning with the 1995 data, this file is produced in two formats. The file is released first as a period data file and later as a cohort file. In the birth cohort format, it includes linked vital records for infants born in a given year who died in that calendar year or the next year, before their first birthday. In the period format, the numerator consists of all infant deaths occurring in one year, with deaths linked to the corresponding birth certificates from that year or the previous year. The linked file includes all the variables on the national natality file, as well as medical information reported for the same infant on the death record and the age of the infant at death. The use of linked files prevents discrepancies in the reporting of race between the birth and infant death certificates. Although discrepancies are rare for White and Black infants, they can be substantial for other races. National linked files are available starting with the birth cohort of 1983. No linked file was produced for the 1992 through 1994 data years. Match completeness for each of the birth cohort files is about 98 percent.

For more information, see:

Prager, K. (1994). Infant mortality by birthweight and other characteristics: United States, 1985 birth cohort. *Vital and Health Statistics, 20*(24). Hyattsville, MD: National Center for Health Statistics.

Mathews, T.J., and MacDorman, M.F. (2008). Infant mortality statistics from the 2005 period linked birth/infant death data set. *National Vital Statistics Reports 57*(2). Hyattsville, MD: National Center for Health Statistics.

Information about the National Linked File of Live Births and Infant Deaths is available online at http://www.cdc.gov/nchs/linked.htm.

Agency Contact:
T.J. Mathews
National Center for Health Statistics
Phone: (301) 458-4363

Safe Drinking Water Information System

The Safe Drinking Water Information System (SDWIS) is the national regulatory compliance database for the U.S. Environmental Protection Agency (EPA)'s drinking water program. SDWIS includes information on the Nation's 160,000 public water systems and data submitted by states and EPA regions in conformance with reporting requirements established by statute, regulation, and guidance.

EPA sets national standards for drinking water. These requirements take three forms: maximum contaminant levels (MCLs, the maximum allowable level of a specific contaminant in drinking water), treatment techniques (specific methods that facilities must follow to remove certain contaminants), and monitoring and reporting requirements (schedules that utilities must follow to report testing results). States report any violations of these three types of standards to the EPA.

Water systems must monitor for contaminant levels on fixed schedules and report to the EPA when a maximum contaminant level has been exceeded. States also must report when systems fail to meet specified treatment techniques. More information about the maximum contaminant levels can be found online at http://www.epa.gov/safewater/contaminants/index.html.

EPA sets minimum monitoring schedules that drinking water systems must follow. These minimum reporting schedules (systems may monitor more frequently) vary by the size of the water system as well as by contaminant. Some contaminants are monitored daily, others need to be checked far less frequently (the longest monitoring cycle is every 9 years). For example, at a minimum, drinking water systems will monitor continuously for turbidity, monthly for bacteria, and once every 4 years for radionuclides.

SDWIS includes data on the total population served by each public water system and the state in which the public water system is located. However, SDWIS does not include the number of children served. The fractions of the population served by noncompliant public water systems in each state were estimated using the total population served by violating community water systems divided by the total population served by all community water systems. The numbers of children served by violating public water systems in each state were estimated by multiplying the fraction of the population served by violating public water systems by the number of children (ages 0–17) in the state.

Information about the EPA's SDWIS is available online at http://www.epa.gov/safewater/sdwisfed/sdwis.htm.

Agency Contact:
Jade L. Freeman
Office of Ground Water and Drinking Water
U.S. Environmental Protection Agency
Phone: (202) 564-1935
E-mail: lee-freeman.jade@epa.gov

Survey of Income and Program Participation

Core survey and topical modules. Implemented by the U.S. Census Bureau in 1984, the Survey of Income and Program Participation (SIPP) is a continuous series of national longitudinal panels, with a sample size ranging from approximately 14,000 to 36,700 interviewed households. The duration of each panel ranges from 2 years to 4 years, with household interviews every 4 months.

The SIPP collects detailed information on income, labor force participation, participation in government assistance programs, and general demographic characteristics in order to measure the effectiveness of existing government programs, estimate future costs and coverage of government programs, and provide statistics on the distribution of income in America. In addition, topical modules provide detailed information on a variety of subjects, including health insurance, child care, adult and child well-being, marital and fertility history, and education and training. The U.S. Census Bureau releases cross-sectional, topical modules and longitudinal reports and data files. In 1996, the SIPP questionnaire was redesigned to include a new 4-year panel sample design and the computer-assisted personal interviewing (CAPI) method. The 2004 panel was a 3-year panel sample, and a new 2008 panel is currently in the field and is anticipated to cover a 3-year period.

Information about the SIPP is available online at http://www.sipp.census.gov/sipp.

Agency Contact:
Fertility and Family Statistics Branch
U.S. Census Bureau
Phone: (301) 763-2416

Youth Risk Behavior Surveillance System

The Youth Risk Behavior Surveillance System (YRBSS) was developed in 1990 to monitor priority health risk behaviors that contribute markedly to the leading causes of death, disability, and social problems among youth and adults in the United States. The YRBSS includes national, state, and local school-based surveys of representative samples of 9th- through 12th-grade students. These surveys are conducted every 2 years, usually during the spring semester. The national survey, conducted by the Centers for Disease Control and Prevention (CDC), provides data representative of high school students in public and private schools in the United States. The state and local surveys, conducted by departments of health and education, provide data representative of public high school students in each state or local school district.

The sampling frame for the 2007 national Youth Risk Behavior Survey (YRBS) consisted of all public and private schools with students in at least one of grades 9–12 in the 50 states and the District of Columbia. A three-stage cluster sample design produced a nationally representative sample of students in grades 9–12 who attend public and private schools. All students in selected classes were eligible to participate. Schools, classes, and students that refused to participate were not replaced. For the 2007 national YRBS, 14,103 questionnaires were completed in 157 schools. The school response rate was 81 percent, and the student response rate was 84 percent. The school response rate multiplied by the student response rate produced an overall response rate of 68 percent.

Survey procedures for the national, state, and local surveys were designed to protect students' privacy by allowing for anonymous and voluntary participation. Before survey administration, local parental permission procedures were followed. Students completed the self-administered questionnaire during one class period and recorded their responses directly on a computer-scannable booklet or answer sheet.

Information about the YRBS and the YRBSS is available online at http://www.cdc.gov/HealthyYouth/yrbs.

Agency Contact:
Laura Kann
Centers for Disease Control and Prevention
Phone: (770) 488-6181
E-mail: lkk1@cdc.gov

www.ingramcontent.com/pod-product-compliance
Lightning Source LLC
Chambersburg PA
CBHW081207280526
45787CB00006B/2361